Living with the Party

Yifan Shi

Living with the Party

How Leisure Shaped a New China

Yifan Shi
East China Normal University
Shanghai, China

ISBN 978-981-99-0207-1   ISBN 978-981-99-0208-8 (eBook)
https://doi.org/10.1007/978-981-99-0208-8

© The Editor(s) (if applicable) and The Author(s), under exclusive license to Springer Nature Singapore Pte Ltd. 2023
This work is subject to copyright. All rights are solely and exclusively licensed by the Publisher, whether the whole or part of the material is concerned, specifically the rights of translation, reprinting, reuse of illustrations, recitation, broadcasting, reproduction on microfilms or in any other physical way, and transmission or information storage and retrieval, electronic adaptation, computer software, or by similar or dissimilar methodology now known or hereafter developed.
The use of general descriptive names, registered names, trademarks, service marks, etc. in this publication does not imply, even in the absence of a specific statement, that such names are exempt from the relevant protective laws and regulations and therefore free for general use.
The publisher, the authors, and the editors are safe to assume that the advice and information in this book are believed to be true and accurate at the date of publication. Neither the publisher nor the authors or the editors give a warranty, expressed or implied, with respect to the material contained herein or for any errors or omissions that may have been made. The publisher remains neutral with regard to jurisdictional claims in published maps and institutional affiliations.

This Palgrave Macmillan imprint is published by the registered company Springer Nature Singapore Pte Ltd.
The registered company address is: 152 Beach Road, #21-01/04 Gateway East, Singapore 189721, Singapore

Acknowledgments

My first thanks go to Jeremy Brown and Timothy Cheek for their support and encouragement. They are the best mentors and critics that I can imagine. They have also set up a model for thesis supervision that I can follow in my own academic career. This book cannot be finished without help from other senior scholars. During my field research in Beijing, Chen Donglin, Wang Haiguang, and Yin Hongbiao offered me advice on my project and helped me find interviewees. At conference panels, Han Gang, Jan Kiely, Xin Yi, Yang Kuisong, and Zhang Jishun provided their comments and feedback on early drafts of my chapters.

A lot of people also helped me navigate my project. During my first field trip, a librarian at the Peking University Library, an archivist at the Peking University Archives, and a staff member at the Peking University Alumni Association kindly introduced to me their collections, which precipitated my decision to give up an immature project about the everyday life of Peking University students under Mao. I would also like to thank staff members at the Universities Service Centre at the Chinese University of Hong Kong, archivists at the Beijing Municipal Archives, librarians at the National Library and the Capital Library, vendors at Panjiayuan Flea Market, and people who helped me digitize all materials.

I thank the institutions that provided financial support for my book. The research was supported by a Simon Fraser University Graduate International Travel Award and an Esherick-Ye Family Foundation Fellowship. Writing during my final year at SFU was supported by a Simon Fraser

University Community Trust Endowment Funds Graduate Fellowship, a Simon Fraser University President's Ph.D. Scholarship, and a Simon Fraser University Graduate Fellowship.

Chapter 3 is derived in part from "Temporal Politics and the Collectivization of Young People's Leisure Time in Early Maoist Beijing," *Politics, Religion & Ideology* 22, no. 3–4 (2021): 329–350 © Taylor & Francis, available online: https://www.tandfonline.com/doi/10.1080/21567689.2021.1995715. Portions of Chapter 6 are from "Exiting the Revolution: Alternative Ways of Life in Beijing, 1966–1976," *Modern China* 48, no. 6 (2022): 1238–1264 © SAGE Publications, Inc., available online: https://journals.sagepub.com/doi/abs/10.1177/00977004221106101.

Contents

1 Introduction   1
2 A Happy New World: The Communist Takeover
  of Leisure   29
3 Temporal Politics in Beijing, 1949–1956   67
4 Youth Subcultures, Leisure Regulation,
  and Community Life, 1955–1962   107
5 Anxiety About Difference: Politicization
  and Stratification in Leisure, 1962–1966   151
6 Exiting the Revolution: Alternative Ways of Life
  and the Institutionalization of Leisure, 1966–1976   193
7 Epilogue   235

References   249
Index   269

Acronyms

BMA Beijing Municipal Archives
CCP Chinese Communist Party
RMRB Renmin Ribao [People's Daily]
YSD Youth Service Department

List of Figures

Fig. 2.1	Cover page of *American Way of Life*	34
Fig. 2.2	Back cover of *American Way of Life*	35
Fig. 2.3	Cover page of Tan Youshi's *How to Ballroom Dance* (1951)	47
Fig. 2.4	Cover page of *How to Learn Ballroom Dancing* (1953)	48
Fig. 2.5	"Balance Movement"	49
Fig. 2.6	Promoting Officials, New Society Version	56
Fig. 2.7	"Resist America and Aid Korea" chess	58

List of Tables

Table 2.1	Private Ball Game Clubs in Beijing, 1950–1952	42
Table 2.2	Schedule for Dancing Club Activities in the Summer Vacation of 1951	52
Table 2.3	Schedule of Beijing People's Radio Station No. 2, January 1952	55
Table 3.1	Activities planned by the committee for summer vacation life in June 1950	76
Table 3.2	Weekly schedule of leisure activities in Beijing Knitting Mill (1956)	89
Table 3.3	Revised weekly schedule of leisure activities in Beijing Knitting Mill (1956)	100

CHAPTER 1

Introduction

Q: Did you observe any "backward" elements in young workers' leisure activities?
A: During that time, we thought that playing poker was the most backward... I really did not sense anything unhealthy during the Cultural Revolution. There were many [collective] recreational and sporting activities, so people all played together. Almost no one played poker during the Cultural Revolution.
Q: Because people were afraid of doing so?
A: Not necessarily. For example, I did not play poker because I thought that playing poker was not as interesting as playing ball games.
Q: How did you feel living in the Mao Zedong era?
A: At that time, I felt it was very pleasant. Now I still maintain that.[1]

Sitting in Old Zhang's capacious living room in his three-storied villa in suburban Beijing, I chatted with him about his life from the late 1960s to the 1980s. Old Zhang was born to an ordinary worker's family in Beijing in 1954, a year meaning that he would be too young in 1966 to get involved in the Red Guard movement during the early months of the Cultural Revolution. In 1967, he entered junior high school without interruption after graduating from his elementary school and then was assigned to work in the Beijing Heavy-Duty Electric Machinery

---

[1] Interviewee 1, October 24, 2018.

© The Author(s), under exclusive license to Springer Nature Singapore Pte Ltd. 2023
Y. Shi, *Living with the Party*,
https://doi.org/10.1007/978-981-99-0208-8_1

Factory three years later when factories in Beijing started to recruit young workers. To a large extent, Old Zhang can be considered as a man with "vested interests" who benefited a lot from China's economic reform since the late 1970s. In the 1980s, with Deng Xiaoping's call to promote "younger, better educated, and better professionally qualified" cadres, Old Zhang got a degree in enterprise management in a workers' university and became one of the promising young leaders in his factory. In 2001, after devoting three decades to his factory as administrative and Party heads, he altered his track and started to work as a deputy manager of a share-holding enterprise. Perhaps for this reason, during our conversation, Old Zhang could not help but talk about his experience in the 1980s with great zest. It was interesting to hear opinions on Mao and the Mao era from a man who benefited so much from Deng's policies.

Was Old Zhang a typical conformist who had been used to doing what he was told? Perhaps not, because although Old Zhang was promoted into the Youth League Committee in his workshop in 1973, he still participated in the mass mourning of the late Premier Zhou Enlai in April 1976 (which would soon be labeled as "counterrevolutionary") by helping transport a huge self-made iron wreath to Tiananmen Square. His idea that "skill came first" was inconsistent with the official propaganda of being both "red and expert" during that time. In many ways, however, Old Zhang was not rebellious at all. During the 1970s, he felt annoyed by his colleague's unconventional comments on one of Mao's poems; in the 1980s, as the head of the Youth League Committee in his factory, he was keen on organizing collective leisure activities for workers, and he truly believed that workers could be better educated through organized leisure than by entertaining themselves.

The regime under the Chinese Communist Party (CCP) has made indelible marks that cannot be removed from Old Zhang: although elements that do not match the official propaganda might be found, many of his behavior patterns have clearly been "formatted" by the Party. This ambivalence leads to a general question: to what extent has the CCP influenced people's behavior patterns in their everyday life, and through what means? To answer this question, this book examines how the CCP attempted to create an attractive way of life as an alternative to the influential way of life in the "capitalist" world. I argue that the party-state achieved this goal by adopting an interventionist approach in the seemingly most private sphere of people's everyday life—leisure.

Although young people might not have fully accepted the Party's ideological jargon or welcomed persistent political movements, their behavior patterns were incorporated into the way of life favored by the Party as a result of the party-state's constant regulation of people's leisure time and leisure activities.

Existing Interpretations of State-Society Relations

In terms of the relationship between ordinary people and state power in China under the CCP, two approaches have dominated the debate: first, the totalitarian model in which the party-state suffocates society; second, the resistance model in which the party-state faces unavoidable difficulties inside and outside the Party.

The totalitarian model, which originated during the Cold War years but has remained full of life after the Cold War, stresses the role of terror and brainwashing when answering the question of how the CCP could consolidate its power. In early studies of the Chinese Communist Party, influenced by the totalitarian model in Soviet studies, scholars usually portrayed the CCP as a totalitarian political party similar to its Soviet counterpart, featuring all-round infiltration and omnipresent control of politics, economy, and society. One presumption underlies this model: the CCP is a tightly-organized and centralized "organizational weapon" operated by a small group of ruling elites; relations between people under Communist rule are remolded into an ideology-oriented way advocated by the Party.[2] In post-1949 China, society itself was reorganized and supervised by Party ideology and organizations, and it was constantly renewed by "ideological activities" as well as political purges because of the Party's rejection of "routinization."[3] Since the early years of the Cold War, China observers have paid special attention to the role of terror (state violence) such as mass execution and imprisonment of people's "enemies" and regarded it as a fundamental way of control. In his comprehensive study of the history of the People's Republic of China, Maurice

---

[2] The notion of "organizational weapon" was first introduced by the sociologist Philip Selznick in a report submitted to the Rand Corporation published in 1952. See Philip Selznick, *The Organizational Weapon: A Study of Bolshevik Strategy and Tactics* (New York: McGraw-Hill Book Company, 1952), 2–8.

[3] Franz Schurmann, *Ideology and Organization in Communist China*, 2nd ed. (Berkeley: University of California Press, 1968), 108.

Meisner states that the Campaign to Suppress Counterrevolutionaries launched by the Party in 1951 successfully achieved its purpose to "create a public climate of fear and terror" during which a large number of people were executed or sent to labor camps.[4] Subsequent studies show that to terrorize the Chinese people, Mao himself even worked out a killing quota for different regions to expedite mass executions.[5] State violence continued throughout the Mao era. During the Cultural Revolution, it caused more human loss than any factional warfare.[6] Apart from mass killing, the Party's thought reform project transformed Chinese people's private lives and created a new social morality known as "comradeship."[7] The totalitarian model did not fade away completely after the Cold War. One recent example is Lucien Bianco's comparative study of Russian and Chinese revolutions in which Bianco depicts China under Mao as a country full of "lies, fear, and debasement."[8]

The resistance model, on the contrary, highlights the party-state's inability to control every aspect of its people as scholars have found tensions between the Party's goals on paper and its actual implementation in reality. The outbreak of the Cultural Revolution greatly subverted the totalitarian model when scholars began to recognize that China was far from a monolithic entity supervised by a unanimous totalitarian political party.[9] As more detailed studies emerged, scholars discovered that the CCP's social transformation project faced considerable tensions at the grassroots level. For example, the Party's authority in rural base areas was eroded by local ties throughout the Communist revolution.[10] The post-1949 work unit system in factories became a hotbed of patron-client

---

[4] Maurice Meisner, *Mao's China and After*, 3rd ed. (New York: Free Press, 1999), 72.

[5] Yang Kuisong, "Reconsidering the Campaign to Suppress Counterrevolutionaries," *The China Quarterly* 193 (March 2008): 108–109.

[6] Andrew G. Walder, *China Under Mao: A Revolution Derailed* (Cambridge, MA: Harvard University Press, 2015), 271–277.

[7] Ezra F. Vogel, "From Friendship to Comradeship: The Change in Personal Relations in Communist China," *The China Quarterly* 21 (January–March 1965): 46.

[8] Lucien Bianco, *Stalin and Mao: A Comparison of the Russian and Chinese Revolutions*, trans. Krystyna Horko (Hong Kong: Chinese University Press, 2018), 347–350.

[9] Joseph W. Esherick, Paul G. Pickowicz, and Andrew G. Walder, eds., *The Chinese Cultural Revolution as History* (Stanford, CA: Stanford University Press, 2006), 1–3.

[10] Edward Friedman, Paul Pickowicz, and Mark Selden, *Chinese Village, Socialist State* (New Haven, CT: Yale University Press, 1991), xv.

relations that undermined the Party's political control over society.[11] The CCP had to deal with continuities of Chinese traditions and Nationalist rule, and on many occasions, it did not win this battle.[12] If this reluctant "culture of accommodation" can be seen as a result of "passive resistance" from the society, scholars have also noticed direct defiance against the authorities both in ideology and in action since the Mao era.[13] This model echoes studies of other totalitarian regimes. Scholars argue that regimes that have been labeled as "totalitarianism" were not omnicompetent at all when they discover that "Hitler's regime was disorganized, and many lived throughout his tenure with little change in their day-to-day lives"; "in the Soviet Union, party rule varied from place to place." Radical critics of the totalitarian model even suggest that the term "totalitarianism" be abandoned.[14]

These two models are problematic in two aspects. First, both indicate a dichotomy between state and society in which ordinary people either support or resist state power. This is considered unsatisfactory by scholars such as Gail Hershatter, who argues that in China under Mao, state and society intertwined in the sense that a labor model in rural Shaanxi in the 1950s could be treated both as a state agent and as a member of

---

[11] Andrew G. Walder, *Communist Neo-Traditionalism: Work and Authority in Chinese Industry* (Berkeley: University of California Press, 1986), 7.

[12] James Z. Gao, *The Communist Takeover of Hangzhou: The Transformation of City and Cadre, 1949–1954* (Honolulu: University of Hawai'i Press, 2004); Jeremy Brown and Paul G. Pickowicz, eds., *Dilemmas of Victory: The Early Years of the People's Republic of China* (Cambridge, MA: Harvard University Press, 2010); Aminda M. Smith, *Thought Reform and China's Dangerous Classes: Reeducation, Resistance, and the People* (Lanham, MD: Rowman & Littlefield, 2013).

[13] Jeremy Brown and Paul Pickowicz raise the notion of "culture of accommodation" to indicate practices of many nonparty elites who did not resist or flee China but collaborated with the new regime in many ways hoping to get some political and material rewards. See Brown and Pickowicz, *Dilemmas of Victory*, 10. Yiching Wu uncovers marginal ideas during the Cultural Revolution that debunked the Mao-type socialism by criticizing that the Party failed to bring social equality. These ideas led to a real political crisis that Mao did not expect before they were finally cracked down on. See Yiching Wu, *Cultural Revolution at the Margins: Chinese Socialism in Crisis* (Cambridge, MA: Harvard University Press, 2014), 12. On social resistance after the Mao era, see Elizabeth J. Perry and Mark Selden, eds., *Chinese Society: Change, Conflict and Resistance*, 3rd ed. (London: Routledge, 2010).

[14] A. James Gregor, *Marxism, Fascism, and Totalitarianism: Chapters in the Intellectual History of Radicalism* (Stanford, CA: Stanford University Press, 2009), 15–16.

the local community.[15] Second, although the resistance model belies the traditional assessment that ordinary Chinese submitted to the state under coercive means wielded by the Party, it tends to exaggerate the difficulties the Party encountered. This highly ideal depiction of resistance leads to a dilemma similar to what post-colonial scholars are facing, where, in Leo Ching's words, "colonial discourse is deemed not so invincible, and anticolonial resistance is more readily available." "Does the mere presence of the colonized," asks Ching, "necessarily entail the destabilizing of the colonial regime?... If colonial discourse is so ambivalent and colonial resistance so ubiquitous, then why does colonialism persist?"[16] As a matter of fact, scholars have acknowledged that discontent and protests in contemporary China are unable to challenge the ruling position of the CCP, indicating the resilience of the party-state.[17]

Toward a New Model

In this book, to explain why some interventionist regimes can persist despite tensions between reality and its goals and to better understand the CCP's interventionist regime, I wish to fuse these two models together to develop a new model called "participatory totalitarian model."[18] Does the

[15] Gail Hershatter, *The Gender of Memory: Rural Women and China's Collective Past* (Berkeley: University of California Press, 2011), 13.

[16] Leo T. S. Ching, *Becoming "Japanese:" Colonial Taiwan and the Politics of Identity Formation* (Berkeley: University of California Press, 2001), 134–135.

[17] Perry and Selden, *Chinese Society*, 20.

[18] All kinds of interventionist regimes require a certain degree of mass participation. Nevertheless, as expressed by Mao's theory of "mass line," the CCP was extremely obsessed with establishing a participatory regime. This could be reflected by the differences in policies against internal "enemies" between China and the Soviet Union. While the Soviets adopted a combination of state-led coercive means such as forced migration and labor camps ("Gulag"), the CCP preferred the "dictatorship of the masses" (*qunzhong zhuanzheng* 群众专政), meaning letting one part of Chinese citizens monitor and regulate another part. For research on Mao's mass line, see Mark Selden, *China in Revolution: The Yenan Way Revisited* (Armonk, NY: M. E. Sharpe, 1995). For the implementation of the "dictatorship of masses" at the grassroots, see Wang Haiguang 王海光, *Zhizao fangeming: Liu Xingfu an yu wenge shiqi de jiceng fazhi shengtai* 制造反革命: 柳幸福案与文革时期的基层法制生态 [Making a counterrevolutionary: the case of Liu Xingfu and China's grassroots legal system, 1949–1979] (Hong Kong: Chinese University of Hong Kong Press, 2021). In an essay published in 2004 reviewing Stephen Kotkin's monograph *Magnetic Mountain: Stalinism as Civilization*, Astrid Hedin coined the term "participatory totalitarianism" when she suggests that Kotkin's contribution in his book is to provide two new

seemingly outdated term "totalitarianism" still have interpretative power? Is it necessary to use this term again in the twenty-first century? My answer is: it is necessary to "revisit" this term, not to "repeat" it. As challenged by the works from the resistance model, the classic totalitarian model fails for two reasons: first, it relies on a very broad definition of totalitarianism which includes some elements that may not be the essence of the regime; second, it offers a simplistic depiction of the life of ordinary people under totalitarian regimes, which makes it easy to find counterexamples to support the resistance model.

Most scholars of totalitarianism usually view mass terror as a key element for these regimes to achieve totalitarian control. In *The Origins of Totalitarianism*, Hannah Arendt devotes a full chapter entitled "Ideology and Terror: A Novel Form of Government" when she tries to explain how totalitarian regimes could control a large number of people. As Arendt says explicitly, "terror is the essence of totalitarian domination."[19] In their six-point definition of totalitarianism, political scientists Carl Friedrich and Zbigniew Brzezinski stress the existence of "a system of terror, whether physical or psychic, effected through party and secret-police control."[20] Raymond Aron regards the Soviet law system as a legal way to exercise terror on its own citizens, accompanied by the practice of the deportation of the whole population of those labeled as enemies.[21] Even Arendt herself, however, notices the limitation of her theory when she examines the case of China. As Arendt wrote in 1966, "a much more serious question is whether a study of totalitarianism can afford to ignore what

---

perspectives on Soviet history: competing modernities and participatory totalitarianism. While Kotkin argues that people participated in the Soviet enterprise because they truly believed in official discourse from the government, my theory does not examine whether the official discourse really permeated the society. Instead of studying whether people believed in official propaganda, this book focuses on how people got used to the way of life under Communist rule regardless of whether they were ideologically affected. See Astrid Hedin, "Stalinism as a Civilization: New Perspectives on Communist Regimes," *Political Studies Review* 2 (2004): 166–184.

[19] Hannah Arendt, *The Origins of Totalitarianism* (New York: Harcourt Brace Jovanovich, 1973), 464.

[20] Carl J. Friedrich and Zbigniew K. Brzezinski, *Totalitarian Dictatorship and Autocracy*, 2nd ed. (Cambridge, MA: Harvard University Press, 1965), 22.

[21] Raymond Aron, *Democracy and Totalitarianism*, trans. Valence Ionescu (London: George Weidenfeld and Nicolson, 1968), 185–191.

has happened, and is still happening, in China."[22] On the one hand, the CCP's "totalitarian traits have been manifest from the beginning." On the other hand, Mao's 1957 speech "On the Correct Handling of Contradictions Among the People" seemed to open up a new way to organize the society because it offered some kind of normal life instead of mass killings. Arendt concludes that Mao's ideas "did not run along the lines laid down by Stalin (or Hitler, for that matter), that he was not a killer by instinct."[23]

With the wind of de-Stalinization in the Soviet Union, more scholars started to doubt the role terror played in regimes that they considered totalitarian. As Juan Linz observes, in the 1970s, the Soviet Union was on the track of constructing "totalitarianism without terror" when the Soviets were reforming their legal system to introduce a "socialist legality" in which the "arbitrary power of the police" could be limited by some legal procedures.[24] Linz, therefore, concludes: "Terror is neither a necessary nor sufficient characteristic of totalitarian systems."[25] Of course, Linz's assertion that the Soviet legal system could place some restrictions on its own power is still debatable, but his discussion on the absence of political terror in some totalitarian regimes is noteworthy.

Linz's study reminds us that there are different types of political systems in totalitarian regimes. We need to refine the meaning of "totalitarianism" with minimal factors that can best grasp the essence of the term. As Sujian Guo suggests, we need to distinguish the "essential components" of totalitarianism from many "operative" features, because "only the 'essential components' account for the *origins*, the *dynamics*, and the *essence* of totalitarianism, while the *operative* features…largely account for the functioning of totalitarianism."[26] Terror, in this sense,

---

[22] Arendt, *The Origins of Totalitarianism*, xxvi.

[23] Arendt, *The Origins of Totalitarianism*, xxvi–xxvii.

[24] Juan J. Linz, *Totalitarian and Authoritarian Regimes* (Boulder, CO: Lynne Rienner Publishers, 2000), 101.

[25] Linz, *Totalitarian and Authoritarian Regimes*, 74.

[26] Sujian Guo, "The Totalitarian Model Revisited," *Communist and Post-Communist Studies* 31, no. 3 (1998): 280. Guo also illustrates three essential components of totalitarianism: utopian goal, ideological commitment, and dictatorial party-state system. Other components, including but not limited to the means of social control, the way of mobilization, economic system, and policymaking process, are operative features. Changes in operative features do not mean a system becomes more or less totalitarian. Totalitarianism

is one of the operative features for many totalitarian regimes to maintain power. In fact, as Linz states, a totalitarian regime "could be based on the identification of a very large part of the population with the rulers, the population's active involvement in political organizations controlled by them and at the service of their goals." People could be manipulated with "a mixture of rewards and fears" rather than mere political terror.[27]

When we treat terror as an operative feature instead of an essential component of totalitarianism, the term "totalitarianism" has more interpretive power. For a long time, the classic totalitarian model has been unable to explain the nostalgia that emerges in many places after the downfall of totalitarian regimes.[28] By stripping terror off the essence of totalitarianism, scholars can pay more attention to the diversity of the toolbox that leaders in interventionist regimes possess. In this sense, emphasizing repression and terror can only downplay the power of interventionist states. While for some people, repression and terror remained keywords in their everyday life, for others who did not become the target of the regime, their life was quite "normal." Mary Fulbrook describes the mentality of many East Germans after the demise of the Communist regime: "they were baffled by the analyses of the political scientists who told them they had been victims or, worse, accomplices in a dictatorship comparable with that of Hitler. Many thought, by contrast, that they had been able to lead what they considered to be 'perfectly ordinary lives'."[29]

The second problem of the classic totalitarian model is that it only provides an oversimplified explanation of the operation of interventionist regimes. This is an epistemological question: we can always find counterexamples when studying people's everyday life under interventionist regimes. How should we deal with these tensions between the goals of the interventionist regime and the reality at the grassroots, as described in studies from the resistance model? Do these tensions mean that the state actually achieved nothing?

---

is sustained as long as the essential components remain unchanged. Guo, "The Totalitarian Model Revisited," 281–282.

[27] Linz, *Totalitarian and Authoritarian Regimes*, 66.

[28] Eckhard Jesse, "Reflections on Future Totalitarianism Research," in *Totalitarianism and Political Religions Volume I: Concepts for the Comparison of Dictatorships*, ed. Hans Maier, trans. Jodi Bruhn (London: Routledge, 2004), 230.

[29] Mary Fulbrook, *The People's State: East German Society from Hitler to Honecker* (New Haven, CT: Yale University Press, 2015), 3.

Linz notices that while ordinary German people could show their discomfort with Hitler's regime in private or unnoticeable ways, many of them still spontaneously participated in the state violence against enemies of the *Volksgemeinschaft* (people's community) such as the Jews. Therefore, when discussing the literature on everyday life under Hitler, Linz argues that although these works proved "the limits of Hitler's power" and highlighted "people's ways of evading the politicization of everyday life," they "do not call into question the distinctive characteristic of a totalitarian regime (in contrast to other types of nondemocratic rule), nor the shaping of society, behavior patterns, and values by the system. They only question a simplistic view of totalitarianism that extrapolates from an ideal type a society totally penetrated and shaped by those in power."[30] For Linz, although people might not be ideologically loyal to the Nazi regime, they were still used to the life under it, because "in a nondemocratic and particularly in a stable totalitarian society, many ordinary people are not necessarily aware of their lack of freedom; for them, that is the way life is."[31]

This simplistic view usually overestimates the effect of propaganda, assuming that it could change people's behaviors through a transformation in people's minds. Scholars from the resistance model, on the contrary, are good at finding discrepancies in people's everyday life that contradicted official propaganda, celebrating them as showing the incompetence of the regime. Nevertheless, we must realize that the effect of propaganda should not be assessed by to what extent people were "brainwashed." In his studies on propaganda, Jacques Ellul points out that "if the classic but outmoded view of propaganda consists in defining it as an adherence of man to an *orthodoxy*, true modern propaganda seeks, on the contrary, to obtain an *orthopraxy*."[32] For Ellul, a good propagandist could make people act properly in public without trying to change their

---

[30] Linz, *Totalitarian and Authoritarian Regimes*, 27–28.

[31] Linz, *Totalitarian and Authoritarian Regimes*, 28. This is also the case for people living under Stalin. See Sheila Fitzpatrick, *Everyday Stalinism: Ordinary Life in Extraordinary Times: Soviet Russia in the 1930s* (New York: Oxford University Press, 1999).

[32] Jacques Ellul, *Propaganda: The Formation of Men's Attitudes*, trans. Konrad Kellen and Jean Lerner (New York: Vintage Books, 1973), 27.

opinion.[33] In this sense, propaganda works when people act as what the regime wants them to do, regardless of what people's real intentions are.

An example of the effectiveness of Soviet propaganda comes from Peter Kenez's study on Komsomol activities. Kenez states that the purpose of the Komsomol during the years of the New Economic Policy was to teach "a generation of young people to think and speak in a communist fashion."[34] Like many scholars following the resistance model, Kenez finds "tensions" between the manifested goals of Soviet propagandists and the actual operation of the propaganda work on Soviet citizens: young people who participated in political reading sessions organized by the Komsomol did not become Marxists. Kenez, however, still considers that the Soviet regime succeeded in changing people's behaviors in many ways: it prevented "the formation and articulation of alternative points of view" because the Bolsheviks suppressed freedom of speech; it forced its citizens to take part in state-organized activities because independent organizations had been destroyed; and it made its people learn how to live like a Soviet citizen through participating in organized activities, even though people "often had only the vaguest understanding of Marxist philosophy or even the immediate goals of the regime."[35] In other words, tensions between the ultimate goal of the Communist propaganda and the reality at the grassroots did not jeopardize the agenda of the state in forging Soviet citizenship.

My analysis of the two major problems of the classic totalitarian model suggests that a new direction for studies on interventionist regimes is necessary. Unlike the classic totalitarian model, this direction, which I call the participatory totalitarian model, acknowledges the limits of coercive measures such as political terror in consolidating and maintaining state power, as shown by the abundant scholarship following the resistance model. Unlike the resistance model, however, the participatory totalitarian model pays more attention to what the regime actually achieved in regulating people instead of dwelling on the incompetence of the state. We need to admit that this kind of regime has a certain kind of resilience, not because it successfully "brainwashed" or terrorized its people, but

---

[33] Ellul, *Propaganda*, 34.

[34] Peter Kenez, *The Birth of the Propaganda State: Soviet Methods of Mass Mobilization, 1917–1929* (Cambridge: Cambridge University Press, 1985), 16.

[35] Kenez, *The Birth of the Propaganda State*, 252–254.

because it had some "attractive sides" that could achieve "seduction, mobilization and integration of the people."[36]

From the perspective of state-society relations, I define totalitarianism as any regime aiming at fulfilling absolute regulation of both public and private spheres of individuals. This kind of regime, which I call interventionist regime, does not necessarily rely only on terror. Instead, it can use other means such as pleasure as long as it can facilitate its goal of total control. What I am showing in this book is that for most people living under interventionist regimes, their behavior patterns cannot be explained as the outcome of coercion as many of them did not feel the terror at all. While tensions between goals and realities can be observed, the participatory totalitarian model does not interpret these tensions simply as resistance from the grassroots. It will examine whether these tensions could actually jeopardize the general project of the regime.[37] In the case of China, the participatory totalitarian model has one obvious advantage: it bridges the gap between the Mao era and the post-Mao era by highlighting the capacity of state power. While many people agree that China under Mao was totalitarian, when it comes to the nature of the Chinese regime after Mao, there have been diverse opinions. Most people argue that with the exit of mass terror and the introduction of the market economy, China has transformed from totalitarianism to authoritarianism.[38] If we identify the most essential feature of interventionist regimes as the ambition to achieve absolute regulation of individuals by

---

[36] Eckhard Jesse, "Reflections on Future Totalitarianism Research," in Maier, *Totalitarianism and Political Religions*, 230.

[37] Margaret Roberts' book on censorship in China reminds us that some seemingly deficiencies in its censorship system are actually the outcome of sophisticated design of the state. Although for many people, censorship is circumventable, the whole system still has an important influence on information access. The state uses "customized" measures strategically to make its censorship system most efficient: instead of direct repression, the state can affect most people's access to information "simply by inconveniencing them, without interfering so much to cause widespread public backlash." See Margaret E. Roberts, *Censored: Distraction and Diversion Inside China's Great Firewall* (Princeton, NJ: Princeton University Press, 2018), 4–14. Daniel Mattingly likewise shows that civil society, which is usually considered as a sphere for public resistance, can be cultivated and used to achieve some "hidden forms of coercion" on citizens. See Daniel C. Mattingly, *The Art of Political Control in China* (Cambridge: Cambridge University Press, 2020), 3–5.

[38] For a scholarly debate on the nature of the post-Mao regime, see Sujian Guo, *Post-Mao China: From Totalitarianism to Authoritarianism?* (London: Praeger, 2000). Using

the state, we will agree that state power has never retreated from people's most private sphere in post-Mao China. Following the participatory totalitarian model, we need to explore the role of measures other than terror in the post-Mao regime's attempt to regulate people.

POSITIONING LEISURE IN CHINA

In this book, I use leisure as an analytical tool to examine the operation of the Chinese state because it can reflect the very essential nature of the regime: the intervention in and regulation of the private sphere by state power.

The meaning of "leisure" has three dimensions. First, leisure means a period of time beyond working and school hours. In this sense, the CCP's regulation of leisure first means the regulation of how people spend their spare time. Activities happening during leisure time might not seem to be leisurely, as the CCP was in favor of using leisure time to study. In 1961, Deng Tuo, one of China's most prominent propagandists, started a column in the Party-operated *Beijing Evening News*, and his first article, entitled "One-Third of Your Life," expressed his ambition of teaching his readers how to spend their leisure time. In this article, Deng regards "evening hours" as "one-third of your life" and suggests that people should cherish every minute in their life to "labor more, work more, and study more."[39] Deng's article can be understood as an echo of the Chinese tradition of using leisure time to achieve self-cultivation.[40] The difference between leisure in ancient China and China under Mao, however, is that people witnessed a prominent political interference in their leisure time during the Mao era. Propaganda machines constantly organized discussions in newspapers and magazines, telling young people how to spend their time correctly. Even in the 1980s, the mouthpiece of the Beijing Municipal Youth League Committee organized a discussion

---

his method of distinguishing between essential and operative features, Guo argues that post-Mao China is still totalitarian because essential features remain the same.

[39] Deng Tuo 邓拓, "Shengming de sanfen zhiyi" 生命的三分之一 [One-third of your life], in Ma Nancun 马南邨, *Yanshan yehua* 燕山夜话 [Evening chats at Yanshan] (Beijing: Beijing chubanshe, 1961), 1–3.

[40] For an introduction to the traditional Chinese view on leisure, see Huidi Ma and Er Liu, *Traditional Chinese Leisure Culture and Economic Development: A Conflict of Forces* (New York: Palgrave Macmillan, 2017), 52–53.

entitled "how to spend one-third of your life," claiming repeatedly that the Youth League should "help" young people "enrich their everyday life."[41]

Second, leisure means a "combination of free time and the expectation of preferred experience."[42] This dimension of leisure stresses people's initiative in choosing the activities they prefer. Emotional factors play an important role in this dimension as scholars have argued that to have real leisure, people need to have the freedom to choose what they want to do. As Adorno points out, people need to "successfully follow their own desire for happiness" so they can enjoy leisure in their free time.[43] For interventionist regimes, this dimension of leisure is extremely important because all of these regimes promise a happy life. For example, the name of the Nazi Party's leisure organization, *Kraft durch Freude* (strength through joy), suggests the key role of pleasure in the Nazi movement.[44] To achieve this "Nazi Joy," National Socialists preferred voluntary participation to coercive means. By letting people feel happier in organized leisure activities, the Nazi regime not only strengthened its ideal "people's community," but also consolidated its power.[45] The CCP regarded pleasure as part of its "revolutionary optimism" before it came to power in 1949. The "eight-character" motto of the Anti-Japanese Military and Political University, "united, alert, serious, lively" (*tuanjie, jinzhang, yansu, huopo* 团结、紧张、严肃、活泼), suggests that to be a qualified revolutionary soldier, people must learn how to live a joyful life. As a pamphlet published in 1961 for militia training states, "wherever the People's Liberation Army appears, there is a lively atmosphere and loud sound of singing; everyone is happy… During the war years, although life was hard, recreational and sporting activities were very active…This lively situation cannot be achieved without the leadership of the people's

---

[41] See, for example, *Beijing qingnian bao*, May 7, 1982.

[42] Douglas A. Kleiber, *Leisure Experience and Human Development: A Dialectical Interpretation* (New York: Basic Books, 1999), 4.

[43] Theodor W. Adorno, *Critical Models: Interventions and Catchwords*, trans. Henry W. Pickford (New York: Columbia University Press, 2005), 171.

[44] Pamela E. Swett, Corey Ross, and Fabrice d'Almeida, eds., *Pleasure and Power in Nazi Germany* (Houndmills: Palgrave Macmillan, 2011), 1.

[45] Julia Timpe, *Nazi-Organized Recreation and Entertainment in the Third Reich* (London: Palgrave Macmillan, 2017), 1–10.

army led by the Communist Party."[46] For these regimes, being happy in people's leisure time was not only a means of control but also the ultimate goal.

Third, leisure is related to governmentality. The Foucauldian usage of the term "governmentality" emphasizes that to make the state operate smoothly, modern liberal states direct people into modern citizens through the regulation of a variety of social institutions including medicine, education, social reform, demography, and criminology. In this process, people gain modern citizenship and learn to govern themselves as free subjects.[47] In many interventionist regimes, governments use leisure as a way to transform people into ideal subjects who can make their regimes work. Some scholars link the role of leisure with the formation of a state-recognized political culture.[48] The CCP, too, underscored the importance of promoting Communist ideology through leisure activities. During a meeting on trade union's "club work" in 1955, Lai Ruoyu, the head of the Party-led All-China Federation of Trade Unions, expressed his ambition to educate people in their everyday life: "Everyday life means activities other than work, including relaxing, watching films, watching operas, studying, playing ball games, skating, etc. These activities are called leisure activities. When we say that we want to influence the masses by the spirit of communism in everyday life, we mean that we should imbue these activities with the spirit of communism. This influence is huge even before people realize it."[49]

Having said that, the real effect of ideological indoctrination through leisure is debatable because it is always difficult to transform people's

---

[46] Jiefangjun Nanjing budui zhengzhibu renmin qunzhong gongzuobu 解放军南京部队政治部人民群众工作部, ed., *Minbing zhengzhi jiaocai* 民兵政治教材 [Textbook for political training for civilians] (Shanghai: Shanghai renmin chubanshe, 1961), 98–99.

[47] Chris Baker, *The SAGE Dictionary of Cultural Studies* (London: SAGE Publications, 2004), 78. Sam Binkley, "Governmentality and Lifestyle Studies," *Sociology Compass* 1 (2007): 118.

[48] The Italian Fascists used leisure organizations to create a "popular consensus" for Mussolini's regime. See Victoria de Grazia, *The Culture of Consent: Mass Organization of Leisure in Fascist Italy* (New York: Cambridge University Press, 1981). Rather than giving German people abstract lectures, the Nazi Party indoctrinated its ideology by organizing its people to participate in collective leisure activities organized by its leisure organization *Kraft durch Freude*. See Timpe, *Nazi-Organized Recreation and Entertainment in the Third Reich*, 214–216.

[49] *Gongren ribao*, January 19, 1955.

minds.[50] Moreover, when ideological zest began to wane, political preaching faded from leisure because even political leaders themselves did not believe that people would be indoctrinated. In many cases, leisure under interventionist regimes degenerated from a field of ideological indoctrination to a tool of intoxication.[51] Nevertheless, like Kenez's study on the role of the Komsomol in the early 1920s, although achieving a thorough ideological transformation through leisure is almost impossible, for interventionist regimes, participating in state-organized leisure activity itself is a way of leisure governmentality because it can make people understand how to live under the interventionist regime. As Lai Ruoyu said in his 1955 report, "club activity itself is collectivist… [Participating in] club activities itself is a form of education for workers."[52] Lai's argument is very close to Robert Putnam's theory of accumulating social capital in leisure organizations and activities to make democracy work.[53] Although state-sponsored leisure activities in interventionist regimes are very different from community life in societies that Putnam has described, they both have a similar effect of making their respective regimes operate more smoothly by letting people *experience* how the system works.

[50] For example, following the resistance model, Matthew D. Johnson discovers that in the early 1950s, although the CCP tried to establish its legitimacy through cultural governance in leisure activities, in reality, the Party constantly met with "coexisting practices of cooptation, rejection, and counter-cultural creation." See Matthew D. Johnson, "Political Culture in the Archive: Grassroots Perspectives on Party-State Power and Legitimacy in 1950s Beijing," *The PRC History Review* 3, no. 1 (October 2018): 1–36.

[51] After 1968, the Czechoslovak Communist Party planned and approved a popular TV series that attracted a large audience. Leisure facilitated the stability of the Czechoslovak regime in the sense that it distracted people from thinking about "any political or economic alternative to the existing system." See Ondřej Daniel, Tomáš Kavka, and Jakub Machek, eds., *Popular Culture and Subcultures of Czech Post-Socialism: Listening to the Wind of Change* (Cambridge: Cambridge Scholar Publishing, 2016), 14. TV programs also played an important role in post-Khrushchev Soviet Union when the Communist Party started to explore new ways of creating "new sources of social solidarity." See Christine E. Evans, *Between Truth and Time: A History of Soviet Central Television* (New Haven, CT: Yale University Press, 2016).

[52] *Gongren ribao*, January 19, 1955.

[53] Robert D. Putnam, Robert Leonardi, and Raffaella Nanetti, *Making Democracy Work: Civic Traditions in Modern Italy* (Princeton, NJ: Princeton University Press, 1993); Robert D. Putnam, *Bowling Alone: The Collapse and Revival of American Community* (New York: Simon & Schuster, 2000).

Lifestyle and Youth Subcultures

Leisure is always relevant to lifestyle (ways of life) and subculture (alternative ways of life). Although there is not a consensus on the meaning of the term "lifestyle," in this book, I define it as a combination of individual choices and collective norms. Lifestyle is reflected by leisure activities and tastes. As Featherstone shows, "one's body, clothes, speech, leisure pastimes, eating and drinking preferences, home, car, choice of holidays, etc. are to be regarded as indicators of the individuality of taste and sense of style of the owner/consumer."[54]

The meaning of the term "subculture" is also debatable as there are diverse definitions of "culture." Traditionally, culture is understood as a "whole way of life" that "make the world intelligible to its members."[55] Following Dick Hebdige's emphasis on the role of "style" in subcultures, I define subculture as a kind of behavior different from the existing social norms, which is usually reflected by distinctive styles.[56] In this sense, subcultures can be understood as "lifestyle choices that depart from the mainstream," and these alternative lifestyles might include "alternative ways of thinking about society."[57] Subcultures have been treated by interventionist rulers as a threat to the ideal way of life favored by the regime, and thus, they have been targeted and hit hard.[58]

These correlating terms of leisure, lifestyle, and subculture are useful in investigating how interventionist regimes operate at the grassroots. On the one hand, leisure is used by the state to forge an ideal way of life that its people should be accustomed to even if they might not be supporters of those official ideologies. On the other hand, as in Western

---

[54] Mike Featherstone, "Lifestyle and Consumer Culture," *Theory, Culture and Society* 4 (1987): 55.

[55] Baker, *The SAGE Dictionary of Cultural Studies*, 193.

[56] For Hebdige's discussion of style in subculture, see Dick Hebdige, *Subculture: The Meaning of Style* (London: Routledge, 1979).

[57] Laura Portwood-Stacer, *Lifestyle Politics and Radical Activism* (New York: Bloomsbury, 2013), 4–5.

[58] For example, in the 1930s, the Nazis launched a campaign to terminate "degenerate art" and "degenerate music" because they thought that Avant-Garde paintings and some kind of popular music (i.e. jazz) were not in accordance with the desired way of life in a National Socialist Germany. See Olaf Peters, ed., *Degenerate Art: The Attack on Modern Art in Nazi Germany, 1937* (Munich: Prestel, 2014); Erik Levi, *Music in the Third Reich* (New York: Palgrave Macmillan, 1994).

countries, subcultures (alternative ways of life) that contradict ideological or aesthetic standards of the ideal way of life always exist in people's everyday life under interventionist regimes. How should we evaluate the role of subcultures?

For decades, scholars of subculture studies have usually followed the resistance model when it comes to state-society relations. Studies by the Birmingham School underline the "objections and contradictions" against mainstream cultures in capitalist systems.[59] For the Birmingham School, youth subcultures in post-war Britain have four features: first, subcultures generate from the working class; second, subcultures take shape around loosely or tightly bounded groups; third, the meaning of subcultures is expressed in "style" such as music, writing, clothing, and haircut; and finally, people who engage in subcultures are expressing their resistance against the mainstream.[60] Likewise, in the Soviet bloc, resistance appeared in tensions between subcultures and state-sponsored cultures. In Czechoslovakia, for example, the Communist Party's campaign against the subcultural group *vlasatci* ("longhairs") gave rise to more influential underground defiant movements around the rock group Plastic People of the Universe and the activism of *Charta 77*.[61] During the final stage of the Cold War, youth subcultures became "the heady medium of expression for protest against the establishment, against corruption and alienation of the personality."[62]

More scholars challenge the traditional approach that treats youth subcultures only as a means of resistance. Younger generations from the Birmingham School argue that previous studies had an "unqualified equation of post-war patterns of youth consumerism with notions of working-class resistance" in the sense that "the issue of young people playing their 'subcultural' roles for 'fun' is never really considered."[63] Soviet youth had a more ambiguous attitude toward the regime when they enjoyed subcultures. Anne Gorsuch suggests that "youth cultures can

---

[59] Hebdige, *Subculture*, 17.

[60] Stuart Hall and Tony Jefferson, eds., *Resistance Through Rituals: Youth Subcultures in Post-War Britain*, 2nd ed. (London: Routledge, 2006), 6–7.

[61] Filip Pospíšil, "Youth Cultures and the Disciplining of Czechoslovak Youth in the 1960s," *Social History* 37, no. 4 (November 2012): 477–500.

[62] Jim Riordan, ed., *Soviet Youth Culture* (Basingstoke: Macmillan, 1989), viii.

[63] Andy Bennett and Keith Kahn-Harris, eds., *After Subculture: Critical Studies in Contemporary Youth Culture* (New York: Palgrave Macmillan, 2004), 7–8.

be conformist as well as defiant" because in the era of the New Economic Policy, "some communist youth supported the Soviet project, even as they resisted the Bolsheviks' paternalist attitude toward youth."[64] Although youth in late Stalinist years dressed and danced provocatively, held underground poetry reading clubs, and listened to the BBC, they "did not see themselves in opposition to the system." Rather, they "bypassed it."[65] Hooligans in the Khrushchev period were "accidental deviants" instead of conscious anti-regime resistance.[66] The socialist project did matter to Soviet citizens, although at the same time they were doing things considered subversive by the authorities, by foreign observers, and by scholars.

Following the participatory totalitarian model, my research in this book shows that in the case of China, we should not overestimate the role subcultures played as a way of resistance, even though we can constantly find tensions between the ideal way of life that the CCP wanted its people to live and alternative ways of life that were actually followed by Chinese youngsters. Instead of interpreting the tensions as limits of interventionist rule, we should delve into the mentalities behind those young people with alternative ways of life to show what actually remained between widespread subcultures and the Party's leisure regulation.

The CCP's lifestyle politics created three layers of leisure. First, the Party wanted a "politicized leisure" in which people could live as official ideology required. This is, of course, a highly ideal way for people to spend their leisure time as it required all people to become ideological supporters of the Party's socialist project. Second, the Party directed people to have a "collectivized leisure," which means that although people did not become ideologically obedient, they were still used to attending state-organized collective leisure activities such as club activities organized in work units or schools. Through these activities, people actually transferred their right to allocate their leisure time to the state. Third, even if many people still had free time to do what they wanted to do and their activities were not favored by the Party (in other words,

---

[64] Anne E. Gorsuch, *Youth in Revolutionary Russia: Enthusiasts, Bohemians, Delinquents* (Bloomington: Indiana University Press, 2000), 7.

[65] Juliane Fürst, *Stalin's Last Generation: Soviet Post-War Youth and the Emergence of Mature Socialism* (Oxford: Oxford University Press, 2010), 3, 345.

[66] Brian LaPierre, *Hooligans in Khrushchev's Russia: Defining, Policing, and Producing Deviance During the Thaw* (Madison: University of Wisconsin Press, 2012), 11.

they were engaging in subcultures), these activities had been "institutionalized" by the regime in the sense that although these activities broke some rules, they did not jeopardize the regime's overall agenda and sometimes, people who engaged in subcultures actually benefitted from the institution or were hoping to join the establishment. As Chapter 6 shows, we can test the effect of institutionalization in people's leisure by observing a variety of alternative ways of life during the Cultural Revolution. Although some people did not actively participate in the political movement and they led an idle life by learning how to play musical instruments, their real intention was to get accepted by official troupes and become members of the establishment. The state could also use people's leisure choices for its own needs. For example, fishing became a popular leisure activity in the 1980s, but it was used by the government to promote public diplomacy. In May 1983, China hosted the first "Sino-Japanese fishing competition" and Wang Zhen, a veteran revolutionary, attended the opening ceremony. Three months later, the Chinese Fishing Association was established, with several well-renowned veteran revolutionaries as its consultants or honorary president.[67]

Examples in this book show that while a thoroughly "politicized leisure" was not popular among many young people, most of them did not reject "collectivized leisure" because they were used to participating in collective leisure activities. People who offered their recollections of recreational activities in the early 1950s usually had some certain kind of nostalgia because they thought that during that time, interpersonal relations in these activities were simple and pure, even though they might not like the political elements of collective leisure. The institutionalization of leisure took place imperceptibly, showing that people's leisure was still regulated and used by the regime, even if collectivism had faded away. It is noteworthy that politicization, collectivization, and institutionalization of leisure did not appear linearly; they could coexist and were spotlighted respectively in different periods. The differentiation of three layers of leisure challenges the traditional description of the trajectory of

---

[67] Wang Shaoguang 王绍光, "Siren shijian yu zhengzhi: Zhongguo chengshi xianxia moshi de bianhua" 私人时间与政治: 中国城市闲暇模式的变化 [Private time and politics: changes in the leisure mode in Chinese cities], *Zhongguo shehui kexue jikan* (Summer 1995): 117; "Zhongguo diaoyu xiehui chengli Ye Jianying ren mingyu zhuxi" 中国钓鱼协会成立叶剑英任名誉主席 [The Chinese Fishing Association has been set up with Ye Jianying as its honorary president], *Xinhuashe xinwengao* 4973 (1983).

leisure modes in the People's Republic of China that regards the demise of the political presence in people's leisure time since China's economic reform as rehabilitation of "the legitimacy of private time."[68] A highly politicized leisure was never popular among Chinese people and thus was the most inefficient way to achieve absolute control. Although people did resist the politicization of their leisure, their leisure was still institutionalized unconsciously in people's everyday practices. In this sense, the CCP's leisure regulation has greatly changed people's behavior patterns in a subtle way.

Sources and Methods

I focus on Beijing youth because the state invested substantial resources and produced profound data. Beijing was one of the first cities where the CCP attempted to organize state-sponsored leisure activities for young people and archival documents are relatively accessible.[69] Youth subcultures in urban Beijing can also ensure diversity among the group of youth that I choose because among the historical actors there were children of senior officials (which were rare in other cities), children of junior officials, and children from working-class families. Thus, urban Beijing can provide an ideal case study on the connection between leisure and social stratification under state socialism.

The definition of youth varies in different spatial and temporal contexts. In a 1989 volume, Jim Riordan stresses the divergence in the notion of youth in Western and Soviet writings. For Western scholars, youth refers to the teenage years, while for Soviet writers, it is set to a category of 14- to 32-year-old people.[70] From a biological perspective, youth is "an unavoidable period in the development of the individual between childhood and adulthood," during which adolescents prepare themselves for "the adult roles of work and family, so as to be able to continue

---

[68] Wang Shaoguang, "Siren shijian yu zhengzhi," 108–125.

[69] From September 1948, following the takeover of major cities in the Civil War, the CCP established "youth service departments" (also known as "social service departments" in some places) in Jinan, Beiping (Beijing), Tianjin, Shenyang, Shanghai, Wuhan, and Chongqing, with the purpose of educating young people through organized leisure activities. "Yinian lai de qingnian fuwu gongzuo jiankuang" 一年来的青年服务工作简况 [Summary of the youth service work in this year], 1950, BMA, 100-003-00025-0009.

[70] Riordan, *Soviet Youth Culture*, ix.

and reproduce the society."[71] In China between 1949 and the early 1980s, however, young people were outlined in an ideological dimension, whose aim was to assist the Party "to strengthen its ruling power and to achieve national independence and unity."[72] To avoid ambiguity, this project uses a simple way to circumscribe this group, with an emphasis on both biological and ideological perspectives: youth refer to those whose daily activities are regulated by the Chinese Communist Youth League (CCYL). Although the CCYL is an organization of "advanced youth" (*xianjin qingnian* 先进青年), it still aims at revolutionizing the Chinese youth by "nurturing numerous people's loyalty to the cause of the laborers" among a broad group of "young workers, young peasants, young soldiers, young clerks and young intellectuals."[73]

To examine the CCP's leisure regulation and the diverse mentalities of young people living alternatively since the 1950s, following the methodology of triangulating different levels of documents, I use three kinds of primary sources in this book. First, documents generated by the state, including but not limited to archives, published collections of official policies, biographies and chronicles of relevant officials, local gazetteers, newspapers, and magazines. The Beijing Municipal Archives has a significant number of documents about how the CCP and the Youth League organized leisure activities for young people, which are usually under the title of "mass cultural work" (*qunzhong wenhua gongzuo* 群众文化工作). The "Internal Reference" (*neibu cankao* 内部参考) held by the Universities Service Centre for China Studies at the Chinese University of Hong Kong provides details about the prevalence of youth subcultures (which were often condemned as "hooliganism" and "bourgeois lifestyle") in Beijing in the 1950s. The strengths of this sort of source are obvious: they can provide a general development of the Party's "youth work"

---

[71] Thomas B. Gold, "Youth and the State," *The China Quarterly* 127 (September 1991): 595.

[72] Ngan-Pun Ngai, Chau-Kiu Cheung, and Chi-Kei Li, "China's Youth Policy Formulation and Youth Participation," *Children and Youth Services Review* 23, no. 8 (2001): 652.

[73] "Zhongguo xin minzhu zhuyi qingniantuan gongzuo gangling" 中国新民主主义青年团工作纲领 [Working Guidelines of the Chinese New Democracy Youth League], RMRB, May 6, 1949. For a general introduction to the CCYL's function of promoting political socialization among the Chinese youth, see James R. Townsend, *The Revolutionization of Chinese Youth: A Study of Chung-kuo Ch'ing-nien* (Berkeley: Center for Chinese Studies, 1967), 9–13.

(*qingnian gongzuo* 青年工作); newspaper and magazine articles include vivid descriptions of people's everyday activities; the Party's concern about the "bourgeois lifestyle" (*zichanjieji shenghuo fangshi* 资产阶级生活方式), "petit bourgeois sentiment" (*xiao zichenjieji qingdiao* 小资产阶级情调) and "spiritual pollution" (*jingshen wuran* 精神污染) among young people led to public discussions. Nevertheless, these sources tend to over-interpret the activities of their people by labeling them as "problematic," "backward," or "reactionary" and categorize all behaviors into a polarity of support or subversion. What's more, as David Ownby observes, before the 1980s, public discussions in the magazine *China Youth* followed a style of Yan'an rectification: the authority of official ideology could not be questioned, and thus, the discussions were predetermined and biased.[74]

Second, personal accounts such as diaries, letters, blog articles, and memoirs can provide local and personal experiences of ordinary people that official documents neglect, misread, or over-interpret for some purposes, as mentioned above. This category of sources also has its pitfalls. Memories can be wrong because of the remoteness of the past; authors of such sources sometimes organize their accounts based on their personal emotions of affection or hatred.[75]

Third, oral interviews that I conducted in Beijing. Similar to memoirs, interviews allow historians to go deep into individual stories of those who do not write their own recollections while at the same time have the problem of self-justification or self-glorification. In this project, I follow a "semi-structured" style, which means that the interviewees have the initiative to shape the dialogue, but some of my questions validate details and avoid digression.[76] I also managed to find several authors of blog articles and asked them directly about their mentalities when they engaged in youth subcultures during the Cultural Revolution.

---

[74] David Ownby, "The Audience: Growing Alienation Among Chinese Youths," in *China's Establishment Intellectuals*, eds. Carol Lee Hamrin and Timothy Cheek (Armonk, NY: M.E. Sharpe, 1986), 212–246.

[75] Shen Zhihua 沈志华, "Jinshen shiyong huiyilu he koushu shiliao" 谨慎使用回忆录和口述史料 [Use memoirs and oral materials cautiously], March 11, 2013, http://dangshi.people.com.cn/n/2013/0311/c85037-20742242.html.

[76] Ning Wang offers a protocol of doing "semi-structured" interviews in China. See Ning Wang, *Banished to the Great Northern Wilderness: Political Exile and Re-education in Mao's China* (Vancouver: UBC Press, 2017), 199–200.

OUTLINE OF CHAPTERS

This book is organized thematically and, on most occasions, chronologically, which means that instead of providing a linear historical narrative of leisure regulation under the CCP, I discuss a certain topic in each chapter, but these chapters are ordered in chronological order. This does not mean that the topic discussed in each chapter did not happen in other time periods. On the contrary, the repetitiveness of certain topics shows the continuity of the CCP's tight regulation of leisure. Chapter 2 investigates the interventionist nature of the Communist regime through its visions and strategies toward young people's leisure following its takeover of Beiping (later renamed Beijing) in 1949. For the CCP, leisure was important in several ways: theoretically, Marxist doctrine placed leisure (free time) in a key position in its program of cultivating all-round developed new people; in practice, as reflected by the attack on the "American way of life" and the praise of the "Soviet way of life" from the Party's propaganda machine, diverse state-sponsored leisure activities symbolized the supremacy of socialism over capitalism; moreover, the CCP wished young people under its regime to have vigorous and lively personalities. Thus, the Party wanted young people to voluntarily take part in state-organized collective and participatory leisure activities, as it believed that instead of being a passive member of the audience, through participating in leisure activities in person, young people could "liberate" themselves culturally. To take over Beijing's leisure landscape, instead of a thorough control and transformation, the CCP adopted a "decentralized" approach to people's leisure choices. Private ball game clubs were laid aside by the Party, and they gradually declined. Self-organized dancing was redirected into officially organized group dancing. Radio entertainment and popular games that contradicted the Party's policies or tastes were banned and replaced by government-offered versions. The Party also offered new leisure in the newly established Beijing Youth Service Department. The decentralized approach toward leisure changed people's way of spending their leisure time without noticeable complaints about losing freedom in their private time.

Chapter 3 examines the Party's regulation of leisure through its "temporal politics," which is defined as the process of seizure and allocation of private time by political power. This process was achieved through collective leisure activities. Following the CCP's takeover of Beijing, authorities at first started to offer a variety of leisure activities in long vacations and days off. From 1953 to 1956, the regulation of people's private time came to its first climax when the Party introduced organized activities in everyday leisure. Young people were unsatisfied with the tight schedule in their leisure time, and as a result, in 1956, the Party adopted the policy of letting people plan their leisure time freely. While asking grassroots institutions to reduce excessive meetings and stop compelling people to participate in organized leisure activities, the CCP did not abandon its presence in people's private time. On the contrary, what the Party wanted was to rationalize the "problems" in its leisure regulation. As a result of the CCP's temporal politics, young people in Beijing became accustomed to the presence of political power in their leisure time and they were silently incorporated into the collective way of life favored by the Communist regime. This chapter discusses the collectivized leisure.

Chapter 4 deals with leisure as a form of social capital. On the one hand, the Communist regime remained vigilant to any kind of spontaneous activities and organizations, even in people's leisure time. On the other hand, the CCP worked very hard to forge an ideal way of life through organized leisure. Starting from 1955, worried about the increasingly prominent youth subcultures, the Party launched a campaign to rectify the influences of alternative ways of life in young people's leisure time. Although these subcultures were more or less available because of official policies and they were not subversive in nature, what the Party really wanted to achieve was to destroy old social connections embodied by these subcultures. Apart from eliminating existing subcultures, the CCP tried to develop a new way of life by mobilizing people to attend collective leisure activities that included participatory activities such as writing poems or singing songs. Political interference into private time also reached into people's dormitories when grassroots institutions were asked to carry out Party policies in housing units. From this perspective, although the Great Leap Forward failed economically, it did have a long-term social impact. Party-organized collective leisure activities and leisure groups during this time can be conceived as a Communist version of social capital to make its regime run smoothly by rooting out existing social connections and creating new interpersonal relations in controllable spaces. This Communist version of social capital laid the foundation of the institutionalization of leisure.

Chapter 5 discusses the relationship between leisure/lifestyle and social stratification in a self-claimed socialist country. With its ambition to create a classless utopia by eliminating the "three major differences" (the difference between industrial workers and peasants, between city and countryside, and between manual workers and mental workers), the CCP was very sensitive about any signs of social stratification under its rule. Although theoretically, three major differences should be eliminated through economic means, in reality, the Party tried to extinguish some superficial symbols of differences regarding people's everyday way of life such as alternative styles in clothing and haircuts. The campaign to revolutionize people's everyday way of life did have a huge impact on many people when they cut their hair short or refused to wear colorful clothes mostly from their own will. Although superficial differences were eliminated, the Party's politicization of leisure failed in two ways. First, it targeted the wrong objects because those who seemed to have been influenced by bourgeois lifestyle might not be ideologically alienated from Party doctrines. Second, the egalitarian politicization of leisure led to the emergence of the difference between children of officials and people with ordinary family backgrounds in the sense that children of officials formed friendship groups in some organized leisure activities exclusive to them. This chapter argues that the politicization of leisure was not as effective as the CCP had imagined because ironically, leisure became one of the sources of social stratification under state socialism.

Chapter 6 tests the effect of the Party's leisure regulation by showing how young people's leisure and lifestyle were greatly institutionalized by the regime. The Cultural Revolution freed many young people when it paralyzed the temporal discipline that had gradually been established since the Communist takeover of Beijing. Young people, therefore, felt that they had time to do things that they wanted to do. Not surprisingly, many young people at once devoted all their time and energy to the Cultural Revolution as they regarded editing and printing tabloids as their career. As the Cultural Revolution proceeded, however, diverse alternative ways of life emerged. Although rebels and members of the Central Cultural Revolution Group criticized these lifestyles as a violation of the revolutionary spirit, those who chose to live alternatively actually had very different intentions. The "decadent lifestyle" of children of officials derived from their reluctance to be politically marginalized. Some participated in self-organized choruses to avoid factional struggles, but at the same time, to participate in the Cultural Revolution in a way that they thought was correct and meaningful. A significant number of people formed a group of bystanders (*xiaoyao pai* 逍遥派) whose way of life was constantly criticized by radicals. While some bystanders were politically indifferent from the start, there were others who chose to live alternatively to wait for a better opportunity to come back to the mainstream. Overall, living alternatively did not become a means of "passive resistance." People might have resisted the chaotic practices of the Cultural Revolution, but they did not resist the regime as a whole because the regime actually greatly facilitated their alternative ways of life.

Piecing these chapters together, this book suggests that the CCP achieved an interventionist rule through the regulation of people's leisure and lifestyle. Although people might have loathed the politicization of their leisure and engaged in diverse forms of subcultures—alternative ways of life—they did not refuse to calibrate their activities to meet the requirements of the regime. The CCP successfully made people get familiar with and accustomed to how to live with the Party.

CHAPTER 2

A Happy New World: The Communist Takeover of Leisure

On November 26, 1950, a young man named Yang Zhenping boarded a train from Beijing to Shanghai without informing anyone he knew.[1] As a student at Chongde High School in Beijing, Yang had just been accepted as a member of the Chinese New Democracy Youth League in April because of his good performance in study and student work.[2] He, however, had a startling secret: he was no longer willing to continue his Youth League membership and wished to go back to his Shanghai home. Yang's decision to quit the Youth League directly originated from his maladjustment to the rules of the League. "I knew almost nothing about the Youth League when I joined," confessed Yang in a letter he left to a friend. "It was okay at the beginning, but as time goes by, I became disappointed because I felt constrained." In his self-criticism to his League branch, Yang admitted that he was extremely envious of life

---

[1] The following paragraph on Yang Zhenping is from Youth League Punishment File (19501210 Yang), author's collection.

[2] The Chinese New Democracy Youth League was renamed as the Chinese Communist Youth League in May 1957. In this book, when it is necessary to address its full name, I use the Chinese New Democracy Youth League to denote this organization before May 1957. In most cases, I simply use "Youth League" or "League" for short. For a brief introduction to the Youth League, see: "Zhongguo gongchanzhuyi qingniantuan" 中国共产主义青年团 [The Chinese Communist Youth League], http://web.archive.org/web/20191020231320/http://www.gov.cn/test/2005-06/28/content_18105.htm.

© The Author(s), under exclusive license to Springer Nature Singapore Pte Ltd. 2023
Y. Shi, *Living with the Party*, https://doi.org/10.1007/978-981-99-0208-8_2

in Europe and the United States. Although Yang was keen on having fun (*ai wan* 爱玩), he could not get real pleasure when participating in activities organized by the League. The outcome of Yang's sudden departure was grave: the Beijing Municipal Youth League Committee expelled Yang from the League in December, accusing him of "having a thought of admiring the American way of life."

Yang's inability to reconcile his own taste for entertainment with the way of life that the new regime had been advocating was not unique. In early 1951, Li Min, a government employee and also a reader of a Shanghai-based weekly titled *Outlook* (*Zhanwang* 展望), expressed his concerns about how his young colleagues spent their Saturdays and Sundays in a letter to *Outlook*:

> We have dozens of young people in our office who are very busy working and studying every day. They get up at six o'clock in the morning and cannot go to bed until ten or eleven at night, so their life is very tense. On Saturdays and Sundays, people seem to be relieved. During this period of time, everyone goes to take care of their personal affairs. Some comrades think that since this is their own time, they should use this time to "have fun (*xiaoqian* 消遣)." People have different ways to kill time: one comrade was so obsessed with *Dream of the Red Chamber* that he did not want to eat meals; one played poker until midnight; one dressed up "beautifully" and hung around the street; one had to catch three movies or dramas within a day...³

Li Min's article sparked a discussion among *Outlook* readers about "should I have fun?", and within a month, 449 replies were received by the editorial department.⁴ It is worth noticing that although most readers agreed that there should be a good rest after a week of intense work, such a good rest must not be perceived merely as "having fun." "'Pastime' was a thing of the leisure class in the old society who were worried that they had nothing to do and tried every means to 'idle away' their time," wrote a reader. "Today, now that we are very busy with our

---

³ Li Min 李敏, "Yinggai 'xiaoqian' me?" 应该 "消遣" 么? [Should I have fun (in leisure time)?], *Zhanwang* 13 (1951): 25.

⁴ Editor, "Yinggai xiaoqian ma taolun zongjie" "应该 '消遣' 吗" 讨论总结 [A summary of the discussion "should I have fun"], *Zhanwang* 17 (1951): 25.

work and study, where can we find time to 'have fun'?"[5] Another reader pointed out that "'having fun' indulgently is a way of life that is sufficient to erode the revolutionary initiative of the youth," and therefore, such activity was "backward."[6]

The examples above indicate that in the early years of the People's Republic of China, how people spent their leisure time was a serious issue to the newly established regime. This chapter focuses on the scale of the penetration of political power into young people's leisure time in Beijing in the early 1950s.[7] I explain the rationale behind the Chinese Communist Party (CCP)'s constant interest in people's leisure and the principles the Party preferred when organizing leisure activities. I then discuss the Party's multifaceted tactics toward the sphere of leisure. Without a coherent and unified agenda, multiple Party and government institutions dealt with existing leisure activities separately and differently. These tactics, along with the state-sponsored new leisure forms, shaped the space of leisure that young people in Beijing would encounter in the following decades.

THE COMMUNIST VIEW ON LEISURE

The Chinese Communists, who vowed to pursue the perfect society in human history, had a utopian vision of what people should do in their

---

[5] Lin Yongjiang 林永江, "Weile gongzuo yangjing xurui" 为了工作养精蓄锐 [Save our energy for work], *Zhanwang* 15 (1951): 24.

[6] Xue Lai 薛莱, "Fandui luohou de 'xiaoqian' sixiang" 反对落后的 "消遣" 思想 [Opposing the backward thought of "having fun"], *Zhanwang* 16 (1951): 26.

[7] A traditional way to study leisure in the early years of the People's Republic is to juxtapose leisure options that were available during a certain period of time and examine the tensions between entertainment and political indoctrination. See, for example, Zhou Jing 周静, "Xin Zhongguo 'shiqi nian' Beijing dazhong de yule shenghuo yanjiu" 新中国 "十七年"北京大众的娱乐生活研究 [Research on popular entertainment in Beijing during new China's first seventeen years] (master's thesis, Capital Normal University, 2008). Another approach usually focuses on the transformation of certain kinds of entertainment by highlighting how actors or writers that had become famous before the CCP came to power experienced the new regime. See Perry Link, "The Crocodile Bird: *Xiangsheng* in the Early 1950s" and Paul G. Pickowicz, "Acting Like Revolutionaries: Shi Hui, the Wenhua Studio, and Private-Sector Filmmaking, 1949–52," in Brown and Pickowicz, eds., *Dilemmas of Victory*, 207–231, 246–287. This chapter follows this grassroots approach and looks at how ordinary people's leisure options were shaped by the Chinese Communist Party.

leisure time with the faith that the Communist enterprise aimed to create not only a collective personality but also a happy one. Theoretically, the Party's solicitude for leisure can be tracked back to the highly idealist Marxist view of the future Communist society. For Marx, as a result of the abolition of the division of labor, any person can become an all-round developed individual who will be able "to do one thing today and another tomorrow, to hunt in the morning, fish in the afternoon, rear cattle in the evening, criticize after dinner."[8] This transformation toward all-round development, as stated by Marx, would be possible through cultivations in "free time."[9] Accordingly, to transform the youth into all-round developed individuals, the CCP took on the responsibilities to organize all kinds of leisure activities for the youth in their leisure time, such as book reading, professional training, amateur drama, and singing groups.[10]

In practice, diverse state-sponsored leisure activities symbolized the supremacy of socialism over capitalism, during which people could not only be educated but also have real fun. In the early 1950s, Chinese propagandists usually portrayed the "American way of life" as corrupt, morbid, and degenerated with money as the determining factor. In the United States, "no matter young or old, people go to pubs every Saturday night, where the drunken people dance and shout wildly," a pamphlet about the United States published in Shanghai in 1951 wrote scornfully. "People have no sense of belonging to a collective, and thus they don't get any real pleasure."[11] In 1951, famous Chinese philosopher Jin Yuelin criticized the American way of life by offering his reflection on individual freedom:

> If there is a so-called democratic way of life with individual freedom, it is shown in the deterioration and lack of discipline in the trivia of everyday life. This kind of individual freedom is not real freedom, but the freedom of indulgence and being wild, in which people look down

---

[8] Karl Marx, "The German Ideology," in *Karl Marx: Selected Writings*, ed. David McLellan (Oxford: Oxford University Press, 2000), 185.

[9] Marx, "Grundrisse," in McLellan, *Karl Marx*, 419.

[10] Feng Wenbin jinian wenji bianjizu 冯文彬纪念文集编辑组, ed., *Feng Wenbin jinian wenji* 冯文彬纪念文集 [Collected writings commemorating Feng Wenbin] (Beijing: Zhonggong dangshi chubanshe, 2001), 101.

[11] Peng Ruifu 彭瑞夫, *Meiguo mianmianguan* 美国面面观 [An overview of the United States] (Shanghai: Liantong shudian, 1951), 32.

upon life with serious disciplines and seek only excitement. Pornographic novels and movies about robbery flood the market, alcohol-related crimes emerge one after another, and mental disorders become the most common diseases[12] (Figs. 2.1 and 2.2).

On the contrary, the "Soviet way of life" was joyful, tasteful, and meaningful. A member of the All-China Federation of Trade Unions who visited the Soviet Union in 1950 noticed that "people live a tasteful and civilized happy life. Everyone coming out of factories, farms, schools, and government buildings will enjoy good cultural leisure by entering any club, cinema, concert hall, dance hall, library, stadium, and cultural park…This is the product of the superior Soviet system."[13] Facilities for cultural leisure (*wenhua xiuxi* 文化休息), which was the Soviet term for state-sponsored leisure activities, were also places that the Soviet hosts preferred to display to their visitors. Huge urban "cultural leisure parks" in the Soviet Union were always impressive to Chinese travelers. Different from "amusement parks" in capitalist countries in the sense that while amusement parks were only places for people to have fun without realizing that they were "intoxicated" and "lured to degeneration" by the ruling class, cultural leisure parks offered the laboring masses relaxation and education at the same time.[14]

Furthermore, in the CCP's vision of youth, instead of being downhearted and dull like they usually were in the "old society," young people should be vigorous and lively under the new regime. During the Second National Congress of the Chinese New Democracy Youth League in July 1953, Hu Yaobang, then head of the Youth League, asserted that the

[12] Jin Yuelin 金岳霖, *Cong duoluo dao fandong de Meiguo wenhua* 从堕落到反动的美国文化 [American Culture from being degenerate to being reactionary] (Shanghai: Pingming chubanshe, 1951), 10.

[13] Chen Xiwen 陈希文, *Fang su zaji* 访苏杂记 [Scattered records of visit in the Soviet Union] (Beijing: Gongren chubanshe, 1951), 66.

[14] Chen, *Fang su zaji*, 95. Cultural leisure parks, or parks for culture and leisure (парк культуры и отдыха), were a new kind of cultural and educational infrastructure that appeared during the Soviet Cultural Revolution. The first cultural leisure park in the Soviet Union, the Gorky Central Park for Culture and Leisure in Moscow, was opened in 1928. Usually, a Soviet cultural leisure park has theaters, amusement areas, places for music and dancing, auditoriums, reading rooms, chess rooms, rooms for group activities, gyms, and bowling alleys. See *Gongchanzhuyi jiaoyu cidian* 共产主义教育词典 [Dictionary for communist education] (Chengdu: Sichuansheng shehui kexueyuan chubanshe, 1986), 291–292.

Fig. 2.1 Cover page of *American Way of Life* (Shanghai: Shidai she, 1950)

youth should be educated to become a generation that would be "patriotic, loyal to the people, literate, disciplined, brave, hardworking, and vigorous."[15] A cadre in the Beijing Municipal Youth League Committee

[15] RMRB, July 6, 1953.

Fig. 2.2 Back cover of *American Way of Life*

argued that because of the long-lasting "feudal shackles," young people used to live a monotonous life, which made their personality "unliberated," like a "thermos, being cold on the surface but hot in the heart." He observed that during interactions with foreign friends, foreigners, no matter young or old, could dance and sing, but the Chinese could only give boring talks about politics.[16] Therefore, it was vital and necessary for the Party to nurture more and more vigorous young people through various kinds of leisure activities.

From the perspective of the CCP, successful leisure activities should follow three principles. The first and most fundamental principle was that people should join voluntarily. Official guidelines on leisure activities repeatedly stressed that these activities must match the real interests and hobbies of young people so that they would take part voluntarily. For example, in 1951, the Beijing Municipal Youth League Committee proposed in a report that "cultural activities should be carried out on a voluntary basis and appeal to young people."[17] A cadre from the Youth League Central Committee also reminded activists in Beijing that when organizing leisure activities, all work units should set up different kinds of amateur groups so that young people could join voluntarily based on their own interests and hobbies.[18]

The second principle was that leisure activities should be organized collectively. Collective leisure is a form of entertainment that the CCP tried to promote in young people's leisure time. From the table of contents of various pamphlets published in the 1950s to guide young people's recreational activities such as the *Youth Club* in Beijing and the *Youth Cultural Palace* in Shanghai, collective activities including group dancing, group games, and choruses always occupied the most important position. The Party recognized that with "the spirit of friendship and unity of the working class," collective leisure activities could enhance the comradeship among participants in an imperceptible way.[19] These collective leisure activities, however, must be organized under the leadership of the Party, the Youth League, labor and trade unions, cultural palaces, or

---

[16] "Liu Daosheng tongzhi zai Beijingshi zhongdeng yishang xuexiao qunzhong wenhua huodong jiji fenzi dahui shang de baogao" 刘导生同志在北京市中等以上学校群众文化活动积极分子大会上的报告 [Comrade Liu Daosheng's report during the conference of mass culture activists in secondary and post-secondary schools in Beijing], November 15, 1953, BMA, 100-001-00118-0001.

[17] "Beijingshi qingnian qunzhong wenhua gongzuo zongjie baogao ji wuyi nian xiabannian gongzuo fangzhen jihua cao'an" 北京市青年群众文化工作总结报告及五一年下半年工作方针计划 (草案) [Summarizing report on mass culture work among Beijing youth and working plans for the second half of 1951 (draft)], 1951, BMA, 100-003-00045-0001.

[18] *Feng Wenbin jinian wenji*, 103–104.

[19] *Gongren ribao*, January 19, 1955.

other such official organizations. Collective activities that were organized spontaneously were not advocated.

The final and perhaps the most important principle was that successful leisure activities must be participatory. Instead of being satisfied with performances offered by professional organizations at the grassroots level, young people should participate in leisure activities by compiling their own scripts, performing their own plays, and singing their own songs. From the perspective of organizers of leisure activities, although labor and trade unions in capitalist countries could also hand out free movie tickets to workers or invite theatrical troupes and bands to factories, workers could only passively "watch" the intoxicating arts because they did not actually "do" them. And therefore, they were not "liberated" culturally under the CCP's standard.[20]

From the analysis above, we can find out why "having fun" could become a problem and aroused a public discussion in *Outlook* in the early 1950s. On the one hand, similar to "having fun," the Communists also considered leisure activities they organized as a means of letting people spend their leisure time with pleasure. On the other hand, the aim of these organized leisure activities was not just to let people "have fun" meaninglessly. They must be organized with educational purposes to make participants free from being "intoxicated" as they were when purely having fun. To implement their view on leisure after the takeover of Beijing, the CCP adopted several tactics toward existing leisure activities.

DEALING WITH EXISTING LEISURE ACTIVITIES: THREE TACTICS

When the CCP took over Beijing in 1949, they found that the city was awash with all kinds of spontaneously organized leisure activities, as ordinary people found ways to share sports, dancing, and games. The Party, therefore, set out to bring these uncoordinated and possibly degenerated activities under its "guidance." The Party employed three major tactics to achieve its goal: putting aside, redirecting, and replacing.

---

[20] A Ying 阿英, *Gongchang wenyu gongzuo de lilun yu shijian* 工厂文娱工作的理论与实践 [Theory and practice of cultural and recreational work in factories] (Beijing: Shenghuo dushu xinzhi sanlian shudian, 1950), 8.

Putting Aside: Private Ball Game Clubs

Private ball game clubs (*qiushe* 球社) flourished in Republican Beijing (Beiping) as venues of both physical exercise and leisure entertainment. According to a tourist guidebook published just before the Sino-Japanese War, as an important part of "entertainment venues," ball game clubs offered places and equipment for billiards, bowling, table tennis, and even golf. By the time of 1937, there were nine famous ball game clubs scattered across downtown Beijing.[21] Ball game clubs were ranked into three levels based on the quality of the equipment they could provide, and rates were charged by the hour. Customers should also tip scorekeepers and sparring partners serving them.[22] By the end of the Nationalist rule, the number of private ball game clubs in Beijing increased to twenty-two.[23]

For the Communists, ball game clubs bore ambivalent meanings: on the one hand, the initial purpose of these clubs was to entertain through sports, which was quite tasteful; on the other hand, the nature of ball game clubs as commercial businesses made it inaccessible to the poor. According to a survey conducted by the Beijing Municipal Bureau of Industry and Commerce shortly after the takeover of Beijing, ball game clubs belonged to "proper entertainment," but they also had serious "problems." As observed by Party officials, although it seemed easy to run ball game clubs in Beijing, the actual situation was quite complicated because to make a profit, the owners of ball game clubs had to get connected with people from different classes, which made these clubs hodgepodges of both good and bad.[24]

Party officials considered the "atmosphere" of ball game clubs unacceptable in the new society because of their way of doing business. For a long time, one of the major selling points of ball game clubs was the existence of waitresses who served as scorekeepers or sparring partners. In the 1930s, ball game clubs started to recruit such waitresses to solicit

---

[21] Ma Zhixiang 马芷庠, *Beiping lüxing zhinan* 北平旅行指南 [Beiping guidebook] (Beiping: Jingji xinwen she, 1937), 259.

[22] Bai Zhaojie 白肇杰, "Jiuri Beijing de digunqiu he taiqiu" 旧日北京的地滚球和台球 [Bowling and billiards in old Beijing], *Beijing tiyu wenshi* 4 (1989): 15.

[23] Xi Wuyi 习五一 and Deng Yibing 邓亦兵, *Beijing tongshi di jiu juan* 北京通史 第九卷 [General history of Beijing, vol. 9] (Beijing: Beijing yanshan chubanshe, 2012), 203.

[24] "Qiushe ye zongjie" 球社业总结 [Summary of the ball game club industry], 1949, BMA, 022-010-00084-014.

more customers, and not surprisingly, some customers went to ball game clubs not to play ball games, but to flirt with those waitresses.[25] This was still the case when an investigation of Beijing's private ball game clubs was conducted in 1949 by officials who were in charge of industry and commerce in this city.[26] "Ball game clubs were vibrant during the Japanese and Nationalist rule when people from the wealthy leisure class came up with many ideas to kill time and spend their easy money," the investigators wrote in a contemptuous tone. "Few of them, however, actually went there to play ball games. Their real purpose was to hunt for those waitresses taking care of pitches. They tipped the waitresses several times higher than hourly rates [of ball game clubs]. As this bad atmosphere deepened day by day, people seeking real recreational purposes did not dare to visit ball game clubs at all." As a result, ball game clubs became hotbeds of those "monkeying around" (*youshou haoxian* 游手好闲), and even local bullies and hooligans. In addition, for the waitresses working for ball game clubs, making a living on tips encouraged a kind of "parasitic thinking" (*jisheng sixiang* 寄生思想) in the sense that they did not get paid from decent labor. Furthermore, the owners of ball game clubs only served a small number of people from the "leisure class," which made it difficult for them to realize that it would be more joyful "serving the majority."

The investigators concluded that private ball game clubs "could and should exist" by nature, and they had a promising future in "raising general awareness of proper entertainment among the masses." To deal with the problems observed in ball game clubs, investigators suggested that political education should be promoted among waiters and waitresses to let them recognize that this kind of business was "painful, dark, and abnormal" so that they could abandon their "parasitic thinking." The owners of ball game clubs should also be inspired to understand that proper entertainment was supposed to be close to the proletariats instead of serving a few wealthy people. The investigators predicted optimistically that once the problems of ball game clubs were solved, whether the waiters and waitresses still worked there or were assigned to factories, they would finally become good laborers and no longer lead a "parasitic life."

---

[25] Ma, *Beiping lüxing zhinan*, 259.

[26] The following paragraphs on ball game clubs are from "Qiushe ye zongjie," 1949, BMA, 022-010-00084-14.

Generally speaking, the Party's strategy toward private ball game clubs was "putting aside"—clubs did not get support from the government, but they were not closed either. Nevertheless, the gradual transformation of female scorekeepers and sparring partners did have a huge impact because they were the reasons people had been going there. Huixian Ball Game Club, with pitches of several different kinds of ball games, was one of the most profitable private clubs in Beijing. As recalled by an old Beijing resident, before the 1950s, "the most attractive thing [about Huixian Ball Game Club] was that there were scorekeepers, all of whom were very beautiful ladies wearing the same uniforms to help you record your points. If you did not go there with your friends and felt bored playing alone, the scorekeepers could also spar with you. You could even take them out of the club." The business, however, became slack after the service of female scorekeepers and sparring partners was discontinued.[27] During a survey conducted by the Beijing Municipal Bureau of Industry and Commerce in 1953, Yuying Ball Game Club reported that only clubs with a "flavor of the old society" (which means clubs that still had female scorekeepers and sparring partners) could make a satisfactory profit. On the contrary, those clubs with fewer female scorekeepers and sparring partners were facing bankruptcy.[28]

The decline of ball game clubs was also related to the establishment of state-sponsored recreational venues as well as their poor attitude in customer service. Also, in the 1953 survey mentioned above, Yuying Ball Game Club noticed that because work units and schools across Beijing started to provide sports equipment, people became less interested in spending time in private ball game clubs because of the expensive hourly rate and deposit.[29] For example, two high school students in Beijing went to Huixian Ball Game Club to play table tennis in the winter break of 1954 and had a very unpleasant experience there:

---

[27] Zhao Heng 赵珩, "Huiyi jiushi de Beijing shangye zhongxin" 回忆旧时的北京商业中心 [A Recollection of the old business center of Beijing], April 5, 2015, http://web.archive.org/web/20191022231036/https://cul.qq.com/a/20150409/027355.htm.

[28] "Diaocha liaojie Beijingshi wenyuchang yingye qingkuang baogao" 调查了解北京市文娱场营业情况报告 [Report on the investigation of situation of cultural recreational venues in Beijing], June 1953, BMA, 022-010-00713-037.

[29] "Diaocha liaojie Beijingshi wenyuchang yingye qingkuang baogao," June 1953, BMA, 022-010-00713-037.

The waitress was sitting cross-legged, busy knitting by the fire in the corner of the room. After noticing that the customers were two high school students, she kept an indifferent attitude and said "four *mao* an hour" without raising her head. After we clubbed together four *mao* and put the money on the counter, the waitress added, "deposit, two *yuan*." We were astounded: two *yuan* at that time was equal to the money of a monthly traffic pass. I asked: "Why do you charge a deposit after we pay the hourly rate?" The waitress came over carelessly and said, "what if the rackets and table are damaged by you?" I said: "We bring our own rackets." "What if the table is broken?" The waitress replied. I was speechless and said, "can I use my student ID as collateral?" The manager showed up and said, "no, we have never done this before." My friend had to take off his leather jacket as collateral. The manager said reluctantly, "next time, bring enough money." We played with the utmost care for an hour with the fear of causing any damage to the table. After one hour, the waitress came over and inspected the table carefully. She returned the leather jacket to my friend after finding no damage to the table.[30]

Consequently, during the first three years of the takeover of Beijing, the number of ball game clubs and people working there decreased rapidly. At the end of 1950, there were still eighteen ball game clubs in Beijing, but in October 1952, only one-third of them survived[31] (Table 2.1)

Redirecting: Self-Organized Dancing

In 1952, people in Beijing found a new way to spend lovely summer nights: they went dancing in Tiananmen Square. Since the May Day of that year, hundreds of workers, students, cadres, soldiers, and sales clerks participated in dancing enthusiastically every weekend, and some of them even went dancing every night during workdays. People were positive about dancing. "With the improvement of their living standard, cultural and recreational activities (*wenhua yule huodong* 文化娱乐活动) have become an indispensable part in the lives of the liberated Chinese

[30] "Wo zai jiefang chu de qiushe jingli" 我在解放初的球社经历 [My experience in a ball game club shortly after the liberation], November 25, 2003, http://web.archive.org/web/20191022235344/http://www.sport.org.cn/sfa/2003/1125/80717.html.

[31] Beijingshi qiushe ye tongye gonghui choubei weiyuanhui 北京市球社业同业公会筹备委员会, "Siying shangye diaocha baogao (qiushe ye)" 私营商业调查报告 (球社业) [Investigation on private business (ball game clubs)], November 27, 1952, BMA, 126-001-00197-0308.

Table 2.1 Private Ball Game Clubs in Beijing, 1950–1952

	Number of Ball Game Clubs	Number of Workers
End of 1950	18	160
End of 1951	15	150
October 1952	6	45

Source Data adapted from Beijingshi qiushe ye tongye gonghui choubei weiyuanhui 北京市球社业同业公会筹备委员会, "Siying shangye diaocha baogao (qiushe ye)" 私营商业调查报告 (球社业) [Investigation on private business (ball game clubs)], November 27, 1952, BMA, 126-001-00197-0308

people," wrote one reader in his letter to *People's Daily*. "Everybody is singing and dancing with great excitement. People need this kind of entertainment after working intensely for a whole week."[32] What the dancers did not know was that the Beijing authorities had been keeping a close eye on their activities. In July 1952, the Beijing Municipal Youth League Committee submitted a report to the Beijing Municipal Party Committee on this spontaneous dancing carnival. The authorities wanted to know who went dancing, who organized them, what they danced, what music they used for accompaniment, why they danced, and whether this activity had any social impact.[33]

According to the report, most of the dancers had very decent personal backgrounds. Among those who went dancing every night, there were around 300 workers (including four Youth League members), 30 sales clerks (including two or three Youth League members), and dozens of high school students. Twenty or so workers only went dancing on Saturdays and Sundays; most of them were labor union activists. There were even army and navy soldiers, police officers, and government workers among the dancers. Group dancing (*jiti wu* 集体舞) and ballroom dancing (*jiaoji wu* 交际舞 or *jiaoyi wu* 交谊舞) were both performed. The report confirmed that most of the dances were "healthy": some were

---

[32] RMRB, June 8, 1952.

[33] The following paragraphs on dancing at Tiananmen Square are from Qingniantuan shiwei 青年团市委, "Qingniantuan Beijing shiwei guanyu zai Tiananmen qian tiaowu qingkuang ji chuli yijian de baogao ji Zhao Fan de pishi" 青年团北京市委关于在天安门前跳舞情况及处理意见的报告及赵凡的批示 [Report on dancing in front of Tiananmen and opinions on how to handle this issue by the Beijing Municipal Youth League Committee, with Zhao Fan's comments], July 8, 1952, BMA, 001-006-00651-00016.

accompanied by folk songs "singing the praises of Chairman Mao from ethnic minorities in Xinjiang," and others were accompanied by songs "singing the praises of New China." Most of the dancing steps were fine, except some "very unhealthy" poses such as "shouting strangely with heads tilted to one side" and "raising body to embrace waist" while singing "we are so happy." As for whether there were organizers behind the scene, the Municipal Youth League Committee admitted that they were unable to make a conclusion at the moment, but they had noticed that when dancing in circles, there were always two or three people in the middle of the circles leading the dance or accompanying with harmonicas. The Municipal Youth League Committee attributed the dancing activities to three reasons: first, after the Five-anti Campaign, workers had little work to do, and labor discipline became lax; second, there was a lack of organized study sessions or cultural and recreational activities; third, a small number of "backward" youth went dancing to find girlfriends.

The Municipal Youth League Committee had an ambiguous attitude toward dancing on Tiananmen Square. First and foremost, as the reader's letter to *People's Daily* indicated, there was no reason to forbid dancing because it was considered a "proper requirement" from the masses. From the perspective of Party officials, however, some of the steps, poses, and even music accompaniments were far from satisfactory. What's more, such kind of self-organized activities, even if they were only for recreational purposes without any political intentions, still made the Party uneasy because they did not want any spontaneous activities going out of their own control. In September 1952, the Cultural Enterprise Management Office of the Beijing Municipal Government drafted a three-step plan to mobilize the dancers to dance inside the government-run Workers' Cultural Palace near Tiananmen Square. The first step was to launch a propaganda campaign by publishing readers' letters opposing dancing on Tiananmen Square in newspapers. Then, the Cultural Enterprise Management Office, the Cultural Palace, and amateur art schools would send people to persuade the dancers to leave the square by explaining that "group dancing is good, but it is inappropriate to dance on Tiananmen Square because cultural and art departments cannot lead you to improve your level of dancing." Finally, if the measures described in the first two steps did not work, the Public Security Bureau would start the "exhortation."[34]

[34] "Niding dongyuan Tiananmen wudao qunzhong dao wenhuagong qu de baofan de qianbao" 拟定动员天安门舞蹈群众到文化宫去的办法的签报 [Application for mobilizing

The example above shows the first layer of redirection: the Party redirected spontaneous dancing into an officially organized leisure activity that must be held in a proper venue. If this layer of redirection mainly focuses on the location of dancing, forms and contents of dancing were also a major target for leisure redirection. In the early years of the People's Republic, as a common way of leisure entertainment, ballroom dancing was still popular among people in Beijing. Ballroom dancing had its own rules that were not defined by the Party. In June 1951, Tan Youshi, a ballroom dancing educator in Beijing who had been famous since the Republican years, published his *How to Ballroom Dance* (*Zenyang tiao jiaoji wu* 怎样跳交际舞), which was the first book about ballroom dancing after 1949.[35] In his book, Tan introduced eleven types of ballroom dancing, including blues, quicksteps, waltz, quick waltz, tango, rumba, slow foxtrot, jitterbug, samba, one step, and conga.[36] Tan also attached fourteen tips about dancing etiquette at the end of his book, basically for male learners:

1. Two men can dance together when learning how to dance, but in ballrooms, a man should dance in pairs with a woman.
2. Wear proper suits and shoes, but do not dance with hats.
3. If the woman takes a male partner or parents with her, the man should ask for their consent when inviting her to dance.
4. If you go dancing with a female partner, you should not dance with others and let her sit alone (except when your partner wants to quit dancing).
5. If you bring more than one female partner, you should invite them to dance in rotation.
6. If you go dancing with a female partner, you should dance at least three times: at the beginning, in the middle, and at the end of the dancing party.
7. If a man invites a woman to dance, it would be improper for the female to reject.

---

the masses dancing in front of Tiananmen to the Working People's Cultural Palace], September 11, 1952, BMA, 011-002-00146-001.

[35] Gu Yewen 顾也文, *Jiaoyi wu qutan* 交谊舞趣谈 [Amusing remarks on ballroom dancing] (Shanghai: Xuelin chubanshe, 2003), 68.

[36] "Table of Contents" and "Preface," Tan Youshi 谈有时, *Zenyang tiao jiaoji wu* 怎样跳交际舞 [How to ballroom dance] (Beijing: Minzhi shudian, 1951).

8. If the daughter of the hostess is present at the party, you should invite her to dance to pay your tribute.
9. When the music starts to play, walk to your female partner and bow for around fifteen degrees while waiting for her to stand up.
10. After you start to dance, you should not stop until the music stops.
11. If the music continues to play for a second time, you should not go back to your seat or find another partner when the first time ends.
12. If you collide with your partner during dancing, both of you should apologize to each other.
13. After you dance with your female partner, send her back to her seat and thank her; the female partner should reply with a nod.
14. You may leave before the dancing party ends. Do not disturb the host. If the host approaches you, however, you should thank him as a farewell.[37]

According to Tan in his preface, this book originated from his notes for ballroom dancing crash courses as more and more people wanted to master ballroom dancing because government offices, factories, and schools often held dancing parties in leisure time after the "liberation."[38] Although Tan wished to introduce ballroom dancing to his readers within the ideological and narrative preference of the Party, critical letters from several readers from Tianjin were sent to the News and Publication Office of Beijing Municipal Government in early 1952. After consulting the Chinese Dancers Association, it was concluded that Tan's book was "publicizing bourgeois ballroom dancing." The cover page of the book, according to the Chinese Dancers Association, was depicting a "lady and gentleman" couple dancing together from the bourgeois class. By "singing the praises of their lifestyle consciously or unconsciously," Tan forgot that such a lifestyle came from the exploitation of workers and peasants. Tan's tips for ballroom dancing beginners were just "hypocritical etiquette rules and rituals" that would deceive young revolutionary cadres. As for the genres introduced in Tan's book, jitterbug, samba, and conga were considered representatives of "decadent emotions in capitalist

---

[37] Tan, *Zenyang tiao jiaoji wu*, 116.
[38] Tan, *Zenyang tiao jiaoji wu*, 1.

societies," while other relatively "formal" genres such as waltz, blues, and foxtrot were "useless" for Chinese because they were foreign[39] (Fig. 2.3).

There is no document showing whether Tan's 1951 book was criticized publicly, but he must have learned of the Chinese Dancers Association's comments. In 1953, Tan published his revised version of *How to Ballroom Dance* with a new title *How to Learn Ballroom Dancing* (*Zenyang xuexi jiaoyi wu* 怎样学习交谊舞), and also with a new cover page on which the woman's clothes were changed into a Soviet-style one piece, or *bulaji* in Chinese, and her hair was plaited into a long braid.[40] The shoes of the dancing pair also became less formal (see Fig. 2.4). What's more, when introducing some basic dancing movements, Tan even added illustrations of a man wearing a much more revolutionary Sun Yat-sen suit (see Fig. 2.5).

The fourteen tips for beginners that were condemned as "hypocritical" were removed in the 1953 edition along with several genres of ballroom dancing. To redirect his book to the course of the new regime, Tan added a short essay, "A Proper Understanding of Ballroom Dancing that We Should Have," at the beginning of the book, claiming that ballroom dancing actually originated from folk dances that were created by the laboring masses. Thus, with "natural, pure, healthy, and beautiful" characters in nature, it was welcomed by the masses as a "cultural recreation serving the laborers." Tan admitted that in the "old society," like many other kinds of "popular arts," ballroom dancing was "eroded." Nevertheless,

> Now, it's the age of the people, and also the time when ballroom dancing should go back to the laboring masses… We should know about it, study it, popularize it, and improve it to make it more popular as a means of cultural recreation so that it can better serve the production and labor of the people.[41]

---

[39] Zhonghua quanguo wudao gongzuozhe xiehui 中华全国舞蹈工作者协会, "Guanyu Tianjin duzhe laixin piping ruhe tiao jiaojiwu yishi de chuli yijian" 关于天津读者来信批评如何跳交际舞一事的处理意见 [Opinions on how to handle reader's letter from Tianjin criticizing *How to Ballroom Dance*], March 14, 1952, BMA, 008-002-00014-0006.

[40] For the popularity of Soviet-style one piece among Chinese woman in the early 1950s, see Yan Li, *China's Soviet Dream: Propaganda, Culture, and Popular Imagination* (London: Routledge, 2018), 119–132.

[41] Tan Youshi 谈有时, *Zenyang xuexi jiaoyi wu* 怎样学习交谊舞 [How to learn ballroom dancing] (Beijing: Unknown publisher, 1953), 2.

Fig. 2.3 Cover page of Tan Youshi's *How to Ballroom Dance* (1951). Note the man's high collar and the winkle-pickers as well as the woman's permanent wave, formal long skirt, and high heels

Fig. 2.4 Cover page of *How to Learn Ballroom Dancing* (1953)

No matter how much effort Tan took, the image of ballroom dancing in the People's Republic was still connected with a decadent lifestyle that would fritter away young people's energy.

平衡動作

平衡動作是舞術上最基本的要素。當你單獨練習舞步的時候，往往不能移走得平穩。如果和舞伴同舞，則更感到困難。這完全是你不能正確去支配身體的重心。所以當你前進或後退時，必須兩腿從大腿骨開始。同時身體必須保持自然直立，重心向前；但不要傾撲向前。當你前進時把後面的腳跟提起重心移向前面，在前面的腳跟一踏實地面，則重心介於後面腳的腳掌和前面腳的腳跟中間。繼即把前腳放平，重心換到前面的腳上（見圖一）。當後退時應先用腳趾，及至後面的腳放到腳掌時，再把前面的腳趾從地面上略微提起，此時重心介於前面腳跟和後面腳掌中間。繼即將重心換到後面的腳掌上。在前腳未經過後腳時，後腳腳跟不可落地（見圖二）。此種平衡動作須要特別注意練習。

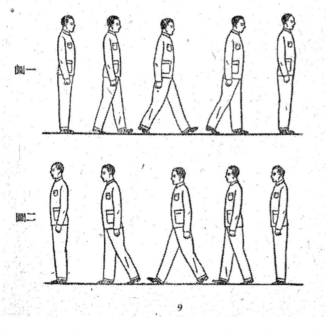

Fig. 2.5 "Balance Movement" *How to Learn Ballroom Dancing*, 9

In the early 1950s, another kind of dancing—group dancing—was advocated and promoted by the Party both as a means of leisure entertainment and as a type of performing arts. Different from the self-entertaining ballroom dancing, group dancing, according to its advocates, had multifaceted meanings. One pamphlet about group dancing published in 1951 classified dancing into two kinds: "one kind is to make oneself happy by joining dancing alone. There is also another kind of dancing that is intended for the audience to enjoy." Editors suggested in the pamphlet that whereas in the "old society," the two kinds of dancing were "hostile and unrelated," in the new society, the two kinds could influence and benefit from each other because they were both well suited to the needs of the people. "The relationship between these two kinds of dancing is the relationship between improvement and popularization. The performing dancing is more focused on improvement, while the self-entertaining dancing is more focused on popularization."[42]

In fact, from the perspective of ordinary people, the distinction between group dancing and ballroom dancing lies not in their meanings or steps, but in the number of people dancing together: group dancing involves more people in which they need to dance in rehearsed formations, and ballroom dancing only requires one man and one woman in pair.[43] Although born to be a type of "proper cultural and recreational activities," ballroom dancing was condemned as "stinky" and "unhealthy" in the sense that it was used by the Western bourgeoise to "reflect their degenerate emotion and style." When it spread to China, after combining with the "corrupt and dissipated lifestyle in semi-colonial metropolises," ballroom dancing finally became a mixture of "degenerated pastime" and "tool for seduction."[44] In contrast, group dancing, as a mixture of *yangge* in Communist-controlled Northwest China and folk dances in the Soviet Union and Eastern Europe, had a more revolutionary origin.[45]

---

[42] Pu Siwen 濮思温 and Guan Yulin 管玉琳, *Xin jiti wu* 新集体舞 [New group dancing] (Beijing: Shenghuo dushu xinzhi sanlian shudian, 1951), 6–7.

[43] Interviewee 1, October 24, 2018. This interviewee was born in 1954 and started to work in a factory in Beijing after graduating from junior high school in 1970. He liked to participate in leisure activities in the factory and became a part-time Youth League cadre in 1973.

[44] Gu Yewen 顾也文, *Guoji jiaoyi wu* 国际交谊舞 [International ballroom dancing] (Shanghai: Wenyu chubanshe, 1953), 1.

[45] Pu and Guan, *Xin jiti wu*, 1–5.

In Beijing, Party officials strived to redirect "decadent" ballroom dancing into the "spirited" group dancing that could meet the high emotional standard of the new regime. On the one hand, steps of different group dances were promoted in recreational handbooks such as *Youth Club* compiled by the Beijing Municipal Youth League Committee. The first volume of *Youth Club*, published in May 1950, included six group dances with musical accompaniments and steps. Most of these group dances, which were compiled by amateur and professional dancers in Beijing, had strong political implications. One group dance titled "Wind from the Northeast" was designed to be set to the lyrics "Our leader Mao Zedong led us to get liberated. When the sun rises up, the sky is all red. Our Mao Zedong, oh oh oh…".[46]

Group dancing activities and training were also offered among high school students in the summer break of 1951, as planned by the Committee for Summer Vacation Life (*shuqi shenghuo weiyuanhui* 暑期生活委员会). These activities and training were mainly designed for dancing activists (*wudao jiji fenzi* 舞蹈积极分子) and mainstays of mass culture (*qunzhong wenhua gugan* 群众文化骨干) in Beijing high schools to let them communicate with and learn from each other to promote group dancing in their own schools. As a schedule for dancing club activities shows, organizers also offered theoretical and practical training for participants. Demonstration performances were also used to spur students from those schools with weak dancing activities[47] (Table 2.2).

Although many young people in factories, government offices, and schools welcomed group dancing, sometimes, the mass campaign promoting group dancing did backfire. In some schools, even though people became interested in group dancing at first, after they were organized in leisure time to learn group dancing regularly, many people got bored and just participated passively. The advocates of group dancing had to appeal to dancing educators to "avoid forcing people to dance when they don't want to; avoid teaching dances that people don't like."[48]

---

[46] Beijing qingnian she 北京青年社, ed., *Qingnian julebu di yi ji* 青年俱乐部 第一辑 [Youth club, vol.1] (Beijing: Beijing qingnian she, 1950).

[47] "Beijingshi yijiuwuyi nian shuqi shenghuo weiyuanhui gongzuo jihua" 北京市一九五一年暑期生活委员会工作计划 [Working plans of the Summer Vacation Life Committee in 1951], July 5, 1951, BMA, 100-001-01,036-0001.

[48] Pu and Guan, *Xin jiti wu*, 14–15.

Table 2.2 Schedule for Dancing Club Activities in the Summer Vacation of 1951

Time and Date	Participants and Contents	Schedule
7:30–10:30 pm, July 28	Dancing activists from various schools, around 800 people	Section One: Report by Comrade Zhao Yunge I. Why should we dance? How do we understand dancing? II. Promote group dancing activities Section Two: Evening Party I. Performances from dancing clubs in different high schools II. Group dancing
7:30–10:00 pm, August 20	Dancing party, attended by dancing activists and mainstays of mass culture from various schools, around 2,000 people	Group dancing: produced by students and professionals
Evenings, August 20–25	Comprehensive evening parties and demonstration performances	Programs produced by dancing clubs in different schools

Source "Shuqi wuzaozu jihua" 暑期舞蹈组计划 [Plans for dancing club activities in summer vacation], BMA, 1951, 100-001-01036-0012

Replacing: Radio Entertainment and Games

For some people in Beijing, listening to the radio was easy and convenient way leisure entertainment. Before the Japanese invasion in 1937, there were several government-owned and private radio stations in Beiping, offering entertainment programs such as Peking opera, storytelling (*pingshu* 评书), cross-talks comedy (*xiangsheng* 相声), and even Western music. During the Japanese occupation, only one radio station was permitted to continue broadcasting, and most of its programs were pure entertainment. Between 1945 and 1949, radio entertainment in Beiping flourished again.[49]

---

[49] Yu Na 于娜 and Yu Jia于嘉, *Dangdai Beijing guangbo shihua* 当代北京广播史话 [History of broadcasting in contemporary Beijing] (Beijing: Dangdai zhongguo chubanshe, 2013), 6–14. Beiping was the name of Beijing after the Nationalist Party set

Communist troops entered Beiping on February 3, 1949. On that evening, a young faculty member in Peking University named Yu Shichang turned on his radio and tuned in to the Xinhua Radio Station owned by the CCP. He was surprised to find that this radio station only broadcast news and articles. The lack of entertainment programs such as music or opera made him experience "another way of life."[50] Although the Party-owned radio station established a "new broadcasting style," during this period, private radio stations were still on the air and continued to broadcast entertainment programs that were considered extremely "poisonous" by the Party. "If you listened to pop songs on those private radio stations, almost all of them are about love and flirtation," wrote one article on *People's Daily*. "We suggest that the government should forbid those radio stations from broadcasting such songs."[51]

Echoing the voices above, *People's Daily* published an editorial on May 5, 1949, explaining why "decadent music" (*mimi zhiyin* 靡靡之音) should be banned on Beiping's private radio stations. According to *People's Daily*, as a modern means of propaganda, radio, with its close ties with the audience, was a "powerful weapon to educate the masses." Therefore, people would be greatly influenced if radio stations spread anything "pernicious." During Nationalist rule, radio stations lured the audience through the entertainment of "bad taste" to make a profit by "poisoning" people.[52] As of October 1949, three of the four remaining private radio stations were forced to close because of their alleged connection with the recently defeated Nationalist Party. The other one was put under the supervision of the Communist authorities.[53]

---

its capital in Nanjing in 1928. On September 27, 1949, Beiping was renamed as Beijing under a resolution of the Political Consultative Conference. See RMRB, September 28, 1949.

[50] Yu Shichang 喻世长, *Jianguo riji* 建国日记 [Diary during the founding of the republic] (Beijing: Dongfang chubanshe, 2009), 262.

[51] RMRB, April 20, 1949.

[52] RMRB, May 5, 1949.

[53] Beijingshi danganguan 北京市档案馆 and Zhonggong Beijng shiwei dangshi yanjiushi 中共北京市委党史研究室, eds., *Beijing shi zhongyao wenxian xuanbian* 1948.12–1949 北京市重要文献选编 1948.12–1949 [Selection of important documents of Beijing, 1948.12–1949] (Beijing: Zhongguo dangan chubanshe, 2001), 708–710; Beijing renmin guangbo diantai 北京人民广播电台, ed., *Beijing renmin guangbo diantai zhi* 1949–1993

Following instructions from the News Agency of the Central People's Government in April 1950 that there should be three tasks for radio propaganda (news reporting, social education, and entertainment), government-run radio stations in Beijing started to broadcast entertainment programs of their own.[54] In 1950, Beijing People's Radio Station No. 2, 3, and 4 were established, with a specific focus on entertainment. The programs, including local folk arts such as Peking opera, storytelling, and Hebei clapper opera (*bangzi* 梆子), were mostly undertaken by private troupes and actors under the guidance of staff from the radio station. The radio station also formed its own band, choir, Peking Opera troupe, and radio opera troupe[55] (Table 2.3).

Another leisure activity that was replaced by the new regime was board games. In early 1951, when walking on the street, a Beijing resident suddenly noticed that Promoting Officials (*shengguan tu* 升官图), a kind of board game that was popular among people in Beijing during the Spring Festival, had taken on a new look (Fig. 2.6).[56] In this new version of Promoting Officials, traditional Chinese official ranks were replaced by a combination of government systems in Republican China and those under the Communist Party. Starting from "commoner," players would become "student" and then "study overseas." After graduation, players would go back to China to enter the bureaucratic system from staff in "county government" and "municipal government," to heads of offices and bureaus, and finally, become the head of the "provincial government" and officials in the central government. The publisher of this game was obviously not familiar with the changes in government institutions after the Communists came into power because although the final victory of

---

北京人民广播电台志 1949–1993 [Annals of the Beijing People's Radio Station] (n.p., 1999), 255.

[54] Beijing difangzhi bianzuan weiyuanhui 北京地方志编纂委员会, ed., *Beijing zhi xinwen chuban guangbo dianshi juan guangbo dianshi zhi* 北京志 新闻出版广播电视卷 广播电视志 [Annals of Beijing, volume of news, publication, radio, and television, annals of radio and television] (Beijing: Beijing chubanshe, 2006), 6; *Beijing renmin guangbo diantai zhi*, 74.

[55] *Beijing renmin guangbo diantai zhi*, 74.

[56] Quite similar to *Monopoly*, the game Promoting Officials was invented in Tang Dynasty in the ninth century with an objective of getting the highest possible rank in the bureaucratic system. See Sung Ping-jen 宋秉仁, "Shengguan tu youxi yange kao" 升官图游戏沿革考 [The evolution of Chinese Promotion Game], *Taiwan shida lishi xuebao* 33 (2005): 27–78.

Table 2.3 Schedule of Beijing People's Radio Station No. 2, January 1952

9:25–9:30	Preview of upcoming programs of the day	15:30–16:00	Ping Opera (*pingxi* 评戏)
9:30–10:00	Peking Opera	16:00–16:30	folk arts by Folk Arts Troupe of the Institute of Chinese Opera
10:00–10:30	songs and music	16:30–18:00	Peking Opera by Radio Peking Opera Troupe in the Capital
10:30–11:45	live theater	18:00–18:30	Storytelling with a Chinese hammered dulcimer (*qinshu* 琴书) by Guan Xuezeng 关学增
11:45–12:45	storytelling: *Three Kingdoms* by Lian Kuoru 连阔如	18:30–19:00	*xihe dagu* 西河大鼓 by Ma Zengfen 马增芬
12:45–13:45	radio opera	19:00–20:00	songs and music
13:45–14:15	storytelling with one Chinese lute (*danxian* 单弦) performance by Cao Baolu 曹宝禄	20:00–20:30	programs from the Central People's Radio Station
14:15–15:00	songs and music	20:30–23:00	live theater
15:00–15:30	folk arts by Folk Arts Work Team of Blind Performers in the Capital	23:00–23:05	guide for tomorrow's programs

Source *Beijing renmin guangbo diantai zhi*, 202–203

the game was marked by becoming "Commander in Chief Zhu [De]" and "Chairman Mao," on the chessboard, there were still "Legislative Yuan" and "Administrative Yuan" that only existed under the Nationalist rule. Beijing authorities found it extremely "disrespectful" to Mao himself because in the game, once "Chairman Mao" accepted a bride, he would be downgraded to "Vice-Chairman."[57] Government officials in charge of publication purchased several different kinds of Promoting Officials games for screening purposes, and they concluded that most of these games should be removed from the market and replaced by other new games.[58]

---

[57] Shi Kan 石侃, "Guanyu qudi huangmiu xuanchaunpin wenti de han" 关于取缔荒谬宣传品问题的函 [Letter on banning absurd publicity materials], February 21, 1951, BMA, 008-002-00149-0006.

[58] Shencha zu 审查组, "'Shengguan tu' yanjiu baogao" "升官图"研究报告 [Research report on Promoting Officials], March 5, 1951, BMA, 008-002-00149-0015.

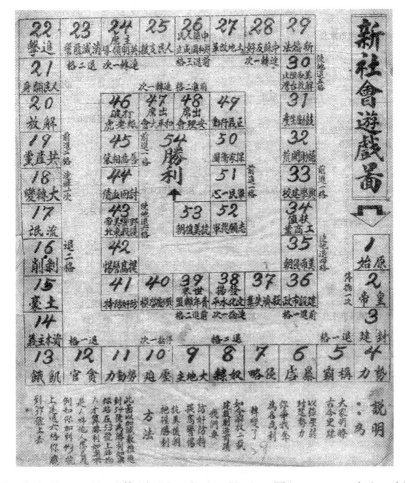

Fig. 2.6 Promoting Officials, New Society Version. This game was designed in accordance with the Communist narrative of social development from "primitive [society]" (box 1) to "feudalism" (box 3) to "capitalism" (box 14), and to "liberation" (box 20) after the establishment of the "Communist Party" (box 19). Boxes 26 to 53 were major events in China after 1949 with very positive descriptions. According to government officials, what was wrong with this game was that the "slave" (box 8) could be promoted to "big landlord" (box 9), and "hooligans" (box 17) could become the "Communist Party" (box 19). The "misinformation could be very harmful" to players. (*Source* Chuban shencha ke 出版审查科, "'Xin shengguan tu' lei chubanwu de yanjiu baogao" 新升官图"类出版物的研究报告 [Research report on publications like "New Promoting Officials"], April 3, 1951, BMA, 008-002-00149-0019)

Similarly, another board game about the Korean War was banned in early 1953 because of several "errors of principle (see Fig. 2.7)."[59]

While the authorities examined board games designed and sold by private publishers strictly, people could still come up with other forms of games by themselves. In 1954, an "International Game" prevailed in many places in China including Beijing. The game proceeded by writing letters. Anyone who received a letter from a participant should send a painting, photo, or postcard to the address of the letter within three days of receiving it and then send four letters with the same content as the original one to their friends at home and abroad. According to its rule, in a very short period of time, everyone participating in the game could get 256 paintings, photos, or postcards as well as friendship from strangers. *China Youth* published an article persuading its readers not to take part in this "International Game" because "it would be a great waste" of paper and postage. Ideologically, trading four letters and one picture with 256 photos or postcards embodied "bourgeoisie thinking of exploitation" in the sense that it "lured the youth to exchange the minimum price for the maximum benefit." What's even worse, this game could give "bad elements with hidden agendas" an opportunity to "develop relationships far from normal" that might cause damage politically.[60]

What the Party advocated was the "group game" or collective games with educational and ideological meanings. For example, in the first volume of the recreational guidebook *Youth Club* published in 1950, 31 collective games were introduced, including "Constructing the Motherland, Excavating Mineral Resources," "Sending the Liberation Army to Take Over Taiwan," "Passing a Red Flag," and "Sharpening Your Vigilance." The instruction of a game named "Friendly Call" reads:

> Sit in a circle. One person stands up and says "Sino-Soviet friendship." The two people sitting beside him should stand up quickly, shaking hands with each other and chanting "long live!" Then, the second person on the right side of the first person stands up and shouts "long live" and then

---

[59] "Shifu guanyu chajin zhishou kangmei yuanchao qizi de tongzhi" 市府关于查禁制售抗美援朝棋子的通知 [Notification from the Municipal Government on banning the production and sale of Resist America and Aid Korea chess], March 24, 1953, BMA, 022–012-01156.

[60] "Buyao zaiwan 'guoji youxi'" 不要再玩"国际游戏" [Stop participating in the "International Game"], *Zhongguo qingnian* 23 (1954): 32–33.

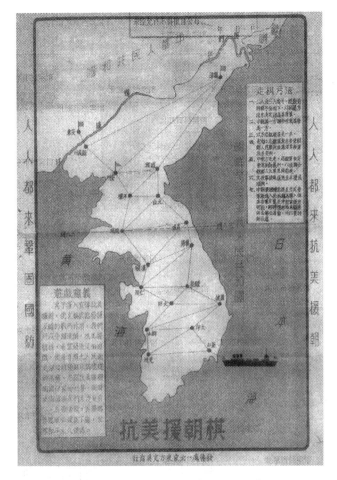

Fig. 2.7 "Resist America and Aid Korea" chess. In this game, one plays as Chinese/North Korean military forces and another plays as US military forces. The slogans on the two sides of the board read: "Everybody Join the Resist America and Aid Korea Campaign" and "Everybody Come to Strengthen the National Defense." This game was considered inappropriate because "the fact that in a game there will be winners and losers is not compatible with faith that we will definitely win." Another reason was the imbalance of military strength between US and Chinese/North Korean sides in the game design: the Chinese/North Korean side did not have naval bases while the US side did, which made it easy for the US side to raid the rear of the Chinese/North Korean side. (*Source* "Shifu guanyu chajin zhishou kang Mei yuan Chao qizi de tongzhi," March 4, 1953, BMA, 022-012-01156)

sits down. The second person on the left side of the first person stays still. Then move to the right side like that. People who forget to shake hands or move slowly will be penalized.[61]

In the second volume of the Youth Club, more outdoor collective games were introduced. A game called "Flying Hero" should be played in the following way:

> Four people form a team. First, three people stand in a circle hand in hand, and one of them bends down to the arms of the other two and stretches his two arms to hold their hands. The fourth person should lift the legs of the people in the middle to form a shape of an airplane. After every team gets prepared, begin to run forward from the starting point. The team reaching the finish line first wins.[62]

Providing New Leisure: The Beijing Youth Service Department

With the takeover of major cities, the Chinese Communist Party started to set up "youth service departments" (*qingnian fuwu bu* 青年服务部) to attract more young people by providing different kinds of leisure activities.[63] Located in a three-story building at No. 16 East Changan Avenue near the Wangfujing District in central Beijing, the Beijing Youth Service Department was jointly established by the Central Committee of the Youth League and the Beijing Municipal Youth League Committee in December 1949.[64] The aim of the Youth Service Department (YSD), according to its regulations published upon its establishment, was to "serve the masses" by organizing four kinds of activities. First, carrying out social education (led by the YSD's Social Education Unit) through

---

[61] *Qingnian julebu di yi ji*, 25–26.

[62] Qingnian tuan Beijing shiweihui wenhua yishubu 青年团北京市委会文化艺术部, ed., *Qingnian julebu* di er ji 青年俱乐部 第二辑 [Youth club, vol.2] (Beijing: Qingnian chubanshe, 1950), 25.

[63] "Yinian lai de qingnian fuwu gongzuo jiankuang" 一年来的青年服务工作简况 [Summary of the youth service work in this year], 1950, BMA, 100-003-00025-0009.

[64] RMRB, December 18, 1949; He Lu 赫鲁, "Xiao bai lou tiyu huodong yihua" "小白楼"体育活动忆话 [Recollections of sports activities in the "Little White Building"], *Tiyu wenshi*, Z1 (1984): 18–19. "Little White Building" was the nickname of the building of the Beijing Youth Service Department.

youth lectures, remedial schools, information desks, reading rooms, and exhibitions of cultural relics. Second, providing recreational activities (led by the YSD's Recreation Unit) by hosting evening parties and running recreational venues such as amusement centers, skating rinks, basketball, and volleyball courts. Third, holding artistic activities (led by the YSD's Arts Unit) such as research groups on opera, music, fine arts, and dancing. Finally, recruiting and connecting "Friends of the Youth Service Department."[65]

The name of the "Youth Service Department" indicated that the essential purpose of the YSD is to serve young people by providing venues for cultural and recreational activities in their leisure time based on their real needs. As a matter of fact, the Beijing YSD, when established, claimed that its three goals were to "improve physical and mental health, enrich the contents of life and improve knowledge and skills." In the beginning, the Beijing YSD publicized itself in newspapers, and sometimes, the YSD even made advertisement-style promotions to attract more young people. For example, on April 3, 1950, Beijing YSD peddled its activities in *People's Daily*:

> Want to learn group dancing?
> Want to play group games? Want to learn singing and playing harmonica?
> Sign up at the Youth Service Department!
>
> To assist associations and government organs in Beijing to hold cultural and recreational activities, the YSD is organizing a special "seminar on cultural and recreational work in government organs" teaching how to do group dancing, group games and evening parties on Tuesdays and Thursdays from 6:30 to 8:30 pm. At the same time, the YSD also offers a "singing and conducting class" (from 6:30 to 8:30 pm every Thursday) and a "harmonica class" (from 6:30 to 8:30 pm on Mondays, Wednesdays, and Fridays). Young people from all walks of life are welcome.[66]

In the eyes of a staff member, it was crucial that the youth could all find their niche in the YSD. Ideally, a typical day during opening hours of the YSD should be:

---

[65] "Qingnian fuwu bu gognzuo tiaoli" 青年服务部工作条例 [Working regulations of the Youth Service Department], December 3, 1949, BMA, 100-001-00039-0057.

[66] RMRB, April 3, 1950.

As the "indoor square" of the Youth Service Department, the hall is important not only because of the availability of newspapers and recreational equipment but because of the existence of an information desk as a formal reception on behalf of the YSD. It answers people's questions and guides them to find the activities they need. So, from the information desk, people disperse in all directions like lights.

People show up in the reading room…They show up in political education classes, Russian language classes, bookkeeping classes, fine arts classes, harmonica classes, teahouses, and even general offices. People show up in every corner of the YSD, chatting, discussing, and playing group games.[67]

In the early days of the YSD, when organizing leisure activities, political education was usually ranked as the first priority. Staff members simply considered that in youth service, "to serve means keeping the YSD open, so it's good as long as people continue to come here."[68] For example, before the end of January 1950, the YSD often held informal dancing parties, which young people were free to attend at any time and "dance whenever they came."[69] At the same time, instead of perceiving it as a place that might involve political implications, most of the young people who participated in YSD activities regarded the YSD only as a place of entertainment. As of February 1950, three-quarters of the regular attendees of YSD activities were students, who were "politically backward in the sense that they did not like to keep a close relationship with Youth League branches and student unions at their own schools." Besides, judging from the clothes they wore, most of these students were not from underprivileged families. During their stay in the YSD, the ice rink, amusement center, and ball game pitches were their favorite place because they could "have fun" there. Skaters reflected that they came to the YSD ice rink only because compared with other rinks, "it's more convenient to retrieve clothes in YSD rink's changing room."[70]

[67] RMRB, April 6, 1950.

[68] "Qingnian fuwu bu sange yue gognzuo zongjie" 青年服务部三个月工作总结 [Summary of the work of the Youth Service Department in the past three months], 1950, BMA, 100-001-00039-0071.

[69] "Qingnian fuwu bu yiyuefen gongzuo jianbao" 青年服务部一月份工作简报 [Summary of the work of the Youth Service Department in January], February 1, 1950, BMA, 100-003-00016-0011.

[70] "Qingnian fuwu bu sange yue gognzuo zongjie," 1950, BMA, 100-001-00039-0071.

This entertainment-oriented approach, however, did not last very long. In May 1950, in a report, the primary goals of YSD were changed from the 1949 version "improving physical and mental health, enriching the contents of life and improve knowledge and skills" into "raising political awareness, learning productive knowledge, improving physical and mental health, and enriching the content of life." The YSD also made it clear that all of its work should concentrate on "political education, production education and cultural education" by "closely integrating youth service work with production and construction through various kinds of leisure activities" among unemployed and out-of-school "unorganized youth."[71]

In November 1950, the YSD again stated that "although unorganized youth from all walks of life have different requirements, the most common and immediate problem is the demand for studying and working." Therefore, to "chop off some unnecessary work and concentrate on several of the most effective key tasks," the YSD reorganized itself under the principle of "focusing on social education." The original three units (Social Education Unit, Recreation Unit, and Arts Unit) were reorganized into four offices: Office of Social Education, Office of Physical Education, Office of Arts, and Office of General Services, with a separate Steering Committee on Reading. The former amusement center and activities such as evening parties under the charge of the former Recreation Unit were curtailed and managed by the Service Section under the Office of General Services as miscellaneous activities. Research and guidance on cultural and recreational activities in government organs were abandoned completely.[72]

The "Public Lecture" became the new favorite of the YSD after the focus of its "service" moved from recreational activities to social and political education. As a leisure activity held by the YSD since its inception, the initial purpose of the "Public Lecture" was to enrich people's knowledge by inviting "celebrities and experts from all walks of life to meet the needs of the broad masses of young people through lectures." Held once a week, "Public Lecture" offered fresh information about current affairs, literature and art, as well as natural science. Starting from 1951, to carry out patriotic and internationalist education, the YSD designed a more

---

[71] "Qingnian fuwu bu gaikuang" 青年服务部概况 [General overview of the Youth Service Department], May 19, 1950, BMA, 100-003-00025-0001.

[72] "Qingnian fuwu bu gongzuo fangzhen" 青年服务部工作方针 [Working principles of the Youth Service Department], November 23, 1950, BMA, 100-003-00025-0073.

systematic schedule for Public Lectures. Meanwhile, people started to be mobilized to attend the lectures.[73] In 1951, under the call of the Youth League Committee in a district in Beijing, "lecture organizers," who were responsible for mobilizing students in their own schools to attend lectures, were recruited and assigned to high schools in that district. After May 1951, with the recognition of the Beijing Municipal Youth League Committee, this "lecture organizer" system became a city-wide practice. The major task of the lecture organizers was to collect and report people's ideological condition, their questions and needs to the YSD in a timely manner, and then "mobilize the masses to attend the lectures with the cooperation from school leaders and student unions in their own schools."[74]

In addition to educating young people by organizing lectures, to get those "free" and "slack" young men who "just came out of the old society" and "never participated in collective life" to go to work as soon as possible, the YSD tried to "raise their political awareness" by "uniting them through cultural and artistic ways" in leisure activities. For example, many young people, who did not intend to receive political education when they came to attend collective activities, only expected to "sing and have fun" in the YSD choir. Having observed such a tendency among the youth, the YSD choir made use of every activity to carry out political education. During the Resist America and Aid Korea Campaign starting from 1950, the YSD choir combined patriotic education with songs such as "Driving Out American Wolves," "Defending the Motherland," and "Defending the Fruits of Victory." The YSD found that through political instillation in songs, many members in the choir started to care about the ongoing Korean War. They even began to "conduct political learning in the harmonica team and choirs, hoping that the members could show political concern and establish a system of criticism and self-criticism." At the same time, many people were always late or absent for choir activities because they were used to "going to bed as late as one or two o'clock in the night, getting up at eleven in the morning, and doing whatever they want to do." The YSD cadres took this opportunity to teach these young

---

[73] "Liangnian lai de dazhong jiangzuo gonzuo" 两年米的大众讲座工作 [The work of Public Lecture in the past two years], December 9, 1951, BMA, 100-003-00045-0040.

[74] "Shejiao ke jiangzhan zu bannian gognzuo zongjie" 社教科讲展组半年工作总结 [Summary of the half year's work by the Lecture and Exhibition Group of the Social Education Unit], July 1951, BMA, 100-003-00045-0085.

people about collectivism and told them that "in a group, individual life must be subject to organizational discipline, that is, if you join this organization, you must abide by the regulations laid down by everyone." The YSD observed with satisfaction that under the influence of collective leisure activities, many young people "seemed to have become someone totally new."[75]

Conclusion: The Decentralized Takeover of Leisure in Beijing

The takeover of leisure shows the interventionist nature of the new regime in the sense that the Chinese Communist Party was not satisfied only with the occupation and transformation of government institutions and ownership, but also aspired to mold the emotions of people according to the Party's vision that in a socialist country, people must live both joyfully and meaningfully in their leisure time. Unlike the conventional historical narrative of urban takeover in the early 1950s, during the takeover of leisure, there was not a unified leading organ to instruct Party officials on how to do that, nor were there specific general guidelines on such an issue. After all, there was not a campaign aiming directly at transforming people's leisure time.

Because of this decentralized character, variegated tactics were adopted consciously or unconsciously by different Party and government institutions to influence the landscape of leisure in Beijing. Private ball game clubs were put aside and declined gradually. Self-organized dancing was redirected into officially organized group dancing. Radio entertainment and popular games with contents not in accordance with the Party's taste were replaced by government-offered versions. At the same time, the Party established the Beijing Youth Service Department as a new kind of leisure complex. The decentralized character in the takeover of leisure made it less noticeable than major political movements that stormed the city during this time. People were not banned from having fun, nor were they forced to make confessions about their leisure choice. Nevertheless, for people who experienced this period like Yang Zhenping, Tan

---

[75] "Qingnian fuwu bu wenyi ke yinyue xiju zu bannian gongzuo zongjie chugao" 青年服务部文艺科音乐戏剧组半年工作总结初稿 [Summary of the half year's work by the Music and Drama Group of the Arts Unit of the Youth Service Department (draft)], August 1951, BMA, 100-003-00045-0046.

Youshi, and Yu Shichang, something did happen to their everyday life and brought actual changes as they gradually experienced leisure options favored by the Party.

Regulating ordinary people's leisure time was not unique in the postwar Socialist Bloc. Large-scale enterprises in Europe and the United States gradually accepted the idea that systematic arrangements of workers' off-duty hours were important for improving their efficiency at work after the First World War. As for government-level actions, the Fascist regime in Italy set up the National Recreational Club (*Opera Nazionale Dopolavoro*) in 1925, followed by a more powerful and influential Nazi version leisure organization named Strength through Joy (*Kraft durch Freude*) in 1933. National recreational agencies sprung up in right-wing regimes such as Portugal, Greece, Bulgaria, Romania, and Spain in the 1930s and by the mid-thirties, the traditional liberal policy that let people spend their leisure time freely seemed to be outdated, even among observers and policymakers in democratic countries.[76]

Struggles between pleasure and education continued as the Party considered that both of them were vital, but worried that they could undermine each other. The fate of the Beijing YSD offers an example: in May 1952, during a reorganization of the Beijing Municipal Youth League Committee, the Beijing YSD was merged with Culture and Arts Department. Seven months later, in December, the YSD was dissolved.[77] The institutional change, however, did not mean that the Party found itself incapable of organizing young people's leisure time. For the Party, the early 1950s was only the start of a long march toward a revolution of lifestyle as it launched its program of collectivizing young people's leisure time.

---

[76] For the National Recreational Club, see De Grazia, *The Culture of Consent*. For the Strength through Joy, see Timpe, *Nazi-Organized Recreation and Entertainment in the Third Reich*. For the rise of national recreational agencies and the decline of the liberal way of mastering individual's leisure time freely, see De Grazia, *The Culture of Consent*, 239–240.

[77] Gongqingtuan Beijing shiwei wenhua tiyu bu 共青团北京市委文化体育部 and Gongqingtuan Beijing shiwei qingyun shi yanjiu shi 共青团北京市委青运史研究室, eds., *Jidang yu huisheng: Beijing gongqingtuan wenhua tiyu gongzuo sishi nian* 激荡与回声：北京共青团文化体育工作四十年 [Surges and echoes: forty years of cultural and sports work of the Beijing Youth League] (Beijing: Beijing gongye daxue chubanshe, 1992), 6.

CHAPTER 3

Temporal Politics in Beijing, 1949–1956

On an autumn day in 1955, among the peddlers, storytellers, and acrobats in a crowded fair, an unexpected foreign guest showed up in Beijing's southern district: Simone de Beauvoir, who had just arrived in the capital of the People's Republic in September as a result of Zhou Enlai's "come and see" invitation at Bandung earlier that year. Accompanied by another two French visitors, the well-renowned French writer and feminist visited Tianqiao, the most famous urban recreational center in Beijing since the Qing dynasty, to experience how Beijing residents spent their leisure time. The frugal way people entertained themselves impressed Beauvoir deeply: open-air restaurants were rudimentary but clean; classic operas were performed faultlessly by amateur performers with very basic facilities; admission fees were extremely low. Nevertheless, one disturbing rumor made her uneasy: a Soviet-style cultural leisure park, like the Gorky Park in Moscow, was going to replace the existing recreational venues in Tianqiao. "It is a pity," writes Beauvoir in her recollection of the China trip. "For my part I hope that…their diversions won't become too stringently organized."[1]

---

[1] Simone de Beauvoir, *The Long March: An Account of Modern China*, trans. Austryn Wainhouse (London: Phoenix Press, 2001), 78–80.

Although a cultural leisure park was never built in Tianqiao district, Beauvoir's concern of a "stringently organized" leisure was quite understandable, considering that in capitalist countries such as France, people were used to treating leisure as a completely private issue. As E. P. Thompson suggests, one of the major features of a mature capitalist society is a clear-cut boundary between "work" and "life" as well as rigid time-related disciplines and labor rhythms based on that boundary.[2] Individuals, with the distinction of work and life, can consequently keep apart private and public spheres. In this sense, as the impetus of the "institutionalization of privacy," the establishment of accurate and predictable schedules becomes an important organizational principle for a modern society that facilitates individuals to switch between different "roles" when engaging in multiple social involvements.[3]

From a sociological perspective, because temporality is a product of social construction, in different societies there are diverse ways in which people perceive and organize their time.[4] One example comes from the comparison between capitalist and socialist countries. In her study of Romania in the 1980s under Nicolae Ceaușescu before his sudden downfall in December 1989, Katherine Verdery investigates an intangible but substantial way of governance that she calls "temporal politics" in which "regime policies created struggles over time, as people were subjected to and resisted new temporal organizations."[5] Through policies concerning time directly and indirectly, from increasing working hours arbitrarily to organizing mass rallies, the Romanian Communist Party gradually deprived Romanian people of much of their right to control their own time. Verdery implies that whereas the purpose of the capitalist way of organizing time is to create more profits, in Ceaușescu's Romania, time

---

[2] E. P. Thompson, "Time, Work Discipline, and Industrial Capitalism," *Past and Present* 38 (1967): 90–93.

[3] Eviatar Zerubavel, *Hidden Rhythms: Schedules and Calendars in Social Life* (Berkeley: University of California Press, 1985), xv.

[4] For an introduction to the social constructionist view of time, see Helga Nowotny, "Time and Social Theory: Towards a Social Theory of Time," *Time & Society* 1, no. 3 (1992): 421–454.

[5] Katherine Verdery, *What Was Socialism, and What Comes Next?* (Princeton: Princeton University Press, 1996), 39.

turned out to be "the medium for producing not profits but subjection, for immobilizing persons in the Party's grip."⁶

While Beauvoir considered the plan to replace a traditional center of entertainment with a state-run recreational complex as a signal of the coming of organized leisure, I examine this issue from a more microscopic level: the inconspicuous process of the collectivization of leisure time. Following the perspective of "temporal politics" proposed by Verdery, this chapter explores the Chinese Communist Party's attention to "leisure problems" among young people in Beijing from 1949 to 1956. I then explain how the Party's actions on leisure affected people's control and use of their private time. Borrowing David Easton's classic concept of politics as "the authoritative allocation of values for a society," here I define "temporal politics" as the authoritative allocation of time by political powers.⁷ While "leisure time" denotes the private sector of time away from workplace or school that is supposed to be spent and allocated freely by individuals, it should also be noted that there was not a private/public dichotomy in Party documents regarding people's leisure time. In public discussions, too much emphasis on the private nature of leisure time was often dismissed as "employee thinking" (*guyong sixiang* 雇佣思想) because after the Communist victory in 1949, from the perspective of the Party, the relationship between work and leisure had already been changed. One article in the 1951 "Should I Have Fun" discussion mentioned in Chapter 2 made it clear that "if you say that weekends and Sundays are your 'private' time, you must be implying that you sell yourself to your work unit during weekdays." Now that "the state has become our own state," work and leisure should both be organized under public needs favored by the government.⁸ In this sense, leisure time was collectivized in theory with the Communist Party coming into power. In reality, however, it was impossible to achieve this process of collectivization overnight. This chapter, therefore, examines how the Party's "temporal politics" was understood, accepted, and challenged in young people's everyday life at the grassroots.

---

⁶ Verdery, *What Was Socialism*, 40–57.

⁷ For Easton's definition of politics, see David Easton, *The Political System: An Inquiry into the State of Political Science* (New York: Knopf, 1953), 129.

⁸ Xue Lai 薛莱, "Fandui luohou de 'xiaoqian' sixiang" 反对落后的 "消遣"思想 [Opposing the backward thought of "having fun"], *Zhanwang* 16 (1951): 26.

The perspective of "temporal politics" helps uncover stories beyond political movements while refusing to ignore the role of the state. Emerging scholarship on everyday life under China's state socialism seeks to answer the question of what ordinary people actually did rather than what the intentions of top officials were.[9] Although rich in details from the grassroots, this bottom-up approach has been challenged by other scholars as overlooking the big picture by engaging inadequately with the Party-state and its policies.[10] Echoing this scholarly pursuit of investigating people's everyday life beyond political movements, "temporal politics" emphasizes intangible influence from the state at the same time. The regulation of young people's leisure time was not the major target of any political movement in the early 1950s. Instead, leisure regulation proceeded in parallel with other movements. In this regard, examining temporal politics in the early 1950s can showcase the enduring interventionist nature of the CCP even before political movements became a more prominent factor in ordinary people's everyday life after the mid-1950s.

Leisure Time: The Sphere of Temporal Politics

In this chapter, I divide leisure time into two categories for analytical purposes: first, leisure time over a relatively long period such as vacations and weekends; second, the everyday off-duty and after-school hours. According to a vacation arrangement published in *People's Daily* on December 24, 1949, in the early 1950s, people in China could enjoy four nationwide public holidays: New Year's Day (one day off on January 1); the Spring Festival (three days off for the lunar New Year); Labor Day (one day off on May 1); and the National Day (two days off on October 1 and 2). Furthermore, women had a half day off on International Women's Day (March 8), students above secondary schools had a half day off on Youth Day (May 4), children had a half day off on International Children's Day (June 1), and members of the military forces had a half day off on August 1.[11]

---

[9] Jeremy Brown and Matthew D. Johnson, eds., *Maoism at the Grassroots: Everyday Life in China's Era of High Socialism* (Cambridge, MA: Harvard University Press, 2015), 2.

[10] Elizabeth J. Perry, "The Promise of PRC History," *Journal of Modern Chinese History* 10, no. 1 (2016): 117.

[11] RMRB, December 24, 1949.

Daily off-duty hours correlate with the working system the Party adopted. To ensure workers' right to rest in their leisure time, the Party proposed the eight-hour working day system shortly after its establishment.[12] After it came into power, the CCP announced in the Common Program in 1949 that "public and private enterprises should generally implement an eight-hour to ten-hour working day system."[13] A decision made by the Government Administration Council in 1952 required that "all larger public and private industrial, mining, and transportation enterprises should implement the eight-hour working day system as soon as possible," that "state-owned shops and cooperatives in large and medium-sized cities and industrial and mining areas should also implement the eight-hour working day system," and that "for jobs that are detrimental to health, working hours should be less than eight hours a day." Working overtime was also restricted rigidly.[14] Government employees in Beijing worked eight hours a day, but they needed to arrive at their offices one or one and a half hours before the start of working hours to attend political study sessions. In spring (March, April, and May) and autumn (September, October, and December), government employees had to start their study sessions at 7 am, begin to work at 8:30, have lunch break between 12:30 and 1:30 pm, and get off work at 6 pm. In the summer months, study sessions started half an hour earlier, and in winter months, half an hour later.[15]

Apart from public holidays and regular weekends, young students also had long summer and winter vacations and short spring vacations. In a preliminary school calendar issued by the Ministry of Education in August 1950, high school students could enjoy a fifty-five-day summer vacation (from July 11 to August 31), a twenty-three-day winter vacation (from

---

[12] *Xin Shenbao*, May 24, 1922.
[13] RMRB, September 30, 1949.
[14] RMRB, August 4, 1952.
[15] RMRB, April 6, 1952.

January 24 to February 15), and an additional three-day spring vacation (starting from April 3).[16] University students had a similar vacation system.[17]

Vacations and Weekends: Temporal Politics at the First Stage

The Summer of Liberation for Beijing Students

Following the Communist takeover of Beijing, Party officials initiated the first stage of "temporal politics" featuring the gradual presence of political power in relatively long periods of leisure time including vacations, public holidays, and weekends. Upon the takeover, Party officials found out immediately that because of the long-lasting revolution, young people in Beijing became quite "slack" (*sanman* 散漫) in the sense that after engaging in student movements during the Nationalist rule, students were not used to going back to normal school life. As Jiang Nanxiang, then a member of the Secretariat of the Youth League Central Committee, described in a report in summer 1949, now that Nationalist rule had been overthrown in the city, students should "go back to classrooms" and focus only on their school work at school instead of organizing and participating in mass movements. Nevertheless, the boundary of school

---

[16] "Zhongdeng xuexiao zanxing xiaoli (caoan)" 中等学校暂行校历 (草案) [Preliminary calendar for high schools (draft)], in *Jiaoyu wenxian faling huibian 1949–1952* 教育文献法令汇编1949-1952 [Collection of documents and decrees on education], ed. Zhonghua renmin gongheguo jiaoyubu bangongting 中华人民共和国教育部办公厅 (n.p., 1958), 172.

[17] According to the "Calendar for Institutions for Higher Learning" issued in June 1950, university and college students had a 62-day summer vacation, a 14-day winter vacation, and a 3-day spring vacation. A slightly revised version was issued on August 17, 1954. See "Gaodeng xuexiao xiaoli" 高等学校校历 [Calendar for institutions for higher learning], in *Gaodeng jiaoyu wenxian faling huibian 1949–1952* 高等教育文献法令汇编 1949–1952 [Collection of documents and decrees on higher education], ed. Gaodeng jiaoyubu bangongting 高等教育部办公厅 (n.p., 1958), 175; "Gaodeng jiaoyubu wei banfa gaodeng xuexiao xiaoli ji feizhi 1950 nian zhongyang jiaoyubu banfa de gaodeng xuexiao xiaoli de mingling" 高等教育部为颁发高等学校校历及废止1950年中央教育部颁发的高等学校校历的命令 [Order on issuing calendar for institutions for higher learning and nullifying the calendar for institutions for higher learning issued by the Central Ministry of Education in 1950], in *Zhonghua renmin gongheguo zhongyao jiaoyu wenxian* 中华人民共和国重要教育文献 [Important documents on education in the People's Republic of China], ed. He Dongchang 何东昌 (Haikou: Hainan chubanshe, 1998), 366.

hours and free time became obscure because after the People's Liberation Army entered Beijing, "everyone felt that they were free and did not go to classes. Instead, they hold meetings all day long."[18] To help the youth switch to a normal calendar favored by the Party, the Beijing authorities used the first summer vacation after 1949 to let the youth make sense of how they should live under the new regime.

In the first summer vacation after the Communist takeover, Beijing students could choose to attend two kinds of summer programs including the Summer Study Group of High School and University Students (*shuqi dazhong xuesheng xuexi tuan* 暑期大中学生学习团) and the Youth School (*qingnian xueyuan* 青年学园) that were organized under the leadership of the newly established Committee for Summer Vacation Work (*shuqi gongzuo weiyuanhui* 暑期工作委员会).[19] With the same goals of implementing political education during summer vacation, to attract more students, these two programs were different in formats. Compared with the Study Group, the Youth School, with five separate branches across the city, was to offer more diverse and flexible activities including a fair number of recreational activities in which participants could attend or quit at their own will. The Study Group, on the contrary, was similar to a short-term summer school during which the participants were required to live together and take mandatory courses and discussions.[20]

On July 13, 1949, the Youth School commenced officially. Although in his opening remarks, Peng Zhen, the head of the Beijing Municipal Party Committee, hoped that young participants could "study well and play well" in the Youth School, his focus was still on the educational purpose of the School by emphasizing that students must "study for the people" and "learn the method of dialectical materialism" from various leisure activities.[21]

---

[18] "Jiang Nanxiang tongzhi baogao xuexiao gongguo" 蒋南翔同志报告学校工作 [Comrade Jiang Nanxiang's report on work in schools], working notes of Zhang Youcheng, author's collection. Zhang Youcheng was then the leader of the Party committee in Beijing No. 1 Boys' High School. For a brief description of Zhang, see his own account in Wang Jintang 王晋堂, ed., *Guxiao maixiang 21 shiji Beijing yizhong xiaoshi gao 1644–1990* 古校迈向21世纪: 北京一中校史稿 1644–1990 [Old school marching to the twenty-first century: a draft of the history of Beijing No. 1 High School, 1644–1990] (Beijing: Huayi chubanshe, 1990), 208.

[19] RMRB, June 28, 1949.

[20] RMRB, June 30, 1949.

[21] RMRB, July 14, 1949.

The underlying purpose of the Youth School was to let young people in Beijing get accustomed to the collective lifestyle under the new regime. For example, many students did not have any experience in organizing after-lecture discussions. As a result, during discussion sessions, they just "looked at each other and remained speechless." To activate these students, one Youth School branch organized icebreaker collective games before the discussion to create a more engaging atmosphere.[22] They also proposed that students could form "homes" with cohorts from their own schools and lead a collective life.[23] According to *People's Daily*, after the end of the Youth School one month later, attending collective leisure activities was effective because through these summer activities, young students received ideological education, and thus they became supporters of collectivism:

> Through the report "From Apes to Man," students have understood that working people are masters of history, that people's thought is the result of the accumulation of labor experience, that labor, not idea, creates everything, and that intellectuals should learn from the laboring masses. Students have also established the viewpoint of serving the working people. After listening to the report about the five modes of production, students have recognized the past and future of social development. They have understood that the driving force of social progress was the contradiction between productive forces and relations of production. The report "Collective Freedom and Individual Freedom" made students review their lax style in the past. They have criticized the habit of absolute individual freedom and have understood that individual freedom can only be achieved through collective freedom, which will in turn also become the guarantee of individual freedom. [They have realized that] collective freedom has to be obtained through a long struggle and to strive for permanent and greater freedom, young people should organize themselves by returning to their own organization—the New Democracy Youth League and consider themselves as screws in the revolutionary struggle. Recognizing that people will have strength through organizations, many students have understood the relationship between the individual and the collective, and thus they became close to the Youth League voluntarily and happily.[24]

---

[22] RMRB, August 18, 1949.
[23] RMRB, August 3, 1949.
[24] RMRB, August 18, 1949.

Another portion of the summer program was the Study Group, which lasted for nearly one month from July 14 to August 11 and concentrated more on direct political education. The Committee for Summer Vacation Work planned to recruit 2,000 students for the Study Group, and finally, 1,934 students signed up.[25] Participants had different purposes such as learning Marxist theory and making sense of the policies of the Party when they joined the Study Group, but they soon discovered that it was designed for thought reform through political education and collective life. During the first phase of the Study Group, Ai Siqi, one of the top Party theorists, delivered a speech about how to learn historical materialism, in which he emphasized that during the study session, students should connect the theory with practice and their own thoughts by implementing criticism and self-criticism. In another report, the speaker made it clear that the purpose of this Study Group was to "dig out non-Marxist-Leninist erroneous thinking and plant Marxist-Leninist thinking." Students were also encouraged to practice self-management and improve their study conditions by themselves. In the second phase of the Study Group, reports on labor, class struggle, revolutionary outlook on life, Party history, and international relations were offered by various speakers including senior Party figures such as Yang Fu, Hu Sheng, Hu Qiaomu, Qian Junrui, and Bo Yibo. After that, students spent two whole days summarizing what they got from these reports. Finally, in the third phase of the Study Group, students who wished to join the Youth League were tested on their opinions on labor, class struggle, and how to serve the people. Eventually, 505 students of the Study Group were admitted to the Youth League.[26] Apart from listening to reports, students in the Study Group were organized to attend collective labor such as cleaning dorms, repairing roads, and washing dishes.[27]

---

[25] RMRB, June 30, 1949; RMRB, September 28, 1949.

[26] Wang Hu 王浒, "Yichang zhuoyou chengxiao de qiming jiaoyu ji 1949 nian shuqi da zhong xuesheng xuexituan" 一场卓有成效的启蒙教育——记1949年暑期大中学生学习团 [An effective enlightening education: recollections on the Summer Study Group of High School and University Students of 1949], in Zhang Dazhong 张大中, *Wo jingli de Beiping dixiadang* 我经历的北平地下党 [The Beiping underground Party that I experienced] (Beijing: Zhonggong dangshi chubanshe, 2009), 257–264.

[27] RMRB, September 28, 1949.

Teach Students How to Rest Properly

In 1950, the regulation of Beijing students' summer vacation continued as the Committee for Summer Vacation Life (*shuqi shenghuo weiyuanhui* 暑期生活委员会) was launched on June 10, 1950, under the cooperation of the Beijing Municipal Youth League Committee, Beijing Municipal Student Federation, Beijing Municipal Bureau of Culture and Education, and Municipal Union of Educators. This committee had an overarching aim of "organizing a variety of cultural, recreational, and sports activities that meet the needs of young people, which are also meaningful and beneficial to their physical and mental health, so that young students can get appropriate rest and exercise from these activities, and thus can make progress ideologically and culturally." According to a brief introduction posted in *People's Daily*, during the summer vacation of 1950, various kinds of activities including lectures, singing competitions, sports, and camping would be organized[28] (Table 3.1).

Table 3.1 Activities planned by the committee for summer vacation life in June 1950

Categories of summer vacation activities	Details
Lectures	Youth lectures on current affairs to be held in districts respectively
Artistic activities	City-wide chorus; massive chorus, singing and drama competition participated in by over 1,000 people
Instructions from youth cadres about how to organize in-school activities	Instructions about organizing in-school literature, drama, and dancing activities
Sports competitions	Youth swimming team; ball game competitions
Study groups	Assistance on in-school study groups of current affairs, history, and radio
Camping	Organized camping activities participated in by youth and children
Other	Excursions; film screenings

Source RMRB, June 14, 1950

---

[28] RMRB, June 14, 1950.

Compared with the Committee for Summer Vacation Work, the Committee for Summer Vacation Life made more detailed plans on leisure activities. This was because the major aim for the summer vacation of 1950 was different from that of 1949 in the sense that activities in 1950 focused less on direct political education and more on providing organized recreational activities. As Zhang Dazhong, the vice director of the Committee for Summer Vacation Life, reported during a joint meeting in July with people who were in charge of student unions, Youth League committees, and propaganda groups in various schools in Beijing, because of the political atmosphere and the ideological indoctrination after the takeover of Beijing, students had made huge progress in their thinking and started to establish a revolutionary outlook on life. Therefore, the "basic spirit for this year's summer vacation activities" was to "lead students to have a good rest through activities that are good for their health."[29] Zhang also offered seven requirements for students on what they should do during the summer vacation:

> First, you should have sufficient rest, and at the same time, pay attention to exercise, and improve your health.
> Second, you should participate in one or two kinds of leisure activities or sports based on your own interests and hobbies to make your summer life relaxing and joyful.
> Third, you should read one or two revolutionary literary works and attend lectures that you like, so as to cultivate your interest in literature and art and expand your field of knowledge.
> Fourth, it is necessary to review your previous lessons, study your favorite subjects, and read some natural science books, to deepen and enrich your knowledge of the major courses at school.
> Fifth, you should make a simple and feasible timetable. Get up and rest on time and live regularly. Develop the habit of reading newspapers and listening to the radio every day.
> Sixth, you should establish a close friendship with your classmates and spend a good summer life collectively.
> Seventh, you must prevent any way of life that is harmful to your body and mind, and not read novels with improper contents.[30]

[29] RMRB, July 16, 1950.
[30] RMRB, July 16, 1950.

Zhang Dazhong's seven requirements depicted an extremely ideal way of spending summer vacation, but they also reflected the Party's ambition to teach students how to rest. The real effect of the Party's regulation of students' vacation, however, was questionable. Although in official propaganda, students in Beijing led very happy and productive life during summer vacations after 1949 by participating in leisure activities organized by various work units in Beijing and also their own schools, the Party and the Youth League still found themselves unable to make students live in a disciplined way in their leisure time. For example, on July 8, 1955, *Beijing Youth Daily*, the official newspaper run by the Beijing Municipal Youth League, published a cartoon criticizing the undisciplined ways of life led by students during the summer vacation in which one boy did not get up until noon, went to the swimming pool every day, read dozens of novels but forgot to do his homework; another boy got up early in the morning, kept studying all whole day but got sick when the new term started.[31]

Another article titled "Do Not Slack" under the column "Brief Comments on Summer Vacation Life" in *Beijing Youth Daily* criticized the "slacker thinking" in some students' mind:

> It is said that "a good beginning makes a good ending." These students, however, were slacking at the beginning of the summer vacation, and let their slacker thinking gain the upper hand. When they wish to make plans for summer life, this slacker thinking will tell them: the current way of life is so good! Why bother making plans to restrain yourself?...[32]

Both the cartoon and the article explicitly explained that undisciplined summer vacation was completely incompatible with youth in New China who should know how to live a vigorous and meaningful life. Nonetheless, these articles suggest that the problem still existed.

Visitors and Performers: Spending Days off in Park Festivals

In the early 1950s, the Party not only strived to plan leisure time for young students in their summer vacations but also for young people from all walks of life during their regular days off. Park festivals (*youyuanhui* 游

---

[31] *Beijing qingnian bao*, July 8, 1955.
[32] *Beijing qingnian bao*, July 15, 1955.

园会) were a kind of state-organized large-scale leisure activity that usually happened during weekends and public holidays. The first park festival that was held in Beijing after 1949 was the "Chinese Youth Day Park Festival" in Zhongshan Park in the afternoons from May 4 to May 6, 1950, to commemorate the May Fourth Movement.[33] Organized professional and amateur cultural troupes, folk vocal art artists, and military bands performed during the park festival. More than ninety-five kinds of collective games and collective dances were offered. According to a count made by the Beijing Municipal Youth League Committee, to let the park festival proceed smoothly, the organizer mobilized 585 performers from thirty-two work units, in addition to 143 guides and 736 staff members who acted as leaders in collective games. The park festival, under the principle of "offering various entertainments and making people feel happy," was aiming at attracting as many young people as possible to attend organized activities in their leisure time during public holidays, and at the same time popularize the Party's ideology through entertainment. From the summary report submitted by the organizer, the Youth League was apparently very satisfied with the effect of their first attempt to organize such kind of activity in Beijing:

> People who went to the park festival took part in different activities based on their own interests. They watched all kinds of performances happily and played all kinds of games joyfully. Driven by the enthusiasm of young people, some older men also began to dance with them. Foreign friends sang and danced hand in hand with Chinese students and workers. The performers came down from their stages to celebrate together with the audience. After the end of the park festival, people were still singing and laughing and did not want to leave until it was getting dark.

Such a lively atmosphere might not be exaggerated in the sense that the state-organized park festival was truly welcomed by young people in Beijing. A young soldier expressed his feelings in the visitor's book: "the nine of us had a really good time!" Many students reported that "this is the best time I have ever enjoyed, and [from the park festival] I feel a

---

[33] The following paragraphs on the "Chinese Youth Day Park Festival" are from an internal report from the Beijing Municipal Youth League Committee, "Guanyu jinian wusi qingnianjie tongzhi zongjie deng" 关于纪念五四青年节通知总结等 [Notifications, summaries and others regarding the commemoration of the May Fourth Youth Day], 1950, BMA, 100-003-00021.

new atmosphere in which I could be happy and positive." Some students asked for more frequent park festivals in the future. In a letter written by a student after the park festival, the writer, on behalf on dozens of his friends, suggested that this kind of park festival should be organized every two weeks.

If young people attending the May 4 park festival of 1950 could actually have some fun as pure visitors during their leisure time, on some other occasions (which were usually called "organized park festivals"), they spent their leisure time as organized performers to show how happy Chinese youth were. Beijing youth had more opportunities to become performers in park festivals because the capital city welcomed more foreign guests than other cities. For instance, the park festival on May 4, 1954 was an example of a well-organized Potemkin village. Although in a report published in *People's Daily*, there were only normal descriptions of happy Chinese young men and women dancing with foreign guests from the Soviet Union and other socialist countries with no sign of being organized, the Chinese attendees were actually carefully selected from factories, government offices, universities and schools, and military forces to make the venue safe and noisy.[34]

The first thing to notice is that not all young people in Beijing were allowed to enter the Zhongshan Park to celebrate their own holiday with Soviet friends. According to a working plan made by the Beijing Municipal Youth League Committee, only those who were "politically reliable and relatively active in personality" could get admission tickets from their schools or workplaces. Additional time was wasted in the sense that although the park festival started at 7 pm, the attendees had to arrive one-and-a-half hours earlier to wait for the Soviet delegation. The Chinese attendees were deployed into five separate sections in the park, and no one could join activities in other sections without permission from the organizing headquarters.[35] Young people with the extra mission of "lining

---

[34] A newspaper report of this park festival can be found in RMRB, May 6, 1954. The organization of the party is recorded in "'Wusi' qingnianjie Zhongshan gongyuan youyuan lianhuan wanhui qunzhong huodong jihua" "五四"青年节中山公园游园联欢晚会群众活动计划 [Plan for mass activities of the garden evening party in Zhongshan Park on May Fourth Youth Day], 1954, BMA, 100–003-00084–0064.

[35] "'Wusi' qingnianjie Zhongshan gongyuan youyuan lianhuan wanhui qunzhong huodong jihua," 1954, BMA, 100–003-00084–0064.

the streets to welcome foreign guests" received more detailed instructions on what they should do when foreigners arrived such as "when welcoming, people can throw flower bunches, paper flowers, and colorful paper ribbons; can wave your headscarves, handkerchiefs or just applaud; or can cheer and sing. But you must make sure that foreign guests can pass quickly."[36]

Although young people were not allowed to spend their leisure time freely in these "organized park festivals," for many of them, this was not a problem. As mentioned above, during the preparation of the May 4 park festival of 1954, because only reliable attendees could get tickets from schools or workplaces, those who were qualified could easily feel the trust from the Party, especially those who were supposed to be excluded for such kind of event. For instance, some young capitalists in Beijing who were invited were "greatly flattered." A young business owner said, "I never thought that I could have a stake in such an event!"[37] This example shows that rather than opposing political power from entering their leisure time, many young people embraced politicized leisure as an honor.

Problematizing Youth Leisure

Although leisure activities were regularly organized during vacations and weekends in Beijing after 1949, in the eyes of Party and Youth League leaders, the results of the state-organized leisure activities were far from satisfactory. As revealed by Party documents, a great number of youth cadres still found it hard to handle the boundary between political indoctrination and leisure entertainment, some even thought that the purpose of those leisure activities was to "play" and since there was a lot of other work to do with the incipient regime, "where can we find the time to play with the youth?" Some cadres even considered that "young people

---

[36] "Zhongshan gongyuan youyuan wanhui jiadao huanying qunzhong de zuzhi he jihe shusan banfa" 中山公园游园晚会夹道欢迎群众的组织和集合、疏散办法 [Solution for the organization, assembly and evacuation of the masses lining the street to welcome (guests) during the garden evening party in Zhongshan Park], 1954, BMA, 100–003-00084–0074.

[37] Qingniantuan Beijing shiwei tongzhanbu 青年团北京市委统战部, "Guanyu zuzhi wufangmian qingnian canjia 'wusi' qingnianjie huodong de qingkuang baogao" 关于组织五方面青年参加"五四"青年节活动的情况报告 [Report on organizing young people from five categories to participate activities on May Fourth Youth Day], May 25, 1954, BMA, 100–003-00084–0001.

naturally love to play, it would be disastrous to lead them to play."[38] Apart from neglect from the cadres, with irregular work arrangements and vague requirements, the Beijing Municipal Youth League Committee itself did not pay enough attention to organize leisure activities. As a result, a great number of cadres organizing leisure activities could not focus on their duties and felt that they were mere "fourth-class cadres."[39] Furthermore, long school hours for students and additional meetings for activists reduced their own leisure hours bit by bit.[40]

Aware that young people were leading a tense life, in June 1953, when meeting with the presidium of the second National Congress of the Youth League, Mao Zedong said that "young people should play more, have more entertainment, and hop and bounce around energetically. Otherwise, they will not be happy." "We should pay close attention to both ends, with study and work at one end, and sleep, rest and entertainment at the other," Mao urged. "In the past, we only grasped one end firmly, leaving the other end not grasped or only half-heartedly grasped. Now… this end should be firmly grasped, too." Mao also raised his famous "three good" requirements that youth should "be in good health, study well, and work well."[41]

In addition to Mao's requirements, the Beijing Municipal Youth League Committee did consider it necessary to organize more leisure activities because of the existing "problems" in young people's leisure time. Wang Zhaohua, the second secretary of the Beijing Municipal Youth League Committee claimed that young people felt so bored that they only messed about on Saturdays and Sundays idly:

[38] "Liu Daosheng tongzhi zai Beijingshi zhongdeng yishang xuexiao qunzhong wenhua huodong jiji fenzi dahui shang de baogao" 刘导生同志在北京市中等以上学校群众文化活动积极分子大会上的报告 [Comrade Liu Daosheng's report during the conference of mass culture activists in secondary and post-secondary schools in Beijing], November 15, 1953, BMA, 100-001-00118-0001.

[39] *Jidang yu huisheng*, 136–137.

[40] Mao Zedong, "Qingniantuan de gongzuo yao zhaogu qingnian de tedian" 青年团的工作要照顾青年的特点 [The work of the Youth League must take the characteristics of youth into its consideration], in Zhonggong zhongyang wenxian yanjiushi 中共中央文献研究室 and gongqingtuan zhongyang 共青团中央, eds., *Qingnian gongzuo wenxian xuanbian shang* 青年工作文献选编 上 [Selected documents on youth work, vol. 1] (Beijing: Zhongyang wenxian chubanshe and zhongguo qingnian chubanshe, 2012), 342.

[41] Mao, "Qingniantuan de gongzuo yao zhaogu qingnian de tedian," in *Qingnian gongzuo wenxian xuanbian shang*, 342–343.

Some college students say that their daily life is like a parallelogram (dining hall, classroom, library, and dormitory), or "three points in a line" (dining hall, classroom, dormitory). Some young workers say, "Life is the same every day, just working, meeting, and sleeping." On Sundays, they "get up, have face washed, and wait for breakfast, then wander around until eleven at night." Some young government employees sleep all day on Sundays. Young people are energetic and they can always find something to do. Some disassemble their bicycles on Saturday and then clean the parts for a whole day on Sunday; some go out by bike and turn around aimlessly whenever they see an alleyway for half a day. Some female comrades, who have no place to go on Saturday night, dress up and look at themselves in the mirror all night.[42]

More seriously for the Party and the Youth League, although some young people did have their own plans for leisure time, they tended to be lured by "degenerate" lifestyles. In a survey conducted by the Youth League Committee in Shijingshan Iron and Steel Plant in 1954, while most young workers had nothing to do after they came back to their dormitories after work, there were still some workers playing poker without self-restraint. They played poker until dawn after the night shift, and some gambled with cigarettes when playing and were even arrested by the police. Some other workers performed traditional storytelling (*pingshu* 评书) in their dormitories, including "Three Knights-errant with Swords" (*san xia jian* 三侠剑), "Wang Zuo Breaks His Arms" (*Wangzuo duan bi* 王佐断臂), and "Myths" (*shenhua* 神话). Most of the listeners were young, including students. Some people even considered that listening to *pingshu* was "more fascinating than taking Youth League classes." As for leisure reading, "old" novels such as *The Investiture of the Gods* (*Fengshen bang* 封神榜), *Red Apricot Coming out of the Wall* (*Hongxing chuqiang ji* 红杏出墙记), *Unfinished Destiny* (*Weiliao yuan* 未了缘), *Xuegang Rebels against the Tang Dynasty* (*Xuegang fan Tang* 薛刚反唐), and *Meng Lijun* were still popular among young workers. Few of them had ever read books advocated by the Party such as *Lovely China* (*Ke'ai de Zhongguo* 可爱的中国) by a Communist martyr named Fang Zhimin and *Stories of Zoya and Shura* (*Zhuoya he shula de gushi* 卓娅和舒拉的故事) about two Soviet heroes translated from Russian.[43]

---

[42] *Jidang yu huisheng*, 135.

[43] "Qingniantuan Shijingshan gangtiechang weiyuanhui guanyu diaocha yu gaijin jiti sushi zhuangkuang de baogao" 青年团石景山钢铁厂委员会关于调查与改进集体宿舍状况

In the early 1950s, youth cadres were constantly problematizing young people's allocation of their leisure time, which suggests that Party officials considered it necessary to regulate young people's leisure activities. Concerned about "problematic" ways of spending leisure time among the youth, the Beijing Municipal Youth League Committee concluded in a 1953 report that young people "did not know how to live." They were unable to rest well because they were indulgent in "degenerate" lifestyles in off-duty hours, which in turn resulted in an increase of absence and accidents in factories. Therefore, they needed to be guided in their leisure time.[44] In addition to scrutiny from the top, young people themselves also wrote to newspapers and magazines complaining about the dullness of their leisure time. In 1954, Ma Tieding, a columnist writing for the column "essays on [people's] thoughts" of *Changjiang Daily* who had a nationwide reputation in the early 1950s, received a letter from a young man named Sun in which he said that his leisure time was extremely "quiet and boring." Every day, he and his colleagues just went to work, ate meals, and went to bed routinely, and only occasionally there would be someone playing the game of Novuss (*kelang qiu* 克郎球, a game similar to billiard ball which became popular during the Republican era) in the evening. Another young man said that he would rather "work endlessly" because as soon as he left his work, he "felt bored and had nothing else to do." Because of this, he became "most afraid of Sundays and vacations."[45]

As a political organization that had claimed to adopt a "mass line," the CCP did not forget to mention young people's own initiative in seeking help from youth cadres when they were too bored in their leisure time. Although it was difficult to assess how many young people would actually request the Party to take over their leisure time or how they wished the Party to regulate their leisure activities, the scenario of young people

---

的报告 [Report by the Youth League Committee in Shijingshan Iron and Steel Plant on investigating and improving conditions in communal dormitories], December 1, 1954, BMA, 100–001-00160–0001.

[44] "Liu Daosheng tongzhi zai Beijingshi zhongdeng yishang xuexiao qunzhong wenhua huodong jiji fenzi dahui shang de baogao," November 15, 1953, BMA, 100–001-00118–0001.

[45] Ma Tieding 马铁丁, "Wenhua de xiuxi" 文化的休息 [Relaxing with culture], *Zhongguo qingnian* 12 (1954): 29. "Ma Tieding" was a communal pen name used by Chen Xiaoyu, Zhang Tiefu, and Guo Xiaochuan. They published nearly 500 essays under this pseudonym. See Tan Zheng 谭征, *Xunzhao Ma Tieding* 寻找马铁丁 [In search of Ma Tieding] (Beijing: Haiyang chubanshe, 2009), 1–4.

turning to the Party for help would give the CCP a great excuse to wield its power over young people's private sphere. A journalist from the Youth League's mouthpiece *China Youth Daily* claimed in his book that young people often raised questions to him about how to organize their own leisure time. They demanded that "the organizations of the Party, the administrative offices, the labor unions, and the Youth League committees should organize not only their eight-hour working hours but also the rest of their time." The journalist recorded the "distress" among young workers and young technicians:

> Chairman Mao teaches us to "be in good health, study well, and work well." But now we can only do well in our work. Apart from work, there seems to be nothing else in our everyday life. But work only accounts for one-third of our time. We don't know how to organize the rest of the one-third except for sleeping time. We forget anything else during work time when concentrating on production, but as soon as we get off work, we feel distressed, especially on Saturdays and Sundays. We cannot just work, attend meetings, eat meals, and sleep all day long. We are all young people. Who doesn't want to have a good leisure time and make ourselves happy? But we just don't know how to have fun...[46]

According to the journalist, young people felt that they "led a socialist way of life at work," but "seemed to lead a 'capitalist' way of life after work" because they had nothing else to do other than "desultory chats, or talking about food, drink, and clothing."[47] From the perspective of this journalist, organizing more state-sponsored leisure activities was not a top-down infiltration of political power in people's private time, but came from youth themselves: young people were eagerly inviting official organizations to take over their leisure time for their own good.

---

[46] Feng Yuqin 冯玉钦, *Tantan qingnian yeyu shenghuo* 谈谈青年业余生活 [Talking about young people's leisure life] (Wuhan: Hubei renmin chubanshe, 1957), 1.

[47] Feng, *Tantan qingnian yeyu shenghuo*, 1–2.

"Life Should Be Planned:" Temporal Politics Deepened

More Regulations of Everyday Leisure Time

In 1954, after receiving complaints from young people about their leisure time, Ma Tieding wrote an essay titled "Relaxing with Culture" as a response. He believed that "relaxing with culture" should be advocated by "organizing beneficial cultural, recreational, and sports activities to attach our rest with more a positive meaning." Ma justified his statement from a biological point of view: people needed to have some rest, "just as tightened strings will break, excessively tense nerves will go wrong." Therefore, people should relax for better performance at work, not for the sake of having fun.[48] Obviously, although many young people did wish to have more organized recreational activities, not everyone, including organizers, was aware of the purpose of these activities. One example was that dancing parties in factories sometimes lasted late into the night. *China Youth Daily* had to instruct young people that "first of all, to play well and rest well is to work better" and "all leisure activities that can help achieve this goal should be advocated; all that that cannot help achieve this goal should be corrected."[49]

For the Party, the ideal way of life should be working diligently in working hours and relaxing with culture during leisure. Leisure activities should never hinder work and study. Therefore, from the perspective of youth cadres, it was not a minor problem if young people did not know how to rest in their leisure time. One article in *China Youth Daily* analyzed that the problem with these young people was that they did not understand the principle that "life should have norms and also should be planned" so that "they were always unable to control themselves" and became "weak-willed people." Incompetence of planning their leisure time was a big issue in the sense that "at present, our country should gradually realize socialist industrialization and the transition to socialism…The

---

[48] Ma, "Wenhua de xiuxi," *Zhongguo qingnian* 12 (1954): 29.

[49] Chen Dong 陈东, "Wenyu huodong shi weile shenme?" 文娱活动是为了什么? [What is the purpose of cultural recreational activities?], in *Youyi de mianli: Zhongguo qingnian bao sixiang erritan xuanji* 友谊的勉励: 中国青年报 "思想二日谈" 选集 [Encouragement of friendship: selected essays from "Talking about thought every two days" column of *China Youth Daily*] (Beijing: Zhongguo qingnian chubanshe, 1955), 64–65.

socialist construction should be carried out in accordance with an accurate and rigid plan." As qualified future socialist builders, the youth must "pay attention to arranging their own time in a planned way."[50] "Youth, be the master of your life," appealed *Beijing Youth Daily* to its young readers in 1955. "Master your leisure time!".[51]

The underlying claim of these articles was that state intervention in young people's leisure time helped them better allocate their time. One youth cadre believed that, with "very inadequate knowledge and experience about life," youth needed to be guided effectively. They observed that during working hours, young people could work in a cheerful mood with "the help and support of their leaders," but after work, when "time was at their own disposal," they were unable to arrange their leisure properly. This phenomenon could only lead to the conclusion that "the leadership and help of Youth League organizations are vital for young people to live a good leisure life."[52] This kind of opinion resonated with a report drafted by the Beijing Municipal Youth League Committee in 1954 on the League's role in organizing leisure activities since 1949. The League discovered that before the second National Congress of the Youth League in 1953, because the League organizations mainly "focused on political education," leisure activities were not properly organized. During this period, Youth League organizations basically gave up their leadership on young people's leisure time in the sense that although large-scale activities such as park festivals and art festivals were held during summer vacations and public holidays, "everyday activities" were ignored.[53]

Along with the propaganda campaign to persuade people that young people's leisure "problems" could not be solved without state intervention, from 1953 to 1955, the Youth League adopted a more interventionist approach toward young people's leisure time when it required its grassroots organizations to extend power into people's daily activities. In 1953, the second National Congress of the Youth League required

---

[50] Huang Lin 黄磷, "Cong guohao xingqitian tanqi" 从过好星期天谈起 [Speaking about spending Sundays properly], in *Youyi de mianli*, 63.

[51] *Beijing qingnian bao*, October 14, 1955.

[52] Feng, *Tantan qingnian yeyu shenghuo*, 41.

[53] Tuanshiwei xuanchuanbu 团市委宣传部, "Wunianduo lai qunzhong wenhua gongzuo de fazhan jiankuang" 五年多来群众文化工作的发展简况 [A brief introduction to the development of mass culture work in more than five years], 1954, BMA, 100-001-00188-0018.

League organizations at all levels that apart from existing large-scale activities, they should make more effort to organize "small-scale and scattered" activities, which indicated the Youth League's ambition to expand its presence from vacations and days off to people's everyday leisure time.[54] Youth cadres, however, were not satisfied with the implementation of the League's policy. The Beijing Municipal Youth League Committee found in 1954 that although after the second National Congress of the Youth League, League-organized leisure activities had improved a little bit, there was still a lack of "regular and specific guidance at the grassroots level." In 1955, the Youth League Central Committee issued *Resolution on Strengthening Youth Cultural Work during Leisure Time*, calling for leisure activities to be carried out as an "important and regular" work of the Youth League. The Central Committee believed that leisure activities were not widely organized in many grassroots organizations, and even in places where there were League-organized leisure activities, these activities were not frequently organized. The Central Committee also criticized that these activities were not rich in their contents, not diverse in their forms, and could not attract participants from a wide range of backgrounds. To prevent young people from "pursuing improper entertainment" in their leisure time, the Youth League organizations at all levels were asked to plan leisure time more extensively for the youth by promoting literacy campaigns among the illiterate, organizing reading clubs, and organizing leisure artistic activities and sports.[55]

Under the guidance of these principles, factories and schools in Beijing carried out pilot projects to organize everyday leisure activities. In factories, workers were organized to attend recreational activities, play sports, participate in education sessions offered by the Party, the Youth League, and the labor union in their leisure time. They were also required to take after-work literacy classes. The Beijing Knitting Mill, for example, planned leisure time for its workers on a daily basis. Based on archival documents, we can make sense of how workers' leisure time was spent (Table 3.2):

---

[54] Tuanshiwei zhongxuebu 团市委中学部, "Ba banji de wenhua xiuxi gongzuo kaizhan qilai shida nü fuzhong kaizhan banji wenhua xiuxi huodong de jingyan" 把班级的文化休息活动开展起来——师大女附中开展班级文化休息活动的经验 [Develop in-class activities for cultural leisure: experience from the Beijing Normal University Girls' High School on developing in-class activities for cultural leisure], 1955, BMA, 100-003-00186-0001.

[55] RMRB, April 20, 1955.

Table 3.2 Weekly schedule of leisure activities in Beijing Knitting Mill (1956)

Monday	Attend activities organized by sports association, singing club, and amateur troupe in the factory
Tuesday	Literacy class; do homework
Wednesday	Labor union activities (basically listening to propaganda reports from district-level labor union)
Thursday	Literacy class; do homework
Friday	Party and Youth League activities
Saturday	Literacy class; do homework
Sunday	Party education sessions; discussions on Party education sessions

Source "Yeyu shijian fenpei qingkuang" 业余时间分配情况 [Situation on the arrangement of leisure time], 1956, BMA, 038-002-00205-029

According to archival documents, workers in the Beijing Knitting Mill worked for nine hours a day, from 7:00 am to 5:30 pm, excluding a lunch break for one and a half hours. Nevertheless, individual workshops would usually expropriate the lunch break to discuss problems regarding production. Also, workers could not go to bed after literacy classes that ended at around 10:10 pm because there would be meetings for the selection of advanced workers after literacy classes that would last until midnight. On Monday evenings after 8:30 pm, Party and Youth League cadres needed to attend meetings if necessary.[56] This schedule indicates that there was hardly any time left that could be planned by workers themselves in the Beijing Knitting Mill.

The Model of the Beijing Normal University Girls' High School

In universities and high schools, everyday leisure activities usually included cultural and recreational activities, physical exercise, voluntary labor, study sessions on current affairs, meetings held by Party and Youth League branches, and class meetings. The Beijing Normal University Girls' High School was a model for organizing everyday leisure activities.[57] Before the second National Congress of the Youth League

---

[56] "Yeyu shijian fenpei qingkuang" 业余时间分配情况 [Situation on the arrangement of leisure time], 1956, BMA, 038-002-00205-029.

[57] The following paragraphs on recreational activities in the Girls' High School are from "Ba banji de wenhua xiuxi gongzuo kaizhan qilai shida nü fuzhong kaizhan banji wenhua xiuxi huodong de jingyan," 1955, BMA, 100-003-00186-0001.

in 1953, instead of organizing "small-scale and scattered" recreational activities at school, the Girls' High School preferred to organize large-scale school-wide activities such as Evening Party Commemorating the October Revolution and New Year's Eve Party. According to the school's own assessment, however, organizing these large-scale recreational activities required plenty of people and energy, therefore they could not be held very often. From 1953 to 1955, under the guidance of organizing more "small-scale and scattered" leisure activities from the Youth League Central Committee, the Girls' High School shifted from organizing school-wide activities to organizing more daily class-wide activities.

Individual classes in the Girls' High School organized four kinds of class-wide activities: activities during breaks, activities during weekly fixed cultural and recreational hours, group activities, and weekend activities. Activities during breaks were organized during the ten-minute breaks between lectures to "make the cerebral cortex get adequate rest." The school assumed that if students did not organize recreational activities during class breaks, they would "be busy preparing for the next lecture, or continue to think about contents from the previous lecture," which would "seriously influence the absorption of new knowledge in the next lecture." The school believed that although the ten-minute break might not be suitable for holding large-scale events, classes could still organize small-scale activities such as storytelling and quick collective games. The following paragraph is a description of a typical ten-minute break with recreational activities:

> When the bell rang, all students put their books used in the previous lecture back into their desks and quickly prepared things for the next lecture and arranged them at the left corner of the desks. Students on duty for the day cleaned the blackboard and opened the windows to let in some fresh air. Then students started their joyful recreational activities during this time... What is most important when organizing recreational activities during breaks is that we should rely on activities that already exist in different classes. During the ten-minute break, singing clubs in classes can start practicing actively. Dancing clubs can practice poses. Musical instrument clubs can practice their musical instruments.

While a ten-minute break might be too rushed, in the Girls' High School, there were other fixed hours for cultural and recreational activities every week. During this period, student cadres in individual classes organized activities such as ball games or chess competitions. Apart from these competitions, students also organized music appreciation activities. One class introduced the life and achievements of the Russian musician Tchaikovsky accompanied by his music. Another class organized a club-style recreational party during which all classmates could chat with each other while eating snacks and listening to music.

The third kind of activity—group activity—was organized based on in-class clubs such as dancing club, singing club, flute club, and harmonica club. After activists in classes made proposals, clubs would be established, and they would have group activities once a week under the guidance of instructors. Finally, on weekends, rather than organizing school-wide activities, the school usually treated students to a movie, allowing them to "spend their time and organize activities freely." Class-wide collective activities, however, would also be organized on weekends. In some classes, activists mobilized their classmates to attend an exhibition. Youth League members in some other classes went out of town to conduct geological surveys. In the evening, students living on campus "got together to talk about their ambitions," some even "talked about each other's shortcomings." Some Youth League groups held evening parties.

"LEISURE TIME DOES NOT BELONG TO US"

From the perspective of the Youth League, by 1956, with the efforts of its organizations at all levels, young people seemed to be leading a highly planned and regular life in their leisure time as many youth cadres expected. At the same time, however, cadres also reported that some young people felt overburdened by organized leisure. These findings might not be the result of the trend of de-Stalinization from the Soviet Union in early 1956 because internal surveys addressing young people's tight schedule were conducted as early as 1955.[58] Nevertheless, the relatively free atmosphere in 1956 when official newspapers and magazines were allowed to publish people's discontent made this

---

[58] See, for example, "Jianzhu dangwei guanyu zhigong yeyu huodong shijian de yijian (cao'an) ji youguan cailiao" 建筑党委关于职工业余活动时间的意见（草案）及有关材料 [Draft from the Party committee in building industry regarding workers' leisure time and relevant materials], June 1955, BMA, 001-020-00060. For the CCP's reaction of Khrushchev's condemnation of Stalin, see Meisner, *Mao's China and After*, 162–165.

new problem more visible.[59] As a result, newspaper and magazine articles started to call for a more reasonable allocation of young people's leisure time. For example, in April 1956, *China Youth Daily* published an editorial entitled "Give Leisure Time Back to the Youth." After citing young people's complaints that "leisure time does not belong to us," the author suggested that "Youth League branches should try to give leisure time back to the youth."[60] More articles published in newspapers and magazines during this period as well as investigations conducted by the Beijing Municipal Youth League Committee in schools, factories, and shops attributed youths' sense of losing control of their leisure time to three main reasons: mandatory activities, unnecessary school work, and forced participation in collective activities.

Mandatory Activities

A plethora of mandatory activities, including mandatory meetings held by Party branches, Youth League branches, labor unions, and classes in schools as well as activities aiming at raising political awareness such as mandatory labor and study sessions on current affairs, seized too much leisure time from young people. These activities, which were too frequently organized, took up their already limited leisure time, making it impossible for young people to have a good rest, let alone take part in recreational activities. In early 1956, a satirical article published in *Chinese Workers* revealed how workers had no alternative but to attend a long and meaningless meeting held by the labor union during off-duty hours on New Year's Eve:

> It will be a new year in only half an hour. Usually, on New Year's Eve, you should hang out with your friends or have a rest. Hundreds of us, however, are doing something else. Alas, we are still sitting here for a meeting.
> It is said that the heroic labor models are now working on the production quota of the year 1958. Nevertheless, if we had competed with them on the quota of holding meetings, we might have got ahead of them!
> ......

---

[59] For the political situation in early 1956 and the subsequent "Hundred Flowers Campaign" launched by Mao, see Meisner, *Mao's China and After*, 159–161, 165–180.

[60] *Zhongguo qingnian bao*, April 15, 1956.

President Meng of the labor union has been talking for more than 300 minutes since the start of the meeting at 7:00 pm. No one can match his "eloquence." Every report—even a report about "don't write graffiti on walls in washrooms"—is divided into at least three parts, and each part has four or five sections, and each section has key points. Today's meeting is to summarize the work of the labor union in 1955. How important it is! This is the way it is...

"Today's meeting, extended a little bit though (Oh dear! It's past 11:00 pm!), is very fruitful. We not only summed up our previous work but also assigned new tasks. Our experience proves that this is a way to kill two birds with one stone." Chairman Meng took a sip of tea which had already cooled down like ice. He glared at the sleepy comrades who were in charge of making the meeting go smoothly.

"Therefore, the meeting must continue, and let's cheer up! Stick to the end! It's a matter of organizational principle."

......

"Dismissed"—what a beautiful and seductive word. At last, we were not disappointed when the meeting finally ended at 1:26 am, January 1, 1956.

Many people slept on the benches in the meeting room and said helplessly: "It will be dawn if we walk back home. Just make do here for a night!"[61]

Apart from workers in factories, university students also faced numerous meetings for reports and mobilization, some of which were even convened with no advance notice. A student named Lin Ding complained that after the slogan "marching towards science" was issued in early 1956, he, along with his enthusiastic classmates, had to attend countless meetings immediately, which "made his head spin." He described one week that had meetings everyday including Saturday and Sunday:

> On Monday afternoon, we attended a mobilizing meeting, in which the president and the provost gave mobilizing reports. On Tuesday, Party and Youth League branch held meetings to discuss how to carry out the call from the president. On Wednesday, my class held another meeting with similar contents with meetings on Tuesday. On Thursday there were liaison meetings between the masses and the Party and Youth League members to expose our erroneous thoughts during the "marching towards science" movement under the arrangement of the Youth League Committee. On

---

[61] Zhu Mo 朱墨, "Kai le liangnian de 'wan' hui" 开了两年的 "晚" 会 [A late meeting that was held for two years], *Zhongguo gongren* 5 (1956): 24.

Friday, the Youth League Committee organized a meeting in which the secretary of the Youth League delivered a report about several typical incorrect thoughts based on Thursday's meetings. On Saturday, the university invited a scientist to give us a lecture. The Youth League Committee required that all League members and activists should attend. As a matter of fact, all students, including those who were not League members, went to listen to the report because no one wanted to fall behind. There was also a meeting on Sunday night discussing the report delivered by the secretary of the Youth League on Friday.[62]

In addition to various meetings, activities such as mandatory labor and study sessions on current affairs also took up a large portion of students' leisure time. In 1955, the fourth "school work conference" held by the Youth League Central Committee demanded that to promote the "Communist Saturday" spirit proposed by Lenin among students, mandatory labor should be organized in factories, construction sites, farms, and cooperatives, but with a limitation that "each student, in general, should undertake mandatory labor for over two or three hours a month."[63] In reality, however, many students had to take part in mandatory labor for three hours in one week on average.[64] As for study sessions on current affairs, in most high schools and some universities, all students were required to listen to newspaper reading and take notes in a designated period of time. When having meals, students had to listen to on-campus radio broadcast, which was full of news and all kinds of criticism and praise.[65]

---

[62] Lin Ding 林丁, "Hui: yi ge xuesheng de zishu" "会": 一个学生的自述 [Meeting: personal account from a student], *Zhongguo qingnian* 11 (1956): 6.

[63] "Peiyang wei shehui zhuyi shiye zhongcheng fuwu de laodong zhishi qingnian—Hu Keshi tongzhi zai qingniantuan zhongyang di si ci xuexiao gongzuo huiyi shang de baogao" 培养为社会主义事业忠诚服务的劳动知识青年——胡克实同志在青年团中央第四次学校工作会议上的报告 [Foster laboring educated youth serving the socialist enterprise faithfully—Comrade Hu Keshi's report on the fourth school work conference of the Youth League Central Committee], in *Peiyang wei shehui zhuyi shiye zhongcheng fuwu de laodong zhishi qingnian* 培养为社会主义事业忠诚服务的劳动知识青年 [Nurture laboring educated youth serving the socialist enterprise faithfully], ed. Qingniantuan zhongyang xuexiao gognzuobu 青年团中央学校工作部 (Beijing: Zhongguo qingnian chubanshe, 1956), 27–28.

[64] Shang Qi 尚琪, "Guanche ziyuan yuanze gengjia fengfu duocai de kaizhan kewai huodong" 贯彻自愿原则,更加丰富多彩地开展课外活动 [Carry on the principle of participating voluntarily and develop more colorful extracurricular activities], *Zhongguo qingnian* 17 (1956): 9.

[65] Shang Qi, "Guanche ziyuan yuanze gengjia fengfu duocai de kaizhan kewai huodong," *Zhongguo qingnian* 17 (1956): 9.

Unnecessary Student Work

Even if the workload of mandatory activities was relatively reasonable for high school and university students, because of the existence of a large number of on-campus student groups, students had to undertake unnecessary work in their leisure time. In August 1956, a teacher from Beijing No. 4 High School reported at the fourth Congress of the Beijing Municipal Youth League that in his school, there were numerous student organizations including the Youth League, the Student Committee, the Young Pioneers, the Sports Association, the Young Red Cross, extracurricular research groups, the Department of Sports, groups of national defense sports, sanitary inspection groups, artistic clubs, film groups, and distribution stations of newspapers and magazines. Even the Public Security Bureau set up a bicycle group in the school. Each organization, with dozens to hundreds of student cadres, had regular work and activities. This high school teacher pointed out that organizations such as the Sports Association, the Young Red Cross and newspaper distribution stations did not need to be run by students at all because these jobs should be done by the administrative staff at school.[66]

Similarly, according to a survey conducted by the Committee of University Work of the Beijing Municipal Youth League Committee in 1956, besides the Ministry of Higher Education, the Municipal Party Committee, and the Municipal Youth League Committee, multiple government institutions and other work units also assigned extra work directly to universities, including the Municipal Sports Committee, the Central National Defence Sports Club, the People's Committee of Haidian District, governments of nearby counties, agricultural cooperatives, post offices, and even Xinhua bookstores. As a result, university students had to pick cotton seeds for agricultural cooperatives and distribute newspapers for post offices in their leisure time.[67]

---

[66] *Beijing qingnian bao*, August 28, 1956.

[67] Qingniantuan Beijing shiwei daxue gognzuo weiyuanhui 青年团北京市委大学工作委员会, "Guanyu Beijingshi gaodeng xuexiao xuesheng kewai huodong de qingkuang ji jinhou yijian chugao" 关于北京市高等学校学生课外活动的情况及今后意见 (初稿) [On the situation of extracurricular activities of university and college students in Beijing and our opinion the future (draft)], August 7, 1956, BMA, 100-001-00361-0011.

Forced Participation in Collective Activities

For many cadres, organizing collective leisure activities was a way to achieve the Party's goal of making new people.[68] Between 1955 and 1956, to forge more all-round developed young people, some youth cadres raised high standards in leisure activities by asking students to participate in activities they organized. Under the slogans such as "develop cultural tastes" and "for the honour of the collective," students had to participate in collective activities even if they were unwilling to do so in their hearts. Even worse, after the administrative staff and Youth League organizations in universities encouraged "100 percent participation of class-organized activities," forced participation became a norm when students who did not attend dancing parties, film screenings, or other recreational activities would be criticized. In Beijing Mining Institute, one class even intended to launch a special section on their blackboard bulletin called "Weekend Deserters," but their plan was not approved by their Youth League committee.[69]

The battle to take over young people's entire leisure time met considerable difficulties. In 1956, many young people wrote to *China Youth*, a journal run by the Youth League Central Committee, to complain about their experience of being forced to attend collective recreational activities at school or in work units. On closer examination of these articles, it is highly possible that this was part of the CCP's propaganda campaign because they followed a similar pattern: asking for more rationalized state allocation of leisure time instead of challenging the legitimacy of the state intervention itself. Nevertheless, these articles suggested the CCP's concern that forced collective activities might not be effective in creating new people.

A young journalist named Fan Qun revealed that he was unable to see his wife even during weekends because she had to attend collective recreational activities organized by her school. As a member of the Youth League, Fan's wife used to work in a government office, but was admitted to a university in the summer of 1955. As scheduled, she was supposed

---

[68] Creating new people is a common goal in diverse socialist countries as a result of the philosophical desire to reshape human nature since the Enlightenment. See Yinghong Cheng, *Creating the "New Man:" From Enlightenment Ideals to Socialist Realities* (Honolulu: University of Hawai'i Press, 2009).

[69] "Guanyu Beijingshi gaodeng xuexiao xuesheng kewai huodong de qingkuang ji jinhou yijian chugao," August 7, 1956, BMA, 100-001-00361-0011.

to live on campus during weekdays and come back home every Saturday afternoon. Nevertheless, Fan discovered that his wife often came back very late on Saturdays and sometimes even needed to go out on Sundays. As Fan described, his wife's tight schedule greatly affected their family life:

> In deep silent nights, my wife came home late with regret, kissed the sleeping kid, and asked me affectionately when I came back. She explained to me again and again that she wanted to go home early but was delayed by film screenings or collective singing activities organized by the university. Sometimes she felt particularly embarrassed because, despite the kid's crying to be with her mother, she had to leave home early on Sunday morning to go out for a collective excursion with her classmates.[70]

Fan concluded that his wife was "forced to attend" these activities because in her university, there was an opinion that "everyone should participate in all extracurricular activities, otherwise you are an individualist who separates yourself from the collective and the masses." Fan's wife was condemned as "having a deep family consciousness" (*jiating guannian nonghou* 家庭观念浓厚) after being absent from two collective activities. Fan's brother, similarly, was also suffering from collective activities. He wanted to read more books in his leisure time after a one-year leave from school because of lung disease but was criticized as "conceited" and "sabotaging the collective." As a boy who could not sing in tune and a patient recovering from his lung disease, he was forced to sing songs and jog together with his classmates.[71]

For some people who preferred to stay alone in their leisure time, forced participation in collective activities could make them feel stressed. Zhu Yiming, a young man working in a government office, seldom attended collective leisure activities because he liked to read books alone or play Go with his friend. Sometimes Zhu and his friend would go to the club run by his work unit, but after seeing others playing table tennis, playing poker, and having a lot of fun dancing, they still remained uninterested. Therefore, the two of them usually ended up playing Go alone

---

[70] Fan Qun 范群, "Keyu huodong buyao qiangqiu jitihua" 课余活动不要强求集体化 [Do not force people to attend extracurricular activities collectively], *Zhongguo qingnian* 10 (1956): 5.

[71] Fan Qun, "Keyu huodong buyao qiangqiu jitihua," *Zhongguo qingnian* 10 (1956): 5–6.

because nobody else knew how to play. Their behavior aroused criticism in their work unit. Some people said that they "separated themselves from the masses and were lacking the spirit of collectivism." His leaders told him that "if you do not participate in collective activities with others in your leisure time, you will separate yourself from the masses." Pressure from his colleagues and leader made Zhu begin to reflect on his behavior: "Now that everyone says so, it must be my mistake. Just correct it!" He started to spend a lot of leisure time participating in collective recreational activities and even learned how to play poker. Sometimes he even played table tennis. But deep down, Zhu was not interested in these activities because he thought that they were not as interesting as reading books. He went to these collective activities because he had no alternative: "I did so only because the leader and other comrades said that I was wrong. Now I even have concerns when reading books in my leisure time. As for Go, I stopped playing it a long time ago." These episodes in his leisure time made Zhu anxious:

> I am confident to say that although I have some shortcomings in my thought, I do not have any ideas of complacency or contempt for others. In my daily work, I often discuss with leaders and comrades around me how to improve my work with an open mind to opinions from them. The comrades are relatively satisfied with my work. I have been praised by the leader.[72]

Zhu could not understand why a cadre, who did his job so well, should be criticized for planning his leisure time life according to his own interests. He asked in his article: "Can a cadre allocate his leisure time freely based on his own hobbies? How should people deal with hobbies and interests in leisure time? If a person does not attend collective activities in leisure time, does it mean that he lacks the spirit of collectivism?".[73]

The articles of Fan and Zhu resonated among readers of *China Youth*. A Beijing student wrote a letter about how the teacher in charge of his class elevated leisure time issues to the level of ideology. Every spring

---

[72] Zhu Yiming 朱一明, "Ying bu yinggai you geren de yeyu xingqu he aihao?" 应不应该有个人的业余兴趣和爱好? [Should I have personal hobbies in leisure time?], *Zhongguo qingnian* 10 (1956): 39.

[73] Zhu Yiming, "Ying bu yinggai you geren de yeyu xingqu he aihao?", *Zhongguo qingnian* 10 (1956): 39.

vacation, his school would either organize a group excursion or a group visit. In spring 1956, students in his class had various ideas about the destination of this year's spring vacation, including the Great Wall, the Summer Palace, Biyun Temple, Beihai Park, and the Temple of Heaven. Some students also wanted to go to construction sites or farms to sketch. Diverse as the destinations were, his classmate Li Lingyu proposed that "now that we have different interests and requirements, why not organize several different 'spring excursion' groups instead of all going to one place?" Considering it a reasonable proposal, his classmates began to sign up for different groups and prepare for spring break activities respectively. Mr. Kang, the headteacher of the class, said: "No way! If you think differently and do not act consistently, how can we do a good job in the class during the spring vacation?" Mr. Kang started his "persuasion and dissuasion" immediately by talking about preconditions of the class as a collective and analyzing the erroneous tendency of "being weak in collective thought." Finally, after the repeated "persuasion and mobilization" from Mr. Kang, it was decided that the whole class would go to Taoranting Park, a place that nobody had ever proposed, for a "collective spring excursion."

The matter did not end there. As the initiator of forming different groups in the spring vacation, Li Lingyu faced additional pressure from the headteacher. Mr. Kang spoke personally to Li and "helped" her realize the "origin and bad influence" of her "incorrect thought." Mr. Kang even charged Li of having a "serious tendency of liberalism" after Li refused to admit her "mistakes," which had made Li cry. During the first class meeting after the spring vacation, Mr. Kang not only publicly criticized the students who acted "without organization and discipline" during spring vacation activities but also made this statement:

> Thinking only of oneself and not taking care of others is incompatible with the spirit of collectivism and thus violates the principles of the class as a collective. Now you are still students, but what will you do in the future after you start to work? Gao Gang and Rao Shushi embarked on the road of opposing the Party and the people because of their growing individualism! You must take it as a warning. You should criticize yourselves thoroughly from the perspective of ideology...[74]

---

[74] Guo Lin 郭林, "Wei shenme yiding yao qiang qiu yizhi?" 为什么一定要强求一致?[Why force us to act collectively?], *Zhongguo qingnian* 12 (1956): 30.

THE STRUGGLE OVER LEISURE TIME: THE POLICY OF "FREE ALLOCATION OF LEISURE TIME"

Along with public discussions about overburdened youth in leisure time, in 1956, the Party introduced an overhaul of its previous leisure regulation during which all work units were required to ensure that young people could have enough free time for themselves. Of course, the Party did so not for the sake of individual freedom, but for the practical reason of letting young people work more effectively after adequate rest. As the *China Youth Daily* editorial published in April 1956 claimed, the purpose of "giving leisure time back to youth" was not to leave leisure time unattended, but to let young people "enrich their knowledge" by studying in leisure time during the movement of "marching towards science."[75]

The first measure was to reduce redundant meetings in people's leisure time, which became the key part of the implementation of the so-called "free allocation of leisure time" (*ziyou zhipei shijian* 自由支配时间) policy. Many work units made specific arrangements for meetings in their new leisure schedules. The Beijing Knitting Mill, for example, required that "the administrative staff shall not expropriate workers' leisure time for meetings," and the activities organized by the Party and Youth League branches should also be reduced. The revised version of the weekly schedule of leisure activities in this factory was as follows (Table 3.3):

Table 3.3 Revised weekly schedule of leisure activities in Beijing Knitting Mill (1956)

Monday	Labor union activities
Tuesday	Literacy class
Wednesday	Planned by workers freely (but Party branches, Youth League branches, and labor union committee can hold meetings during this time)[a]
Thursday	Literacy class
Friday	Party and Youth League activities
Saturday	Planned by workers freely
Sunday	Planned by workers freely

[a]Meetings should be held on time, and each meeting should last no more than two hours
Source Gongsi heying Beijing zhenzhichang dangzhibu 公私合营北京针织厂党支部, "Gongsi heying Beijing zhenzhichang dangzhibu zhigong yeyu shijian anpai jihua yijian" 公私合营北京针织厂党支部职工业余时间安排计划意见 [Opinions on the arrangement of workers' leisure time by the Party branch in the joint public–private enterprise Beijing Knitting Mill], August 2, 1956, BMA, 038-002-00461-033

[75] *Zhongguo qingnian bao*, April 15, 1956.

Another measure was the reaffirmation of the principle of voluntary participation among students, which was, according to the Beijing Municipal Youth League Committee, "one of the basic differences between leisure activities and in-class teaching." Leisure activities should be "organized according to the interests and needs of the masses" and if not, they would become "taking classes in disguise."[76] The Municipal Youth League Committee stressed that "the major task for students is to study at school, and therefore leisure activities should only play a cooperative and auxiliary role. There should be strict rules for studying at school, but students should also be allowed to participate in leisure activities voluntarily without any mandatory requirements." While the Municipal Youth League Committee still maintained that large-scale collective leisure activities should be sustained, other forms of leisure activities were permissible such as "playing chess, boating or taking a walk with one or two people." The Municipal Youth League Committee even articulated particularly that "reading books alone was also fine."[77]

From the perspective of leisure activities organizers, when implementing the policy of "free allocation of leisure time," the key was to strengthen the unified leadership of the Party in the sense that the Party could make overall plans of the organized leisure activities to avoid overlapping time expropriation. Before initiating the policy of "free allocation of leisure time," different agencies such as labor unions, Party branches, and Youth League branches could not coordinate their leisure activities because of the lack of an arbitrator. For example, on a Saturday in April 1956, in a factory in Beijing, there was a dispute between the labor union, the Youth League, and the administrative staff over who could use Saturday's leisure time to hold a meeting. All of the three parties were unwilling to compromise because they all considered their meeting important. In the end, the director of the factory was extremely unsatisfied and said angrily: "Okay, we will hold our meeting during working hours!".[78]

---

[76] Shang Qi, "Guanche ziyuan yuanze gengjia fengfu duocai de kaizhan kewai huodong," *Zhongguo qingnian* 17 (1956): 9.

[77] "Guanyu Beijingshi gaodeng xuexiao xuesheng kewai huodong de qingkuang ji jinhou yijian chugao," August 7, 1956, BMA, 100–001-00361–0011.

[78] "Yeyu shijian fenpei qingkuang," 1956, BMA, 038–002-00,205–029.

To solve similar issues, in a document titled "Regulations of Leisure Time" issued in June 1956, the Party committee in the Beijing Municipal Supply and Marketing Cooperative emphasized that "leisure time is uniformly controlled by the Party committee."[79] In August 1956, the Beijing Knitting Mill required that "the Party committee shall make overall plans of leisure activities organized by the labor union, and the Youth League."[80] More specific instructions were made by another factory in September 1956 that "to control the usage of people's leisure time, the Youth League, the labor union and the administrative staff should submit the plans of meetings to be held next month to the Party committee for unified arrangements."[81] Similar regulations were introduced in universities. The Committee of University Work of the Beijing Municipal Youth League Committee believed in a survey that because of the lack of unified leadership in leisure activities organized in Beijing universities, although the activities "seemed to be good when being examined individually," when organized together, it was impossible for students to take part in all the leisure activities that were "designed scientifically" from the top. As a result, the leisure activities that "were designed for entertainment, rest and the improvement of physical and mental health" became heavy burdens for students. Therefore, to "plan more rigorously and avoid disorder," leisure activities "should strive for the unified leadership and control of Party committees."[82]

Nevertheless, the policy of letting young people plan their leisure time freely did not guarantee their freedom to control all of their leisure activities. As an article in *China Youth* summarized, the principle of voluntary participation did not apply to activities such as Party and Youth League

[79] Zhonggong shi gongxiaoshe zhibu weiyuanhui 中共市供销社支部委员会, "Guanyu yeyu shijian de guiding" 关于业余时间的规定 [Regulations of Leisure Time], June 15, 1956, BMA, 088-001-00124-0009.

[80] Gongsi heying Beijing zhenzhichang dangzhibu 公私合营北京针织厂党支部, "Gongsi heying Beijing zhenzhichang dangzhibu zhigong yeyu shijian anpai jihua yijian" 公私合营北京针织厂党支部职工业余时间安排计划意见 [Opinions on the arrangement of workers' leisure time by the Party branch in the joint public–private enterprise Beijing Knitting Mill], August 2, 1956, BMA, 038-002-00461-033.

[81] Xiangli dangzhibu 祥利党支部, "Xiangli zhibu yeyu shijian guihua" 祥利支部业余时间规划 [Plans for leisure time by the Party branch in Xiangli Factory], September 3, 1956, BMA, 038-002-00461-031.

[82] "Guanyu Beijingshi gaodeng xuexiao xuesheng kewai huodong de qingkuang ji jinhou yijian chugao," August 7, 1956, BMA, 100-001-00361-0011.

organizational life meetings (*zuzhi shenghuo hui* 组织生活会) for Party and Youth League members because they were obliged to participate in these meetings according to Party and Youth League constitutions. For activities that applied to this principle such as mandatory labor and study sessions of current affairs, organizers should not take a laissez-faire attitude. Instead, organizers must "inspire" (*qifa* 启发) students to participate in these activities voluntarily because "young people with consciousness shall not be absent from these activities."[83]

Examining the Impacts of "Temporal Politics"

On the one hand, the CCP never abandoned its leisure regulation. On the other hand, young people in Beijing did not seem to reject the presence of political power in their leisure time. One reason was that for many young people, being admitted to state-organized leisure activities such as park festivals was a sign that they were accepted politically. Another important reason was that leisure activities organized by the Communist Party were indeed better than those offered by the Nationalist Party. As recollected by a Beijing resident who was a high school student in 1949, after the end of the first semester of the 1948–1949 school year, the Nationalist Party organized mandatory winter camps for all high school students. Locked in campuses, students took military training every morning and they could not even eat meals on time. In contrast, when he attended the Summer Youth School organized by the Communist Party about half a year later, he felt "revolutionary enthusiasm and joyful atmosphere." Although both the winter camp and the Youth School were collective activities organized by political parties, the latter one was easily accepted by him and his classmates who had lived through the Nationalist rule.[84] In addition, when people could only choose between leisure activities organized by their work units, recreational activities, at least, were not as boring as other activities such as meetings. One cartoon published in *Beijing Daily* in 1955 revealed that even among cadres, watching dramas organized by the labor union was far more popular than attending meetings.[85]

---

[83] Shang Qi, "Guanche ziyuan yuanze gengjia fengfu duocai de kaizhan kewai huodong," *Zhongguo qingnian* 17 (1956): 9.

[84] Zhang Baozhang 张宝章, "Sijiu nian shenghuo manyi" 四九年生活漫忆 [Scattered recollections of life in 1949], *Haidian wenshi xuanbian* 11 (1999): 89–92.

[85] *Beijing ribao*, January 8, 1955.

The impacts of "temporal politics" can be further proved by oral interviews conducted several decades later. The interviewees were eleven Beijing residents who were workers, office employees, soldiers, salesclerks, teachers, and housewives in the 1950s. When these ordinary people recalled their leisure time in the early years of the People's Republic, no matter what their jobs were, collective activities organized by their schools, factories, or neighborhood committees including park festivals, collective dancing, film screening, singing contests, and sports games were a major part in their leisure activities. Keywords such as "interesting," "lively," and "colorful" frequently appeared when they described collective leisure activities they had attended. To be sure, there were interviewees who thought that they did not have enough time to relax, or their leisure activities were too politicized. They still, however, welcomed leisure activities offered by work units as they thought that while being too politicized was irrational, any form of leisure activity should include political elements to be "educational." For them, it was the degree of politicization of their leisure time that was problematic, not the existence of political power.[86] This nostalgia indicates that people's way of life has been forged by the Party's regulation of leisure time.[87]

Conclusion: Temporal Politics and the Forging of a New Pace of Life

After the Chinese Communist Party's military victory in 1949, authorities in Beijing offered collective leisure activities in long vacations and days off with different purposes such as political education, developing young people's habit of relaxing with culture, or propagandizing the happiness

---

[86] Interviews of eleven Beijing residents, in Liang Jinghe 梁景和, ed., *Zhongguo xiandangdai shehui wenhua fangtanlu di si ji* 中国现当代社会文化访谈录 第四辑 [Collection of interviews on social culture of modern and contemporary China, vol. 4] (Beijing: Shoudu shifan daxue chubanshe, 2014), 119–145; 215–227.

[87] To collect more oral history materials from the grassroots, during my field research in Beijing in 2018 and 2019, I talked to several people who were in their teenage years in the early 1950s. Unfortunately, except for the fact that they attended many collective activities, most of them could not remember what they did in their leisure time in detail as most of the interviewees were in their late 80 s when I interviewed them. From another perspective, however, the vague memories show that at least the collectivization of leisure time was "normal" for my interviewees because they usually had relatively fresh memories about things that they considered special.

of young people living under the new regime. From 1953 to 1956, interference and control of people's private time by political power reached its first pinnacle in the sense that the regulation of leisure time overwhelmed everyday leisure. At the same time, the CCP found that a tight schedule in leisure time might affect the efficiency of political education and everyday work. In 1956, the Party initiated the policy of "free allocation of leisure time," hoping to rectify chaos in young people's leisure by reducing excessive meetings, reiterating the principle of voluntary participation in collective leisure activities, and strengthening the overall leadership of Party committees in grassroots work units.

Temporal politics, as defined at the beginning of this chapter, is the process of seizure and allocation of private time (i.e., leisure time) by political power. Both the attempt to achieve a full takeover of everyday leisure and the subsequent policy of "free allocation of leisure time" were related parts of the CCP's "temporal politics" during which the Party claimed its sovereignty over young people's private time. For those living in Beijing in the early 1950s, "temporal politics" seemed to become a "normal" practice in the sense that they were accustomed to the presence of political power in their leisure time. The success of "temporal politics" should not be assessed by whether young people really got educated ideologically through leisure activities. It was embodied in the very fact that it was the Party that had the right to problematize, collectivize, and rationalize young people's leisure time, and the very fact that young people were unwittingly incorporated into the pace of life advocated by the new regime: doing the right things at the right time, in the right place.

CHAPTER 4

Youth Subcultures, Leisure Regulation, and Community Life, 1955–1962

Hua Yong, a 23-year-old deputy technician working for the First Bureau of Design under the Ministry of the First Machinery Industry in Beijing, led an extremely busy but joyful leisure life during the year of 1957. Born to a poor family of seven, Hua worked diligently in his workplace, while enthusiastically participating in labor union activities. The labor union trusted Hua and asked him to help organize dancing parties in the bureau, which were usually held in the bureau's dining hall and only open for colleagues from their own work unit. Nevertheless, Hua's seemingly promising life changed dramatically. After organizing several joint dancing parties with other government offices nearby in capacious auditoriums in grandiose hotels in Beijing before the Spring Festival of 1957, Hua realized that the previous bureau-wide dancing parties were somewhat tiresome. He, therefore, decided to organize large-scale dancing parties in luxury venues. To attract more people, Hua hired a bunch of "amateur bands" that were active in Beijing such as "Xidan Band," "Donghuamen Band," "Overseas Chinese Band," and "Light Music Band." Because his workplace would certainly not reimburse such huge expenses, Hua started to sell admission tickets for the dancing parties to keep a balance between income and expenditure. The business turned out to be astonishingly lucrative. On Saturday nights and Sundays, young people in Beijing flocked to Hua's dancing parties, during which men and women wearing fancy clothes "wiggled their hips" and "embraced tightly" on the dancing floor with the accompaniment of "yellow music" such as jazz. As the boss of the self-proclaimed "Dancing Party Trust," Hua not only enjoyed himself in dancing parties but also made great profits from them. He started to buy good leather shoes and eat in restaurants.[1]

Along with other young people who were frequent visitors to the dancing parties, Hua was exposed during the political storm of the "rectification movement" in 1957. According to a report in *Beijing Daily*, by January 1958, Hua had lost his Youth League membership and was waiting for an administrative punishment from his work unit because of his "degeneration" from an "honest" young man to a "bad element hooligan" who "sought a life of pleasure." Although Hua's dancing parties did not last very long, the report in *Beijing Daily* admitted that they had formed an "unhealthy trend" affecting over 100 work units in Beijing.[2]

"Hooligans" (*liumang* 流氓) like Hua became notable from the mid-1950s in China and other countries as a worldwide phenomenon during the early Cold War era.[3] In China, from late 1954, after the publication of a *China Youth Daily* report about "hooliganism" conducted by a young man in Shanghai named Ma Xiaoyan, people became increasingly aware of examples of urban youth deviancy as the campaign of Nurturing Communist Morality among Youth and Opposing the Corruption of Capitalist Ideology unfolded. Scholarship about "hooliganism" in the early years of the People's Republic of China usually consider this campaign as the inception of massive suppression of hooliganism and emphasize the flexibility of the category of "hooligan" and "hooliganism."[4] This chapter

[1] *Beijing ribao*, January 18, 1958; Beijingshi wenhuaju 北京市文化局, "Beijingshi huangse yinyue yu huangse gequ liuxing de gaikuang" 北京市黄色音乐与黄色歌曲流行的概况 [A brief survey of the prevalence of yellow music and yellow songs in Beijing], March 3, 1958, BMA, 022-012-02517-00001.

[2] *Beijing ribao*, January 18, 1958.

[3] Y. Yvon Wang, "Heroes, Hooligans, and Knights-Errant: Masculinities and Popular Media in the Early People's Republic of China," *Nan Nü* 19 (2017): 326.

[4] In Shanghai, for example, because of the ambiguous recognition of hooliganism by different Party and government agencies, the policy toward hooligans always swayed between a soft line of "positive education" and a hard line of criminalization from 1949 to 1965. See Liu Yajuan 刘亚娟, "Shanghai a-fei: gundong de huayu luoji yu jiceng shijian zouxiang (1949–1965)" 上海 "阿飞": 滚动的话语逻辑与基层实践走向 (1949–1965) [Shanghai "A-fei:" The rolling logic of discourse and grassroots practical trends], *Zhonggong dangshi yanjiu* 5 (2018): 59–71. Y. Yvon Wang stresses that the Party deliberately expanded the category of hooliganism from the 1950s to the 1960s to remind the people that anyone could be labeled as a hooligan. See Y. Yvon Wang, 325–326.

does not seek to clarify whether certain behaviors should be categorized as "hooliganism" or reaffirm the Party's suppressive power on "hooligans" by detailing additional examples of urban "hooliganism." Official documents and newspaper reports from the mid-1950s to the early 1960s have made it clear that although the campaign of Nurturing Communist Morality was triggered by youth crimes connected with "hooliganism," it was actually a nationwide campaign not targeted specifically at "hooligans," but instead, at all young people. According to an article in *China Youth* in December 1954, the Party had a rigid definition of "hooligan:" it only denoted a very small number of young people who "are professional in theft, swindling, insulting women and so on." Young people who engaged in "hooligan behaviors" or had "hooligan style" occasionally in their daily life should not be considered as "hooligans."[5] For the CCP, however, every young man and woman was supposed to participate in this campaign even if they did not act like "hooligans" because they were considered highly vulnerable to those "corrupt and degenerate" behaviors in their daily life, especially during their leisure time. In this regard, instead of treating the strike on hooliganism in isolation, I see this campaign as the start of the state's long-lasting attempt of forging a new way of life among young people through a direct mass politicization of leisure and private space, with the hope to eliminate any potential or existing youth subcultures that might undermine the lofty socialist program. This attempt culminated during the Great Leap Forward as young people were mobilized to participate in collective leisure activities during which they were expected to become unconscious participants in the Party's political agenda even in their leisure time. During the subsequent famine, the Party's political indoctrination extended to people's dormitories under the "balancing work and rest" (*laoyi jiehe* 劳逸结合) policy with an ostensible emphasis on people's freedom in their leisure time.

The importance of leisure was demonstrated in the Party's own accounts. Leisure occupied a major role in the battle against youth subcultures from the start of the Nurture Communist Morality campaign because it was considered as a formidable sphere in which young people were exposed to unfavored temptations everywhere. For example, as Liu

---

[5] Wen Lan 文蓝, "Guanyu peiyang qingnian de gongchanzhuyi daode wenti" 关于培养青年的共产主义道德问题 [On nurturing communist morality among youth], *Zhongguo qingnian* 24 (1954): 7.

Daosheng, a member of the Secretariat of the Youth League Central Committee stated in *People's Daily* in October 1954, young people living under the new regime were still facing grave danger in their leisure time in the sense that "second-hand bookstores, bookstalls, and backward entertainment venues…still had a wide position to spread feudal, superstitious, mysterious, erotic, and robbery thoughts." He criticized "backward" entertainment venues as "dens for promoting bourgeois lifestyle and propagating sex and violence." To nurture Communist morality among the youth, instead of "only regulating the eight hours at work and ignoring the whole twenty-four hours," it was vital for the Youth League to collectivize young people's "private life" and teach them how to "live correctly."[6]

Nevertheless, the CCP was never satisfied with the collectivization of young people's leisure. What they strived to achieve was a politicized leisure, meaning young people could willingly live as the Party wished. While in most cases, the connotation of leisure includes an implication of "respectability, self-control, and constraint" and people usually associate leisure with "responsible freedom,"[7] if we perceive the nature of leisure as passing time with pleasure, it is useful to emphasize the emotional dimension of leisure by including any activities with sensual attraction, no matter how they are defined, to leisure activities regardless of moral assessment.[8] Young people might have conducted activities that were considered deviant by the Party, but most importantly, they did them for fun, and of their own will. In Maoist China, tensions between the Party's high expectations and the youth initiatives were not rare in the sense that with a self-claimed mission to forge "new people," the CCP favored an idealist, and to some extent unapproachable, morality in people's everyday life.[9] The question here is not whether young people spent their leisure time "properly," but how they spent the time "willingly," and even "happily." As Ban Wang observes, the Party's utopian political agenda, along

---

[6] RMRB, October 30, 1954.

[7] Chris Rojek, Susan M. Shaw and A. J. Veal, eds., *A Handbook of Leisure Studies* (New York: Palgrave Macmillan, 2006), 12–13.

[8] Rojek, Shaw, and Veal, *A Handbook of Leisure Studies*, 290–302.

[9] Yu Miin-ling 余敏玲, *Xingsu "xinren": Zhonggong xuanchuan yu Sulian jingyan* 形塑 "新人": 中共宣传与苏联经验 [Forging "new man": the Chinese Communist Party's propaganda and the Soviet experience] (Taipei: Zhongyang yanjiuyuan jindaishi yanjiusuo, 2015).

with other political programs in twentieth-century China, was carried out not only through political means, but also through "aesthetic experience and activities" that involved "bodily, sensuous, and emotional dimensions of the individual's lived experience."[10] In other words, any political agenda could not be achieved without the happy and unconscious participation of the targeted people. In this sense, leisure time, when people always wanted to choose a pleasurable way to pass time, was the ultimate touchstone of the effectiveness of the Chinese Revolution, and that is why the Party paid huge attention to where people went to entertain themselves, what music they listened to, what kind of clothes they wore, or what leisure readings they preferred.

The CCP never achieved a full politicization of leisure. Nevertheless, from a sociological perspective, the Party's leisure regulation could still expedite the making of an interventionist regime when we recognize that in any society, spontaneous leisure activities can act as lubricant in people's community life and thus facilitate the sustainable development of the political system. Robert Putnam hails the everyday "informal connections" in leisure time that form a typical American community life, which include "getting together for drinks after work, having coffee with the regulars at the diner, playing poker every Tuesday night, gossiping with the next-door neighbour, having friends over to watch TV, sharing a barbecue picnic on a hot summer evening, gathering in a reading group at the bookstore, even simply nodding to another regular jogger on the same daily route."[11] These connections, although less "formal" than organizations such as political parties, civic associations, churches or unions, are as important as formal connections in accumulating "social capital" that makes the political system work. For the Chinese Communist Party, however, during its enterprise of establishing a highly organized Party-state, formal connections were taken over, swept away, or transformed. As a natural extension of the Party's logic, informal connections in people's leisure time, or possible bases of youth subcultures, became so suspicious and even detrimental that the very existence of these subcultures, no matter their real intentions, required the Party's vigilance. Therefore, I

---

[10] Ban Wang, *The Sublime Figure of History: Aesthetics and Politics of Twentieth Century China* (Stanford, CA: Stanford University Press, 1997), 8.

[11] Robert D. Putnam, *Bowling Alone: The Collapse and Revival of American Community* (New York: Simon & Schuster, 2000), 99.

see the Party's battle against youth subcultures as a process of demolishing existing social connections and at the same time creating a new form of "social capital" by developing its own way of life as a community.[12]

Targets: Inappropriate Joyfulness and Unfavorable Connections

Since the commencement of the campaign of Nurturing Communist Morality, youth cadres in Beijing faced the problem of losing the focus of the campaign when they implemented political agendas in their own work units because the meaning of "communist morality" was ambiguous and target of the campaign could include anything cadres were uncomfortable with. During a report delivered in December 1954 by Yang Shu, the head of the Department of Propaganda of the Youth League Central Committee, communist morality had broad connotations with special emphasis on labor and collectivism. As Yang suggested, the moral outlook of young people hinged first on their attitude toward labor and whether they abided by laboring discipline. Second, communist morality favored collectivism in everyday life. Yang explained with examples such as "cutting illustrations from books borrowed from public libraries is a violation of [public] order. [On the contrary,] giving up a seat on a bus is not only a matter of politeness but also a matter of collectivism... It is not rare to see young people not taking off their hats in the cinema, drawing on books, making noises when others are sleeping, and not living a regular life. These are the behaviors that hinder other people."[13] In practice, however, because of the wide scale of communist morality, when grassroots cadres educated young people about this issue, what they were actually looking at were "deviant" ways of life such as theft, flirtation, or disrespect toward seniors instead of abstract moral flaws or deficiencies

---

[12] The application of social capital theory in this chapter challenges traditional wisdom that highlights the important role of thought reform in creating new interpersonal relations in Maoist China. See, for example, Ezra F. Vogel, "From Friendship to Comradeship: The Change in Personal Relations in Communist China," *The China Quarterly* 21 (January–March 1965): 46–60.

[13] "Guanyu peiyang qingnian gongchanzhuyi daode wenti Yang Shu baogao jilu" 关于培养青年共产主义道德问题 杨述报告记录 [On nurturing communist morality among youth: records of Yang Shu's report], 1954, BMA, 100-001-00168-0015.

in workspace morale.¹⁴ Some cadres, for example, liked to pay special attention to interactions between men and women with the idea that "to develop a friendship (between men and women) is to fall in love, and to fall in love is to have chaotic sexual relations."¹⁵

More specifically, various investigation reports on "morally corrupt" youth submitted by multiple work units in Beijing from early 1955 show that officials mostly focused on inappropriate leisure activities by young people in which the lack of "communist morality" was said to be apparent. The first activity that officials were extremely cautious about was young people's leisure reading. During the second congress of the Chinese People's Political Consultative Conference in December 1954, Shen Yanbing (i.e., Mao Dun), head of the Ministry of Culture, mentioned in his conference speech that the power of inappropriate leisure reading could not be underestimated. Through bookstores and stalls that rented "yellow books," about 1.5 million to 2 million people, including children, youth, and adults, got "poisoned and corrupted" every day across the country.¹⁶ In January 1955, Beijing authorities conducted a survey on bookstores that provided rental service. According to the report, there were sixty-five book renting stores in total across the city, with seventy thousand books on rent. Among these books, about 90 percent were "old books" with romantic, martial arts, and detective contents that were welcomed by a large readership consisted of workers, cadres, students, and sales clerks. Apart from these book renting stores, there were another 239 smaller stores that rented picture books.¹⁷ These bookstores attracted many more readers than public cultural facilities. While state-run public libraries, cultural centers, and cultural stations in Beijing only had 5,000 readers a day, about 15,000 readers visited book renting stores that provided "old books."¹⁸

---

¹⁴ Daxue gongzuo weiyuanhui 大学工作委员会, "Guanyu Yang Shu tongzhi suozuo gongchanzhuyi daode jiaoyu wenti baogao de yixie fanying" 关于杨述同志所作共产主义道德教育问题报告的一些反映 [Some feedbacks on Comrade Yang Shu's report on the education of communist morality], January 19, 1955, BMA, 100-001-00287-0049.

¹⁵ "Guanyu peiyang qingnian gongchanzhuyi daode wenti Yang Shu baogao jilu," 1954, BMA, 100-001-00168-0015.

¹⁶ RMRB, December 24, 1954.

¹⁷ Neibu cankao, January 19, 1955.

¹⁸ RMRB, March 28, 1955.

A worker named Zhang Chunhua in a private iron wire factory became a negative model in a report by the Qianmen District Youth League Committee because of his indulgence in romantic and martial arts novels. In the past three years, Zhang read over three hundred novels, which allegedly affected his performance at work. Obsessed with the plots, Zhang could not stop reading novels during the daytime when he worked the night shift, so during the night, he fell asleep when sitting by the machine. Zhang's recognition of the meaning of life was also affected by these novels when he started to think that life was all about "eating, drinking, making merry" and "money and beauty." As a great admirer of martial arts "heroes," Zhang believed that these heroes were still alive and planned to learn martial arts from a swordsman in mountain caves and then become a hero that could travel around the world. His colleague, a Youth League member named Zhang Henian, was also a fan of romantic and martial arts novels. After reading over one hundred novels, his physical health was "seriously damaged" and he always "felt dizzy" because he ruminated about the "erotic stories every day." Romantic and martial arts novels were so prevalent in this factory that in a survey, fourteen out of fifteen young people had experience reading them. The only one who did not read these novels was illiterate.[19]

The prevalence of inappropriate leisure reading was partly because when dealing with romantic and martial arts novels, cadres discovered that the boundary between the "classic" and the "erotic" was obscure. Young people could always find the contents they were interested in even if they could only get access to books that might not seem to have "problems" from the perspective of cadres. In May 1955, when drafting a plan to tackle "reactionary, obscene, and absurd books, magazines, and picture books," the Ministry of Culture warned local authorities to "rigidly grasp the standard and deal with books and magazines with different rate of toxin differently." The Ministry suggested that those with "extremely reactionary and extremely obscene contents" should be confiscated directly from booksellers. These books included political propaganda of Nazis and the Nationalist Party such as *Mein Kampf*,

---

[19] Qingniantuan Qianmenqu gongzuo weiyuanhui 青年团前门区工作委员会, "Siying dalu basi gongchang qingnian shou zichanjieji sixiang qinshi de qingkuang" 私营大陆拔丝工厂青年受资产阶级思想腐蚀的情况 [The situation of young people in Private Dalu Iron Wire Factory being corrupted by bourgeois thoughts], February 21, 1955, BMA, 038-002-00175-038.

The Destiny of China (by Chiang Kai-shek), and *The Struggles of Mr. Chiang Kai-shek* (*Jiang xiansheng fendoushi* 蒋先生奋斗史); martial arts novels that contradicted the Party's policy toward ethnic minorities such as *Wind and Cloud in the Soil of Miao* (*Miaojiang fengyun* 苗疆风云); and pornographic pictures (*chungong tupian* 春宫图片). Other "obscene erotic novels and absurd martial arts novels" should be replaced by "new books" favored by the Party. The Ministry of Culture listed a third category of books that should be reserved and allowed to circulate, including classic books with mysterious or martial arts contents published before the May Fourth Movement of 1919 such as *The Investiture of the Gods, Journey to the West, Strange Stories from a Chinese Studio, Legend of the White Snake,* and *The Seven Heroes and Five Gallants*. Books that should not be confiscated also included: vernacular popular novels published after the May Fourth Movement such as those written by Yu Dafu and Shen Congwen; romantic novels by the Mandarin Ducks and Butterflies School such as Zhang Henshui's famous fiction *Fate in Tears and Laughter*; books aiming at "exposing the darkness of the old society" but containing erotic scenes; detective novels such as the Sherlock Holmes series; mythology, fairy tale, and picture books adapted from these books such as *One Thousand and One Nights, Robinson Crusoe,* and *Gulliver's Travels*; and scientific books on sex education such as *Marriage and Health*.[20] In March 1956, the Ministry of Culture sent telegrams to Bureaus of Culture in eight major cities reiterating the boundary of dealing with these "problematic" books.[21]

Apart from inappropriate leisure readings, Beijing officials were also concerned about self-formed organizations among young people. The Beijing Municipal Youth League Committee specified in a report in

---

[20] "Wenhuabu dangzu guanyu chuli fandongde yinhuide huangdande shukan tuhua wenti de qingshi baogao" 文化部党组关于处理反动的、淫秽的、荒诞的书刊图画问题的请示报告 [Report for instructions by the leading Party members group in the Ministry of Culture on dealing with reactionary, obscene, and absurd books, magazines, and cartoons], May 20, 1955, in *Chuban gongzuo wenxian xuanbian (1949–1957)* 出版工作文献选编 (1949–1957) [Collection of documents on publication work], ed. Wenhuabu chuban shiye guanliju bangongshi 文化部出版事业管理局办公室 (n.p., 1982), 165–166.

[21] Wenhuabu, "Guanyu ge shengshi chuli fandong yinhui huangdan shukan gongzuo zhong de yixie wenti" 关于各省市处理反动、淫秽、荒诞书刊工作中的一些问题 [On problems when dealing with reactionary, obscene, and absurd books, magazines, and cartoons in various provinces and cities], March 13, 1956, in *Chuban gongzuo wenxian xuanbian (1949–1957)*, 189–195.

early 1955 that among high school students, "there were many small organizations with various names such as 'Four Junior Knights-Errant Intimidating the East' (*zhendong sixiaoxia* 镇东四小侠) or 'Five Duckweed and One Plum' (*wu ping yi mei* 五萍一梅)." From the perspective of youth cadres, these organizations were different from hooligan gangs in the sense that the members of those small organizations usually had their own occupations, either as workers or as students. Youth self-formed organizations, however, were still notable because of the deviant lifestyle of their members.[22] Young members of these organizations seemed to be inspired by both the mainstream political culture favored by the Party and their leisure readings of martial arts novels. In some of these self-formed organizations, internal hierarchical orders such as "squadrons," "detachments," and "brigades" similar to the Party-affiliated Chinese Young Pioneers were established, but in some other organizations, members were under the command of "Chiefs" (*zhaizhu* 寨主) and "High Officials" (*daguan* 大官) paralleling plots in traditional Chinese novels about grassroots rebels.[23] The self-formed organizations were not exclusive to boys. A student named Ma Yumei from the No. 5 Girls' High School even participated in several organizations simultaneously, including "Teasing Girl Team" (*douniudui* 逗妞队) and "Two Dragons and One Phoenix" (*shuanglong yifeng* 双龙一凤), with a nickname "A Stalk of Flower" (*yizhihua* 一枝花).[24] Young people with decent jobs could also be members of these organizations. An accountant working for an iron plant

[22] Qingniantuan Beijingshi weiyuanhui 青年团北京市委员会, "Tuanshiwei guanyu jiaqiang qingnian de gongchanzhuyi daode jiaoyu dizhi zichanjieji sixiang qinshi de baogao" 团市委关于加强对青年的共产主义道德教育、抵制资产阶级思想侵蚀的请示报告 [Report for instructions by the Municipal Youth League Committee on strengthening the Communist Morality Education and Resisting the Corruption of Capitalist Ideology among youth], February 2, 1955, BMA, 100-001-00264-0001.

[23] Y. Yvon Wang, "Heroes, Hooligans, and Knights-Errant: Masculinities and Popular Media in the Early People's Republic of China," *Nan Nü* 19 (2017): 334.

[24] Zhonggong Beijing Qianmen quwei bangongshi 中共北京前门区委办公室, "Qianmen quwei guanyu bufen qingnian zhong daode baihuai qingkuang de baogao" 前门区委关于部分青年中道德败坏情况的报告 [Report by the Qianmen District Party Committee on some young people being morally corrupted], March 8, 1955, BMA, 038-001-00128-009.

joined an organization called "Five Thugs of Xisi" (*Xisi wuhei* 西四五黑) and was once detained for fighting.[25]

In addition to self-formed organizations, the CCP also paid special attention to young people's interpersonal relations in their leisure time. Officials assessed youth subcultures as a "great harm to social order, production, as well as physical and mental health of the youth."[26] Nevertheless, just like practices in other cities like Shanghai, instead of criminalizing those young people, Beijing authorities considered those deviant youth, excluding professional hooligans, as "victims" of the remnants of the old regime and because of the lack of proper guidance by Youth League organizations.[27] Almost all reports on "degenerated and corrupt" young people would emphasize that they lost control over themselves and started to pursue the "corrupt" way of life from improper connections with capitalists or "backward workers." According to a report from a private iron wire factory, although most of the young workers in this factory came to Beijing from poor rural families, they were "seriously eroded by bourgeois ideology over the past few years" because of "the courtship and temptation of the capitalists, the corrosion of backward entertainment venues, pornographic books, and magazines, as well as the weak ideological education work of labor union and the Youth League."[28]

One way capitalists established cordial personal connections with young male workers was to invite them to hang out with other women such as sex workers who were not employed by brothels (*yeji* 野妓) and waitresses working in ball game clubs as shown in Chapter 2. For example, the boss of the Dalu Iron Wire Factory often took young workers to visit sex workers. At first, workers just watched what their boss was doing and

---

[25] Zhonggong Beijing Qianmen quwei bangongshi, "Qianmen quwei guanyu bufen qingnian zhong daode baihuai qingkuang de baogao," March 8, 1955, BMA, 038-001-00128-009.

[26] "Qianmen quwei guanyu bufen qingnian zhong daode baihuai qingkuang de baogao," March 8, 1955, BMA, 038-001-00128-009.

[27] In Shanghai, young people working in factories with peculiar behaviors were treated differently compared with jobless ones in the mid-1950s before the Anti-Rightist Movement. See Liu Yajuan, "Shanghai a-fei," 61–67.

[28] "Siying dalu basi gongchang qingnian shou zichanjieji sixiang qinshi de qingkuang," February 21, 1955, BMA, 038-002-00175-038. In the early and mid-1950s, rather than an abstract political label as it was in the Four Clean-ups and the Cultural Revolution, "capitalists" simply referred to owners of private businesses.

made fun of him, but gradually they started to visit sex workers, too. The fifteen young workers in this factory all had experience visiting sex workers, and three of them became frequent visitors. A young worker call Liu Zhenkui visited sex workers three or four times a week and usually went back to his factory dormitory after midnight. He always told his colleagues that "it is fruitless to go to a park without finding a girl (i.e., prostitute)." He was so acquainted with sex workers that when he went to parks, some of the sex workers greeted him by saying "Little Liu, buy me a meal with your money!".

As for Youth League and labor union members working in this private factory, their boss invited them to have fun in places that might not seem to offend public decency such as ball game clubs but would introduce waitresses to them. For some young people, ball game clubs became a place to waste their salary. A young worker called Liu Qinghai went to play billiards at a ball game club near the center of Beijing and usually spent a lot of money when socializing with waitresses there. Some young workers even exchanged messages about how to attract waitresses in a ball game club.[29] Female capitalists had their own way of establishing relations with female workers. Wang Yuqin, a waitress working for a ball game club, had a close relationship with her boss in her leisure time. She never considered her boss as a "stranger," and they always went to restaurants and theaters together. She even sought her boss' advice on which clothes she should buy when she went shopping.[30]

The CCP did not conceal its attention to unfavorable social connections between youth and "degenerate" people or places, especially the close relationship between workers and capitalists, because it had observed that unfavorable social connections would alienate young people from the ideal way of life that the Party advocated. In some private enterprises, young people were so obsessed with pursuing joyfulness in their own leisure time that labor union and Youth League could not hold meetings. Young workers were also reluctant to attend Youth League

---

[29] "Siying dalu basi gongchang qingnian shou zichanjieji sixiang qinshi de qingkuang," February 21, 1955, BMA, 038-002-00175-038.

[30] Beijingshi Qianmenqu gonghui 北京市前门区工会, "Beijingshi Qianmenqu qugonghui guanyu siying qiye zhigong jinxing gongchanzhuyi daode jiaoyu de baogao," 北京市前门区区工会关于向私营企业职工进行共产主义道德教育的报告 [Report by Qianmen District Labor Union in Beijing on educating workers in private enterprises about communist morality], June 29, 1955, BMA, 026-001-00046-00018.

education sessions; some even did not pay their mandatory labor union dues. Because of the friendly relationship between workers and capitalists in their leisure time, workers "gave up monitoring capitalists." In early 1954, after the government did not allow the capitalist in the Dalu Iron Wire Factory to give a salary raise to his employees, workers immediately started to bombard the government with fierce words, and someone even threatened to "beat the bastards in government offices to death." A member of the Youth League declared that he would withdraw his membership after the Youth League branch criticized him for scolding the government. When banks and tax bureaus came to collect loans and taxes, workers even insulted their staff. Labor Union and Youth League organizations in this factory lost their credentials to monitor capitalists because of the non-cooperative attitude among workers.[31]

Pressurizing Everyday Life

Worrying that youth subcultures had become a social problem that would eventually undermine the Party's socialist program at the everyday front, in late 1954, Beijing officials decided that it was vital to launch education about communist morality to a broader range of young people. In a notification issued on December 27, 1954, the Beijing Municipal Youth League Committee urged its grassroots organizations to launch an educational campaign among urban youth to make young people, both in and outside the Youth League, understand "the situation of class struggle during the period of transition" and "raise their vigilance against degenerate bourgeois ideas." The notification listed several "good qualities" young people should have, including "caring about the collective, loving labor, taking good care of public property, abiding by public order, frugality, loyalty, and honesty." The Municipal Youth League Committee clarified that although launching a campaign was necessary, the nurturing

---

[31] "Siying dalu basi gongchang qingnian shou zichanjieji sixiang qinshi de qingkuang," February 21, 1955, BMA, 038-002-00175-038. Joel Andreas views the participation of workers in factory affairs (under the supervision of the CCP, of course) since the founding of the People's Republic as the process of creating an "industrial citizenship" based on self-management. In this sense, unfavorable social connections between workers and business owners would greatly undermine the creation of this "industrial citizenship" because workers did not form a community like what the CCP wished. For the development of "industrial citizenship" since 1949, see Joel Andreas, *Disenfranchised: The Rise and Fall of Industrial Citizenship in China* (New York: Oxford University Press, 2019).

of communist morality could not be achieved through one-time centralized education. Instead, young people must develop their new morality through "regular labor, study, and everyday life."[32] This campaign was different from other campaigns such as thought reform in the sense that the Municipal Youth League Committee emphasized a soft line against youth deviancy. During the education, grassroots Youth League organizations should not call for massive self-criticism on young people's own thoughts. Instead, they were supposed to educate young people in an active way by organizing more leisure activities including recreational activities and sports. In addition, the Youth League must guide young people's leisure reading to pull them away from "yellow books."[33]

Despite the Municipal Youth League Committee's strategy of nurturing Communist morality through everyday practice gradually instead of through fierce struggles, when the campaign actually started, it was impossible to circumscribe its scope. In many work units, leaders were preparing to treat this campaign as a political movement by digging out negative models in their workplaces respectively and asking young people to write reports of self-criticism. Some work units sent all young people with deviant behaviors to the court. Most importantly, because of people's ambiguous understanding of "hooliganism," in grassroots practices, cadres tended to "pin a big label" (*damaozi kouren* 大帽子扣人) on young people by treating all suspicious behaviors as hooliganism, which caused a tense atmosphere in everyday life. At Peking University, for example, a male student was accused of "peeping at female classmates" when he took off his clothes in his room toward a window facing a women's dormitory. The Youth League branch in Peking University criticized another Youth League member for conducting hooliganism when he pulled a female student's hand to check the time on her watch.[34] A piece in *China Youth* revealed that in order not to be labeled as having

---

[32] "Qingniantuan Beijingshiwei guanyu ruhe peiyang qingnian de gongchanzhuyi daode pinzhi de tongzhi" 青年团北京市委关于如何培养青年的共产主义道德品质的通知 [Notification by the Beijing Municipal Youth League Committee on how to nurture communist morality among youth], December 27, 1954, BMA, 100-001-00168-0001.

[33] "Qingniantuan Beijingshiwei guanyu ruhe peiyang qingnian de gongchanzhuyi daode pinzhi de tongzhi," December 27, 1954, BMA, 100-001-00168-0001.

[34] "Tuanshiwei guanyu jiaqiang qingnian de gongchanzhuyi daode jiaoyu dizhi zichanjieji sixiang qinshi de baogao," February 2, 1955, BMA, 100-001-00264-0001.

"bourgeois thoughts," some young couples even drafted outlines of questions on political issues for them to discuss when they met with each other so that they would not risk talking about love.[35]

In May 1955, the Department of Propaganda of the Beijing Municipal Party Committee reiterated in its plan for intensifying the education about communist morality that "education about communist morality is a regular and arduous task, which should be carried out continuously in all kinds of daily struggles, production, study, and life. Do not make this education a movement criticizing people's thought. Do not use simple and impatient means. In general, grassroots organizations should not criticize negative models randomly... Avoid criticizing trivia in daily life as violations of communist morality."[36]

One of the "trivia in daily life" that once became a nationwide spotlight of moral denunciation was the matter of wearing colorful clothes. During 1955 and 1956, as a key symbol of the dress reform proposed by culture cadres in Beijing, newspapers and magazines declared that wearing colorful clothes and pursuing a beautiful appearance was not a violation of the aesthetic favored by the new regime. In March 1955, *Guangming Daily* published a short article justifying the opinion that Chinese women should wear skirts more frequently because compared with trousers, skirts were more economical to make, more convenient for walking, more customary among Chinese, and above all, more attractive.[37] In January 1956, the Youth League Central Committee and the Women's Federation even held a forum on reforming women's clothing with a focus on improving women's physical appearance.[38] The reason for promoting dress reform was ideological: now that the whole country was "flourishing," people should dress more colorfully to reflect their happy

---

[35] Wei Junyi 韦君宜, "Cong hua yifu de wenti tanqi" 从花衣服的问题谈起 [Speaking from the issue of colorful clothes], *Zhongguo qingnian* 5 (1955): 21.

[36] "Shiwei xuanchuanbu guanyu jiaqiang dui dangyuan he laodong renmin de gongchanzhuyi daode jiaoyu de jihua," 市委宣传部关于加强对党员和劳动人民的共产主义道德教育的计划 [Plan for intensifying the education of Communist morality among Party members and laboring masses by the Department of Propaganda of the Municipal Party Committee], May 1955, BMA, 001-005-00183-00021.

[37] Antonia Finnane, *Changing Clothes in China: Fashion, History, Nation* (New York: Columbia University Press, 2008), 207.

[38] Li, *China's Soviet Dream*, 130.

and joyful life, especially to foreign visitors.[39] During the communist morality education, however, officials usually linked taste in clothes as a sign of being "corrupted" by bourgeois thoughts. In some places, a young woman was condemned as having "bourgeois thought" because she wore colorful clothes. The broad notion of "bourgeois thought" even included putting the neck of a shirt outside the uniform jacket.[40] In a factory, a worker was refused entry to a factory-organized evening party simply because she wore colorful clothes.[41] A twenty-year-old young woman wrote to *China Youth* complaining that when she wore an imported green sweater with patterns of flowers, she received gossips and even criticism from her colleagues:

> Some comrades in our office disliked my clothes. They talked behind my back, saying that I got dressed up to find a boyfriend. Some people satirized me publicly that "she is not satisfied with clothes produced by our country and did not shrink from the toil and hardship to get an imported one. Her pursuit of beauty shows her dirty heart." What made me feel more outraged was that during a meeting that week, one comrade from our group criticized me that it was a lifestyle matter (*zuofeng wenti* 作风问题) that people should all pay attention to. When analyzing this issue, he said that "laboring masses are very frugal and simple, and only the parasites from the exploiting class in the old society dressed themselves up every day and sought to look good."

This young woman did not accept these opinions and wanted to know that "when our motherland is taking on a new look every day and young people living in this beautiful era wish to beautify their everyday life, is it a dirty and shameful idea to dress ourselves up in accordance with the look of new China?".[42]

Party officials were aware and anxious about the arbitrary explanation of what could be labeled as having relations with "bourgeois thought" among everyday behaviors. As early as May 1955, the Party called for a more cautious interference in people's private life. A *People's Daily* article

---

[39] *Zhongguo qingnian bao*, February 12, 1956.

[40] Wei Junyi, "Cong hua yifu de wenti tanqi," *Zhongguo qingnian* 5 (1955): 21.

[41] *Zhongguo qingnian bao*, February 12, 1956.

[42] Xiao Rui 小锐, "Wo xihuan hua yifu" 我喜欢花衣服 [I like colorful clothes], *Zhongguo qingnian* 1 (1956): 38.

titled "Lead Workers to Live a Progressive Life" stated that "when we say organizing everyday life of workers, we do not mean to interfere too much in their private life like what some people have done. They were even against proper behaviors such as having a perm, wearing colourful clothes, socializing, dancing, dating, and so on." According to this article, this kind of arbitrary interference in people's private life would only lead to "a non-political tendency" among workers, which would finally "convert them into overcautious and mediocre people who do not pay attention to politics," and thus would "jeopardize the political enthusiasm and the spirit of enterprise among workers."[43] Nevertheless, the official separation of wearing colorful clothes from bourgeois lifestyle led to another unexpected outcome, which was similar to when it was criticized as opposition to communist morality. When public media propagated the importance of wearing colorful clothes as a new aesthetic standard that people should follow, those who did not wish to change their plain clothes suddenly felt pressure from their peers. In April 1956, the Beijing Municipal Party Committee noticed that "there are some side effects since the propaganda of dress reform in Beijing newspapers and magazines started in March." Some newspaper articles overrated the issue of dress reform as a political issue and used cartoons to satirize those who still preferred Lenin suits.[44] A university student in Beijing reported that some departments in his university mocked students not wearing colorful clothes on blackboard bulletins. Someone even wrote a poem saying that "be brave and take off your blue suit; wear colourful clothes and our boys will all praise you as a good girl!".[45]

[43] RMRB, May 21, 1955.

[44] "Zhonggong Beijingshiwei guanyu gaijin fuzhuang xuanchuan wenti xiang zhongyang de baogao" 中共北京市委关于改进服装宣传问题向中央的报告 [Report from the Beijing Municipal Committee of the Chinese Communist Party to the Central Committee on the propaganda of dress reform], April 2, 1956, in *Beijing shi zhongyao wenxian xuanbian 1956 nian* 北京市重要文献选编 1956年 [Selection of important documents of Beijing, 1956], ed. Beijingshi danganguan 北京市档案馆 and Zhonggong Beijingshiwei dangshi yanjiushi 中共北京市委党史研究室 (Beijing: Zhongguo dangan chubanshe, 2003), 201.

[45] "Buyao mianqiang bieren gaijin fuzhuang" 不要勉强别人改进服装 [Do not force others to improve their clothes], *Zhongguo qingnian* 12 (1956): 39.

The "Yellow Songs" Mania

Another form of youth subcultures noticed by the CCP was the prevalence of "yellow songs." Starting from the spring of 1957, especially since the Hundred Flowers Movement, so-called "yellow songs" spread across the whole country and attracted many young people. "Yellow songs," according to a pamphlet published in 1958, were mostly songs popular during the Republican years in major cities, especially in Shanghai as a combination of Western dance music and Chinese folk songs. Japanese-controlled cities during the Sino-Japanese War also produced Japanese language "reactionary songs" serving the "Greater East Asia Co-Prosperity Sphere" such as "Shina no Yoru" (Night in China) and "Manshu Musume" (Manchurian Girl). "The degenerate bourgeoise, compradors, enemies, and Han traitors used these songs to entertain themselves, and at the same time, intoxicate the people and corrupt the revolutionary will of the youth."[46] "Yellow songs," however, sometimes also referred to any songs that might lead to unfavorable emotions and behaviors among people. For example, in some articles, "yellow songs" even included "Awaara Hoon," a song from the popular Indian film *Awaara*.[47] Songs in Party-produced mainstream films were also facing the danger of being criticized as "yellow songs."[48]

The Party's relatively loose policy toward literature and arts during the Hundred Flowers Movement propelled the popularity of these songs among young people to some extent. Famous songwriters, including Liu Xue'an and Chen Gexin, called for a reassessment of pop songs they had written in Republican years. In Tianjin, the Tianjin People's Radio Station broadcast five "concerts rebroadcasting old songs" within one month to introduce pop songs from before 1949, and this practice turned out to

---

[46] Li Ling 李凌, *Rang xinde yinyue shenghuo huoyue qilai pipan huangse gequ jiangzuo tigang* 让新的音乐生活活跃起来——批判黄色歌曲讲座提纲 [Invigorate the new musical life: Outline for lectures criticizing yellow songs] (Beijing: Yinyue chubanshe, 1958), 1–2.

[47] *Neibu cankao*, December 27, 1957.

[48] From 1958 to 1959, musicians and amateur music fans participated in several discussions on whether songs in Party-produced films such as "Jiujiu yanyang tian" (99 Days of Bright Sunlight) and "Xiao yanzi" (Little Swallow) were "yellow songs." See Feng Changchun 冯长春, "Jianguo shiqinian guanyu shuqing gequ de piping yu pipan" 建国十七年关于抒情歌曲的批评与批判 [Critiques and criticism on lyric songs during the seventeen years after the founding of the People's Republic of China], *Xinghai yinyue xueyuan xuebao* 1 (2017): 67–70.

be a big hit among ordinary people. In the entire city, during the time the People's Radio Station played old pop songs, "nearly every family turned on their radios. In many homes, the whole family, including boys and girls, young and old, sat around the radios and listen. Stores set up loudspeakers, and near every loudspeaker, crowds of people, including workers and students, gathered there. Pedicab drivers stopped soliciting customers because they enjoyed the music sitting on the saddles. Many people hummed with the tune."[49]

In major cities across the country, the remaining network of private businesses played an important role in popularizing old pop songs by selling disks, song sheets, and pictures of pop stars active in Republican era. In Shanghai, for example, speculations in disks of old pop songs flourished as their price was forty times higher than the price of disks of new songs. In Shenyang, customers could buy more than sixty kinds of pop song sheets in markets.[50] In Beijing, during November 1957, many peddlers sold pictures of old pop stars publicly near Tiananmen and Qianmen. According to an investigation conducted by public security bureaus, six photo studios in Beijing participated in printing photographs, among which five were private businesses. The remaining one was a joint public–private enterprise, whose boss "found old negatives from the bottom of his trunk without the permission from the leader from the public side, and processed photographic films massively, trying to make colossal profits." The sales network distributed in the center of Beijing, including the Dongan Market, the Xidan Market, the gate of the Beijing Zoo, the area in front of the Beijing Exhibition Center, Tiananmen and Qianmen. Most of the customers were young people, including workers, students, cadres, and most surprisingly, soldiers and officers from the People's Liberation Army.[51] Retailers even developed an inter-city commercial network. A disk shop in Shanghai recycled a large

---

[49] Li Xi 李溪, "Yinyuejie yinggai guanxin 'jiuge chongfang' de wenti" 音乐界应该关心 "旧歌重放"的问题 [Musical circles should pay attention to problems in "rebroadcasting old songs"], in Wenhuabu yishu shiye guanliju 文化部艺术事业管理局, *Yinyue wudao gongzuo cankao ziliao 2: huangse gequ wenti zhuanji* 音乐舞蹈工作参考资料 (二): 黄色歌曲问题专辑 [Reference materials for the work of music and dancing, vol. 2: special collection on the problem of yellow songs] (n.p., 1958), 31–32.

[50] *Neibu cankao*, December 27, 1957.

[51] "Beijingshi huangse yinyue yu huangse gequ liuxing de gaikuang," March 3, 1958, BMA, 022-012-02517.

number of disks of old pop songs from the market and took over 1000 of them to Guangzhou for sale within June 1957.[52] People could also mail order pictures of pop stars from retailers in Beijing.[53]

People did not conceal their preference for "yellow songs" when they had channels to express their real ideas. For example, the Tianjin People's Radio Station received 493 letters from its audience, among which only thirteen listeners opposed the station's practice of rebroadcasting old pop songs. Many respondents considered that although there were "poisonous weeds" in old songs, there were also "fragrant flowers" among them, which should be "a part of the musical legacy of our motherland." Therefore, the policy of labeling all these songs as "yellow songs" was unfair and harsh. A staff member of the Music Group of the Tianjin People's Radio Station admitted that people liked old pop songs because they were indeed attractive when compared with "new songs" produced after 1949. Before 1957, although people did not dare to listen to and sing old pop songs in public because of an "intangible pressure," they still enjoyed these songs inside their own homes. When the radio station started broadcasting, the audience immediately "felt resonance."[54] In schools, young students did not like the song "Socialism is Good" when instructors organized them to learn it. Instead, they learned old pop songs such as "Siji ge" (Song of the Four Seasons) and "Tianya genü" (The Wandering Songstress) spontaneously without any instructions. During a lecture titled "Eradicating Yellow Songs," the speaker delivered this lecture by explaining and at the same time, playing the "yellow songs" being criticized to avoid preaching in hollow words. The audience was extremely focused when the speaker played "yellow songs" at first, but after the speaker started to play "socialist red discs" in comparison with these "yellow" ones, people began to leave. When the speaker announced "eight crimes" of "yellow songs," only half of the audience stayed.[55]

[52] *Neibu cankao*, December 27, 1957.

[53] "Beijingshi huangse yinyue yu huangse gequ liuxing de gaikuang," March 3, 1958, BMA, 022-012-02517.

[54] "Beijingshi huangse yinyue yu huangse gequ liuxing de gaikuang," March 3, 1958, BMA, 022-012-02517.

[55] Peng Chao 澎潮, "Yao duoshu shehuizhuyi jitizhuyi zhiqing: tan zhishi qingnian chang shenme ge" 要多抒社会主义集体主义之情——谈知识青年唱什么歌 [We should express more socialist and collectivist emotions: on what songs the educated youth sing], *Renmin yinyue* 5 (1958): 8.

Instead of singing privately, young people's mania for pleasant pop music led to the public presence of "yellow songs" in many cities. For "yellow songs" produced before 1949 that were forced to circulate underground or in private previously, during the "yellow songs" mania, people found a way to enjoy them in public by combining their own taste with state-sponsored leisure activities. In Shenyang, during dancing parties organized by the government-run Municipal Cultural Palace, the band usually played "yellow songs" as musical accompaniment. Their practice was so popular that seventeen young dancing enthusiasts even brought them a silk banner with characters of the Mao's "Let a Hundred Flowers Bloom" slogan on it. In a factory, when the Youth League committee refused to let the band play "yellow songs" in a factory-organized dancing party, the members of the band retorted that "the band in the Municipal Cultural Palace could play ("yellow songs"), why can't we?"[56] In Shanghai, many factories, enterprises, and even some government offices played "yellow songs" during get-togethers and daily breaks.[57] In Beijing, young people took a slightly different approach. Hua Yong, the previously mentioned "bad element hooligan," rented auditoriums in hotels under the excuse of labor union clubs organizing cultural recreational activities for the masses and invited amateur bands in different work units to play "yellow songs" for dancing parties. Another band, which was made up of cadres and professional musicians, made profits in their leisure time by playing jazz-style "yellow songs" at the request of "hooligans." The name of the band was "Eight *Yuan* Band" because everyone would be paid a salary of eight *yuan* after their performance. According to a report from the Beijing Municipal Bureau of Culture, from late 1957 to early 1958, fifteen bands accompanying for dancing parties were

---

[56] Gongqingtuan Liaoningshengwei xuanchuanbu 共青团辽宁省委宣传部, "Shenyangshi huangse gequ liuxing qingkuang diaocha baogao" 沈阳市黄色歌曲流行情况调查报告 [Investigation report on the popularity of yellow songs in Shenyang], in *Yinyue wudao gongzuo cankao ziliao 2*, 8.

[57] Shanghaishi wenhuaju 上海市文化局, "Shanghaishi guanyu huangse yinyue changpian wenti de qingkuang" 上海市关于黄色音乐唱片问题的情况 [Situation on the problem of yellow songs discs in Shanghai], in *Yinyue wudao gongzuo cankao ziliao 2*, 10.

active in Beijing.⁵⁸ Some bands even adapted revolutionary songs into "nauseating" jazz-style music.⁵⁹

Some songs that were produced in China after the CCP came to power or by foreign countries having friendly relationships with China might also have "yellow" elements. People were even more bold to perform or learn them publicly because these songs received less ideological criticism from the top. After the Indian film *Awaara* was screened in China, some young people in Beijing imitated scenes in the film by covering their heads in bedsheets and singing the Chinese version of "Awaara Hoon" loudly on streets, with brooms waving in their hands.⁶⁰ Some kids even adapted its lyrics from "roaming everywhere" into "selling stinky tofu" for amusement and sang the adapted version cheerfully in alleyways in Beijing.⁶¹ Young people sang this song because in some cases, it could express their feelings from their deep hearts. One article in *People's Daily* in March 1957 vividly described the author's experience listening to the young man singing "Awaara Hoon" with complicated emotions:

> I traveled to Shanghai for business this January. One night, I went to the Bund. Suddenly, I heard the melody of "Awaara Hoon" behind me. A young man wearing a short jacket without a hat walked slowly past me to a lamppost, stood there facing the river, and sang this song over and over again. His voice was beautiful and bright, but it was also slightly gloomy as if he tried to express his emotions through this song. Shortly afterward, I left, but the young man was still singing…I had an unforgettable experience that night.
>
> I did not talk to this young man. I did not know what kind of man he was and why he sang this song for such a long time. But this experience reminded me of youth, songs, and poems.⁶²

Sometimes, new songs produced after 1949 might also be condemned as "yellow songs" because of their lyrics, melodies, or ways of singing.

---

⁵⁸ "Beijingshi huangse yinyue yu huangse gequ liuxing de gaikuang," March 3, 1958, BMA, 022-012-02517.

⁵⁹ *Neibu cankao*, December 27, 1957.

⁶⁰ *Neibu cankao*, December 27, 1957.

⁶¹ "Biejuyige de yinba gequ," 别具一格的印巴歌曲 [The unique songs from India and Pakistan], January 15, 2013, http://web.archive.org/web/20191204233831/http:/blog.sina.com.cn/s/blog_5f65e6690101b6zg.html.

⁶² RMRB, March 17, 1957.

Before culture officials noticed the "yellow" elements in these songs, they had already spread among young people through official channels. A typical example of this kind of songs was "Jiujiu yanyangtian" (99 Days of Bright Sunlight) from the 1957 film *The Story of Liubao* (*Liubao de gushi* 柳堡的故事). Official music magazines published the lyrics and musical score of this song, which was about the love between a young woman and a young man who later joined the PLA. Some work units also compiled this song into their self-published songbooks.[63] In 1958, when professional artists went to factories to teach revolutionary songs such as "Socialism is Good," they found that workers preferred "Jiujiu yanyang tian" to those revolutionary songs. In factories, radios were playing "Jiujiu yanyang tian," young workers were humming "Jiujiu yanyang tian," and when the professional artists started to teach, workers asked them to sing and teach "Jiujiu yanyang tian" instead.[64]

LIVING AS A SOCIALIST COMMUNITY: THE GREAT LEAP OF EVERYDAY LIFE

In 1958, China suddenly "became the country of poems." Across the country, "from secretaries of county-level Party committees to ordinary people," everyone wrote poems.[65] In addition to writing poems, people also sang songs and drew pictures. As people observed, it was a common scene in many villages that "walls were covered with poems and pictures." It was impossible to tell "how many songs people sang and how many poems people wrote in 1958."[66] This inconceivable and even surreal phenomenon was the product of several small movements during the Great Leap Forward including the "mass singing movement" (*qunzhong*

---

[63] Zhao Di 赵地, "Cong qunzhong geyong huodong kan 'Jiujiu yanyang tian'" 从群众歌咏活动看 "九九艳阳天" [Think about "Jiujiu yanyang tian" from the mass singing activities], *Renmin yinyue* (6) 1958: 25.

[64] Deng Yingyi 邓映易, "Women yingdang ba shenmeyang de gequ gei qingnian" 我们应该把什么样的歌曲给青年 [What songs should we give to young people], *Renmin yinyue* 4 (1958): 18.

[65] *Shikan* bianjibu 《诗刊》编辑部 ed., *1958 Shixuan* 1958 诗选 [1958 selection of poems] (Beijing: Zuojia chubanshe, 1959), 1.

[66] Tian Ying 天鹰, *Yijiu wuba nian zhongguo minge yundong* 一九五八年中国民歌运动 [The Chinese folklore movement in 1958] (Shanghai: Shanghai wenyi chubanshe, 1978), 9–10.

geyong yundong 群众歌咏运动) and the "new folklore movement" (*xin minge yundong* 新民歌运动). Together, these movements became key parts of the "Great Leap of mass culture" paralleling the great leap in other fields that finally resulted in another surge of political interference in people's everyday life.

The dynamics behind the Great Leap of mass culture were multifaceted. From an ideological perspective, this movement shows the Party's consistent emphasis on the mass line and its escalating distrust of experts. During the second session of the 8th National Congress of the Chinese Communist Party in May 1958, Liu Shaoqi announced that "to meet the needs of the revolution in technology, there must be a revolution in culture at the same time." Shortly after the end of the meeting, on June 9, *People's Daily* published an editorial titled "The Revolution in Culture Has Started" (*wenhua geming kaishi le* 文化革命开始了) defining this revolution as "a movement in which all laboring people are emancipated culturally" which resembled the ongoing literacy campaign, but with an emphasis on the leading role of the Party over the experts.[67] As the "revolution in culture" unfolded, however, the aim of the movement soon moved from "popularization" (*puji* 普及) to "improvement" (*tigao* 提高). As Chen Kehan, deputy head of the Department of Culture of the Beijing Municipal Party Committee, explained in November 1958 during a conference about cultural work in Beijing, one aim of the movement was to emancipate the laboring masses from the long-lasting cultural hegemony of "literati and scholars" by letting them produce their own works instead of participating in literacy classes. As he mentioned, "the deceptive propaganda from landlords and bourgeoisie said that only literati and scholars can engage in culture. The purpose (of this propaganda) is to monopolize culture as their private property." As a result, people from the working class themselves "have a sense of inferiority towards culture" and thought that "they cannot master culture, let alone engaging in literary and artistic creation." Therefore, during the real revolution of the Great Leap Forward, it was vital to "eradicate the influence of thoughts from landlords and bourgeoisie and free people from the shackles in their minds" by mobilizing them to participate in the production of cultural works.[68] This idea also resonated with the Party's

---

[67] RMRB, June 6, 1958.

[68] Chen Kehan 陈克寒, "Quandang quanmin ban wenhua kaizhan yi qunzhong yeyu wenhua huodong wei zhongxin de wenhua dapuji yundong (caogao)" 全党全民办文化, 开

ambition to nurture "all-round developed" individuals. "The entire population's engagement in culture…is to make intellectuals become workers and peasants, and at the same time, make workers and peasants become intellectuals" (*zhishifenzi gongnonghua, gongnongfenzi zhishihua* 知识分子工农化, 工农分子知识化), said Chen Kehan. Eventually, the distinction between brain work and manual work would be diminished in the sense that everyone could do both. Chen added that the revolution in culture would finally lead to "the change in the organization of the masses in the sense that laboring organizations will become military organizations, education organizations, sports organization, and cultural organizations at the same time."[69]

A second and practical reason to launch a Great Leap in mass culture was that people needed recreational activities to recover from onerous physical labor. As a slogan in 1958 described, "during the Great Leap in production, culture should play a vanguard role; people are as energetic as fierce tigers, and recreational activities are as varied as the days of the Spring Festival" (*shengchan dayuejin, wenhua daxianfeng, ganjin sai menghu, yüle xiang guonian* 生产大跃进, 文化打先锋, 干劲赛猛虎, 娱乐像过年).[70] This theory was backed by professional musicians such as He Lüting, who confirmed in an article published in *People's Music* in September 1958 after observing a model of the mass singing movement in Anhui Province that "singing not only expressed emotions of the working people but also boosted the morale in production…We (professional musicians) must change the current situation by having a great leap."[71] Culture cadres in Beijing considered that "cultural activities are

展以群众业余文化活动为中心的文化大普及运动 (草稿) [The entire Party and the entire population engage in culture and start a movement of mass popularization of culture focusing on mass leisure/amateur cultural activities], November 1958, BMA, 001-006-01347-00008.

[69] "Quandang quanmin ban wenhua kaizhan yi qunzhong yeyu wenhua huodong wei zhongxin de wenhua dapuji yundong (caogao)," November 1958, BMA, 001-006-01347-00008.

[70] "Yuejin zhong de Beijing qunzhong wenhua huodong" 跃进中的北京群众文化活动 [Mass cultural activities in Beijing are in a great leap], 1959, BMA, 164-001-00214-0052.

[71] He Lüting 贺绿汀, "Xianchang huiyi gei women de qishi" 现场会议给我们的启示 [Our takeaways from the meeting], *Renmin yinyue* 9 (1958): 2.

extremely needed when production, work, and study is strenuous."[72] In reports submitted to the Beijing Municipal Party Committee, examples of people regaining their energy after engaging in activities such as singing are not rare. In Beijing Hardware Factory, workers said that "we no longer feel tired when singing."[73] In an automobile manufacturing factory, although production task was extremely heavy, the leader still required that the time between 12:00 am to 12:30 am should be used to organize cultural activities to "boost morale in production and let workers regain their energy." It was reported that "the director of the factory, the leaders of workshops, ordinary workers and cultural activists were all satisfied with this solution."[74]

Another unclarified but equally important reason was to forge an ideal community life by preventing people from deviant leisure activities. The prevalence of youth subcultures made culture cadres realize that they needed to provide more cultural products to young people and "occupy the battlefield" of youth culture. In February 1958, Qian Junrui, the deputy minister of the Ministry of Culture, stated in a speech that "for any cultural field, if we the proletariats do not occupy, the capitalists will definitely occupy it instead… Today, the prevalence of bad plays, bad books, bad songs, and bad dances indicates that our socialist literary and artistic work still has serious deficiencies. In the future, we must devote 120 percent of our energy to produce a large number of new songs and scripts for the masses, compile good popular books, and launch the socialist mass singing movement… We must firmly occupy

---

[72] "Quandang quanmin ban wenhua kaizhan yi qunzhong yeyu wenhua huodong wei zhongxin de wenhua dapuji yundong (caogao)," November 1958, BMA, 001-006-01347-00008.

[73] "Beijingshi wujin gongchang de qunzhong wenhua gongzuo" 北京市五金工厂的群众文化工作 [Mass cultural work at the Beijing Hardware Factory], September 16, 1958, in *Beijing dang'an shiliao: dang'an zhong de Beijing wenhua* 北京档案史料: 档案中的北京文化 [Archival historical materials of Beijing: the culture of Beijing in archival documents], ed. Beijingshi dang'anguan 北京市档案馆 (Beijing: Xinhua chubanshe, 2012), 167–168.

[74] "Qunzhong wenhua gongzuo youle jinyibu de kaizhan dangqian ying wei qingzhu guoqing guangfan jinxing wenhua xuanchuan huodong" 群众文化工作有了进一步的开展当前应为庆祝国庆广泛进行文化宣传活动 [The mass cultural work has developed a further step; now we should launch mass cultural propaganda activities to celebrate the National Day], September 25, 1958, in *Beijing dang'an shiliao: dang'an zhong de Beijing wenhua*, 171–172.

the battlefield of mass culture with our formidable (cultural) army."[75] In practice, cadres believed that after the commencement of the Great Leap in mass culture, the number of people engaging in deviant activities such as singing "yellow songs" did decrease. According to a report from the Beijing Hardware Factory, before the mass singing movement in April 1958, workers did not pay attention to organized singing activities. "Unhealthy songs" such as "Awaara Hoon" and others about romantic relations between men and women were popular among young workers. After four months of mass singing movement, however, workers began to sing "red songs," and every morning and evening, "sound of singing resounds across the heavens."[76]

Party officials considered the "mass singing movement" as a panacea for eradicating the influence of subcultures, especially "yellow songs" among the youth. A professional musician wrote in an article published in *People's Music* in April 1958 that "right now, the happiest event in the music circle is the surge of socialist mass singing." According to this musician, mass singing had special effects on resisting "unhealthy phenomena." For people who were not professional musicians, mass singing could cure the "disease of being lethargic," the "disease of being apolitical," the "disease of being bureaucratic," and the "disease of being dull." In short, mass singing could act as both a "stimulant" and a kind of "political vitamin" for those who did not have high morale at work or did not care about politics. Mass singing could also lead to the establishment of a new relationship between people as they participated in collective activities together.[77]

In Beijing, the first round of the mass singing movement culminated in May 1958. Around Labor Day, about one million people mastered the "five songs" recommended by the Beijing Mass Art Center.[78] On August

---

[75] RMRB, February 9, 1958.

[76] "Beijingshi wujin gongchang de qunzhong wenhua gongzuo," September 16, 1958, in *Beijing dang'an shiliao: dang'an zhong de Beijing wenhua*, 165.

[77] Xian Di 显谛, "Shehuizhuyi qunzhong geyong yundong neng zhi ba bing" 社会主义群众歌咏运动能治八病 [The socialist mass singing movement can cure eight diseases], *Renmin yinyue* 4 (1958): 5–6.

[78] *Beijing wanbao*, August 14, 1958. The "five songs" include: "Geming ren" (Revolutionary Man), "Shehuizhuyi hao" (Socialist is Good), "Dongfeng yadao xifeng" (East Wind Prevails Over the West Wind), "Ganshang Yingguo" (Catch Up With the United Kingdom), and "Gan! Gan! Gan!" (Do it! Do it! Do it!). See *Beijing wanbao*, March 31, 1958.

14, *Beijing Evening News* reported that the Beijing authorities planned to "set off a second high tide of the socialist singing movement" before the National Day on October 1 by letting 1.5 million people master another five songs.[79] This singing movement was soon merged into the ongoing movement of the Great Leap in mass culture. On August 15, 1958, in a report drafted by the Beijing Municipal Bureau of Culture, culture cadres planned to organize professional cultural groups and send them among the masses to "help and instruct" them according to "the interests and needs of the masses." Officials emphasized the "masses first" principle that "the mass cultural movement must be carried out by the masses themselves… (They should) produce (cultural products) by themselves, organize activities by themselves, and entertain themselves." The general requirement of this mass cultural movement before the National Day of 1958 was to "launch a movement of mass creation and collect literary and artistic works from the masses; start a second high tide of the singing movement and let people learn another five new songs; continue the activities of writing poems and drawing pictures and made walls in urban neighbourhoods and major villages covered by poems and pictures; establish clubs, amateur troupes and reading rooms that can organize regular activities in every county, commune, factory and neighbourhood; set up city-level and district-level amateur art schools and nurture amateur cultural and art backbones vigorously."[80] On August 26, during the "oath-taking rally for the Great Leap in mass cultural work," Chen Kehan reiterated that the mission of the professional cultural groups was not to perform for people at the grassroots, but to "mobilize masses to carry out mass cultural movement" as "work teams." He emphasized the importance of "following the mass line thoroughly" because "culture must be produced, mastered, and used consciously by the laboring masses." In this sense, during the mass cultural movement, the professional art groups were supposed to let people participate in leisure cultural activities actively

---

[79] *Beijing wanbao*, August 14, 1958.

[80] "Beijingshi weihuaju dangzu guanyu diaodong zhuanye wenhuayishu tuanti kaizhan qunzhong wenhua yundong de qingshi baogao (caogao)" 北京市文化局党组关于调动专业文化艺术团体开展群众文化运动的请示报告（草稿）[Report for instruction by the leading Party members group on mobilizing professions cultural and art groups to carry out the mass cultural movement (draft)], August 15, 1958, in *Beijing dang'an shiliao: dang'an zhong de Beijing wenhua*, 152.

and in the end, make everyone know how to "write, perform, sing, dance, and draw pictures."[81]

Different districts in Beijing formulated their own plans for the Great Leap in mass culture. The Dongcheng District named September 1958 as "Month for the Great Leap in Mass Cultural Work" with a plan to establish 150 clubs and 1000 amateur associations within one month. During September, Dongcheng District residents were expected to produce 200,000 pieces of literary and artistic work and learn five songs recommended from the top. Representatives expressed their ambitions during the oath-taking rally held on August 31. A cadre from a neighborhood said that by October 1, they would make "every usable wall covered with poems and pictures" and let everyone in their neighborhood know how to sing. In addition, their neighborhood alone planned to finish 15,000 pieces concentrating on the ongoing Great Leap Forward. They would also organize two large-scale joint performances. A factory planned to establish clubs and reading rooms for every workshop and ask its workers to produce ten poems or pictures within September on average. Similarly, the deputy head of the Chongwen District announced that before October, all work units in this district must establish cultural recreational groups that could organize regular activities. Two million residents of Chongwen District would produce 150,000 pieces of literary and artistic works under a slogan "covering all walls with poems and pictures with attention to both quality and quantity."[82] Some work units planned to organize leisure activities in a militarized way. A factory in Xicheng District required that 100 percent of its workers must finish learning ten songs and 80 percent of them must master ten group dances. The factory also formed an "army of literature and art," with the director of the factory acted as the "army commander," the Party secretary as the

---

[81] "Dongyuan qilai touru zhandou xianqi qunzhong wenhua yundong de gaochao wenhuabu Chen Kehan tongzhi 8 yue 26 ri zai Beijingshi wenhuajie kaizhan qunzhong wenhua gongzuo yuejin shishi dahui shang de jianghua (jilu gao)" 动员起来, 投入战斗, 掀起群众文化运动的高潮!——文化部陈克寒同志8月26日在北京市文化届开展群众文化工作跃进誓师大会上的讲话 (记录稿) [Mobilize, engage in the battle and start a high tide of the mass cultural movement: records of the speech of Comrade Chen Kehan from the Department of Culture during the oath-taking rally for the Great Leap in mass cultural work on August 26], in *Beijing dang'an shiliao: dang'an zhong de Beijing wenhua*, 158–159.

[82] *Beijing wanbao*, September 2, 1958.

"political commissar," and heads of the labor union and the Youth League secretary as "deputy army commanders."[83]

Compared with collective activities before the Great Leap, people were more exhausted because this time, everyone was supposed to become performers as required by the participatory nature of the Great Leap in mass culture. For example, to "sing praises of the new atmosphere of the Great Leap Forward," "literary and artistic activists" in the Beijing Department Store could not go home after business ended at 9:30 pm. People had to arrange and rehearse twenty programs produced by themselves through the night to prepare for their performance the next day. Their programs include a peepshow about new measures taken by the Department Store for the convenience of customers, a piece of Shandong clapper ballad about "good people and good deeds" around the performer, and a chorus adapted from an existing song. The rehearsal did not end until 11:00 pm.[84] In Fusuijing neighborhood, to accomplish the goal of "voice of singing everywhere," residents planned to gather in clubs between 7:00 pm and 8:00 pm every night and sing together.[85]

After the National Day of 1958, the Great Leap did not end. On October 21, 1958, in a draft of "Instructions on Launching the Movement of 'Mass Production of Literary and Artistic Works'," the Beijing Municipal Party Committee required that residents in Beijing should produce 100 million pieces of literary and artistic work by the National Day of 1959 to celebrate the tenth anniversary of the People's Republic. Grassroots Party committees were supposed to take charge of the movement by working out quotas respectively in their own work units. The Municipal Party Committee specifically required that by the end of June 1959, every major factory, enterprise, people's commune, and university must complete at least two works "at a relatively high level." To achieve this goal, grassroots work units, such as workshops, production team classes, should establish their own "mass creating groups" led by "mass creating committees" in their factories, communes, schools, associations, and government offices. The Municipal Party Committee added that to make this movement a "real mass movement," Party committees at all levels must pay great attention and mobilize people to participate,

---

[83] *Beijing wanbao*, August 30, 1958.
[84] *Beijing wanbao*, August 29, 1958.
[85] *Beijing wanbao*, September 3, 1958.

"whoever can write, let them write by themselves; for those who cannot write, let them give oral accounts so that others can help with the transcription."[86] About one month later, in the formal document, perhaps to accentuate initiatives from the people, the Municipal Party Committee changed the sentence "the Municipal Committee requires that …residents in Beijing should produce 100 million pieces" to "the mass army of literary and art in Beijing raised their own quota of producing 100 million pieces; this heroic emotion is worthy of being encouraged."[87] Nevertheless, in some grassroots work units, if not all, it is clear that the quotas were assigned by leaders instead of the masses at first, but during the movement, people might increase their assigned quota. For example, in late 1958, the representative of the Beijing No. 2 Girls' High School promised in a district-level conference that before the National Day of 1959, students in the school would produce twenty thousand pieces of literary and artistic works. Although students had to produce one hundred pieces on average in less than one year, because of their "high enthusiasm," in some classes, students raised their quota to one thousand. The school also planned to establish 120 clubs to train an "army of literature and art" with the purpose of achieving the goal of "publishing compilations (of student-produced literary and artistic works) every month and 'launching satellites' (which means achieving high quotas) in every level" (*yueyue chu xuanji, cengceng fang weixing* 月月出选集, 层层放卫星).[88]

---

[86] "Zhonggong Beijingshiwei guanyu kaizhan qunzhong wenyi chuangzuo yundong de zhishi (caogao)" 中共北京市委关于开展群众文艺创作运动的指示 [Instructions from the Beijing Municipal Party Committee on launching the movement of "Mass Production of Literary and Artistic Works" (draft)], October 21, 1958, in *Beijing dang'an shiliao: dang'an zhong de Beijing wenhua*, 175–177.

[87] "Shiwei guanyu kaizhan qunzhong wenyi chuangzuo yundong de zhishi" 市委关于开展群众文艺创作运动的指示 [Instructions from the Municipal Party Committee on launching the movement of "Mass Production of Literary and Artistic Works"], November 17, 1958, in *Zhongguo gongchandang Beijingshi weiyuanhui zhongyao wenjian huibian 1958 nian* 中国共产党北京市委员会重要文件汇编1958年 [Collection of important documents of the Beijing Municipal Committee of the Chinese Communist Party, 1958], ed. Zhonggong Beijingshiwei bangongting 中共北京市委办公厅 (n.p., 1960), 231.

[88] "Nü Erzhong wenyu huodong yuejin qingkuang" 女二中文娱活动跃进情况 [The situation of the great leap in cultural recreational activities in the No. 2 Girls' High School], 1958, BMA, 100-001-00612-0070.

It was not enough to only *produce* literary and artistic works. More importantly, as discussed above, people must *perform* their works themselves. Holding formal or informal competitions, challenges (*tiaozhan* 挑战) and joint performances (*huiyan* 会演) were among the most regular and effective means of mass mobilization during the Great Leap of mass culture.[89] Under such a heated atmosphere, people had no other choice but to actively participate in the preparation of these competitions, challenges, or performances whenever possible, which inevitably led to a total penetration of political power into people's everyday life, especially leisure time. During the mass singing movement, the Party Committee of Beijing Hardware Factory required that to solve the problem of lacking time, workers should "learn (songs) before and after meetings, sing (songs) both at work and in off-duty hours" (*huiqian huihou xue, shangban xiaban chang* 会前会后学, 上班下班唱) so that "everyone can become singers and the voice of singing can resound in the whole factory" (*renren cheng geshou, gesheng xiang quanchang* 人人成歌手, 歌声响全厂). As a result, more than 95 percent of the workers participated in two joint performances organized in August 1958.[90] In the No. 2 Girls' High School, students did not have a fixed time to produce their own literary and artistic works. Therefore, to meet the requirements from the school that "every class should hold one or two performances every month," some students had to carry a notebook in their pockets to record their inspirations whenever time permits, including breaks between classes and meal breaks.[91]

Moreover, people should not only perform their self-produced works during organized performances but in their everyday life as well. In this sense, the ultimate goal of the Great Leap in mass culture was to transform everyone into the Party's unconscious propagandists that people would encounter every day on the streets or in workplaces, even at home. Using the words of the Beijing Municipal Bureau of Culture in its summary of 1958, the nature of the Great Leap in mass culture was

---

[89] "Qunzhong wenhua gongzuo youle jinyibu de kaizhan dangqian ying wei qingzhu guoqing guangfan jinxing wenhua xuanchuan huodong," September 25, 1958, in *Beijing dang'an shiliao: dang'an zhong de Beijing wenhua*, 172.

[90] "Beijingshi wujin gongchang de qunzhong wenhua gongzuo," September 16, 1958, in *Beijing dang'an shiliao: dang'an zhong de Beijing wenhua*, 167–168.

[91] "Nü Erzhong wenyu huodong yuejin qingkuang," 1958, BMA, 100-001-00612-0070.

a "mass propaganda movement in which everyone performs the central (movement), sings the central (movement), and writes the central (movement)."[92] In suburban Beijing, members of production teams "went to work in the fields while singing and dancing *yangge*." They "sang songs while doing farm works, and during breaks, they started to play gongs and drums, which was noisier than the Spring Festival." Some people even said that "we are not happy if we do not sing; we are willing to express our innermost thoughts by singing!"[93] Changping District proposed that people must "compile by themselves, sing by themselves, say what they want, and entertain themselves" by singing self-compiled songs whenever they spotted "good people and good deeds" in farmlands.[94] By October 1958, four suburban districts, including Miyun, Huairou, Pinggu, and Yanqing had achieved the goal of "everyone can sing songs" (*gechang hua* 歌唱化) and "being covered by wall pictures" (*bihua hua* 壁画化) in the sense that "everyone can be both writers and painters. The walls are covered with poems and paintings. Songs about the Great Leap resound in every county."[95] In urban areas, a factory in Chongwen District announced that their goal was to "let everyone do propaganda work and let everyone get educated."[96] Residents in some urban neighborhoods participated in the movement even at home. In Qiujiajie neighborhood, residents were divided into six "gymnastics and singing groups" based on their locations. Every day, at 7:30 am and

---

[92] "Yuejin zhong de Beijing qunzhong wenhua huodong," 1959, BMA, 164-001-00214-0052. "Perform the central, sing the central, and write the central" (*yan zhongxin, chang zhognxin, xie zhongxin* 演中心、唱中心、写中心) was a common slogan during the Great Leap which indicated that all those self-produced literary and artistic works should focus on publicizing the central movement—the Great Leap Forward.

[93] "Yuejin zhong de Beijing qunzhong wenhua huodong," 1959, BMA, 164-001-00214-0052.

[94] "Muqian benshi qunzhong wenhua gongzuo de qingkuang he wenti" 目前本市群众文化工作的情况和问题 [Situation and problems of the current mass cultural work in our city], September 10, 1958, in *Beijing dang'an shiliao: dang'an zhong de Beijing wenhua*, 162.

[95] "Miyun Huairou Pinggu Yanqing sige xian de wenhua gongzuo jiankuang" 密云、怀柔、平谷、延庆四个县的文化工作简况 [Brief summary of cultural work in the four counties of Miyun, Huairou, Pinggu, and Yanqing], October 3, 1958, in *Beijing dang'an shiliao: dang'an zhong de Beijing wenhua*, 174.

[96] "Muqian benshi qunzhogn wenhua gongzuo de qingkuang he wenti," September 10, 1958, in *Beijing dang'an shiliao: dang'an zhong de Beijing wenhua*, 161.

4:30 pm, "people cleaned the streets first, and then started to do gymnastics and learn songs." As a result, in this neighborhood, women "were singing songs when cooking and doing laundry at home," "there was the merry sound of singing everywhere (in the neighbourhood)."[97]

Accompanying the Great Leap in mass culture, to justify the highly organized leisure activities in China, newspaper articles ridiculed leisure activities that made people "act like buffoons" in other countries to indicate social decay in the West. In December 1958, a short piece in *Beijing Evening News* reported the "hula hoop dance" that prevailed in capitalist countries including the United States, the United Kingdom, France, Japan, West Germany, and Italy. According to this report, bunches of men and women, with specially made circles on their bodies, twisted with "strange music" everywhere on the streets of Western countries. Some people even wore bathing suits when they engaged in "hula hoop dance." Apparently, in the eyes of Party propagandists, this kind of "meaningless" leisure activity could only show the boredom of leisure time among youth in the West.[98]

Propagandists were also scornful of young people in other countries in the Socialist Bloc who were infatuated with "degenerated lifestyles" such as playing "hula hoops." In January 1959, *People's Daily* published a report from Belgrade saying that newspapers and magazines in Yugoslavia were "making great efforts" to promote "the disgusting hula hoops dance popular in capitalist countries." Instead of seeing through the "poisonous" nature of "hula hoop dance," Yugoslav media considered it a leisure activity "suitable for everyone regardless of age and gender" because it could "reduce extra fat around your belly" and "beautify your legs."[99] A poet even wrote a poem mocking Yugoslavia's "degeneration" to an "American way of life" saying that "A new dance is popular in America where people are putting hoops around their bodies. Men and women dance on the streets, twisting their hips like lunatics… [Yugoslavia and America] are birds of a feather, but they still pretend to be decent and do not wish to tear down their masks. How ridiculous!".[100]

---

[97] *Beijing wanbao*, June 6, 1958.
[98] *Beijing wanbao*, December 22, 1958.
[99] RMRB, January 7, 1959.
[100] RMRB, January 9, 1959.

Forging Post-Leap Community Life Through Leisure Regulation

Forging "new men" through the transformation of people's way of life was among the goals of the Chinese Revolution. Under the atmosphere of the Great Leap Forward, discussion about the "communal way of life" (*jiti shenghuo fangshi* 集体生活方式) emerged in newspapers and magazines while "urban people's communes" were widely established across the country. Wang Renzhong, the First Secretary of Hubei Provincial Committee, published a long article in *China Worker* in 1960 to advocate the "communal way of life." He considered that "the collectivization of life and the socialization of housework" was a natural product of the Great Leap Forward in the sense that people's energy would be wasted if they still had to deal with household affairs. "The transformation from the individual way of life to the communal way of life," announced Wang, "will be a revolution in our life and a great change of prevailing habits and customs during the transformation of society… Getting rid of individual domestic life and establishing a communal way of life is most suitable for the need of the socialist communal production."[101] To establish the communal way of life, people should first live together. Although some people said that "living in a communal dormitory is so noisy that people cannot sleep well," Wang maintained that this problem was only a matter of habit because "everyone should obey public rules and should not make noises when others are sleeping." Wang depicted a utopian vision of communal living that "we should build tall apartments that can save raw materials and at the same time, can install heating system, air conditioners, and public bathrooms." In his blueprint, one apartment could accommodate hundreds of families, which would be a residence with a dining hall, club, and library. In leisure time, people could get together, holding dancing parties, playing poker cards, organizing study sessions or poem competitions inside the building. "Isn't this kind of life good?" asked Wang. Wang also considered that those who preferred living alone were not in line with the ideal personality that the Party favored by criticizing those people as "old hermits" who were "willing to live alone,

---

[101] Wang Renzhong 王任重, "Jiti shenghuo fangshi shi zuixingfu zuimeihao de shenghuo fangshi" 集体生活方式是最幸福最美好的生活方式 [The communal way of life is the happiest and brightest way of life], *Zhongguo gongren* 10 (1960): 8.

contemplate and sleep in their leisure time fearing that others will interrupt their peaceful life." That way of life, according to Wang, was not "joyful," and thus "hindered the all-round development of individuals." The communal way of life, instead, was the "happiest" and "civilized" way of life.[102]

Wang's proposal was raised at an inappropriate time because the negative effects of the Great Leap Forward were emerging, and as a result, massive construction of new "communal apartments" was not realized. Nevertheless, people living in school or factory dormitories, who had already experienced the "communal way of life," faced mounting political penetration in their everyday life as the Party introduced a new policy of "balancing work and rest" in 1960. High-sounding words in Party documents indicated that the Party suddenly seemed to want people to have some good rest after years of hard work. In May 1960, the Beijing Municipal Party Committee required that "all enterprises, communes, and schools must make sure that the masses can sleep for eight hours every day. In industrial and mining enterprises, workers must have three weekends for rest every month. Construction enterprises must guarantee their workers two weekends for rest every month. Most workers in neighbourhood commune factories are women, and generally, they should be guaranteed a rest every Sunday."[103] In December, the Municipal Party Committee issued another "urgent notification" on implementing the policy of "balancing work and rest," admitting that the "two-year-long catastrophic natural disaster caused temporary and localized difficulties" and under such circumstances, it was urgent to carry out the principle of "balancing work and rest" to "let the masses get necessary recuperation, regain energy, and protect health."

To balance work and rest, the Party Committee reiterated the requirement on people's sleeping hours and added that strenuous amateur sports

---

[102] Wang Renzhong, "Jiti shenghuo fangshi shi zuixingfu zuimeihao de shenghuo fangshi," *Zhongguo gongren* 10 (1960): 10.

[103] "Shiwei guanyu yange kongzhi zhaoshou renyuan he youguan qunzhong shenghuo de jige wenti de guiding" 市委关于严格控制招收人员和有关群众生活的几个问题的规定 [Regulation from the Municipal Party Committee on the strict control of recruitment and several issues regarding life of the masses], May 17, 1960, in *Zhongguo gongchandang Beijingshi weiyuanhui zhongyao wenjian huibian 1960 nian* 中国共产党北京市委员会重要文件汇编1960年 [Collection of important documents of the Beijing Municipal Committee of the Chinese Communist Party, 1960], ed. Zhonggong Beijingshiwei bangongting 中共北京市委办公厅 (n.p., 1963), 358–359.

activities such as jogging, mountain climbing, weightlifting, boxing, and wrestling should be suspended. Sports competition and performance organized among workers and students should be "moderate."[104] The real reason was that when encountering severe food shortages, people had to take measures to maintain basic physical strength. Qian Liqun recalls that as a young teacher in Guizhou Province, he only had 23 grams of food quota every month during the Great Leap famine, which made him "too exhausted even to teach." At night, he "often could not fall asleep because of hunger, and all leisure activities had to stop."[105] The situation in Beijing was similar. A then Tsinghua University student recalls that although he usually jogged during the fall term in 1960, later, he had to stop jogging because of the great exhaustion of his energy during the food shortage. He switched to less fierce *t'ai chi* for exercise.[106]

After implementing the policy of "balancing work and rest," officials realized that because people now had more leisure time, it was vital to make sure that they could do correct things in their hours of "rest" so that they could save their energy for production and study. A good way to achieve this goal was to reduce individual behaviors that seemed unnecessary to the Party and let their work units plan their usage of physical strength. At the end of 1960, the Beijing Municipal Bureau of Civil Affairs issued an "Opinion on Cultural Recreational Activities for the New Year" and required that to "better carry out the principle of balancing work and rest," work units should arrange time slots to organize cultural activities during the New Year break and guide people to avoid "wasting unnecessary energy and increasing fatigue in hanging out on streets, queueing up, and being packed in buses."

---

[104] "Zhonggong Beijingshiwei guanyu jinyibu guanche zhixing zhongyang guanyu laoyi jiehe zhishi de jinji tongzhi" 中共北京市委关于进一步贯彻执行中央关于劳逸结合指示的紧急通知 [Urgent notification from the Beijing Municipal Committee of the Chinese Communist Party on further implementing Central Committee's instruction of "balancing work and rest"], December 5, 1960, BMA, 100-005-00323-00001.

[105] Qian Liqun 钱理群, *Juehuo buxi wenge minjian sixiang yanjiu biji* 爝火不息: 文革民间思想研究笔记 [Tiny flame does not die out: research notes on grassroots thoughts during the Cultural Revolution] (Hong Kong: Oxford University Press, 2017), 57.

[106] Chen Chusan 陈楚三, *Renjian zhongwanqing yige suowei "hongerdai" de rensheng guiji* 人间重晚晴: 一个所谓 "红二代"的人生轨迹 [People treasure after-rain evening sunlight: the trajectory of a so-called "second-generation red"] (New York: Mirrorbooks, 2017), 128.

Ideally, to let people spend the New Year break happily without wasting their energy, they were supposed to participate in leisure activities in their own work units such as watching television together, holding poem competitions, reading short novels, telling revolutionary stories, or reading picture books borrowed from libraries by their work units.[107] It was not easy, however, to monitor how people used their energy. In a survey conducted by a factory among 387 workers regarding how they spent their increased leisure time in Haidian District in early 1961, cadres found that only thirty-eight workers chose to read books. There were 33 people hanging out in markets, 35 people doing laundry or other housework, 48 people attending meetings or sleeping, and 130 people chatting. Other activities included eating meals together and visiting each other. Some workers "talked about eating and drinking as soon as they reached their dormitory or rushed to markets to shop."[108] Cadres in another factory in suburban Beijing found that some workers "once had erroneous impressions" on the spirit of "balancing work and rest." They thought that in the hours of "rest," the factory could not organize any activities after work. As a result, they "lost energy during production and became undisciplined during leisure time." There was an increasing number of workers sleeping or hanging out on the streets after work. Some people got together "making unreasonable complaints" (*jiang guaihua* 讲怪话) or talking about "pursuing material pleasure" such as eating roast ducks in Bianyifang and dumplings in Duyichu (both were famous time-honored brands in Beijing). Although sufficient sleeping hours were required by the Beijing Municipal Party Committee, sleeping too much was also not advocated. Several workers passed their time in bed, and some even

---

[107] "Beijingshi minzhengju guanyu 1960 [*sic*] nian xinnian wenyu huodong de yijian" 北京市民政局关于1960年新年文娱活动的意见 [Opinion from the Beijing Municipal Bureau of Civil Affairs on cultural recreational activities for the New Year break of 1960], 1960, BMA, 196-002-00062-00080.

[108] Beijing zhiguanchang yeyu xuexiao 北京制管厂业余学校, "Guanyu jiehe sushi huodong jinxing zhengzhi jishu wenhua jiaoyu qingkuang de baogao" 关于结合宿舍活动进行政治、技术、文化教育情况的报告 [Report on implementing political, technological, and cultural education by activities in dormitories], March 1, 1961, BMA, 152-001-00516-0015.

slept for twelve hours every day, which reportedly caused lethargy during working hours.[109]

An ideal way for people to save energy was to spend all leisure time in dormitories under the regulation of their work units, which also allowed the Party to implement political indoctrination among young people in a controllable space. In Beijing Pipe-making Factory, for example, the Party Committee considered that under the principle of "balancing work and rest," after the eight hours of working time, workers would "spend the rest of the fourteen to fifteen hours in their dormitories." Therefore, guiding them to "rest well, produce well, study well, and think well" became an important task. The Factory Party Committee decided to "pay special and intensive attention to life" (*shenru dazhua shenghuo* 深入大抓生活) under the slogan of "politics coming to dormitories" and "cadres coming to dormitories" and aimed at achieving five goals including "militarized tidiness," "militarized atmosphere," "diverse leisure activities," "beautified decorations," and "hygienic space." During the factory-wide "red dormitory" movement, the factory organized seven kinds of in-dormitory activities: telling revolutionary stories, reading newspapers, studying works of Chairman Mao, letting old workers compare current life with that under the old regime, quizzes on current affairs and skills, movie discussions, and studying skills. According to the factory, these activities were effective in stabilizing the mentality of workers. "Political atmosphere" increased in some dormitories where workers attached portraits of Chairman Mao and slogans such as "Long Live the Chinese Communist Party and Chairman Mao" and "Struggling for the Continuous Great Leap in 1961" on the wall.[110]

Cadres were confident that intensified political indoctrination could lead to the lessening of people's suspicion and dissatisfaction with the Party's policies. A factory in Fangshan County set a model by launching a movement of "four comes" (politics, cadres, culture, and study come to dormitories) and "five goods" (good in political atmosphere, good in unity and friendship, good in mutual help, good in organized study, good in obeying discipline and sanitary conditions). After an in-dormitory

---

[109] Fangshanxian gonghui 房山县工会, "Dazhua yeyu shenghuo gaohao zhigong jiaoyu" 大抓业余生活, 搞好职工教育 [Pay special attention to leisure life and do a good job in workers' education], March 25, 1961, BMA, 152-001-00516-0037.

[110] "Guanyu jiehe sushi huodong jinxing zhengzhi jishu wenhua jiaoyu qingkuang de baogao," March 1, 1961, BMA, 152-001-00516-0015.

study session about current affairs, a worker said that "in the past, our whole family had to flee from famine and my father sold me to another family to make a living. Many people left their hometown and died of hunger and cold weather. Today, facing a severe famine in two consecutive years, the Party led us to try every means to make 'substitute food' and let us not only eat well, but also play well and rest well, and sometimes we even have fish to eat. This is nothing like a famine!"[111] News reports of organizing leisure activities in worker and student dormitories frequently appeared in the first two months of 1961 in *Beijing Evening News* to show how happy it was to live under the CCP despite an ongoing famine as a way to relieve people's potential dissatisfaction.[112] In January 1961, the Xuanwu District Culture Center even launched a two-week study session to help grassroots work units train more activists in organizing leisure activities in dormitories. Over sixty people participated in this study session, during which they learned from some factories about their experience of organizing dormitory-wide leisure activities.[113]

Through the "balancing work and rest" policy, dormitories became a space in which leaders in schools and factories could intervene when they wished to do so. In Peking University, for example, to make sure that the eight-hour sleeping time was carried out, university leaders asked students to go to bed as soon as it was dark outside, which not only prevented students from feeling frozen when the heating system malfunctioned but also saved electric energy because lights were turned off. The leader in the Department of Philosophy went to student dormitories at night to check whether they had really gone to bed early.[114] If the example of Peking University can be interpreted as the care for students' physical health from their teachers, extreme examples of unreasonable surveillance and penetration of leisure time and private space were not rare. In March 1961, the Beijing Municipal Party found that in many work

---

[111] "Dazhua yeyu shenghuo gaohao zhigong jiaoyu," March 25, 1961, BMA, 152-001-00516-0037.

[112] See, for example, reports on January 12, January 14, January 26, February 1, and February 21, 1961 in *Beijing wanbao*.

[113] *Beijing wanbao*, January 25, 1961.

[114] Lu Xueyi 陆学艺, ed., *Qingchun suiyue zai Beida: zhexuexi 1957 ji tongxue huiyilu* 青春岁月在北大: 哲学系1957级同学回忆录 [We were in Peking University when we were young: memoirs of Philosophy students entering school in 1957] (Beijing: shehui kexue wenxian chubanshe, 2012), 14–15.

units, people's private matters were spied on and severely interfered in by security guards if they were suspected to have improper thoughts. In the Central Academy of Crafts, members of the Party branch in a department broke into several students' rooms to check their diaries and family letters, hoping to find "reactionary thoughts." In a factory, one night, a nineteen-year-old female worker named Tian Shulan went to her relative's residence and did not go back to her dormitory when she had a fever. The next day, the leader in her factory thought that she went out to have "chaotic sexual relations" and asked her to make self-criticism. After another day, several cadres talked to Tian and asked her "what did you do the night before? Why didn't you stay in your dormitory if you are sick?" A cadre from her Youth League branch found Tian later and said "as a Youth League member, you should be honest. If you admit your mistake, you are still a good Youth League member." Tian insisted that she did nothing wrong, but the cadres did not believe her. Tian attempted suicide by jumping into a well but was saved by local residents.

In another factory, when the security cadre learned that a female worker called Li Youming often went dancing in the Cultural Palace, he began to suspect that Li was engaging in "hooliganism" and went to talk to her. He detained Li for three days and asked her to write a self-criticism. Unsatisfied with Li's written records, the cadre asked Li to write it again and threatened that "if you do not confess, I will put you into a mass debate. Then let's see whether you will confess!" Fearing denunciations from her colleagues, Li committed suicide by drinking hydrofluoric acid.[115] These examples were not uncommon. By May, over one thousand similar events were found in Beijing universities.[116]

[115] "Shiwei guanyu liji jiuzheng zhi'an baowei renyuan zhong weifa luanji xingwei de tongbao" 市委关于立即纠正治安保卫人员中违法乱纪行为的通报 [Circular from the Municipal Committee on correcting unlawful and disciplinary behaviors among security cadres], March 3, 1961, in *Zhongguo gongchandang Beijingshi weiyuanhui zhongyao wenjian huibian 1961 nian* 中国共产党北京市委员会重要文件汇编1961年 [Collection of important documents of the Beijing Municipal Committee of the Chinese Communist Party, 1961], ed. Zhonggong Beijingshiwei bangongting 中共北京市委办公厅 (n.p., 1965), 357–364.

[116] "Shiwei guanyu jiuzheng zhi'an baowei gongzuo zhong weifa luanji xingwei xiang zhongyang huabeiju de baogao" 市委关于纠正治安保卫工作中违法乱纪行为向中央、华北局的报告 [Report submitted to the Central Committee and the Bureau of North China from the Municipal Committee on correcting unlawful and disciplinary behaviors among security cadres], May 4, 1961, in *Zhongguo gongchandang Beijingshi weiyuanhui zhongyao wenjian huibian 1961 nian*, 364.

Conclusion: Accumulating a Communist Version of "Social Capital"

In 2000, Robert Putnam warned Americans that they were losing the most important asset that made American democracy work smoothly: the "social capital" that was accumulated mostly in leisure time. People tended to spend their leisure time watching TV at home or, using the title of his book, "bowling alone." More importantly, the American community declined when people started to become the passive audience of sports and cultural products instead of actively playing music or football together with others.[117] Putnam called for a "re-creation" of social capital by revitalizing community life. One of his suggestions was to let more Americans "participate in (not merely consume or 'appreciate') cultural activities from group dancing to songfests to community theater to rap festivals."[118]

Putnam's suggestion might have seemed redundant for people living in China in the mid-1950s and early 1960s when they participated in a massive cultural movement by performing cultural products generated by themselves instead of just "consuming" or "appreciating." Chinese people were not only banned from engaging in youth subcultures, but also organized to experience what they should do as a socialist community. In this sense, there was a movement to create "social capital," but it was top-down instead of Putnam's bottom-up. Starting from 1955, worrying about the increasingly noticeable subcultures among youth, the Party decided to launch a campaign to rectify the influences of subcultures in young people's daily life. To be frank, the emergence of youth subcultures during this period was quite relevant to the Party's policies, and in this sense, rather than an underground cultural movement that was totally subversive toward the Party line, youth subcultures only reflected people's aesthetic taste. The Party's emphasis on preserving classic novels and popular novels such as romantic fictions of the Mandarin and Butterflies School or detective fictions during the confiscation of "bad" books facilitated the prevalence of inappropriate leisure reading. Wearing colorful clothes, which might be inappropriate to some cadres, was actually advocated zealously by officials in Beijing. The Hundred Flower Movement

---

[117] Putnam, *Bowling Alone*, 121–122.

[118] Putnam, *Bowling Alone*, 448.

stimulated the revival of old "yellow songs" as well as the introduction and creation of new ones. Party officials, of course, did not encourage people to engage in subcultures when they mapped out their political plans. Nevertheless, people could enjoy themselves and pursue what they wanted in a relatively safe atmosphere because of the unexpected effects of Party policies.

The Party's efforts to eliminate youth subcultures by mobilizing people to produce cultural works favored by the Party themselves was unsuccessful in terms of the poor quality of the poems and songs written by the laboring masses. A senior culture cadre admitted in early 1959 that those poems were "absurd" and also led to a shortage of paper.[119] The process of escalating leisure regulation, however, did make some intangible achievements from the perspective of creating "social capital" that could make the Party-state work. If we look at Party documents justifying its policies on intensifying regulations on young people's leisure time, we can find that apart from problems in "thought," the Party worried about unwanted social connections between people, such as self-organized small organizations and personal relationships between workers and capitalists. During the "balancing work and rest," even "drop-in" chats with colleagues living in other dormitories were under the Party's surveillance as a hotbed of undesirable conversations.[120] In this sense, although the Party paid great attention to political indoctrination among young people, what it really achieved was to establish a Communist version of "social capital" by rooting out existing social connections and creating new interpersonal relations in controllable spaces such as dormitories, neighborhoods, schools, and factories under the work unit system. If for Putnam, a diverse group of people can form informal social connections in collective leisure activities, in China, leisure activities were used to accumulate social capital in spaces designated by the Party.

For many ordinary people, the Party's promotion of communal leisure activities in work units was not unacceptable. Old social connections

---

[119] *Dianying zhanbao/Hongdeng bao*, July 22, 1967.

[120] Chat was a major target in some factories when they "occupy the battlefield of dormitory." It was reported that after the "red dormitory movement" in a factory, the percentage of workers who chatted with each other decreased dramatically from 31 to 5 percent. "Guanyu jiehe sushi huodong jinxing zhengzhi jishu wenhua jiaoyu qingkuang de baogao," March 1, 1961, BMA, 152-001-00516-0015.

vanished in the 1950s when people stopped seeing their old friends.[121] Even if people thought that they did not have enough time to relax or leisure activities were too politicized, they still welcomed leisure activities offered by work units. In this regard, Mao's utopian vision of "six hundred million in this land all equal Yao and Shun" in his 1958 poem "Farewell to the God of Plague"[122] was partly achieved: the Chinese people might not have been thoroughly transformed in ideology, but many of them were satisfied with the "communal way of life" under the work unit system, which has become one of the sources of nostalgia for the Mao era today.

[121] Interview of Mr. G (born in 1931, Beijing resident, retired cadre), in Liang Jinghe, *Zhongguo xiandangdai shehui wenhua fangtanlu*, 122.

[122] English translation is taken from https://www.marxists.org/reference/archive/mao/selected-works/poems/poems25.htm.

CHAPTER 5

Anxiety About Difference: Politicization and Stratification in Leisure, 1962–1966

Class struggle among my classmates is getting more and more fierce. On the surface, the situation seems to be very calm, but the struggle is very complicated. I used to be indifferent about it, but now I need to be vigilant and maintain my standpoint. I must crush the conspiracy thoroughly in a short period of time.[1]
—Zhang Baolin, Beijing, November 28, 1965

Class struggle is intangible, but it can be mirrored by behaviors of the youth. Some of my classmates like to dress themselves up to make themselves look good. Some use hair oil. Some like to gossip and make other classmates unable to focus on their schoolwork. Don't they belong to class struggle? Young people: never forget class and class struggle.[2]
—Zhang Baolin, Beijing, January 7, 1966

Small leather shoes, squeak, squeak, squeak, stinking capitalist ideology![3]
小皮鞋, 嘎嘎响, 资产阶级臭思想。
—Popular saying in the early 1960s

---

[1] Zhang Baolin's diary, author's collection. In fall 1965 and spring 1966, Zhang was a grade nine student in a junior high school in Beijing's Dongcheng District.

[2] Zhang Baolin's diary.

[3] This popular saying appears frequently in people's reminiscence of the 1960s. See, for example, Wang Qianrong 王乾荣, "'Jieji' xin gainian" "阶级"新概念" [New concept of "class"], *Zhongguo qingnian bao*, October 9, 2002.

In August 1962, when the nightmarish Great Leap Famine was coming to an end, Mao Zedong reiterated the existence of classes and class struggle in the socialist country he was leading during a meeting held in Beidaihe, the summer resort for the Chairman and his comrades. One month later, his idea was made public following the conclusion of the Party's Tenth Plenary Session of the Eighth Central Committee in Beijing.[4] "The influence from the bourgeoisie and habits from the old society still exist in our society," preached Mao in the Communiqué of the Tenth Plenary Session of the Eighth Central Committee published by the *People's Daily* on September 26, 1962. "Class struggle is inevitable. This is a law of history that has been clarified in Marxism-Leninism long ago. We should never forget."[5]

From the perspective of high politics, Mao's reiteration of class struggle in 1962 is usually interpreted as a result of his clash with his veteran colleagues over a series of socio-economic policies, especially during the recovery from the economic disaster and the famine caused by the Great Leap Forward. Therefore, it is also considered as one turning point in the history of the People's Republic and the prelude of the Cultural Revolution four years later.[6] Meanwhile, from a grassroots perspective, as shown by Zhang Baolin's diary, class struggle also became a central theme in people's everyday life. In his analysis of the play *Never Forget* (*Qianwan buyao wangji* 千万不要忘记, initially known as *Wish You Good Health* [*Zhu ni jiankang* 祝你健康]), Tang Xiaobing captures a collective emotion in China in the early 1960s by stressing that underneath the grand narrative of class struggle, this play actually embodied "a kind of profound anxiety about everyday life during a post-revolutionary period. [Since the performance of this play,] 'everyday life' became a problem that

---

[4] For Mao's change of course on class struggle in the summer and autumn of 1962, see Roderick MacFarquhar, *The Origins of the Cultural Revolution, Vol. 3: The Coming of the Cataclysm, 1961–1966* (New York: Columbia University Press, 1997), 261–296.

[5] RMRB, September 26, 1962. These sentences were added by Mao personally before the communiqué was published. See Mao Zedong, "Dui Zhonggong bajie shizhong quanhui gongbaogao de piyu he xiugai" 对中共八届十中全会公报稿的批语和修改 [Comments and revisions on the draft of the Communiqué of the Tenth Plenary Session of the Eighth Central Committee], in *Jianguo yilai Mao Zedong wengao* 建国以来毛泽东文稿 [Mao Zedong's manuscripts since the founding of the Republic], vol. 10 (Beijing: Zhongyang wenxian chubanshe, 1996), 196–197.

[6] MacFacquhar, *The Origins of the Cultural Revolution, Vol. 3*.

was in dire need of an answer."⁷ Cai Xiang attributes this "anxiety" to the rise of hedonism among young people in terms of material comforts and the Party's fear of losing "cultural hegemony" with the development of the economy in the early 1960s.⁸

While I agree with Tang and Cai that there was a collective "anxiety" in China in the early 1960s, in this chapter, I do not see this anxiety as a result of a "post-revolutionary" sentiment or a lure of consumerism. Neither do I regard this anxiety as something new in the 1960s. As previous chapters have shown, we can see the Party's continuous interference in young people's leisure, regardless of the economic condition or which stage of revolution the country was in. Instead, I see this anxiety as an endogenous corollary of the Party's constant regulation of people's leisure that came from a fear of "differences" in everyday life. The term "difference" here echoes the classic Marxist view that the ultimate purpose of socialism and proletarian dictatorship is to abolish differences in political and economic status between different classes.⁹ For Lenin, these differences are specifically defined as the difference between town and country and the difference between manual workers and brain workers.¹⁰ In Maoist China, the slogan of "abolishing three major differences" became prominent during the Cultural Revolution.¹¹

In Marxist-Leninist writings, "difference" is used along with the theory of class analysis and is bound to be abolished once classes no longer exist. Nevertheless, once such differences had become targets of the Communist revolution, Chinese revolutionaries tended to pay attention to more

---

⁷ Tang Xiaobing 唐小兵, *Yingxiong yu fanren de shidai: jiedu 20 shiji* 英雄与凡人的时代: 解读20世纪 [The era of heroes and ordinary people: an interpretation of the twentieth century] (Shanghai: Shanghai wenyi chubanshe, 2001), 139–140.

⁸ Cai Xiang 蔡翔, *Geming/xushu: Zhongguo shehui zhuyi wenxue-wenhua xiangxiang 1949–1966* 革命/叙述: 中国社会主义文学—文化想象 (1949–1966) [Revolution and narrative: the imagination of Chinese socialist literature and culture, 1946–1966] (Beijing: Beijing daxue chubanshe, 2010), 324–364.

⁹ See, for example, Karl Marx, "The Class Struggles in France, 1848 to 1850," 1850, https://www.marxists.org/archive/marx/works/1850/class-struggles-france/ch03.htm.

¹⁰ Vladimir Lenin, "A Great Beginning: Heroism of the Workers in the Rear 'Communist Subbotniks'," June 28, 1919, https://www.marxists.org/archive/lenin/works/1919/jun/19.htm.

¹¹ The "three major differences" include the difference between industrial workers and peasants, between city and countryside, and between manual workers and mental workers.

conspicuous elements in people's everyday life, rather than the underlying structures of political economy identified by Marx. They considered these daily activities as symbols of social stratification and targets of class struggle that Mao advocated. Leisure and lifestyle, for example, have everything to do with these differences. For some scholars, leisure itself is a privilege for a certain group from an advanced socio-economic class, and thus it can only be enjoyed by this small number of people.[12] Others show that during industrialization, the working class also formed their own leisure taste and lifestyle that were considered rough by the middle class, who made a failed attempt to promote "rational recreation" among the working class.[13] In modern consumer societies, social stratification still has a prominent influence on the formation of different lifestyles.[14]

Maoist China, with a goal to create a utopian classless society, had few similarities with contemporary Western consumer societies, despite the existence of some elements of consumerism.[15] Even compared with countries in the Eastern Bloc where growing indifference to, if not resistance against, the pieties of socialism were spotted among young people who were enjoying underground subcultures with apparent Western influence, young people in China had very few channels to the outside world, not to mention the all-pervasive political movements which had become rare in the Soviet Union and many countries in Eastern Europe.[16] In the context of global Cold War in the 1960s, however, the Party's fear of differences indeed led to a campaign against the so-called "bourgeois lifestyle"

[12] Thorstein Veblen, *The Theory of the Leisure Class* (Mineola, NY: Dover Publications, 1994).

[13] Peter Bailey, *Leisure and Class in Victorian England: Rational Recreation and the Contest for Control, 1830–1885* (London: Routledge & Kegan Paul, 1978). For the case of Germany, see Lynn Abrams, *Workers' Culture in Imperial Germany: Leisure and Recreation in the Rhineland and Westphalia* (London: Routledge, 1992).

[14] Tally Katz-Gerro, "Cultural Consumption and Social Stratification: Leisure Activities, Musical Tastes, and Social Location," *Sociological Perspectives* 42, no. 4 (1999): 627–646; Yannick Lemel and Tally Katz-Gerro, "The Stratification of Leisure: Variation in the Salience of Socioeconomic Dimensions in Shaping Leisure Participation in Two Consumer Societies," *Loisir et Société/Society and Leisure* 38, no. 3 (2015): 399–422.

[15] Karl Gerth, *Unending Capitalism: How Consumerism Negated China's Communist Revolution* (Cambridge: Cambridge University Press, 2020). Gerth stresses that although consumerism existed throughout the Mao Zedong period, it never possessed a dominant position. See Gerth, *Unending Capitalism*, 233.

[16] For the case of the Soviet Union, see Juliane Fürst, *Stalin's Last Generation: Soviet Post-War Youth and the Emergence of Mature Socialism* (Oxford: Oxford University Press,

(*zichanjieji shenghuo fangshi* 资产阶级生活方式). Although bourgeois lifestyle had been criticized since the 1950s, with Mao's reiteration of class struggle, this campaign was more ideology-oriented as all trivial matters in people's leisure, including recreational choices and aesthetic tastes in their everyday life, were all put under the framework of class analysis.

This chapter discusses the CCP's desire to fulfill its mission of ending unjust social differences through the politicization of leisure. Unlike the bold social experiment to accumulate a communist version of social capital through the rebuilding of interpersonal relations during the Great Leap Forward, after the failures of the Leap, the Party became anxious about the possibility of losing young people's hearts and minds in the sphere of leisure and lifestyle when they regarded some superficial symbols as serious political issues. This anxiety came from several channels that might generate alternative ways of life: Party officials started to emphasize the importance of leisure in Beijing's urban planning; young people could learn about Western lifestyle through imported Hong Kong films; the resurgence of commercial networks in Beijing facilitated young people's access to goods not in accordance with the Party's ideal way of life. These signs of differentiation and alienation, along with the fear of a potential "peaceful evolution" in China, made the CCP consider leisure as a battlefield of the competition between the two blocs.

With these political anxieties in mind, Party leaders hastily turned to relatively trivial symbols of "bourgeois lifestyle" in young people's everyday life rather than institutional differences in political economy when they launched a campaign to revolutionize superficial elements of "bourgeois lifestyle" such as clothing, haircut, and other leisure choices that could be broadly construed as lifestyle. The Party's lifestyle politics in the early 1960s did eliminate superficial differences in many ways as many young people regarded distinctive clothing or haircut as bad tastes. The Party's anxiety of social stratification, however, led to an unexpected outcome: the emergence of the differentiation between children of officials and people with ordinary family backgrounds when children of officials formed friendship groups in organized leisure activities exclusive to them.

2010); for the case of Eastern Europe, see Juliane Fürst and Josie McLellan, eds., *Dropping Out of Socialism: The Creation of Alternative Spheres in the Soviet Bloc* (Lanham: Lexington Books, 2016).

The Possibility of Alternative Lifestyles
Positioning Leisure in Urban Planning

For urban residents in Beijing (and also in other cities in China), their ideal way of life under socialism was defined by Mao's remarks on the future role of cities shortly after the People's Liberation Army took over this famous city with a long history of being a political and cultural center. Regarding cities as locations for production, Mao dismissed their role in providing abundant goods for consumers and urged his cadres to transform them into "producer-cities" (*shengchan chengshi* 生产城市), meaning cities with a primary goal of industrial production. "Only when production in the cities is restored and developed, when consumer-cities are transformed into producer-cities, can the people's political power be consolidated," Mao told members of the Central Committee in March 1949 as he was wrapping up the civil war against the Nationalist Party. "Other work in the cities…revolves around and serves the central task, production and construction."[17] The transformation from consumer-cities to producer-cities paralleled with the transformation of urban dwellers' way of life: people's lifestyle must serve the central task of production as well. As a cadre said during a study session held in Tianjin in September 1949, in a producer-city, "during working hours, streets should be empty and quiet. At this time, the market is 'depressed' with very few people buying things. The phenomenon of peddlers cluttering up the streets is impossible to find. Meanwhile, the factories are busy, and most of the people are working there." On the contrary, in a consumer-city, "in the morning (say, until nine o'clock), the streets are sparsely populated with few pedestrians except for students and peddlers. Trams are empty before 10 am, and they are not crowded until midday and afternoon (say, four o'clock). The market is full all day. At night, people are in high spirits; brothels, theatres, dance halls, gambling halls and streets are filled with people, crowding each other."[18]

---

[17] "Report to the Second Plenary Session of the Seventh Central Committee of the Communist Party of China," March 5, 1949, *Selected Works of Mao Tse-tung*, vol. 4, https://www.marxists.org/reference/archive/mao/selected-works/volume-4/mswv4_58.htm.

[18] Li Guofang 李国芳, "Bian xiaofei chengshi wei shengchan chengshi" 变消费城市为生产城市 [Transforming consumer-cities into producer-cities], in *Chengshishi yanjiu* 城市

Based on Mao's proposal on "transforming consumer-cities into producer-cities," in February 1950, Peng Zhen, then Party head of Beijing, announced that the urban planning of Beijing should "serve the people, serve production, and serve the Central People's Government" and later in 1954, this principle was finalized as "serving production, serving the laboring masses, and serving the organs of the Center" (*wei shengchan fuwu, wei laodong renmin fuwu, wei zhongyang ge jiguan fuwu* 为生产服务, 为劳动人民服务, 为中央各机关服务).[19] As a result of this principle, when drafting proposals, city planners in Beijing seldom put everyday life of urban residents under the spotlight. In Peng Zhen's famous 1956 speech on city planning, although he mentioned that planners should consider "what people do during after work hours," he did not talk specifically about his idea on how the city could serve people's recreational needs in leisure time in his thirteen-point proposal.[20]

The neglect of people's everyday life in Beijing's urban planning caused dullness and inconvenience in the daily activities of Beijing residents. One day after Peng Zhen delivered his speech on urban planning, Liu Shaoqi also expressed his view on the lack of basic services and recreational facilities during his visit to an exhibition on Beijing's urban planning. By praising the convenience of life in Shanghai, Liu raised the question of how to improve Beijing's infrastructure to better serve people's life. "There are two-storied grocery stores in Shanghai. Does Beijing have one?" Liu asked. "There are laundry stores, tailors, cobblers, vendors of cigarettes and matches at the entrances of lanes in Shanghai. People can get these daily issues done at the entrances of lanes. Beijing doesn't have [these services]." As for recreational facilities, Liu even proposed that Beijing could transform public revolutionary cemeteries into parks. In addition, parks across Beijing could hold dancing parties for residents in their leisure time. He even had a detailed plan to build boulevards with

史研究 [Studies on urban history], vol. 31, ed. Zhang Limin 张利民 (Beijing: Shehui kexue wenxian chubanshe, 2014), 5–6.

[19] Zhonggong Beijing shiwei dangshi yanjiushi 中共北京市委党史研究室 ed., *Peng Zhen zai Beijing* 彭真在北京 [Peng Zhen in Beijing] (Beijing: Zhongyang wenxian chubanshe, 2002), 394–395.

[20] "Guanyu Beijing de chengshi guihua wenti" 关于北京的城市规划问题 [On the issue of Beijing's urban planning], October 10, 1956, in *Peng Zhen wenxuan* 1941–1990 彭真文选 (一九四一——一九九〇年) [Selected works of Peng Zhen] (Beijing: Renmin chubanshe, 1991), 307–312.

greens like those in Moscow to let people go for a walk in their leisure time. In June 1959, when visiting Beijing's Taoranting Park, Liu encouraged park attendants to organize more recreational activities including drama performances and dancing parties, which he regarded as a "chance for men and women to meet publicly." In a picturesque corner in the park, Liu suggested that a pay tea house could also be set up to serve high-quality snacks for visitors in need. Liu's suggestions would later become his "crimes" for advocating the "lifestyle of old Shanghai" as well as "bourgeois lifestyle" during the early stage of the Cultural Revolution.[21]

In the early 1960s, city life in Beijing would witness a gradual change (at least on paper) as urban planners started to position leisure in socialist urban space. As revealed by rebels among urban planners in Beijing during the Cultural Revolution, from late 1963 to early 1964, the Beijing Municipal Party Committee planned to "reconstruct Chang'an Boulevard" so as to achieve a "solemn, beautiful, and modernized" socialist capital. According to this plan, "non-productive" facilities, including dozens of recreational and commercial facilities such as cinemas, theaters, and department stores, would mushroom along the reconstructed Chang'an Boulevard. It was said that Peng Zhen was extremely satisfied with the plan to build a large shopping mall in Beijing's commercial center Xidan because, in this department store, Beijing residents could "not only go shopping but hang around as well." To facilitate people's life, on the ground floor of this shopping mall, there would be a food court providing meals and snacks from famous Beijing's famous restaurants and other cultural facilities such as a cinema and a Peking Opera theater. This plan was criticized by rebels as imitating capitalist New York and Paris as well as "revisionist" Moscow and Warsaw while the former represented the "corrupt and declining" capitalism, and the latter were "widening the three major differences."[22]

[21] "Chedi qingsuan Liu Shaoqi zai jianzhujie de zuixing" 彻底清算刘少奇在建筑界的罪行 [Liquidating Liu Shaoqi's crimes in the construction circle thoroughly], part 5, Jiangongbu geming zaofan zongbu 建工部革命造反总部, *Fengleiji*, June 6, 1967; "Chedi qingsuan Liu Shaoqi zai jianzhujie de zuixing," part 6, *Fengleiji*, June 22, 1967.

[22] "Gongchan zhuyi de zhaopai xiuzheng zhuyi de heihuo" "共产主义"的招牌 修正主义的黑货" ["Communism" as disguise, revisionism in nature], *Fengleiji*, October 24, 1967. See also Dahpon David Ho, "To Protect and Preserve: Resisting the Destroy the Four Olds Campaign, 1966–1976," in Esherick, Pickowicz, and Walder, *The Chinese Cultural Revolution as History*, 72–73.

The rebels also criticized the Beijing Municipal Party Committee's plan to build "satellite towns" (*weixing zhen* 卫星镇) in suburban Beijing to ease the potential population boom. "Satellite towns" appeared in Peng Zhen's thirteen-point proposal on Beijing's urban planning in October 1956. By introducing the concept of satellite towns, Peng stressed three purposes: first and the most obvious, satellite towns could reduce population density in Beijing; second, as a result of the reduction in population density, satellite towns could facilitate people's daily life by providing basic services not far away from their neighborhood; third, satellite towns could facilitate the preparedness for a future nuclear war as people would be evacuated from Beijing's city center to satellite towns before the outbreak of the war.[23] In the Beijing Municipal Party Committee's plan, these satellite towns not only included compounds with productive purposes such as "iron town," "petroleum town," and "leather shoes town," but also included resorts for leisure activities. The Municipal Party Committee planned to build several "satellite towns for recuperation" (*xiuliaoyang weixing zhen* 休疗养卫星镇) "to meet the need of millions recuperating at the same time." Another bold plan was to connect these "satellite towns for recuperation" with Beijing's city center by four canals in which people who enjoyed aquatic activities could take cruises and motorboats to suburban resorts. The "satellite town" plan would be denounced by rebels during the Cultural Revolution as "pursuing bourgeois lifestyle" and "widening the three major differences between city and countryside, between industrial workers and peasants, and between manual workers and mental workers."[24]

Beijing's urban planning in the early 1960s shows that urban planners were considering incorporating leisure into the socialist capital while still maintaining the principle that Beijing's urban space should "serve the people, serve production, and serve the Center." The change in urban space would presumably bring changes to people's leisure choices and lifestyle, as criticized later by rebels during the Cultural Revolution. Nevertheless, we are unable to examine how urban planning changed Beijing residents' everyday way of life in the early 1960s because the plans were interrupted by the Cultural Revolution. This being said, Beijing

[23] "Guanyu Beijing de chengshi guihua wenti," *Peng Zhen wenxuan*, 310.
[24] "Beijing de weixing zhen" 北京的"卫星镇" ["Satellite towns" in Beijing], *Fengleiji*, October 31, 1967.

residents still had other channels to imagine and even exercise alternative ways of life. These channels were usually made available by official policies and thus they were not experienced as an alternative lifestyle in an underground way like what was going on in the Soviet Union and Eastern Europe.

Imagining an Alternative Way of Life from Hong Kong Films

One window for Beijing residents to learn about an alternative lifestyle was Hong Kong films. To be sure, Hong Kong films were available to Beijing residents since 1950, including the famous 1948 film *Sorrows of the Forbidden City* (*Qinggong mishi* 清宫秘史). From 1950 to March 1963, over twenty Hong Kong films were screened in Beijing.[25] According to a regulation issued in October 1950, films produced in Hong Kong, along with those produced in other capitalist countries, faced harsh censorship on their contents that were considered to "oppose world peace, oppose people's democracy, oppose China's national interest, or publicize pornography, superstition, and terror" by the Ministry of Culture. It was, therefore, extremely hard for Hong Kong films to be imported and screened in mainland China, including those produced by Hong Kong leftist film studios.[26] In October 1960, however, Liao Chengzhi (a senior member of the CCP's International Liaison Department) proposed in a report that there should be an increase in the number of Hong Kong films imported into the mainland in the following years as there were "progressive elements" in these films.[27] Two months later, in December, Chen Huangmei, a Party official in charge of films, suggested that when importing films produced outside, "we

[25] Beijing difangzhi bianzuan weiyuanhui 北京地方志编纂委员会, ed., *Beijing zhi wenhua yishu juan xijui zhi quyi zhi dianying zhi* 北京志 文化艺术卷 戏剧志 曲艺志 电影志 [Annals of Beijing, volume of culture and art, annals of drama, annals of folk vocal art, annals of film] (Beijing: Beijing chubanshe, 2000), 722.

[26] "Wenhua bu guanyu dianyingye wuge zanxing banfa" 文化部关于电影业五个暂行办法 [Five temporary solutions on film industry from the Ministry of Culture], October 24, 1950, in *Zhongguo dianying yanjiu ziliao 1949–1979* 中国电影研究资料: 1949–1979 [Materials for studies on Chinese cinema, 1949–1979], vol. 1, ed. Wu Di 吴迪 (Beijing: Wenhua yishu chubanshe, 2006), 70–71.

[27] "Xianggang dianying jinkou gongsi zongjingli Liao Chengzhi" "香港电影进口公司总经理"—廖承志 [Manager of the "Hong Kong film import company": Liao Chengzhi], *Pi Liao zhanbao*, May 7, 1967.

should also let a hundred flowers bloom." He emphasized the recreational dimension of films: "It would be partial to say that films only have educational purposes. They should be both educational and entertaining."[28] Later, in August 1962, Chen told editors of China's leading film magazine *Popular Cinema* (*Dazhong dianying* 大众电影) that "you should also publicize Hong Kong films. You can point out their advantages. Do not avoid publicizing them because they have side effects."[29]

The immediate result of the relaxation in control of Hong Kong films gave rise to a "Hong Kong frenzy" in young people's leisure time across the country in the early 1960s. As a cadre from the China Film Association observed in early 1962, "nowadays many people are enthusiastic about Hong Kong films." In Beijing, people were enchanted by the touching plot of *The Great Devotion* (*Kelian tianxia fumu xin* 可怜天下父母心). Those who were sent to cinemas by the China Film Association to observe the reactions of the audience reported that "people burst into tears [when watching this film], and there was more than one person crying." When *Girl on the Front Page* (*Xinwen renwu* 新闻人物) was shown in a cinema in Beijing, there was such a big crowd that three glass windows broke and two staff members of the cinema got hurt. Although the cadre admitted that the influence of Hong Kong films "made people doing ideological work anxious," he did not consider it a bad thing as he thought that people could also be educated by "negative examples" and Hong Kong films could be a supplement to the "simplified" official way of ideological indoctrination.[30]

For some young people, Hong Kong cinema was a window for them to learn about fashions of the outside world. In an internal report from the Beijing No. 1 Machine Tool Factory, the head of the Youth League there estimated that about 20% of the young workers in the factory would try every means to secure a ticket whenever a Hong Kong film was to be

---

[28] "Dianyingjie di'erhao fangeming xiuzheng zhuyi toumu Chen Huangmei heihua lu" 电影界第二号反革命修正主义头目陈荒煤黑话录 [Black words of Chen Huangmei, the no. 2 counterrevolutionary revisionist leader in film circle], *Dianying zhanbao/Hongdeng bao*, July 22, 1967.

[29] "Dianyingjie di'erhao fangeming xiuzheng zhuyi toumu Chen Huangmei heihua lu," *Dianying zhanbao/Hongdeng bao*, July 22, 1967.

[30] "Liu Shaoqi shi doushou xianggang dianying de da fandu fan" 刘少奇是兜售香港电影的大贩毒犯 [Liu Shaoqi is a big drug trafficker of Hong Kong films], Beijing hangkong xueyuan 北京航空学院, *Hongqi*, June 6, 1967.

screened. Although for many of them, the mania for Hong Kong films was based on pure curiosity, some young people were extremely interested in the lifestyle presented in these films. As a young worker said explicitly, "Hong Kong films are more interesting than domestically produced films because I can take in some petty-bourgeois lifestyle."[31] As a then junior high school student in Beijing recalls, "before Hong Kong's return to the motherland… Hong Kong was a mysterious land for mainlanders. Nevertheless, people never forgot Hong Kong, and they wished to know Hong Kong's society, economy, local customs and lifestyle from Hong Kong films." Therefore, in the early 1960s, whenever a Hong Kong film was to be screened, people would queue up in the front of the cinema to buy a ticket. "Many people lined up in the queue at midnight, fearing that the tickets might be sold out. Many were anxiously waiting for someone to return their tickets." He even played truant from school to watch *The Great Devotion*.[32] In many cities, young people were obsessed with Hong Kong fashion including jeans, haircuts, and leather shoes with pointed toes. Some tailors and barbers were even organized by their leaders to learn the fashion from Hong Kong films to better serve their customers. It was inevitable for some young people to yearn for life in Hong Kong and it was said that Hong Kong films sparked "a wind of fleeing to Hong Kong" in Guangdong and Fujian.[33] Party and Youth League officials in Shanghai also reported that after watching Hong Kong films, young people there thought that life in Hong Kong was "good" and even got envious of poor people in Hong Kong because they could wear Western clothes.[34]

---

[31] *Neibu cankao*, March 5, 1962.

[32] Li Weiji 李维基, Women de lao Beijing: guxi tuzhu de jinghua suoyi 我们的老北京：古稀土著的京华琐忆 [Our old Beijing: scattered recollections from a native resident over seventy] (Beijing: Zhongguo qinggongye chubanshe, 2015), 187.

[33] "Xianggang dianying jinkou gongsi zongjingli Liao Chengzhi," *Pi Liao zhanbao*, May 7, 1967.

[34] Matthew D. Johnson, "Beneath the Propaganda State: Official and Unofficial Cultural Landscapes in Shanghai, 1949–1956," in Brown and Johnson, *Maoism at the Grassroots*, 220–221.

The Resurgence of Commercial Networks

The Hong Kong channel did not last very long. Recognizing the huge impact of Hong Kong films, in February 1963, Zhou Enlai criticized the loose regulation of film import and screening. The Ministry of Culture ordered a ban.[35] Although the window through Hong Kong films was shut, the resurrection of commercial networks in Beijing also facilitated people's pursuit of alternative lifestyles. One Swedish student studying at Peking University from 1961 to 1962 recalled that life in Beijing was highly divided. On the one hand, students led a militarized way of life on campus in the sense that their daily life was regulated and punctuated by bells and loudspeaker broadcasts: a bell rang at six o'clock asking students to get up, then at 6:30 am they were notified by another bell to go for breakfast. At seven o'clock, students would listen to the first round of news digest and forty-five minutes later, they should sit in their classrooms.[36] On the other hand, in the center of Beijing, she could also find pictures of foreign beauties on sale behind a black door deep in an alley, including a picture of a hot Spanish girl playing guitar. Many men passing by stopped and gazed at these foreign beauties intoxicatedly.[37]

If in 1961 and 1962, selling pictures of foreign beauties was still clandestine, by 1964, this practice became more public and was even under the auspices of government organs. An internal report in September 1964 stated that selling and purchasing of song sheets and pictures of film stars became prevalent in Beijing and Shanghai. Song sheets had lyrics of some "unhealthy songs" and "foreign love songs." As for the film stars in these pictures, they were "seductive and bewitching" (*yaoli yaoqi* 妖里妖气) and equivalent to "film stars in the old society." These song sheets and pictures were very popular. In Shanghai, about 2,000 song sheets and pictures

---

[35] "Liu-Deng wenyi heixian zai jinkou ducao dianying fangmian de zuixinglu" 刘邓文艺黑线在进口毒草电影方面的罪行录 [Record of the crimes of Liu-Deng black line in culture and art on importing poisonous films], *Duiwai wenhua zhanbao*, July 21, 1967.

[36] Lin Xili (Cecilia Lindqvist) 林西莉, *Ling yige shijie: Zhongguo jiyi 1961–1962* 另一个世界：中国记忆 1961–1962 [Another World: Memories of China, 1961–1962] (Beijing: Zhonghua shuju, 2016), 34. Bells and loudspeakers remain a unique memory for many foreign students studying in Maoist China. In a report submitted to the British Council in 1974, a British student complained that bells "made us feel like Pavlovian dogs." See Beverley Hooper, *Foreigners Under Mao: Western Lives in China, 1949–1976* (Hong Kong: Hong Kong University Press, 2016), 200.

[37] Lin Xili, *Ling yige shijie*, 202.

were sold every day, and some vendors even sold them to remote areas including Xinjiang, Inner Mongolia, Yunnan, and Guizhou. A vendor in Beijing's Qianmen District could sell over 100 song sheets and pictures a day during weekdays, and about 250 on weekends. Buyers included high school students, elementary students, young workers, and young soldiers. One major source of these song sheets and pictures was actually the Film Archive Department of the Ministry of Culture.[38] In August 1964, *China Youth Daily* published a letter from a reader asking a ban on this kind of song sheets and pictures because he thought that these things would lure young people into pursuing "bourgeois bad habit" (*zichan jieji huai xiqi* 资产阶级坏习气) when they started to pay too much attention to their appearance.[39]

Fear of a "Peaceful Evolution"

Domestic signs of the influence of the "bourgeois lifestyle" discussed above made the CCP anxious about young people pursuing alternative lifestyles, or even the possibility that the youth might pursue alternative lifestyles. In the early 1960s, the Party's political anxiety aggravated by the fear that its utopian mission would be simultaneously undermined by foreign influence in young people's everyday life when Party leaders became aware of the "peaceful evolution" strategy and its seeming success in Eastern Europe and the Soviet Union.

Everyday life had always been a spotlight in the classic Cold War rhetoric that the battle between the Socialist Bloc and the Capitalist Bloc was a battle for people's hearts and minds over two different ways of life. In an address by Harry S. Truman in March 1947, the president famously announced that "at the present moment in world history nearly every nation must choose between alternative ways of life. One way of life is based upon the will of the majority…The second way of life is based upon the will of a minority forcibly imposed upon the majority."[40]

---

[38] *Neibu cankao*, September 8, 1964.

[39] *Zhongguo qingnian bao*, August 29, 1964.

[40] "Address of the President to Congress, Recommending Assistance to Greece and Turkey," March 12, 1947, https://www.trumanlibrary.gov/library/research-files/address-president-congress-recommending-assistance-greece-and-turkey?documentid=NA&pagenumber=1.

In the early 1960s, "peaceful evolution" as a strategy of subversion came into the view of CCP leaders. During a meeting convened in Hangzhou in November 1959, Mao mentioned US Secretary of State John Foster Dulles' proposal of "peaceful transformation" and warned that China was facing the threat of being "corrupted" and "transformed peacefully" by the United States, although he remained confident that the Socialist Bloc was bound to win.[41] In February 1960, during a report to the Central Committee of the Communist Youth League, Hu Keshi, then a senior leader of the Youth League, vowed to "intensify a communist ideological education" among young people in response to what he called the "strategy to win peacefully" (*heping qusheng de zhanlüe* 和平取胜的战略).[42] Hu was anxious about the behaviors among some young people that had deviated from the "communist style" (*gongchan zhuyi fengge* 共产主义风格). He criticized the growing individualism by citing the case of a young worker in Shanghai who considered that the biggest happiness was to "change into slippers with the help of my wife after getting off work, lie on the sofa, smoke a cigarette, read *Xinmin Evening News* with a cup of tea while listening to the radio, and then have some delicious dishes made by mom." In rural areas in Jilin Province, some young women were pursuing "necklaces, colourful scarves, high heels, and one-pieces." Some other young people were tired of endless campaigns and production competitions. Instead, they thought that these movements had interrupted their everyday life and thus what they were pursuing was "a quiet life." Distressed by these alternative ways of life among young people, Hu recalled the education of the communist morality movement in 1955 and called for a continuous education against bourgeois lifestyle.[43]

---

[41] Lin Ke 林克, "Huiyi Mao Zedong dui Dulesi heping yanbian yanlun de pinglun" 回忆毛泽东对杜勒斯和平演变言论的评论 [Recollections on Mao Zedong's remarks on Dulles' opinions of peaceful evolution], *Dangde wenxian* 6 (1990): 45–46.

[42] "Hu Keshi tongzhi zai tuan de sanjie liuzhong quanhui shang de baogao" 胡克实同志在团的三届六中全会上的报告 [Comrade Hu Keshi's report to the Third Plenary Session of the Sixth Youth League Central Committee], February 27, 1960, in *Tuan de wenjian huibian 1960* 团的文件汇编 1960 [Collection of documents of the Youth League, 1960], ed. Zhongguo gongchan zhuyi qingniantuan zhongyang weiyuanhui bangongting 中国共产主义青年团中央委员会办公厅 (n.p., 1962), 34.

[43] "Hu Keshi tongzhi zai tuan de sanjie liuzhong quanhui shang de baogao," February 27, 1960, in *Tuan de wenjian huibian 1960*, 38–39; 42.

Hu Keshi's speech came after the Youth League submitted a report to the CCP Central Committee suggesting a "socialist education" movement among young people in which the Youth League Central Secretariat regarded young people's pursuit of alternative lifestyles that Hu later mentioned as a reflection of "the struggle between two roads." The Youth League planned to "give young people a deep and vivid education of Marxism-Leninism and Mao Zedong Thought to limit the influence of bourgeois thinking as little as possible."[44] Different provinces adopted different approaches with local features to conduct this education in late 1960. For example, in Shanghai, young people were organized to revisit many historic sites with revolutionary meanings throughout the city to get educated by "revolutionary tradition."[45] In Shaanxi, young people were educated to carry on the "Yan'an style."[46]

The effect of these education movements remained questionable. In 1963, when talking about the "Learning from Lei Feng" movement with cadres in Guangdong Provincial Youth League Committee, Hu Keshi admitted the ineffectiveness of official propaganda when it met with the actual threat of material superiority in the Western world. "Many young people don't actually understand socialism," Hu noted. These young people treated socialism in a hedonist way that "socialism should let us live

[44] "Zhonggong zhongyang zhuanpi gongqingtuan zhongyang shujichu guanyu liaotiao daolu douzheng zai qingnian zhong de fanying he xiang qingnian jinxing shehui zhuyi jiaoyu de yijian de baogao" 中共中央转批共青团中央书记处关于两条道路斗争在青年中的反映和向青年进行社会主义教育的意见的报告 [Report from the Communist Youth League Central Secretariat on reflections of the struggle between two roads among the youth and launching a socialist education among the youth with comments from the CCP Central Committee], February 3, 1960, in *Tuan de wenjian huibian 1960*, 136–137.

[45] "Gongqingtuan zhongyang pizhuan tuan Shanghai shiwei guanyu geng you jihua you zuzhi di xiang qingnian jinxing geming chuantong jiaoyu de qingshi baogao" 共青团中央批转上海市委"关于更有计划有组织地向青年进行革命传统教育的请示报告" [Report asking for instructions from Shanghai Municipal Youth League Committee on conducting education of revolutionary tradition among the youth in a more planned and organized manner with comments from the Youth League Central Committee], September 30, 1960, in *Tuan de wenjian huibian 1960*, 238–244.

[46] "Gongqingtuan zhongyang zhuanfa Zhonggong Shaanxi shengwei pizhuan Gongqingtuan Shaanxi shengwei guanyu xiang qingnian jinxing Yan'an shiqi zuofeng jiaoyu de baogao" 共青团中央转发中共陕西省委批转共青团陕西省委关于向青年进行延安时期作风教育的报告 [Report from Shaanxi Provincial Youth League Committee on conducting education of Yan'an style among the youth with comments from Shaanxi Provincial Party Committee, forwarded by the Youth League Central Committee], December 27, 1960, in *Tuan de wenjian huibian 1960*, 244–250.

better with a light workload, high salary, and the possibility of free development" that allowed the pursuit of individual happiness. Therefore, Hu thought that young people were extremely vulnerable in their everyday life when they see the merchandise and lifestyle in capitalist countries.[47]

More news from the Soviet Bloc that people there were "corrupted" by "bourgeois lifestyle" intensified the anxiety of Chinese leaders about young people at home. The Chinese leaders learned from internal reports that Western films "publicizing bourgeois lifestyle" were extremely popular in the Soviet Union, but revolutionary films had a small audience. In Czechoslovakia, young people were obsessed with swing dance, and they even listened to Western radio looking for music to dance to. Hungarian young people were admiring the West because "almost everyone in the West has their own car." For them, the situation in Romania was also disturbing as Western music and dance were popular among young people there. It was reported that the life goals for many young Romanians were merely family, money, and a decent social status.[48] Chinese leaders believed that Yugoslavia had already been "peacefully evolved" from socialism to "modern revisionism."[49] Thus, Yugoslavia usually appeared on Chinese media as a negative example of deliberately letting its youth be intoxicated by alternative lifestyles to maintain Josip

---

[47] "Zai tuan Guangzhou shiwei tan guanyu xiang Lei Feng xuexi de huodong he lianxiang dao de yidian wenti" 在团广州市委谈关于向雷锋学习的活动和联想到的一点问题 [Talking about the "Learning from Lei Feng" movement and some relating issues at the Guangzhou Municipal Youth League Committee], April 3, 1963, in *Hu Keshi jinian wenji* 胡克实纪念文集 [Collection of essays commemorating Hu Keshi], ed. Hu Keshi jinian wenji bianweihui 胡克实纪念文集编委会 (n.p., 2006), 239–240. Lei Feng was a soldier of the People's Liberation Army who died in an accident in 1962. He was made a role model by the CCP as the embodiment of communist morale with his unselfish commitment to the people and his loyalty to the Party and Mao. For a brief introduction to Lei Feng, see Harold M. Tanner, *China: A History*, vol. 2 (Indianapolis, IN: Hackett Publishing Company, Inc., 2010), 214.

[48] *Neibu cankao*, August 23, 1963.

[49] The nature of the Yugoslav regime became a spotlight during the Sino-Soviet split with the publication of the CCP's "third commentary on CPSU's open letter" entitled "Is Yugoslavia a Socialist Country" in September 1963. This article, along with the other eight "commentaries," influenced a great many young people across China through multiple propaganda channels. See Sun Peidong 孙沛东, "Shiting baoli: jiuping de shengchan chuanbo ji hongweibing yidai de jiyi" 视听暴力：''九评''的生产、传播及''红卫兵一代''的记忆 [Visual-auditory violence: the production and transmission of the "Nine Commentaries" and memories of the Red Guard generation], Harvard-Yenching Institute Working Paper Series, 2018.

Tito's rule. For example, on December 12, 1962, *People's Daily* introduced "the twelfth article exposing the reactionary appearance of the Tito Clique in Yugoslavia by the North Korean Central News Agency" in which Tito, who was depicted as "the faithful slave of the US imperialism," was intentionally importing "American lifestyle" through cultural channels including newspapers, magazines, radio programs, and films.[50] Hu Yaobang, the head of the Communist Youth League, said that Yugoslav young people were becoming "vulgar people" who "only care about life and dismiss politics." Rejecting the "revisionist" slogan that "the ultimate goal of socialism is individual happiness for everybody," Hu urged his colleagues to "raise young people's proletarian consciousness to a new level" during the ongoing "Learning from Lei Feng" movement.[51]

Apart from the potential breakdown of the communist belief in the Socialist Bloc, Chinese leaders also felt that they were facing real threats at home when they found that the Chinese youth were losing their interest in life under socialism. This mentality could be found in public discussions against young people's "wrongful" thoughts organized by different newspapers and journals during this period. In 1963, during the high tide of the movement to "learn from Lei Feng," *China Youth* launched a discussion about what kind of "view of happiness" (*xingfuguan* 幸福观) young people should have. This discussion, which was actually about the meaning of life, reflected the disagreements among young people over what kind of life they wanted to have even if they were all convinced by the official propaganda of Lei Feng. As a reader from Jiangsu Province wrote in his letter to the editors, if people follow Lei Feng's definition of happiness, they should feel happy when "devoting everything to communism." Some people, however, argued that the purpose of communism was to improve people's livelihood, and therefore, pursuing a better living standard ("eat well, dress well, and live well") itself was equivalent to pursuing communism, and this resonated with Lei Feng's spirit essentially.[52] Of course, most of the articles participating in this discussion criticized the "view of happiness" that happiness was equivalent to

---

[50] RMRB, December 12, 1962.

[51] RMRB, April 28, 1963.

[52] Hu Dongyuan 胡东渊, "Qingnian yinggai you shenmeyang de xingfuguan" 青年应该有什么样的幸福观 [What view of happiness should young people have], *Zhongguo qingnian* 7 (1963): 15–17.

eating well, dressing well, and living well. They argued that a communist view of happiness must have a spiritual ambition that abandoned hedonism because hedonism was incompatible with the socialist way of life. As a Shanghai worker said: "Eating and sleeping is the way of life of a pig. It won't be changed into the way of life of a human being by adding dressing and playing!"[53] From August to December 1963, the mouthpiece of the Beijing Municipal Party Committee organized a similar discussion on "how young people can lead an interesting life" to attack the growing individualism and hedonism among Beijing youth.[54]

Party officials also noticed that young people who were unable to stop pursuing alternative lifestyles and material comfort were involved in real "class struggle" cases in the early 1960s after Mao raised the issue of class and class struggle in a socialist country. According to the calculation of Beijing Municipal Public Security Bureau in an internally circulated report in the summer of 1963, Beijing had already become an arena of class struggle. During the first half of the year, the Beijing police uncovered eighty-five "counterrevolutionary cases" including posting slogans, organizing "counterrevolutionary small cliques," fleeing, writing letters to foreign enemies, and participating in religious groups. The Municipal Public Security Bureau found that among these "counterrevolutionaries," 42.2% were young people under twenty-five years old, and many of them engaged in "counterrevolutionary" activities because they were unsatisfied with their life and thought that they could have a better life in another country or without the rule of the Communist Party.[55] In the eyes of Party officials, even though other young people did not engage in "counterrevolutionary" activities, they were still involved in a "battle competing for the youth." In Quanyechang, one of Beijing's department stores, capitalists tried to "compete for the youth" with the Party by telling young workers there that their current life was tense and less comfortable than life before 1949.[56]

[53] *Zhongguo qingnian* 9 (1963): 22.

[54] *Qingnianren zenyang shenghuo caiyou yisi* 青年人怎样生活才有意思 [How can young people lead an interesting life] (Beijing: Beijing chubanshe, 1965).

[55] Shi gonganju 市公安局, "Jinnian shangbannian fangeming pohuai huodong reng buduan fasheng" 今年上半年反革命破坏活动仍不断发生 [Counterrevolutionary sabotage happened continuously in the first half of this year], in *Beijing gongzuo* 北京工作 [Work in Beijing], ed. Zhonggong Beijingshi weiyuanhui 中共北京市委员会, August 12, 1963.

[56] Shi caimaokou wufan bangongshi 市财贸口五反办公室, "Yichang duanbing xiangjie zhengduo qingnian de douzheng" 一场短兵相接争夺青年的斗争 [A close combat competing for the youth], *Beijing gongzuo*, August 12, 1963.

Facing the threat of a real "peaceful evolution" in China, Mao raised the issue of "developing revolutionary successors" (*peiyang geming jiebanren* 培养革命接班人) in June 1964 during a meeting convened in Beijing's Ming Tombs. Unlike the confident remarks, he made in 1959 during the climax of the Great Leap Forward on Dulles' previous speeches, this time Mao became less confident and more anxious. "The imperialists say that [transforming] our first generation is out of the question. The second generation is also impossible to be transformed. But they are hopeful to transform the third and the fourth generation. Will their hope come true? Will their words work?" Mao asked his colleagues and then answered by himself, "I hope that their words will not work. But it is possible that they will work. Khrushchev, the third generation of the Soviet Union, became revisionist. There might be revisionism here at home."[57] Mao's proposal and criteria of revolutionary successors were made public one month later in CCP's ninth commentary on CPSU "On Khrushchev's Phony Communism and Its Historical Lessons for the World" which cited Mao's words "to guarantee that our Party and country do not change their colour, we must not only have a correct line and correct policies but must train and bring up millions of successors who will carry on the cause of proletarian revolution."[58] This article also announced the famous five criteria of such successors:

> They must be genuine Marxist-Leninists and not revisionists like Khrushchev wearing the cloak of Marxism-Leninism.
>
> They must be revolutionaries who whole-heartedly serve the majority of the people of China and the whole world, and must not be like Khrushchev who serves both the interests of a handful of members of the privileged bourgeois stratum in his own country and those of foreign imperialism and reaction.

[57] "Guanyu junshi gongzuo luoshi yu peiyang geming jiebanren de jianghua" 关于军事工作落实与培养革命接班人的讲话 [Speeches on implementing military work and developing revolutionary successors], in *Mao Zedong sixiang wansui 1961–1968* 毛泽东思想万岁 1961–1968 [Long live Mao Zedong Thought, 1961–1968] (Wuhan, 1968), 119. See also Li Jie 李捷, "Mao Zedong fangzhi heping yanbian sixiang shi dui kexue shehui zhuyi lilun de zhongyao gongxian" 毛泽东防止和平演变思想是对科学社会主义理论的重要贡献 [Mao Zedong's idea on preventing peaceful evolution is an important contribution to the theory of scientific socialism], *Zhenli de zhuiqiu* 9 (1991): 9.

[58] "On Khrushchev's Phony Communism and Its Historical Lessons for the World," July 14, 1964, https://www.marxists.org/reference/archive/mao/works/1964/phnycom2.htm.

They must be proletarian statesmen capable of uniting and working together with the overwhelming majority...

They must be models in applying the Party's democratic centralism, must master the method of leadership based on the principle of "from the masses, to the masses," and must cultivate a democratic style and be good at listening to the masses...

They must be modest and prudent and guard against arrogance and impetuosity; they must be imbued with the spirit of self-criticism and have the courage to correct mistakes and shortcomings in their work.[59]

Anxiety about younger generation being incapable of continuing Mao's revolutionary course embedded in the five criteria was well received by China's young people, as they would face challenges in their everyday life.

Revolutionizing Everyday Ways of Life

Mao's reiteration of the existence of classes and class struggle as well as his concern for the dim future of successors of the Party's revolutionary career between 1962 and 1964 triggered another wave of political intrusion into people's everyday life. Although this intrusion was not carried out in a unified political campaign, it affected people's daily life in a more scattered way. Using the title of a discussion organized by the journal *China Youth* in 1964 about class struggle in everyday life, the major theme of the Party's everyday politics in the early 1960s was to "promote the proletarian and extinguish the bourgeois in the sphere of life."[60] In the 1950s, deviant lifestyles such as hooliganism were considered the practice of a small number of young people that would not have a fundamental influence on the regime. In the early 1960s, however, Party propagandists incorporated these activities into Mao's rhetoric of class struggle and examined them as a matter of principle and ideology connected with the fate of the communist movement. This reflected the Party leaders'

---

[59] "On Khrushchev's Phony Communism and Its Historical Lessons for the World," July 14, 1964, https://www.marxists.org/reference/archive/mao/works/1964/phnycom2.htm.

[60] "Zai shenghuo lingyu li yeyao 'xingwu miezi'" 在生活领域里也要"兴无灭资" [We should also 'promote and proletarian and extinguish the bourgeois' in the sphere of life], *Zhongguo qingnian* 18 (1964): 14.

increasing anxiety after the failures of the Great Leap Forward that the next generation was getting skeptical about the official ideology.

Although Mao discussed the issue of revolutionary successors in an ideological way with only several broad principles, in reality, Party officials focused mainly on young people's alternative lifestyles because these were the most noticeable differences between the ideal proletariats and the "backward youth." Instead of a revolution in political and economic structure, this symbolic class struggle in people's everyday life ended up imposing oppressive tyranny in the name of beautiful ideals. Specifically, Party officials were anxious about the tendency among young people to pursue material comfort and not wishing to fight for a utopian goal.

This tendency was not a new thing in the early 1960s. During the Great Leap Forward, the official propaganda machine criticized the "thought of mediocrity" (*zhongyou sixiang* 中游思想) as an opposition to the slogan of "aiming high" (*lizheng shangyou* 力争上游) required by the General Line for socialist construction.[61] This tendency was so persistent that even Liu Shaoqi was worried his own daughter might also fall into the trap of "thought of mediocrity" in the early 1960s. In his letter of advice celebrating his daughter's fourteenth birthday, Liu warned her not to become a "backward element" who "does not have an ambition, does not care about others, and only cares about what to eat, what to wear, and how to play." These kinds of young people, who were indulgent with individual and sensual pleasure, were only "satisfied with mediocrity" (*anyu zhongyou* 安于中游) and thus would never feel happy.[62] In 1965, the Party's propaganda machine started to criticize a new form of the "thought of mediocrity" among some educated youth called "Three *Guo* Thought" (*sanguo sixiang* 三过思想): Be passable in politics, be professional in expertise, and be good in life (*zhengzhi shang guode qu, yewu shang guode ying, shenghuo shang guode hao* 政治上过得去、业务上过得硬、生活上过得好).[63]

---

[61] See, for example, Yang Xiu 杨秀, "Huoshao zhongyou sixiang" 火烧中游思想 [Burn the thought of mediocrity], *Zhongguo qingnian* 22 (1959): 8–10.

[62] Liu Shaoqi, "Gei Liu Pingping de xin" 给刘平平的信 [Letter to Liu Pingping], May 9, 1963, in *Qingnian gongzuo wenxian xuanbian shang*, 559–560.

[63] Zheng Guang 郑洸, ed., *Zhongguo qingnian yundong liushi nian 1919–1979* 中国青年运动六十年 1919–1979 [Sixty years of youth movement in China, 1919–1979] (Beijing: Zhongguo qingnian chubanshe, 1990), 546.

From the CCP's perspective, mediocrity in ideology was accompanied by the pursuit of material comfort in young people's daily life, especially in their leisure time. *Never Forget*, a play that was famous in the early 1960s, became a reflection of the Party propagandists' anxiety over material comfort. As the play writer stated explicitly later, this play was directly aiming at young people's leisure time. "Workers only stay in their factories for eight hours. Ten hours at most if there are meetings. There are, however, twenty-four hours a day and they spend the rest of the time with their families or friends... The education they got in the day might be dissolved by what they learned in their family at night."[64]

The plot of the play is simple: a young worker named Ding Shaochun lives with his wife and mother-in-law after marriage. Influenced by his mother-in-law who used to own a small business, Ding starts to pay attention to food and clothing, and he becomes interested in hunting ducks in his leisure time to make extra money. This makes Ding absent-minded during his work hours and almost causes an accident. Finally, with the help of others, Ding realizes that his way of life is influenced by bourgeois thinking. He decides to correct his mistake and be a good successor of the proletarian revolution.[65] From late 1963 to January 1964, nearly 200,000 people in Beijing went to watch the play *Never Forget*, and according to a report on *Beijing Evening News*, there were still hundreds and thousands of people waiting for their tickets.[66]

From January 1964, *People's Daily* launched a propaganda campaign publicizing the play *Never Forget*. Most of the articles in *People's Daily* expressed the official aspiration to have a tighter grip on people's leisure time. For example, a cadre from an iron factory in Beijing wrote to *People's Daily* after watching the play, expressing the urgent need to revolutionize young workers' off duty hours: "During the class struggle, the bourgeoisie usually appear in an intangible form, and they first appear in leisure time and in dormitories...The life of a typical worker is: work for eight hours, sleep for eight hours, and have another eight hours for free activities. What do workers think and do in their leisure time, whether they are thinking about socialism or capitalism...is a big question for us

[64] Cong Shen 丛深, "Qianwan buyao wangji zhuti de xingcheng"《千万不要忘记》主题的形成 [The formation of the theme of *Never Forget*], *Xiju bao* 4 (1964): 27.

[65] Tang Xiaobing, *Yingxiong yu fanren de shidai*, 140.

[66] *Beijing wanbao*, January 29, 1964.

to ponder."[67] In the following months, the *People's Daily* organized a discussion entitled "How to Spend the Other Eight Hours," targeting leisure time directly. The contents of the discussion were quite similar to the 1951 "Should I Have Fun" discussion (discussed in Chapter 2), but this time it was organized on a much more authoritative platform in a very different time. The conclusion of the discussion, as summarized by the editor, was "leisure time should also be revolutionized."[68]

While similar plays offering "class education" purposes were produced, a novel titled *March Forward Without Hesitation* (*yongwang zhiqian* 勇往直前) published in 1961 was criticized for "publicizing bourgeois lifestyle" in 1964. As the first novel about the life of university students under the People's Republic, *March Forward Without Hesitation* was received by young people favorably.[69] The theme of the novel was actually about how university students were transformed into socialist new people who were in favor of collectivism through struggles with "bad elements" during their campus life.[70] In 1964, however, from the perspective of some critics, the author "vilified" campus life because there was no "class struggle" in his novel. Two students from Zhengzhou University wrote: "What does campus life depicted in *March Forward Without Hesitation* look like? They (i.e., students) are far away from the heated class struggle. They sing merrily and dance gracefully. They flirt with each other. They lead a hedonistic way of life like bourgeois young masters and ladies." This kind of life was nothing similar to the "life of socialist university students" in which "comrades criticize each other" with "serious ideological struggles."[71] Another critic thought that the head of the Communist Party branch in Department of Geography in the novel was corrupted because she "abandoned the cadre suit" and "wore a neat blouse with lattice and a

---

[67] RMRB, January 19, 1964.

[68] RMRB, April 8, 1964.

[69] Guizhousheng xiezuo xuehui 贵州省写作学会, ed., *Zhongguo dangdai xiezuo lilunjia* 中国当代写作理论家 [Writing theorists in contemporary China] (Guiyang: Guizhou renmin chubanshe, 1989), 46–47.

[70] Han Shui 汉水, *Yongwang zhiqian* 勇往直前 [March Forward Without Hesitation] (Tianjin: Baihua wenyi chubanshe, 1961).

[71] Liu Mingchuan 刘明川 and Bi Dianling 毕殿岭, "Yongwang zhiqian waiqu le daxue shenghuo"《勇往直前》歪曲了大学生活 [*March Forward Without Hesitation* vilified campus life in university], *Zhengzhou daxue xuebao* 4 (1964): 93–94.

brown skirt" instead. Because of the woeful leadership of this Party secretary, organized leisure activities that should have included educational purposes, such as get-togethers, New Year's Eve parties, and excursions, became "bourgeois clubs" that only included hedonism. This, according to the critic, "has no whiff of a Party secretary at all!"[72] This novel was labeled as a "poisonous weed" by the Party's Central Department of Propaganda in July 1964 and continued to be criticized publicly.[73]

Although the "revolutionization" of everyday life became a resounding theme in the early 1960s, for many young people, "revolutionization" itself was an empty slogan, especially when they were actually facing trivial matters such as housework. The question remained unanswered: What did "revolutionization" include? The organizer of the *People's Daily* discussion admitted that "we cannot solve all concrete problems during your leisure time in this discussion… As long as you arrange your leisure time with a revolutionary spirit, these concrete problems will be easy to solve." The "revolutionary spirit" denoted nothing more than doing something good to make people "healthy both physically and mentally."[74] An editorial published in *China Youth* in summer 1964 provided a more detailed discussion on the meaning of "revolutionization." By quoting Mao's 1939 speech "On the Orientation of the Youth Movement," the editorial repeated Mao's idea that "How should we judge whether a youth is a revolutionary? How can we tell? There can only be one criterion, namely, whether or not he is willing to integrate himself with the broad masses of workers and peasants and does so in practice. If he is willing to do so and actually does so, he is a revolutionary; otherwise, he is a non-revolutionary or a counter-revolutionary."[75] For editors of the *China Youth*, revolutionization remained an ideological matter in the sense that revolutionization meant the youth must "rely on working class as well as poor and lower-middle peasants; learn from them honestly; represent

---

[72] Hua Dai 华岱, "Yongwang zhiqian shi zenyang waiqu dangde lingdao de"《勇往直前》是怎样歪曲党的领导的 [How does *March Forward Without Hesitation* distort the leadership of the Party], *Hebei wenxue* 11 (1964): 66–67.

[73] Guizhousheng xiezuo xuehui, *Zhongguo dangdai xiezuo lilunjia*, 47.

[74] Guizhousheng xiezuo xuehui, *Zhongguo dangdai xiezuo lilunjia*, 47.

[75] "Qingnian geminghua de shouyao wenti" 青年革命化的首要问题 [The chief problem in the revolutionization of the youth], *Zhongguo qingnian* 12 (1964): 2. English translation of Mao's speech comes from https://www.marxists.org/reference/archive/mao/selected-works/volume-2/mswv2_14.htm.

their interests, serve them wholeheartedly, and stand with them forever in any occasions." Moreover, the youth must "be at one with the masses in their mind with workers and poor and lower-middle peasants" by "loving what they love and hating what they hate."[76]

In practice, however, the Party focused not on essential issues, but on some superficial symbols: the immediate impact of the revolutionization movement went not to their mental state, but to external differences (taste in haircut, clothing, and all elements regarding lifestyle) between young people and the "workers, lower and middle peasants" with whom they were supposed to incorporate themselves. As a then junior high school student in Beijing recalls, one of the most important changes during the revolutionization movement was the change in clothing style among her classmates: the girls "unconsciously" changed their colorful clothes into masculinized gray or blue shirts. One of her friends cut her long hair voluntarily to show that she was revolutionized.[77]

Meanwhile, the propaganda machine noticed the growing differentiation between young people and the "proletarians" in their lifestyle. In September 1964, *China Youth Daily* published a short article about a clash between peasants and a student from Beijing's Central Conservatory of Music when he participated in the "Four Cleanups" in a village. The student was said to spray cologne on himself every day because he could not bear the stinking smell of sweat from the farmers. The farmers were very disgusted with the student, and they told him: "Do you think you smell good after spraying cologne? You don't like the stench from us, but we don't like the stink from you either!" The author of the article criticized the student: "He cannot smell the dirty bourgeois things on his body and thinks that he smells good…They (i.e., the farmers) smell better than those with cologne!"[78]

---

[76] "Qingnian geminghua de shouyao wenti," *Zhongguo qingnian* 12 (1964): 2–3.

[77] Ye Weili 叶维丽, "Yisheng zai sikao" 一生在思考 [I have been pondering for my entire life], in *Huiyi yu fansi: hongweibing shidai fengyun renwu koushu lishi zhi'er* 回忆与反思: 红卫兵时代风云人物—口述历史之二 [Memories and reflections: oral interviews with famous people during the Red Guard Movement, vol. 2], ed. Mi Hedu 米鹤都 (Hong Kong: Zhongguo shuju youxian gongsi, 2011), 151. See also Weili Ye and Xiaodong Ma, *Growing Up in the People's Republic: Conversations Between Two Daughters of China's Revolution* (New York: Palgrave Macmillan, 2005), 62–63.

[78] *Zhongguo qingnian bao*, September 10, 1964.

5 ANXIETY ABOUT DIFFERENCE: POLITICIZATION ...   177

The Party officials in Beijing paid much attention to alternative ways of life among young people and in 1964, several rounds of investigations of young people's leisure activities were conducted by different government agencies. In the summer of 1964, a joint investigation group led by the Rural Work Department of the Beijing Municipal Party Committee submitted their report on the "atmosphere" (*fengqi* 风气) among educated youth who were sent to several farms and forestry centers in suburban Beijing and discovered "unhealthy thoughts and styles" displayed by young people there. According to their report, in a forestry center in the Ming Tombs area, young people were obsessed with "love songs" including songs from Soviet and Indian films. Some of them focused exceedingly on achieving a good physical appearance and a group of female workers even exchanged their clothes so that everyone could have more clothes to wear. A small number of male workers preferred swept-back hair and some even had their hair permed with fire-tongs. When criticized by a farmer about singing a love song in a "weird tune," a male worker retorted: "You know nothing, you bumpkin!"[79] In another forestry center, young workers did not work hard as their leaders hoped. They "went to work late, went to bed late, got up late, and went to meetings late," but "stopped working early."[80]

In urban Beijing, the Beijing Municipal Labor Union discovered elements of "bourgeois thinking, style and taste" among some healthcare workers in a hospital. The "bourgeois lifestyle" mentioned in their report included: (1) Western taste in daily life. Nurse Yang was in a relationship with an overseas Chinese doctor, and they liked to listen to jazz music, drink coffee and milk sent from abroad, and sometimes leaned on the window to enjoy the moon. The nurse often wished to learn some English from others and thought that English was fashionable. (2) Pay attention to clothing. Nurse Sun saved some money from her salary and purchased some good clothes since she started her job. Whenever she attended a meeting, she would choose a seat that could see a mirror. When others

---

[79] "Shisanling linchang huyu zaolindui qingnian zhigong zhong fengqi buzheng" 十三陵林场虎峪造林队青年职工中风气不正 [Unhealthy atmosphere prevails among young workers in Huyu tree planting team in Ming Tombs forestry center], July 2, 1964, BMA, 001-014-00850-002.

[80] "Baihuashan linchang shehui qingnian duo sixiang gongzuo boruo fengqi buzheng" 百花山林场社会青年多, 思想工作薄弱, 风气不正 [There are many unemployed youth in Baihuashan forestry center where the ideological work is weak and the atmosphere is unhealthy], July 2, 1964, BMA, 001-014-00850-008.

were discussing the "Nine Commentaries," she looked around and was intoxicated by her own appearance. (3) Live a "slack and loose" life. Nurse Hu liked to get up late on weekdays, and she would even get up at 10 am on Sundays. She usually walked in the corridor of her dormitory wearing only a bra, a "transparent top," and short underwear in the summer. She hung an "eight-inch big picture of herself leaning her head to one side" (*waibo bacun da xiangpian* 歪脖八寸大相片) on her wall and gazed at her picture alone. Although she did not have a lot of money, she did not like to eat coarse grain and regular food and would eat fruit every day after lunch.[81]

Revolution against people's styles as well as names of stores and roads was a noticeable feature of the Red Guard movement during the early stage of the Cultural Revolution. Before that, however, official-led discussions on alternative tastes in dress, haircut, and even photo style already prevailed in 1964. In this year, the propaganda machines in several major cities simultaneously launched a coordinated propaganda campaign against people's tastes in leisure choices with the goal of wiping out external differences and individual tastes.

In April 1964, the *Tianjin Evening News* initiated a discussion on "haircuts and related issues in life and ideology." A Communist Youth League cadre in the Tianjin Steel Plant wrote to the newspaper, expressing his concerns over some young people's appearance in his factory. In the letter, he said that some young workers liked to have swept-back hair with hair oil. When criticized by other workers for pursuing a bourgeois lifestyle, they replied: "This is a kind of 'beauty.' Where can you find bourgeois thinking? The diverse haircuts and good clothing style show that people's living standard has been increased. Why are you bothered with these trivial matters in life?" The youth cadre suggested that the newspaper organize a discussion to let people "make a clear distinction between right and wrong" and become a revolutionary successor of communism.[82] On the same page, another young female worker, who liked to perm her hair with new styles, wrote in her letter to the

---

[81] "Jishuitan yiyuan bufen hushi zhongji renyuan yeyu shenghuo zhong cunzai zhe yanzhong de zichanjieji sixiang zuofeng qingdiao" 积水潭医院部分护士、中技人员业余生活中存在着严重的资产阶级思想、作风、情调 [Some nurses and media level mechanics in Jishuitan Hospital have severe bourgeois thinking, style and taste in their leisure activities], December 8, 1964, BMA, 079-001-00450-0061.

[82] *Tianjin wanbao*, April 2, 1964.

newspaper: "The goal of our revolution is to increase people's living standard, isn't it? Now I have the conditions to dress better and have a beautiful haircut. Why should it become a problem? How can these trivial matters be connected with pursuing bourgeois lifestyle?"[83] In the following weeks, the newspaper published more letters from its readers. Like many other organized discussions in China, the editor already had their answer in mind beforehand. As they concluded, the discussion on the issue of haircut "is actually a discussion on promoting the proletarian and extinguishing the bourgeois by showcasing people's thoughts from actual-existing examples" (*zhua huo de sixiang* 抓活的思想). As another two articles next to the editor's note stated, the style of hair was a matter of aesthetic taste linked to different classes. The proletariat should have an aesthetic taste different from that of other classes, which usually aimed to differentiate themselves from the working people. Thus, young people must have a "proletarian aesthetic view," such as a preference for tidiness, strength, simplicity, and sublimity.[84]

Also in April 1964, the *Beijing Evening News* organized a discussion entitled "Whom Should Photo Studios Serve" which criticized the "remaining bourgeois aesthetics" among photographers. According to the newspaper, "a small number of" photographers in Beijing were enthusiastic about taking pictures of people "behaving affectedly" (*niuni zuotai* 忸怩作态) and "leaning their heads" (*waitou xielian* 斜头歪脸) because they thought that this style was "art." Some customers even required photographers to take their pictures in this style. A worker summarized the display windows of many photo studios as "three lots and one few": lots of pictures of actors and actresses, lots of pictures of young women, lots of pictures of children wearing expensive clothes, and few pictures of workers, peasants, and soldiers. A middle school student even asked a photo studio to remove the pictures of people dressing expensive clothes from its display window because they could not express people's new fashion of being "diligent and thrifty."[85]

The discussion on what styles photo studios should offer was only a prelude of a campaign against display windows in many stores across Beijing. According to a report in *Beijing Evening News* in October 1964,

[83] *Tianjin wanbao*, April 2, 1964.
[84] *Tianjin wanbao*, April 12, 1964.
[85] *Beijing wanbao*, April 7, 1964.

Beijing's commercial agencies checked and rectified display windows of thousands of stores to eradicate "evil legacies of feudalism and capitalism." The Beijing Department Store replaced mannequins that were dressed like "bourgeois ladies" with domestically produced industrial products including radios, cameras, shirts, and scientific equipment under a banner of "rely on ourselves and go all out to achieve success." These products were held by two giant hands, which were said to "symbolize the heroic mental outlook of Chinese workers." The head of the Party Committee in the Xidan Store organized display window designers to study Mao's "Talks at the Yan'an Forum on Literature and Art" and did not reveal their new design until they thought that it could "reflect the outlook of the socialist era."[86] There was also a name-changing campaign during which the names of some products that were considered inappropriate by the authorities were changed. For example, "foreign liquor" (*yangjiu* 洋酒) was replaced by "domestically produced famous liquor" (*guochan mingjiu* 国产名酒), "Number One Scholar cake" (*zhuangyuan bing* 状元饼) was replaced by "date cake" (*zaoni bing* 枣泥饼), and "sweetheart cake" (*laopo bing* 老婆饼) was replaced by "Guangdong crispy cake" (*Guangdong subing* 广东酥饼).[87]

Another discussion on people's taste came from Shanghai. In June 1964, Shanghai Municipal Party Committee's mouthpiece *Liberation Daily* initiated a discussion on "outlandish clothes" (*qizhuang yifu* 奇装异服), which started from a reader's letter praising workers in a tailor shop who refused to make "outlandish clothes" for a customer. According to this letter, a female customer wanted to make a pair of trousers with narrow legs, and she was unsatisfied with the trousers after trying them on. She complained that the tailor did not meet the customer's needs. The tailor, however, told her that "in a socialist enterprise, we cannot make products harmful to social decency." The editor of *Liberation Daily* confirmed that the tailor was right not to make "outlandish clothes" for the customer. As the editor wrote, "this is not a trivial matter about how to deal with a certain clothing style. It is a big issue on whether to resist bourgeois thinking and bourgeois lifestyle."[88]

---

[86] *Beijing wanbao*, October 20, 1964.
[87] *Beijing wanbao*, October 30, 1964.
[88] *Jiefang ribao*, June 7, 1964.

In October, the Beijing authorities also planned to require tailors not to make "outlandish clothes." The Beijing Municipal Repair Management Bureau drafted a detailed regulation on the style of people's clothes: (1) The leg of male trousers should not be narrower than 6.5 *cun*; (2) the leg of female trousers should not be narrower than 5.8 *cun*; (3) the crotch of male trousers should not be narrower than 9 *cun*; (4) the length of the collar of female jackets should not exceed 4 *cun*; (5) the length of the collar of female coats should not exceed 4.5 *cun*; (6) the wideness of the neckline of female blouses and one-pieces should not exceed 2 *cun*.[89]

These radical plans to revolutionize people's everyday life by wiping out individual tastes faced opposition even among Party officials. In Shanghai, for example, the bombardment on "outlandish clothes" did cause inconvenience to some customers. Party officials in Shanghai raised three "boundaries" (between enriching people's life and promoting simple life; between developing individual features and resisting bourgeois lifestyle, and between "new" and "outlandish") to limit the impact of the movement to resist "outlandish clothes." The Shanghai authorities even encouraged stores to develop their own features and should not follow the same pattern.[90] In Beijing, the draft regulation submitted by the Beijing Municipal Bureau on Repairing Trade Management did not meet an enthusiastic welcome from the top. One official made three comments one month later, stressing that while the government certainly should not encourage "outlandish clothes," there would not be a strict ban and if customers insisted on making "outlandish clothes," tailors had no reason to refuse them.[91] In March 1965, during a working conference organized by Beijing Municipal Youth League Committee, the youth cadres criticized the tendency of blaming every practice that some people did not like as "bourgeois thinking" or "bourgeois lifestyle." In the internal materials distributed during the meeting, there were several examples of "elevating

---

[89] "Beijing shi xiuli shiye guanli ju guanyu weihu shehui fengshang zhunbei zai fuzhuang jiagong hangye shixing jujue jiagong qizhuang yifu de qingshi" 北京市修理事业管理局关于维护社会风尚准备在服装加工行业试行拒绝加工奇装异服的请示 [Asking for instructions from Beijing Municipal Repair Management Bureau on the plan to maintain social decency and not to make outlandish clothes in tailor shops], October 17, 1964, BMA, 075-001-00174-001. 1 *cun* equals to 1.3122 inches.

[90] *Neibu cankao*, September 15, 1964.

[91] "Guanyu fuzhuang jiagong hangye ruhe duidai jiagong qizhuang yifu wenti de jidian yijian" 关于服装加工行业如何对待加工奇装异服问题的几点意见 [Several opinions on how to deal with outlandish clothes], November 24, 1964, BMA, 075-001-00174-012.

trivial matters to the level of principle arbitrarily," which included a doctor who was denounced as pursuing a bourgeois lifestyle because he liked to wear different trousers and polish his shoes, a nurse who was forced to remove paintings from the wall in her dormitory during the movement to revolutionize dormitories, and a young man who was refused to join the Youth League because of his long hair.[92]

POLITICIZATION OF LEISURE EXPERIENCED

How was the CCP's politicization of people's leisure choices perceived by young people in the early 1960s? To what extent did the movement to revolutionize everyday life affect or not affect young people's daily activities, especially what they chose to do in their leisure time? Did the Party succeed in wiping out differences between young people's actual way of life and the ideal communist way of life? In this section, I will approach these questions based mainly on reminiscences of several Beijing youth to examine the real effect of the Party's regulation of people's everyday way of life.

It is certain that the Party's radical plans to wipe out any individual taste did influence young people in Beijing in the early 1960s both physically and mentally, and many of them did not regard it coercive. In this sense, the Party achieved something by politicizing people's leisure choices: establishing a new militarized and uniform style of life by wiping out diverse tastes in young people's minds. Ye Weili became a junior high school student at the famous Beijing Normal University Girls' High School in 1963 and for her, the most impressive thing during her life at the Girls' High was what she called the "revolutionizing movement," which was "different from anything" she had experienced before.[93] As mentioned above, Ye, along with her classmates, replaced their colorful clothes with plain grey or blue shirts. Notably, none of Ye and her classmates realized what was going on with their appearance. The whole

---

[92] "Tuanshiwei gongzuo huiyi jianbao di shisan qi" 团市委工作会议简报 (第13期) [Brief report from the working conference of the Beijing Municipal Youth League Committee, no. 13], March 30, 1965, BMA, 100-001-00937-0059.

[93] Weili Ye and Xiaodong Ma, *Growing Up in the People's Republic*, 56.

process was so "natural" that nobody felt that they were being deprived of the right to wear colorful clothes.[94]

Also in 1963, Ye's friend Ma Xiaodong became a junior high school student at Beijing's No. 8 Girls' High School. Compared with Ye, Ma was more fascinated with beautiful things. As she recalls, she would be "thrilled by the crown and cloak worn by the princess" when watching a foreign film. She liked to wear "beautiful women clad in traditional Chinese costumes" and wear her hair in braids. During the movement to revolutionize everyday life, she had her hair cut short totally out of her own will. She stopped wearing colorful clothes and would prefer clothes with patches, which had become a new fashion among young people during that time.[95]

Boys in Beijing No. 4 High School experienced a similar trend. Chen Kaige entered No. 4 High School in fall 1965. Living in the milieu of the Mao cult, Chen felt that the Chairman's own lifestyle and writings occupied his leisure time and way of life. On many Sundays, Chen and his classmates stayed in their classroom, reading *Selected Works of Mao Zedong* and discussing issues including "revolution," "class," and "dictatorship" in their self-organized "study group of Chairman Mao's works."[96] During that time, young students were keen on imitating the lifestyle of young Mao Zedong, and their understanding of the Chairman's lifestyle was reading and exercising. As Chen recalls, a great number of students in No. 4 High School tried to imitate this imaginary Mao. They "had crewcuts, holding a book in their armpit, and wore very plain clothes. Some had patches even if the clothes were new. Some students did not wear socks even in the winter and did not fix their shoes even if there were holes." In the afternoon, many students walked out of their classroom to exercise on the playground or debate with others over philosophical issues by reciting the works of Marx and Lenin. The food in the school's dining hall was simple, but students paid little attention to food quality.[97]

---

[94] Weili Ye and Xiaodong Ma, *Growing Up in the People's Republic*, 63. See also Ye Weili, "Yisheng zai sikao," in Mi Hedu, *Huiyi yu fansi*, vol. 2, 151.

[95] Weili Ye and Xiaodong Ma, *Growing Up in the People's Republic*, 62.

[96] Chen Kaige 陈凯歌, *Wode qingchun huiyilu* 我的青春回忆录 [Memoir of my youth] (Beijing: Zhongguo renmin daxue chubanshe, 2009), 35–36.

[97] Chen Kaige, *Wode qingchun huiyilu*, 36–37. See also Chen Kaige, "Qingchun jian" 青春剑 [Sword of youth], in Beidao 北岛, Cao Yifan 曹一凡, and Weiyi 维一, eds., *Baofengyu de jiyi 1965-1970 nian de Beijing sizhong* 暴风雨的记忆: 1965-1970 年的北

While the Party succeeded in dictating physical appearance and even behaviors of some young people, for other young students, the austere way of life favored by the Party became a real fashion in their mind. Ma Xiaodong recalls, the biggest influence of the movement to revolutionize everyday life was that she should "work hard, live simply, and break with the bourgeois thinking of gluttony, pleasure-seeking and getting dressed up." For her, "only rich ladies who love leisure, hate hard work, and live idly would adore beautiful things and like to get dressed up."[98] The Party's attempt to wipe out differences between different people's appearance also succeeded in the sense that people became highly aware of any dressing or haircut that was distinctive. As mentioned at the beginning of this chapter, the junior high school student Zhang Baolin showed his vigilance and disgust in his diary in early 1966 toward his classmates who liked to get dressed up and use hair oil. Ma Xiadong also felt "disgusted" when she noticed someone who was "gorgeously dressed" (*huazhi zhaozhan* 花枝招展).[99]

When the famous writer Lao Gui (Ma Bo) was a junior high school student (1960–1963), he once questioned one of his classmates: "Do you really need to wear your hair parted?"[100] Throughout Lao Gui's high school years (1960–1966), he always found the style of his classmates or even his relatives too "distinctive" (*ciyan* 刺眼 or *zhayan* 扎眼) and linked their style to "bourgeois thinking." For example, when he entered senior high school in 1963, he judged his new classmates by their clothes. He considered that a boy who always wore a fashionable blue coat had "strong petty-bourgeois sentiment" because his coat was not "proletarian." A girl usually wore very plain clothes, but she had a very "distinctive" woolen coat in the winter. The colorful clothes worn by repatriated overseas Chinese students from Indonesia were also "distinctive."[101] The sense of not being different from others became prevalent in

京四中 [Memories of the thunderstorm: Beijing No. 4 High School from 1965 to 1970] (Hong Kong: Oxford University Press, 2011), 68–69.

[98] Ye Weili, *Dongdang de qingchun: hongse dayuan de nü'er men* 动荡的青春: 红色大院的女儿们 [Turbulent youth: daughters of red courtyards] (Beijing: Xinhua chubanshe, 2008), 87.

[99] Ye Weili, *Dongdang de qingchun*, 87.

[100] Lao Gui 老鬼, *Xue yu tie* 血与铁 [Blood and iron] (Beijing: Xinxing chubanshe, 2010), 129.

[101] Lao Gui, *Xue yu tie*, 129–131.

people's minds. As recalled by an interviewee who was born in the early 1950s, from his perspective, the term "bourgeois lifestyle" only meant something "different" from ordinary people.[102]

Compared with direct ideological indoctrinations that took place simultaneously with the movement to politicize people's everyday way of life, the Party's project to nurture people who "looked like" revolutionary successors was more effective in the sense that although people who had a certain extent of independent thought might not embrace direct ideological indoctrinations wholeheartedly, they readily adopted the new proletarian clothing fashion. Ye Weili's experience is an interesting example. As she recalls, as a young girl in the early 1960s, she started to feel suspicious about some practices of ideological indoctrination such as asking students to criticize their own parents publicly.[103] Nevertheless, even though she self-identified as being "out of tune with the times," she still did not consider the practice of replacing colorful clothes as a serious matter during that time. She did not realize the drastic transformation in her clothing style until she found and compared two old photos of her classmates taken respectively in 1963 and 1965 several decades later.[104]

To be sure, it was impossible for the Party to wipe out all elements of "bourgeois thinking" and "bourgeois lifestyle" during its politicization of people's leisure choices. This was because the meaning of "bourgeois lifestyle" was so ambiguous that there were disagreements among Party officials when facing specific behaviors of the youth. Another reason was theoretical: although Party propagandists constantly connected "trivial matters in everyday life" (*shenghuo xiaoshi* 生活小事) with big ideological issues by regarding these trivial matters as the first frontline to bear the brunt of a potential attack from the bourgeoisie, this theory itself had some internal contradictions as expressed in the lives of young people. Those who were condemned as hedonists or to have practiced a bourgeois lifestyle might be supporters of the Party's orthodox lifestyle or ideology at the same time. Here is an example from an article published by *China Youth* during a 1961 discussion on "how to be a revolutionary during the period of construction":

---

[102] Interviewee 1.

[103] Weili Ye and Xiaodong Ma, *Growing Up in the People's Republic*, 59.

[104] Weili Ye and Xiaodong Ma, *Growing Up in the People's Republic*, 63.

I think that working hard during working hours means doing well in revolution… Apart from necessary political studies, we should have colourful and diverse leisure activities such as watching movies, going to theaters, and practicing singing or performing in clubs. We do not need to use "devoting everything we have to the communist enterprise" as our slogan every day.[105]

This article was apparently a "negative example" used by the journal to arouse more discussions by demonstrating an opinion that was obviously not in accordance with the official propaganda. The author expressed his idea that compared to the revolutionary years, people should have more time to entertain themselves in peaceful times. Although this kind of idea was in danger of being criticized as hedonism in the early 1960s, we should notice that those leisure activities he mentioned were precisely the "right" and "healthy" activities that the Party wanted them to do. In other words, even though he had some ideas that were not favored by the Party in a particular context, his way of life had already been forged by the Party's "temporal politics" that aimed to train people to do the right things in a right place in their leisure time (see Chapter 3).

Lao Gui's memoir depicts another example of a qualified revolutionary successor who had some elements of "bourgeois lifestyle." Zhang Junman, who was the same boy yelled at by the young Lao Gui for wearing his hair parted, was actually the head of the Youth League branch in his class. In many aspects, Zhang was an antithesis of Lao Gui, although Lao Gui considered himself the revolutionary one. Lao Gui did not like Zhang's haircut because he thought that nobody from the proletarian class would wear their hair parted. Lao Gui liked to imitate the heroes in revolutionary novels while Zhang did not. Zhang even thought that Pavel Korchagin, the hero of the Soviet novel *How the Steel Was Tempered*, had many weaknesses.[106] Despite so many elements of the "bourgeois lifestyle" (from the perspective of Lao Gui), Zhang was

---

[105] Han Yang 汉阳, "Wu tiaojian xianshen geming de yuanze buneng zuowei jianshe shiqi de xingdong kouhao" 无条件献身革命的原则不能作为建设时期的行动口号 [The principle of devoting life to the revolution unconditionally should not be the slogan during the period of construction], *Zhongguo qingnian* 10 (1961): 22–23.

[106] The Soviet novel *How the Steel Was Tempered* became popular and influential among Chinese readers since the 1950s and its protagonist Pavel Korchagin was symbolic embodiment of the socialist "new man." See Donghui He, "Coming of Age in the Brave New World: The Changing Reception of *How the Steel Was Tempered* in the People's Republic

ideologically adamant about communism: he would read anti-revisionist articles published in *People's Daily* very carefully whenever he got the newspaper and then exchange his ideas with Lao Gui.[107]

DIFFERENTIATION DERIVED FROM POLITICIZATION

Although the Party strived to avoid differentiation in lifestyles between youth and the proletariat, a hidden and unexpected result derived from the Party's plan to revolutionize young people's everyday life: the differentiation between children of officials (*ganbu zidi* 干部子弟) and youth from other family backgrounds. Under the façade of uniform plain clothes and haircut, children of officials in Beijing began to form their own circles. The formation of these circles could be attributed firstly to encouragement from their schools. Children of officials could attend events organized exclusively for them, usually in their leisure time.

The first kind of these events was special meetings or study sessions. As a student at the Tsinghua University High School recalls, from the second half of 1964, his school started to organize some "special education" for children of officials. Sometimes, they were summoned to come together on Saturday afternoons to engage in political study. Through this channel, children of officials could get information faster than their classmates. For example, in 1965, they learned about Mao Zedong's conversations with his nephew Mao Yuanxin during the special study sessions.[108] They also learned about Mao's conversation with his niece Wang Hairong from the same channel.[109] This practice did not exist solely in the Tsinghua

---

of China," in *China Learns from the Soviet Union, 1949–Present*, ed. Thomas P. Bernstein and Hua-yu Li (Lanham, MD: Lexington Books, 2010), 393–420.

[107] Lao Gui, *Xue yu tie*, 112–113.

[108] Bu Dahua 卜大华, "Wo suo zhidao de Hongweibing" 我所知道的红卫兵 [The Red Guard movement I know], in *Huiyi yu fansi: hongweibing shidai fengyun renwu koushu lishi zhi'er* 回忆与反思：红卫兵时代风云人物—口述历史之一 [Memories and reflections: oral interviews with famous people during the Red Guard Movement, vol. 1], ed. Mi Hedu 米鹤都 (Hong Kong: Zhongguo shuju youxian gongsi, 2011), 29. In 1964, Mao had two conversations with his nephew about his opinions on education, class struggle, and revolutionary successors. These opinions were frequently cited by the Red Guards during the Cultural Revolution.

[109] Li Weidong 李伟东, *Qinghua fuzhong gao 631 ban (1963–1968)* 清华附中高631班 (1963–1968) [Senior Class No. 631 in Tsinghua University High School], (New York: Cozy Publishing House, 2012), 44.

University High School. In the Beijing Normal University Girls' High School, the school also held a meeting for students from officials' families in the auditorium in which the deputy principal talked about the special responsibilities these students had as offspring of officials. In Beijing No. 4 High School, such meetings were held in their classroom when classes were over on weekends. During this time, children from official families would remain in their seats while others had to leave. Students from other family backgrounds could only guess what happened through the solemn facial expressions of children of officials when they left their classroom after the meeting.[110] This kind of event fostered an intangible differentiation between children of officials and students from other family backgrounds in which a sense of superiority among children of officials was generated.[111]

The second kind of these events was leisure activities. The Tsinghua University High School organized students to attend military training in the Military Engineer Club and then formed a militia shooting team consisting mainly of children from official families. According to Wan Bangru, then principal of the school, although students from other family backgrounds also participated in the school's shooting team, the majority of the team members came from official families.[112] Apart from the shooting team, there were other militia groups attended only by children of officials, such as telegraph teams and militia artillery.[113] There was also such a militia shooting team in the Beijing Normal University Girls' High School.[114] Students from other family backgrounds could feel the difference between them and children of officials in their leisure activities. A student complained bluntly when he was interviewed several decades later: "They (i.e., children of officials) ...took militia training. What the

---

[110] Chen Kaige, *Wode qingchun huiyilu*, 41. See also Chen Kaige, "Qingchun jian," in Beidao, Cao Yifan, and Weiyi, *Baofengyu de jiyi*, 70.

[111] Weili Ye and Xiaodong Ma, *Growing Up in the People's Republic*, 55–56. Not all schools in Beijing held such special meetings for children of officials. Ye Weili's friend Ma Xiaodong could recall such events in her school. See Weili Ye and Xiaodong Ma, *Growing Up in the People's Republic*, 56.

[112] Li Weidong, *Qinghua fuzhong gao 631 ban (1963–1968)*, 47.

[113] Bu Dahua, "Wo suo zhidao de Hongweibing," in Mi Hedu, *Huiyi yu fansi*, vol. 1, 29.

[114] Ye Weili, "Yisheng zai sikao," in Mi Hedu, *Huiyi yu fansi*, vol. 2, 157–158.

hell could you do? We only had one military training in a summer break and did not have other activities. This really hurt my self-respect."[115]

The differences in leisure activities led to the emergence of small friendship groups that would in turn affect young people's patterns of leisure and how they positioned themselves in early 1960s China.[116] Children of officials tended to hang out in their leisure time with others from the same family background. This tendency was vividly reflected in the diary of Song Bolin, who was then a senior student at the Tsinghua University High School. In his diary on January 26, 1966, Song recorded a day during his winter break. On that day, he went to Tiananmen Square along with "children of revolutionary officials" (*gegan zidi* 革干子弟), and they took a lot of pictures together. In the afternoon, they went to Beijing Agricultural Exhibition Center together to watch an exhibition on Dazhai.[117] Song felt that he was more "natural" and "pleasant" with other children of officials, so in March, before he went to the Summer Palace with students from other family backgrounds, he recorded his thoughts in his diary: "Before I went, I learned that I would be the only child of officials. Should I go? Honestly speaking, I did not really want to go with them because I would feel less natural and pleasant." Song, however, still went to the Summer Palace with his classmates only for a practical reason: "Chairman Mao teaches us that we must unite and work with the majority. If I cannot jump out of my small circle [of children of officials], how can I become a revolutionary successor?" To his surprise, he had fun during the excursion.[118]

---

[115] Li Weidong, *Qinghua fuzhong gao 631 ban (1963–1968)*, 45.

[116] On theory of how leisure acts can affect people's self-identity, see Eleni Dimou and Jonathan Ilan, "Taking Pleasure Seriously: The Political Significance of Subcultural Practice," *Journal of Youth Studies* 21, no. 1 (2018): 9–10.

[117] Song Bolin 宋柏林, *Hongweibing xingshuai lu: Qinghua fuzhong lao Hongweibing shouji* 红卫兵兴衰录—清华附中老红卫兵手记 [Ups and downs of the Red Guard: diary of an old Red Guard in Tsinghua University High School] (Hong Kong: Desai chuban youxian gongsi, 2006), 42–43.

[118] Song Bolin, *Hongweibing xingshuailu*, 54. Three months later, however, after the outbreak of the Cultural Revolution, Song thought that his alienation with students from other family backgrounds was justified. He thought that now that the school had been occupied with bourgeois and petty bourgeois elements, feeling at ease in this school could only show that he had been ideologically assimilated by his classmates with bad family backgrounds. See Song's diary on June 22, 1966, in *Hongweibing xingshuailu*, 86–87.

The sense of privilege and mission was reflected by the practice of collective reading of an article entitled "A Letter Full of Revolutionary Affection" (*Yifeng chongman geming ganqing de xin* 一封充满革命感情的信) in early 1966. Written by a young man named Song Xinlu from an official family, this letter was said to be very popular among many students and was, therefore, published by *China Youth Daily* on January 11, 1966.[119] The recipient of the original letter was another child from an official family and in this letter, Song Xinlu raised the question of "what kind of people should our children of revolutionary officials become." Song stressed the duty of children of officials by emphasizing that "if we say children of officials are different from others, we mean that we grew up in the bosom of the Party and were raised all by the dear Party herself. Now that the Party educated us more, we should become politically mature earlier than others, raise our ideological consciousness faster than others, and shoulder burdens heavier than others… We must succeed the revolutionary enterprise from our parents and shall not lose the big banner of revolution from our hands."[120]

Although Song Xinlu's letter was published so that everyone could read it, it was the children of officials who felt strong sympathy from this letter. According to Song Bolin's diary, the "children of revolutionary officials" in his former class in Guangzhou (Song Bolin transferred from Guangzhou to Beijing in 1965 with his parents) convened a meeting in their leisure time to read Song Xinlu's letter together, and everybody burst into tears.[121] In Ye Weili's memory, Song Xinlu's letter, along

---

[119] *Zhongguo qingnian bao*, January 11, 1966. Song Xinlu (宋心鲁) is the son of Song Yangchu (宋养初) and Yang Bin (杨滨). Both of his parents joined the Chinese Communist Party after the outbreak of the Sino-Japanese War. After 1949, Song Yangchu became one of the leaders of the country's economic planning agency, while Yang Bin worked as an educator. By 1966, Yang Bin was the principal of the Beijing No. 4 High School. For information about Song Yangchu, see the obituary published on the *People's Daily* on November 17, 1984. For information about Yang Bin, see Song Xinlu, "Beijing sizhong: wode muxiao, wode muqin" 北京四中—我的母校, 我的母亲 [Beijing No. 4 High School: my alma mater, my mother], July 23, 2017, https://difangwenge.org/forum.php?mod=viewthread&tid=14854&highlight=%CB%CE%D0%C4%C2%B3.

[120] *Zhongguo qingnian bao*, January 11, 1966.

[121] Song Bolin, *Hongweibing xingshuailu*, 40. Song Bolin learned about this issue from a letter written by his former classmate received on January 18, 1966. Considering the speed of mail delivery, it was highly possible that the letter was spread to Guangzhou through channels of other students from official families and was then read by his classmates before it was published.

with the special meetings for children of officials that she attended in her school, aroused their sense of mission that they had special responsibility for the revolution.[122] Another student from an official family linked Song Xinlu's letter to the "unsettled" (*zaodong* 躁动) sentiment among many children of officials before the Cultural Revolution as they started to think about the question of "we should study hard, but for whom do we study hard?"[123]

CONCLUSION: THE LIMITS OF POLITICIZATION

Studies of lifestyle have concluded that as a set of routine choices of everyday practices including but not limited to clothes, food, home decoration, and leisure pastimes, everyday way of life can signify people's self-identity of who they are or who they want to be.[124] People's leisure choices (including both activities and tastes) can thus reflect the differentiation between different groups of people. In the case of China, the Chinese Communist Party, with its goal of establishing a classless egalitarian utopia, was vigilant about any form of potential social stratification. In the early 1960s, within the context of the global Cold War, Mao raised the issue of class struggle to prevent the country from being peacefully evolved. Therefore, the Party became anxious over alternative and distinctive ways of life practiced by its would-be revolutionary successors because it regarded these lifestyles as signs of alienation. The Party, for its part, wished to train more qualified revolutionary successors by eradicating representing elements of differentiation such as dress and haircut to prevent its young people from being corrupted by "bourgeois lifestyles." The Party's project to revolutionize people's everyday life was carried out in a highly politicized manner, meaning that anything in people's everyday life would be put under the spotlight of class struggle. This project aimed to extinguish external differences, and it did influence the lifestyle of many young people in the sense that they abandoned colorful clothes or cut their hair short out of their own will as a new fashion.

---

[122] Ye Weili, *Dongdang de qingchun*, 86.

[123] Wang Jiyu 王冀豫, "Beifu sharen de zize" 背负杀人的自责 [I blame myself for homicide], *Yanhuang chunqiu* 5 (2010): 75.

[124] Laura Portwood-Stacer, *Lifestyle Politics and Radical Activism* (New York: Bloomsbury, 2013), 4.

The CCP's utopian ambition of achieving a classless society through the politicization of leisure had its limits. First, those with elements of bourgeois lifestyle might not be ideologically alienated from the Party's general doctrines after having experienced the Party's all-pervasive regulation and propaganda for many years. Some might even be ardent supporters of the Party's great enterprise. Second, while the Party could celebrate its achievement in abolishing superficial differences as people began to wear uniform clothes, have similar haircuts, or even take pictures of the same style, this achievement was only superficial. The movement to revolutionize people's everyday lives brought about, or deepened, another differentiation, which was the differentiation between children of officials and youth from other family backgrounds. This differentiation generated from various kinds of organized activities designed exclusively for children of officials during their leisure time, and it finally led to small circles or friendship groups of children of officials.

CHAPTER 6

Exiting the Revolution: Alternative Ways of Life and the Institutionalization of Leisure, 1966–1976

It was a sunny Monday in the summer of 1968. Chen Huanren, a Peking University student, found that he was talking about swimming with an official in Kunming Lake at the Summer Palace. The lake was swarmed with swimmers. Workers, students, officials, and residents nearby, who had never met before, were chatting with each other while enjoying themselves in the lake. "The Cultural Revolution is indeed unprecedentedly good," said the official when he was swimming toward the Dragon King Temple beside Chen. "Doing physical exercises, bearing children, playing poker, and traveling across the country. It is indeed unprecedentedly good!" "Don't you need to participate in political movements in your work unit?" asked Chen. "That's their business. They do not allow me to join the revolution, so I have to be a bystander," answered the official.[1]

Like this official, many people stopped participating in political movements during the Cultural Revolution and chose to live alternatively instead. Reflecting on this increasingly acknowledged form of youth subculture, historian Ye Weili provides a metaphoric interpretation: "The revolution had exits. More and more people left the revolution from

---

[1] Chen Huanren 陈焕仁, *Hongweibing riji* 红卫兵日记 [The diary of a Red Guard] (Hong Kong: Chinese University Press, 2006), 544–545.

these exits by not participating in the movement, especially when factional struggles became increasingly fierce."[2]

Ye's metaphor recalls Albert Hirschman's famous thesis on exit and voice. For Hirschman, both "exit (the choice of leaving an organization or not buying a firm's products)" and "voice (the direct expression of dissatisfaction)" are means for customers to express their grievances when they are unsatisfied with the deterioration in performances of firms or organizations.[3] Although this theory applies primarily to economic activities, Hirschman later used a refined version of his theory to analyze the downfall of the German Democratic Republic, when he argued that "exit (out-migration) and voice (protest demonstrations against the regime) worked in tandem and reinforced each other, achieving jointly the collapse of the regime."[4]

Similar to Hirschman's theory, a common explanation of why people exited the revolutionary path and lived alternatively during the Cultural Revolution is to view youth subcultures as a means of resistance against the regime. Radical rebels denounced "bystanders" (*xiaoyao pai* 逍遥派) in Red Guard tabloids for sabotaging the revolution.[5] Some were even criminalized by the state for attending "underground libraries," "underground concerts," "underground studios," or "underground marriage partner introductory services" in the early 1970s.[6] Interestingly, later scholarly research echoed the politicized interpretation of the Cultural Revolution to some extent. For example, Qian Liqun praises the bystanders by stressing that "although their activities were seemingly apolitical on the surface, they resisted and dissolved the mainstream ideology of the Cultural Revolution that put revolution, collectivism, ideology, and struggle above anything else." Their focus on everyday life "formed a de-facto resistance to the institutional control as it destroyed

---

[2] Ye Weili, *Dongdang de qingchun*, 142–143.

[3] Albert O. Hirschman, *Exit, Voice, and Loyalty: Responses to Decline in Firms, Organizations, and States* (Cambridge, MA: Harvard University Press, 1970), 3–4.

[4] Albert O. Hirschman, "Exit, Voice, and the Fate of the German Democratic Republic: An Essay in Conceptual History," *World Politics* 45, no. 2 (January 1993): 177.

[5] See, for example, "Zhengzhi yongren shi zichanjieji sixiang de bianzhong" 政治庸人是资产阶级思想的变种 [Being politically mediocre is a mutation of bourgeois thoughts], *Beijing pinglun*, February 23, 1967.

[6] Roderick MacFarquhar and Michael Schoenhals, *Mao's Last Revolution* (Cambridge, MA: The Belknap Press of Harvard University Press, 2006), 304–306.

and weakened the overall effectiveness of this control."[7] The emergence of alternative ways of life shows the resilience of Chinese society as well as people's disillusion with communist doctrines even under the most repressive conditions.[8] The relationship between the state and people in this "second society" was full of disguise and lies: people had learned "how to parrot the party line in public but keep their thoughts to themselves" and as a result, they could easily switch between two sets of values and lifestyles.[9]

China scholars are not alone in finding seeds of defiance under highly repressive regimes and their research can be incorporated into a larger body of literature on youth subcultures in the Eastern Bloc. Scholars from both East and West reached a consensus even before the end of the Cold War that youth subcultures could play a significant role in political changes in Communist regimes.[10] After the collapse of the Eastern Bloc, scholars paid special attention to the dissident power of youth subcultures including rock music, nudism, yoga, hippiedom, religion, and samizdat reading in former communist countries.[11] In this sense, resistance could be effected everywhere and easily: what people needed to do was simply to exit, because "when people left the socialist stage," the legitimacy of a regime that required wholehearted "emotional investment and participation" was automatically rendered bankrupt.[12]

---

[7] Qian Liqun, *Juehuo buxi*, 1254–1255.

[8] Paul Clark, *Youth Culture in China: From Red Guards to Netizens* (New York: Cambridge University Press, 2012).

[9] Frank Dikötter, *The Cultural Revolution: A People's History, 1962–1976* (New York: Bloomsbury Press, 2016), 285–286.

[10] For example, Dikötter's theory of "second society" comes directly from a 1988 article written by a Hungarian sociologist. See Elemér Hankiss, "The 'Second Society:' Is There an Alternative Social Model Emerging in Contemporary Hungary?" *Social Research* 55, no. 1/2 (Spring/Summer 1988): 13–42. See also Jim Riordan, *Soviet Youth Culture*.

[11] Two early works on rock music in the Eastern Bloc are Timothy W. Ryback, *Rock Around the Bloc: A History of Rock Music in Eastern Europe and the Soviet Union* (New York: Oxford University Press, 1990); Sabrina P. Ramet, ed., *Rocking the State: Rock Music and Politics in Eastern Europe and Russia* (Boulder, CO: Westview Press, 1994). For nudism in East Germany, see Mark Fenemore, *Sex, Thugs and Rock 'n' Roll: Teenage Rebels in Cold-War East Germany* (New York: Berghahn Books, 2007). For an extensive research of a variety of subcultures in the Eastern Bloc, see Juliane Fürst and Josie McLellan, *Dropping Out of Socialism*.

[12] Fürst and McLellan, *Dropping Out of Socialism*, 17–18.

These post-mortem examinations of the Eastern Bloc tend to exaggerate the dissident power of youth subcultures on the basis of a teleological interpretation. Some recent literature has argued that youth subcultures in the Soviet Union and Eastern Europe might not have contradicted the socialist project.[13] The general epistemological problem still exists: While we can always find different kinds of youth subcultures under communist regimes through which young people chose to exit by living alternatively, how should we interpret their behaviors? Here, the question of intentions matters. People could turn to "ordinary weapons" as described by James Scott when they were determined to resist in "everyday forms," but conversely, actions such as foot-dragging, dissimulation, and desertion do not necessarily connote resistance.[14] While it is important and necessary to excavate defiant elements in a sphere of seeming compliance, it is equally worthwhile to examine the underlying motivations behind actions that seem to be defiant.

This chapter does not deny the possibility of resistance during the Cultural Revolution, as has been shown by some scholars.[15] What I wish to achieve is to highlight the idea that many seemingly defiant alternative ways of life may not have been resistance. Living alternatively is neither subversive nor easy. There were diverse intentions behind the option of exiting the revolution that derived from people's inability to follow and understand the rapidly changing political scene during the Cultural Revolution, instead of reflecting their discontent with the regime. Youth subcultures that will be discussed in this chapter can thus showcase the discursive nature of the CCP regime and how young people's leisure

[13] See, for example, Anne E. Gorsuch and Diane P. Koenker, eds., *The Socialist Sixties: Crossing Borders in the Second World* (Bloomington: Indiana University Press, 2013); William Jay Risch, ed., *Youth and Rock in the Soviet Bloc: Youth Cultures, Music, and the State in Russia and Eastern Europe* (Lanham, MD: Lexington Books, 2015); Gleb Tsipursky, *Socialist Fun: Youth, Consumption, and State-Sponsored Popular Culture in the Cold War Soviet Union, 1945–1970* (Pittsburgh, PA: University of Pittsburgh Press, 2016).

[14] For Scott's definition of "everyday form of peasant resistance," see James C. Scott, *Weapons of the Weak: Everyday Forms of Peasant Resistance* (New Haven, CT: Yale University Press, 1985), xvi.

[15] For example, Yiching Wu records potentially subversive thoughts from the grassroots that challenged the Maoist version of socialism, including Yu Luoke's critical analysis of the CCP's systematic discrimination based on class background and Shengwulian's anarchist demand for a People's Commune of China. See Yiching Wu, *Cultural Revolution at the Margins*.

was institutionalized by this regime. My theory is similar to Alexei Yurchak's description of life under what he calls "late socialism" when life in the Soviet Union became increasingly "normalized." Rejecting the binary between "compliance" and "resistance" or "reality" and "mask," Yurchak points out that "for great numbers of Soviet citizens, many of the fundamental values, ideals, and realities of socialist life…were of genuine importance, despite the fact that many of their everyday practices routinely transgressed, reinterpreted, or refused certain norms and rules represented in the official ideology of the socialist state."[16] One example is that although the late Soviet period saw an emergence of young people's favoring of Western culture, this phenomenon did not contradict "the ethics and aesthetics of state socialism" because the prevalence of Western culture was "explicitly produced and implicitly enabled by the socialist project itself" as Soviet socialism celebrated cosmopolitanism and internationalism.[17]

Following Yurchak's analysis of the mentalities of young people in the late Soviet period, in this chapter, I look at the mentalities of Chinese youth behind their alternative ways of life during the Cultural Revolution. I first examine the collapse of the temporal order as a result of the Cultural Revolution, which made it possible for young people to pursue things that they wanted to. Then I discuss different categories of activities conducted by young people during this time and their underlying motivations. I argue that similar to what young people in the Soviet Union were doing in the 1980s, many Chinese young people found a way to lead normal but alternative lives during the Cultural Revolution. While some people exited simply to entertain and socialize, others exited to get a better political position during the Cultural Revolution, and others exited to pursue a meaningful way of life within the scope of orthodox ideology. Exiting the revolution was not an easy option as described in many romanticized accounts. On many occasions, the ability to live alternatively reflected certain young people's privileged access to resources that others could not in the People's Republic.

---

[16] Alexei Yurchak, *Everything Was Forever, Until It Was No More: The Last Soviet Generation* (Princeton, NJ: Princeton University Press, 2006), 8.

[17] Yurchak, *Everything Was Forever, Until It Was No More*, 160.

The Great Revolution in Temporal Order

From the perspective of elite politics, scholarship on the Cultural Revolution usually sees the criticism of the cultural establishment, the removal of several senior Party leaders, and the circulation of the May 16 Notification as the first actions of the Cultural Revolution.[18] At the grassroots, however, the launch of the Cultural Revolution was a sudden thing for many young people in Beijing despite some disturbing harbingers. Newspaper articles denouncing scholars and writers were far away from people's life. Their personal experience of the Cultural Revolution actually started with the breakdown of their daily schedule. As Yin Hongbiao, who was a junior high school student of the Beijing No. 4 High School, recollects, the routine in his school changed in May 1966 as regular classes in the afternoon were replaced by political study sessions. Although this was unusual, Yin did not realize that a more drastic change was on the way.[19] Ye Weili's experience was more dramatic. On the morning of June 1, 1966, Ye went to a public swimming pool to have a swimming class with her classmates. When they left school, everything was normal. When they came back, however, the campus had been covered with big-character posters denouncing their school leaders. Ye's routine was interrupted abruptly, and as she recalls, "the swimming class was my last class before the Cultural Revolution. I had to wait for more than seven years to go back to a real classroom. Most of my classmates' education, however, was permanently terminated."[20]

If we zoom out to a larger picture, the attempt to revolutionize young people's calendars started not from the summer of 1966, but from July 1965 when Mao Zedong proposed that schools should reduce one-third of activities to improve students' physical health.[21] Mao made his proposal after reading an internal report sent from the Beijing Municipal Youth League Committee about their investigation of a class in Beijing

---

[18] MacFarquhar and Schoenhals, *Mao's Last Revolution*, 14–41.

[19] Yin Hongbiao, "Dushu sheng, fengyu sheng" 读书声、风雨声 [The sound of learning and storm], in Beidao, Cao Yifan, and Weiyi, *Baofengyu de jiyi*, 225.

[20] Weili Ye and Xiaodong Ma, *Growing Up in the People's Republic*, 72.

[21] Mao Zedong 毛泽东, "Guanyu xuexiao yao jianqing xuesheng fudan de piyu" 对关于学校要减轻学生负担的批语 [Comments on reducing students' burden at school], in *Jianguo yilai Mao Zedong wengao* 建国以来毛泽东文稿 [Mao Zedong's manuscripts since the founding of the Republic], vol. 11 (Beijing: Zhongyang wenxian chubanshe, 1996), 391.

Normal Institute. In this report, the Municipal Youth League Committee claimed that they conducted a survey among fifty-two students in a class of the Department of History, and to their surprise, twenty-eight of them had various kinds of chronic diseases including neurosis, schizophrenia, hypertension, hypotension, heart disease, stomach disease, pulmonary tuberculosis, hepatitis, arthritis, gynecological disease, and hyperthyroidism. Nearly half of the students were near-sighted.[22]

According to the report, three factors led to the deterioration in students' health condition. First, students felt that they could not finish their readings and assignments because they needed to use their regular school hours to attend political movements and mandatory labor. Second, the school required everyone, regardless of their health condition, to take part in intensive physical education classes. In addition, the school also organized sports competitions frequently. Students had to race to occupy volleyball courts at 5:00 am and practice for the upcoming game for three afternoons every week. Third, students found that other organized activities had exhausted their leisure time and they could not arrange their time freely. Just several days before the survey, students were organized to assess each other's behavior in their own dormitories at night. Even after the lights were switched off, students had to engage in the activity of "thought exposure" during which they needed to talk with their dormmates about their thoughts on current affairs and school issues while lying on their beds. Some dormitories required students to talk about their family history before falling asleep.[23]

The report from the Beijing Municipal Youth League Committee did not exaggerate the strict regulation of young people's leisure time among university students. In Beijing University of Technology, for example, after dormitory lights were switched off at 10:00 pm, students would usually engage in some political activities. According to a student who entered Beijing University of Technology in 1964, over several months, people in his dormitory would study *Selected Works of Mao Zedong* under torchlight after the lights were off. These behaviors, however, were not

---

[22] "Beijing shifan xueyuan yige ban xuesheng shenghuo guodu jinzhang jiankang zhuangkuang xiajiang" 北京师范学院一个班学生生活过度紧张健康状况下降 [Tense life among students in one class of the Beijing Normal Institute leads to the deterioration of their health], *Dongfanghong*, July 3, 1967.

[23] "Beijing shifan xueyuan yige ban xuesheng shenghuo guodu jinzhang jiankang zhuangkuang xiajiang," *Dongfanghong*, July 3, 1967.

the result of requirements from the university. Students did that voluntarily because they were highly influenced by political indoctrination during that time.[24]

In response to Mao's proposal, the education authorities in Beijing convened a meeting attended by Party members in high schools and elementary schools to discuss the issue of implementing "balancing work and rest" among students and teachers. To convince the attendees that "balancing work and rest" was the Party's long-lasting policy rather than an expedient measure, the organizer of the meeting included documents issued by the CCP Central Committee and the Beijing Municipal Party Committee on "balancing work and rest" in 1960 during the Great Leap famine.[25] Cadres from high schools and elementary schools reported during the meeting that there were indeed too many organized activities for both students and teachers, which made it difficult to "balance work and rest." In the early 1960s, high school students in Beijing had to attend mandatory militia training, which was taken very seriously by the organizers. The Party head of the Fengtai District No. 12 High School complained that in the summer vacation of 1965, his students were required to take part in militia training for six hours a day, and consequently, they did not even have time to finish their homework. Some girls fainted after the artillery training. In another school, when the leader of the militia found that some teachers did not attend a planning meeting for the school's militia training because of the conflict with their schedules, he got very angry: "Is the school a special zone? Someone says that he is busy. Who is not busy? Only Chiang Kai-shek is not!".[26]

As a major agenda of the meeting, the Beijing Municipal Party Committee drafted a document on balancing work and rest among students and teachers in high schools and elementary schools, demanding

---

[24] Li Huixiang 李慧祥, "60 niandai zai muxiao" 60年代在母校 [In my alma mater in the 1960s], in *Nanwang de qingchun: beigongda laowujie jishi* 难忘的青春：北工大 "老五届"纪事 [Unforgettable youth: reminiscence from the "old five classes" of Beijing University of Technology], ed. Li Qinglin 李庆林 (Beijing: Dangdai zhongguo chubanshe, 2015), 163.

[25] "Zhongyang shiwei guanyu laoyi jiehe de yixie zhishi" 中央、市委关于劳逸结合的一些指示 [Meeting files No. 2: directions on balancing work and rest from the Party Center and the Municipal Committee], August 12, 1965, BMA, 001-023-00391-002.

[26] "Dui zai zhongxue kaizhan minbing huodong de yijian" 对在中学开展民兵活动的意见 [Opinions on carrying out militia training in high schools], August 1965, BMA, 001-023-00391-051.

that organized activities should be reduced as much as possible.²⁷ The real effect of the implementation of Mao's proposal, however, was debatable. One of my interviewees who entered Beijing No. 31 High School in 1963 maintained that Mao's proposal did not have a real impact on his life because his teachers paid most of their attention to students' grades. He hardly had any free time because he needed to finish his homework first, and as the head of the Youth League branch in his class, he also had to find time to help others who performed poorly in their lessons.²⁸

With the outbreak of the Cultural Revolution, many young students felt that they were emancipated from their tense life. Zhao Zhenkai, who was a senior high school student in Beijing No. 4 High School, cheered with his friends in their classroom after learning that all classes had been canceled. Zhao thanked the Chairman's decision to close all schools because he no longer needed to attend exams.²⁹ The sense of relief was not unique to students performing poorly in exams. Ma Xiaodong's immediate response after learning that there were no more classes was "I'm liberated!" Although she had always been a "good student," Ma never liked the "monotony" in her classroom and thus she wholeheartedly supported Mao's criticism of China's education system.³⁰ An interviewee, who was eager to enter Peking University to be trained as a biologist, also mentioned that the Cultural Revolution freed him from a dull life.³¹

The Cultural Revolution, in this sense, was a revolution on young people's regular way of using their time as it blurred the boundary between working/school hours and leisure time: now they could make use of every minute on their own. Not surprisingly, many students devoted all their time to making revolution. Chen Donglin was a senior high school student at Beijing No. 3 High School by the summer of 1966. In his memory, the Cultural Revolution made young people really become "masters" of their life. Chen, along with other Red Guards in

---

²⁷ "Guanyu zhongxiaoxue shisheng laoyi jiehe de jixiang guiding (caogao gong taolun yong)" 关于中小学师生劳逸结合的几项规定（草稿 供讨论用）[Several requirements on balancing work and rest among teachers and students in high schools and elementary schools (a draft for discussion)], August 1965, BMA, 001-023-00391-013.

²⁸ Interviewee 2, November 2, 2018.

²⁹ Zhao Zhenkai 赵振开, "Zoujin baofengyu" 走进暴风雨 [Walking into the storm], in Beidao, Cao Yifan, and Weiyi, *Baofengyu de jiyi*, 198.

³⁰ Weili Ye and Xiaodong Ma, *Growing Up in the People's Republic*, 72–73.

³¹ Interviewee 3, December 29, 2018.

his school, devoted his time selling Red Guard tabloids along Chang'an Boulevard, only for revolutionary purposes. The weather was hot in the summer, but they refused to use the money they got from selling tabloids to buy some ice cream because that would "let Chairman Mao down."[32]

Michael Schoenhals calls the very early stage of the Cultural Revolution as the "Great Proletarian Information Revolution" as numerous Red Guard publications, including the "current affairs" (*dongtai* 动态) newsletters, started to disseminate information that used to be limited to cadres above a certain level to a much larger audience.[33] Nevertheless, without the possibility of using time freely, this "information revolution" would not be possible. Chen, during a certain period, became a full-time correspondent for the "current affairs" newsletter in his school. He collected information everyday by reading big-character posters in various high schools and even observing factional conflicts on the spot.[34] To accomplish their mission better, Chen and his classmates even slept in the office of the "current affairs" editorial board every day. The motivation for them to devote their time to editing tabloids was that they could give full play to their talent now that Mao gave them a chance to do things freely.[35]

COMPETING FOR LEADERSHIP BY EXITING

In October 1966, Mao reoriented the Cultural Revolution to the Party establishment by attacking the "bourgeois reactionary line." Children from official families, who led the Red Guard movement in Beijing from the beginning of the Cultural Revolution, were confused because they were reluctant to accept Mao's charges against their parents and their parents' close comrades. With the rise of the "rebels," these "Old Red Guards" were facing the danger of being marginalized by the movement. As a result, they had to collaborate with each other to resist the rebels and the Central Cultural Revolution Group. Their first step was to form an organization called Liandong (United Action), but they were soon

---

[32] Interview with Chen Donglin, December 19, 2018.

[33] Michael Schoenhals, "China's 'Great Proletarian Information Revolution' of 1966–1967," in Brown and Johnson, *Maoism at the Grassroots*, 230–258.

[34] Interview with Chen Donglin, December 19, 2018.

[35] Interview with Chen Donglin, December 29, 2018.

cracked down on by the Central Cultural Revolution Group.³⁶ In January 1967, with the arrest and imprisonment of its leaders, Liandong as an organization became defunct.³⁷

Children of officials may have been among the first to exit the revolution and live alternatively. Instead of alienating themselves from the political movement, however, they did so to resist being marginalized by the mainstream. As Ye Weili observes, when children of officials ("Old Red Guards") felt that they were being marginalized, they strived to show their privileged position. As a result, their alternative way of live formed a prominent youth subculture during the Cultural Revolution, usually through collective activities. One of the trademarks of this group was clothing style. In summer 1966, children of officials symbolized their identity by wearing old, even worn-out, army uniforms. At the end of 1966, however, they started to wear their parents' carefully tailored woolen army overcoats, leather boots, and fur hats to distinguish themselves from the flourishing groups of rebels.³⁸

In addition to a different clothing style, children of officials organized activities that were considered "decadent" to remind people of their superiority in the revolution. One of these activities was collective tomb sweeping. On April 6, 1967, Chen Huanren was invited by a classmate from an official family to go to the Babaoshan Revolutionary Cemetery to commemorate revolutionary martyrs. Upon arriving there, Chen noticed immediately and with great surprise that "although many buried in the cemetery are now being denounced, people coming to commemorate them have outnumbered any previous year." Many people from official families came to the cemetery, stood silently in front of the gravestones with tears in their eyes. Some paid tribute by putting white flowers in front of gravestones of someone under denunciation.³⁹ Jiang Qing from the Central Cultural Revolution Group noticed the activity of collective

---

³⁶ Yin Hongbiao 印红标, *Shizongzhe de zuji: wenhua da geming qijian de qingnian sichao* 失踪者的足迹：文化大革命期间的青年思潮 [Footsteps of the missing: youth thoughts during the Cultural Revolution] (Hong Kong: Chinese University Press, 2009), 20–24. See also Andrew G. Walder, *Fractured Rebellion: The Beijing Red Guard Movement* (Cambridge, MA: Harvard University Press, 2009), 184–186.

³⁷ Walder, *Fractured Rebellion*, 192.

³⁸ Weili Ye and Xiaodong Ma, *Growing Up in the People's Republic*, 94. See also Ye Weili, *Dongdang de qingchun*, 145.

³⁹ Chen Huanren, *Hongweibing riji*, 302–303.

tomb sweeping. During a meeting with representatives from universities and high schools in Beijing on April 21, 1967, Jiang criticized official children's "decadent" lifestyle of collective tomb sweeping as a sign of refusing to correct their "mistakes": "Now they are very pathetic. They are following a feudalistic way. They gathered at Tiananmen and paid homage at Babaoshan... Not all buried in Babaoshan are martyrs; some are traitors."[40]

Another activity was collective bike riding. Both Ye Weili and her friend Ma Xiaodong were impressed by crowds of young people with woolen military overcoats whizzing along Beijing streets on their bikes during the Cultural Revolution. As Ye recalls, young people engaging in this activity were actually showing off by displaying their alternative ways of life publicly on the street.[41] The collective bike riding was noticed by opponents of the Old Red Guards. In a short piece published by a rebel organization in May 1967, the author described the ongoing "bicycle movement" in Beijing: "These people with army uniforms gathered in groups and rode on their bicycles. They flashed through the streets like a crowd of grasshoppers with stern looks on their faces." Having realized the political implication of the collective bicycle riding, the author concluded that these youngsters were trying to resist the current orientation of the Cultural Revolution by "firmly embracing the zombies of the Liu-Deng reactionary line."[42]

Some children of officials held parties in restaurants to cherish the memory of their revolutionary passion. Beijing's Moscow Restaurant was popular among those young people who felt that they were later marginalized. A then frequent visitor of the Moscow Restaurant recalled: "The most attractive thing about Lao Mo (the nickname of Moscow Restaurant) was its atmosphere, which was very similar to what was expressed in Russian and Soviet literature as well as Soviet movies. It reminded

---

[40] "Zhongyang shouzhang jiejian Beijing daxuesheng zhongxuesheng daibiao shi de jianghua" 中央首长接见北京大学生中学生代表时的讲话 [Speech from chiefs from the center during their meeting with representatives from universities and high schools in Beijing], April 21, 1967, in Chinese Cultural Revolution Database, Third Edition.

[41] Weili Ye and Xiaodong Ma, *Growing Up in the People's Republic*, 95; Ye Weili, *Dongdang de qingchun*, 145–146.

[42] "Lun 'zixingche yundong'" 论 "自行车运动" [On the "bicycle movement"], *Bingtuan zhanbao*, May 8, 1967.

us of the fervent revolutionary passion."[43] After the Moscow Restaurant resumed offering Russian cuisine in 1969, it soon became a hotspot among many people in Beijing. Luo Yabin, whose parents were ousted by rebels during the Cultural Revolution, also went to the Moscow Restaurant with young people from similar families. In his memory, dressing for a meal at the Moscow Restaurant was a complex affair: "You couldn't dress too casually when going to Lao Mo. People found their fathers' woolen uniforms from their wardrobes, but they did not dare to wear them publicly. Therefore, they covered their woolen uniforms with student uniforms, but revealed their woolen ones with the first button on student uniforms unbuttoned."[44] Dining in Lao Mo became such a distinctive feature of alternative lifestyles of children of officials that even those who did not go there also heard about legends about it. Ma Xiaodong heard a story about a feast organized by a former Old Red Guard in the Moscow Restaurant. In Ma's memory, the Red Guard invited her friends to Lao Mo for her birthday and "wore a white gown for the occasion." For Ma, the Moscow Restaurant was the "most bourgeois restaurant in Beijing."[45]

Although children of officials wished to use alternative ways of life to resist being marginalized, ironically, from the perspective of rebels and members of the Central Cultural Revolution Group, their behaviors justified the necessity of marginalizing children of officials, as rebels connected officials' children's alternative way of life with their privileges before the Cultural Revolution. A pro-rebel article analyzed the mentality of the children of cadres behind their alternative lifestyle: "These 'old' Red Guards are deeply deceived. They have not liquidated the harmful effects from a small handful of capitalist roaders in the Party. They are not willing to wake up… They have nothing to do, have no contact with the vigorously growing class struggle, and have lost their political importance…They

---

[43] Hao Yixing 郝一星, "Chi he shinian: wenge huimou zhi'er" 吃喝十年: 文革回眸之二 [Wining and dining during the ten years: my recollection on the Cultural Revolution, part two], March 21, 2017, https://difangwenge.org/forum.php?mod=viewthread&tid=14104.

[44] "1966: Lao Mo de jifeng zhouyu" 1966: 老莫的疾风骤雨 [1966: Storm in Lao Mo], July 13, 2009, http://news.sohu.com/20090713/n265183788.shtml.

[45] Weili Ye and Xiaodong Ma, *Growing Up in the People's Republic*, 95.

are spiritually empty, decadent, and backward."⁴⁶ When meeting with released Liandong leaders in April 1967, Jiang Qing and Chen Boda from the Central Cultural Revolution Group criticized their "decadent life" and attributed their behaviors to bad influence from their education in schools for children of officials (*ganbu zidi xuexiao* 干部子弟学校).⁴⁷ In early 1967, with the launch of an "exhibition on crimes of Liandong," many visitors realized that the cadre children's alternative ways of life showed their privileged position that needed to be destroyed during the Cultural Revolution.⁴⁸

Waiting for a Better Chance by Exiting

As the political scene of the Cultural Revolution changed rapidly, there were always people who found themselves unable to follow the revolutionary course. "Bystanders," therefore, formed a group of a significant number of people throughout the Cultural Revolution. As Qian Liqun states, they "might have participated in certain Red Guard organizations or peripheral organizations, but they basically adopted a passive or even non-intrusive approach."⁴⁹ The existence of bystanders during the Cultural Revolution attracted attention in early scholarship on the Cultural Revolution when scholars investigated the relationship between factional affiliation and students' family background. A survey conducted in Hong Kong among former students in Guangzhou shows that people's political stance on the Cultural Revolution correlated with their "class" origin: 60% of students from bad class families and 82% of students from middle-class families identified them as bystanders during the Cultural

---

⁴⁶ "Quanjun gengjin yibei jiu, xichu yangguan wu guren: zhi yixie 'lao' gongweibing" 劝君更尽一杯酒，西出阳关无故人——致一些"老"红卫兵 [Have one more cup of wine, there will be no old friends later on: to some "old" Red Guards], *Hongweibing yundong*, September 25, 1967.

⁴⁷ "Zhongyang shouzhang jiejian huoshi 'liandong' fenzi shi de jianghua" 中央首长接见获释的"联动"分子时的讲话 [Speech from chiefs from the center during their meeting with released "Liandong" elements], April 22, 1967, in Chinese Cultural Revolution Database, Third Edition.

⁴⁸ For example, Chen Huanren went to the "exhibition on crimes of Liandong" held at August 1 School in March 1967. Chen did not like the alternative lifestyles performed by children of cadres, and after he visited the exhibition, he felt even more angry with their alternative lifestyles and their privileged life. Chen Huanren, *Hongweibing riji*, 293–294.

⁴⁹ Qian Liqun, *Juehuo buxi*, 1253.

Revolution, while only 34% of students from cadre and working-class families chose to be neither rebels nor loyalists.[50] In Beijing, according to the observation of a then Beijing 101 Middle School student, about one-third to half of the high school students in Beijing were bystanders who "did not participate in Red Guard organizations, did not 'actively' take part in the Cultural Revolution or did not take part in the revolution at all, or became absentminded even if they were affiliated with Red Guard organizations."[51]

There were, of course, bystanders who were politically indifferent and chose not to participate in the Cultural Revolution from the beginning. He Qiu, a student of the Beijing 101 Middle School, discovered that during the "Great Linkup" which was supposed to be an opportunity for the Red Guards to exchange their "revolutionary experience" with people in other places, most people regarded it primarily as a chance to travel across the country for free. As a self-identified bystander himself, He Qiu took this opportunity and joined the team of "Great Linkup" with several students from Tsinghua University. Soon, He Qiu discovered that these Tsinghua University students were all bystanders: their homes were outside Beijing, and their ultimate purpose to take part in the "Great Linkup" was to go home. As a result, the number of people in their team shrank, as people left the team for their homes all along the way.[52] For people who were politically indifferent, going home continued to be a great temptation at the end of 1968 when the Party asked all people not to go home during the coming Spring Festival. In the Beijing Institute of Posts and Telecommunications, activists discovered that many politically indifferent people were trying to go home by fabricating stories that their families got sick. Some people even went home without notifying the school.[53]

---

[50] Anita Chan, *Children of Mao: Personality Development and Political Activism in the Red Guard Generation* (London: The Macmillan Press, 1985), 140.

[51] He Qiu 何求, "Xiaoyao wenge" 逍遥文革 [Being a bystander during the Cultural Revolution], December 25, 2012, https://difangwenge.org/forum.php?mod=viewthread&tid=15771.

[52] He Qiu, "Xiaoyao wenge."

[53] "Zai huoxian shang guoge geminghua de chunjie" 在火线上过个革命化的春节 [Having a revolutionized Spring Festival at the front line], *Beiyou dongfanghong*, November 22, 1968.

Many bystanders actively participated in the Cultural Revolution at first but became disillusioned afterward. For many of them, exiting the revolution was never a great choice: it was actually an expedient measure while they were waiting for opportunities to return to the center stage of the Cultural Revolution. In June 1967, Chen Huanren found that many members of the "New Peking University Commune" became bystanders because they thought that their faction was getting a cold reception from the top. In public, bystanders were living an alternative lifestyle: they either read books alone, or played chess together. Some even started to assemble radios. These bystanders, however, were still paying great attention to the Cultural Revolution by reading tabloids or *People's Daily* and trying to find clues of what to do next.[54] This was not a rare case. Many bystanders who were forced to take a leave from the Cultural Revolution were also frustrated with their own lifestyles. Lu Shuning, a senior high school student at Beijing Normal University High School, wrote in his diary on November 5, 1967:

> Now our life seems to be joyful, carefree, and calm. Every day we kill time by chatting, laughing, playing chess, and reading. When immersed in these things, people are indeed happy because they can forget all other things. After the happiness, however, when the stimulant starts to lose its effect, the anxiety and nervousness [from passing time meaninglessly] ... will come to you, and you will feel spiritually empty. This can only be solved through studying, working, and fighting... Revolution does not allow you to have beautiful dreams in forever peace. The enemies are envying your happiness. The wheel of history will not stop moving forward because of your satisfaction. New struggles are in the making in calmness and leisure. Peaceful life will be interrupted, the calm water will be disrupted, the air full of laughter will be shocked, and the revolutionary melting pot is going to boil again, although there is only a spark of fire under it![55]

Song Bolin, a child of officials, immediately joined the Red Guard in Tsinghua University High School at the beginning of the Cultural Revolution. He led a typical alternative way of life when he started to travel around the country in the name of the "Great Linkup." Song admitted that he was only taking the opportunity to go sightseeing everywhere,

---

[54] Chen Huanren, *Hongweibing riji*, 361–362.

[55] Lu Shuning 卢叔宁, *Jiehui canbian* 劫灰残编 [Fragments from the ashes] (Beijing: Wenlian chubanshe, 2000), 11.

and he was fully aware that his behavior was not in accordance with the course of the Cultural Revolution. "I think that I should not go sightseeing in the name of revolution," wrote Song in his diary in September 1966 after he visited the seashore in Dalian. "But it is not a bad thing to make some mistakes when I am still young."[56]

Song's attitude toward bystanders was ambivalent: on the one hand, he excused himself for traveling around the country in the name of revolution; on the other hand, he disliked the lifestyle of other bystanders. Just one day after he convinced himself that sightseeing was not bad, Song arrived at Lüshun and criticized bystanders in a high school there: "The atmosphere here is pretty bad. People are either playing chess or playing the erhu. Too peaceful. They are falling behind."[57] In summer 1967, Song himself started to play chess, read novels, and go to parks, but he did not alienate himself from the Cultural Revolution. On October 15, 1967, he wrote in his diary: "I am tired of just having fun and reading books. I am going back to school and to participate in the Cultural Revolution."[58]

Bystanders with a bad family background had similar mentalities. Xie Dingguo, who was born to a capitalist family in Shanghai, became a student at Peking University in 1962.[59] Xie was an activist at the beginning of the Cultural Revolution but became tired of on-campus factional struggles one year later. When Xie realized that he wanted to withdraw from meaningless factional confrontations, he felt extremely distressed because he did not wish to reconcile himself to become a bystander. "I am very upset these days," wrote Xie on June 12, 1967. "I cannot have a clear conclusion and always want to drink some alcohol. Sometimes I want to join another faction, but sometimes I just want to be a bystander. This makes me distraught." Although Xie started to go swimming, smoke cigarettes, and drink alcohol, at the same time he paid attention to the

---

[56] Song Bolin 宋柏林, *Hongweibing xingshuai lu: Qinghua fuzhong lao Hongweibing shouji* 红卫兵兴衰录——清华附中老红卫兵手记 [Ups and downs of the Red Guard: diary of an old Red Guard in Tsinghua University High School] (Hong Kong: Desai chuban youxian gongsi, 2006), 138.

[57] Song Bolin, *Hongweibing xingshuai lu*, 139.

[58] Song Bolin, *Hongweibing xingshuai lu*, 322.

[59] Xie Dingguo's experience is from Xie Dingguo 谢定国, "Yige beida xuesheng de wenge riji" 一个北大学生的文革日记 [A Peking University student's diary during the Cultural Revolution], August 17, 2014, https://difangwenge.org/forum.php?mod=viewthread&tid=10029.

situation across the country and refused his parents' suggestion that he should come home to avoid being involved in violent factional conflicts. His diary was still full of his views about the Cultural Revolution.

Unlike Old Red Guards such as Song Bolin who already knew that they had been marginalized, Xie's decision to become a bystander was more a strategy of hibernating for a while and waiting for better opportunities. In his diary of July 12, 1967, Xie recorded Chen Boda's speech when he met with rebels from Peking University. "Comrade Chen Boda said: the sky will not fall down. You should go back to your school and sleep. You must learn how to sleep… Comrade Chen Boda mentioned repeatedly: You must learn how to sleep. He said that this was a rule during the class struggle. I really like that." Because of this strategy, Xie's position shifted regularly between that of an activist and a bystander. For example, on August 1, 1967, Xie joined the "combat group" of the reorganized rebel organization of Peking University. He thought that perhaps his hibernation should end: "I think that I cannot indulge myself any longer. Sleeping, drinking, and smoking will only fritter away my will, energy, and the spirit of hard work." Only ten days later, however, Xie wrote in his diary that during those days, he had been reading a scholarly book about the classic novel *Dream of the Red Chamber*.

At the end of August 1967, Xie finally went back to his Shanghai home and stayed there until mid-October, "doing nothing but reading books and playing chess." Xie's ambivalent attitude toward his lifestyle continued after he went back to Peking University: although he still frequently played chess and drank alcohol, he also participated in regular activities of the rebel organization, and he never considered that the life of bystanders was laudable. After drinking and eating with his classmates during the Spring Festival of 1968, Xie vowed in his diary:

> The reason I indulged in extravagant eating, drinking, and smoking during the Spring Festival is that I want to stop this. The more I was determined to do so, the more alcohol I had. This should stop. I should change my way of life….After the Spring Festival, I must achieve these goals: stop smoking, stop drinking, stop playing poker, and stop chatting meaninglessly with friends.

The third category of bystanders exited the revolution because they wished to resume their normal life before the Cultural Revolution. For example, the activity of raising tropical fish and pigeons was popular in many cities in the early 1960s. Even before the Cultural Revolution, this activity became so popular that it was difficult for the authorities not to notice. A document from Tianjin shows that around May 1966, the Tianjin authorities planned to ban "black markets" selling tropical fish and pigeons. According to this document, there was a fashion among many young people in Tianjin to raise tropical fish and pigeons. As a result, vendors began to sell fish and pigeons in "black markets." Many people were so obsessed with raising fish and pigeons that they could not focus on their regular work and study.[60] During the Cultural Revolution, however, raising pets would be considered as either a "bourgeois lifestyle" or part of the "four olds" and became a target during the house raid. Yu Xiangzhen's home was raided after the outbreak of the Cultural Revolution and as she remembers, people who came to search their house mostly paid attention to three things: whether there was a Mao portrait on the wall, whether there was a plaster statue of Mao on the table, and whether there were pets. During the house raid in her residential compound, many fish tanks were confiscated.[61] Yin Hongbiao recalls his experience of throwing away his pet fish during the "smashing of the four olds": "'Smashing of the four olds' started, and I had to clean the 'four olds' in my home. I needed to sacrifice my treasured goldfish…Seeing the fish struggling at the entrance of the sewer, I did not have the heart to stay. I turned around and left."[62]

The activity of pet raising revived quickly after the turbulence during the early stage of the Cultural Revolution. Raising tropical fish, for example, became popular among many bystanders. In Beijing, there was even a piece of humorous "clapper ballad" (*dagu* 大鼓) that recited the names of various kinds of tropical fish: "Red Arrow, Blue Arrow, and Black Shark; we also have batfish. My poor Black Mary just died tragically; tropical fish got arthritis." A young student remembered that she learned this clapper ballad from a Beijing student on a ship back to Beijing during

---

[60] "Xunsu qudi redaiyu he gezi heishe huodong" 迅速取缔热带鱼和鸽子黑市活动 [Immediately ban black markets selling tropical fish and pigeons], *Tianjin zhengbao* 11 (1966): 10.

[61] Yu Xiangzhen 于向真, "Wo qinli de wenge shinian shi" 我亲历的文革十年 (十) [Ten years of Cultural Revolution that I experience, part ten], January 28, 2016, http://www.hybsl.cn/beijingcankao/beijingfenxi/2016-01-28/56728.html.

[62] Yin Hongbiao, "Dushu sheng, fengyu sheng," in Beidao, Cao Yifan, and Weiyi, *Baofengyu de jiyi*, 230.

the Cultural Revolution.⁶³ A high school girl who later became a famous poet wrote a traditional Chinese poem about her younger brother's tropical fish in the autumn of 1967 entitled "On my brother Kangning's four tropical fish," which depicted the mentality of some bystanders: "I am happy to live in the calm water. Why bother chasing the tide during my entire life? I suggest my dear carp at the Dragon's Gate: I was ambitious at first, but I finally end up decorating people's desks in a bottle." This final sentence about a suggestion from a disillusioned tropical fish to an ambitious carp that they should be satisfied with mediocre life was once popular among Beijing students.⁶⁴

Raising tropical fish required some basic elements: fish and fish tanks. The Cultural Revolution actually facilitated those who wanted to raise tropical fish in an unexpected way. As a then resident of the Broadcast Bureau residential compound recalls: "Children from Building 302 [of the Broadcast Bureau residential compound] looked for tropical fish under the pretext of smashing the four olds. We did not have any experience when we went to confiscate tropical fish for the first time, so we got nothing after fiddling with the tank for a long time. We only left a hole in the fish tank. We were more experienced when confiscating tropical fish for the second time. The whole process was finished in only two or three minutes with our semi-professional fishing equipment."⁶⁵ Tropical fish raisers usually made fish tanks by themselves if they did not have fish tanks surviving the house raid. Materials for fish tanks came from factories or public space in their residence. The windows of the Broadcast Bureau residence, for example, were removed by young people living there to make fish tanks. Their parents did not stop their children from doing so because they thought that it would be better to make fish tanks than hanging out on the streets.⁶⁶ Young workers would use iron and

---

⁶³ "Zouguo qingchun qi chengchuan huijing guonian de lushang" 走过青春 (7) 乘船回京过年的路上 [Walking past my youth, part seven: on my way back to Beijing for the Spring Festival by ship], January 24, 2009, http://web.archive.org/web/201812070 75640/http://blog.sina.com.cn/s/blog_51d095710100ayqt.html?tj=1.

⁶⁴ "Sanshou wenge shiqi de shici suoxiang" 三首"文革"时期的诗词所想 [Thoughts on three poems written during the Cultural Revolution], December 19, 2017, http://web.archive.org/web/20181207080526/https://www.douban.com/note/649696309/.

⁶⁵ Yang Xiaogong 杨小工, "Lao 302 de haidi shijie" 老302的海底世界 [Aquarium in old 302], July 5, 2008, http://web.archive.org/web/20181207075420/http://blog.sina.com.cn/s/blog_531b835401009ucw.html.

⁶⁶ Yang Xiaogong, "Lao 302 de haidi shijie."

glass in their factories to make their own fish tanks. They would even use the official language to justify their behavior: "We laborers are the leading class. We represent the state. Why can't we get some iron from the state property?".[67]

The bystanders' behavior to divert state property to serve their own needs was not limited to tropical fish raising, and this behavior is notable because it shows the subtle relationship between the state and bystanders: the public ownership of property as well as the chaotic situation during the Cultural Revolution facilitated their "hobbies." In this sense, instead of alienating themselves from the state, bystanders were actually dependent on the socio-economic structure of the regime. Apart from raising tropical fish, bystanders diverted state property in activities such as assembling radios and making furniture. In December 1967, the mouthpiece of rebels in the Beijing Institute of Posts and Telecommunications reported that bystanders were busy looking for planks everywhere on campus to make cases for their self-assembled radios. They also dismantled wooden stools and beds deserted in university buildings if they could not find ready-made planks.[68] One year later, the situation became even worse: "Doors of partitions in public washrooms and even wooden plates with Chairman Mao's quotations were missing." They were reportedly made into radio cases by those bystanders.[69]

Factory workers had ample opportunities to divert state properties. After Chen Donglin was sent to a small factory in 1968, he found it necessary to make some furniture by himself as a preparation for his future marriage. Chen made a sofa and a floor lamp using materials from the factory. Chen's friend was sent to another factory and he told Chen that one day, there was an unscheduled blackout during a night shift. After the power was restored half an hour later, people immediately found

---

[67] "Lao Fu tiedaobu dayuan huiyilu 78 yang redaiyu" 老付铁道部大院回忆录78: 养热带鱼 [Old Fu's memory of the Ministry of Railway residential compound, part 78: raising tropical fish], October 27, 2017, http://web.archive.org/web/20181207070131/http://blog.sina.com.cn/s/blog_60f72b1c0102y10k.html.

[68] "Lingren qifen de xiaoshi" 令人气愤的小事 [Trivial matters that make people angry], *Beiyou dongfanghong*, December 1, 1967.

[69] "Shazhu sungong feisi de waifeng: cong tou tianhuaban xiangdao de" 刹住损公肥私的歪风——从偷天花板想到的 [Stop the unhealthy trend of profiting yourself at the expense of the public: thinking from the behavior of stealing the ceiling], *Beiyou dongfanghong*, November 22, 1968.

that many materials in the factory disappeared. Everybody had a tacit understanding with each other that they were diverting state property.[70]

In addition to these three major categories, when everyday life became increasingly "normal" after the end of the Red Guard movement, some people engaged in alternative ways of life because they wished to join the establishment. In this sense, living alternatively did not contradict the pursuit for a better life under the auspices of the regime. In the 1970s, young people in Beijing were obsessed with playing different kinds of musical instruments in their leisure time. As Bao Kun, a young man who was working in a department store during that time, recalls: "Many young people were learning how to play a musical instrument, from the then-fashionable accordion and violin, to clarinet, oboe, and trumpet. Even the guitar, which was denounced as bourgeois decadent music became popular in young people's leisure time… Every night, many music fans gathered near the Forbidden City. Their performance added some romance to Beijing's dull night." Bao Kun attributes this fashion to young people's desire to change their life: "many hoped that they could change their life with their musical talent if they could be recruited by military or civilian troupes."[71]

During the Cultural Revolution, different groups had different views toward the alternative ways of life led by bystanders, and they were not always perceived as natural dropouts of the revolution. For radical rebels, the behaviors of the bystanders could undermine their revolutionary agenda. From 1967, numerous articles denouncing bystanders were published, representing a will of the participants of the Cultural Revolution to incorporate all people into a revolutionary way of life. For example, in February 1967, a rebel tabloid wrote that people who "did not participate in the revolution or only observe the revolution" were "politically mediocre" who needed to be transformed into active participants.[72] The attempt to form a new temporal discipline from the

---

[70] Interview with Chen Donglin, December 19, 2018.

[71] Bao Kun 鲍昆, "Liming qian de yuedong: wo kandao de qishi niandai" 黎明前的跃动——我看到的七十年代 [Pulse before the dawn: the 1970s that I observed], in *Qishi niandai* 七十年代 [The 1970s], ed. Beidao 北岛 and Li Tuo 李陀 (Hong Kong: Oxford University Press, 2008), 189–190.

[72] "Zhengzhi yongren shi zichanjieji sixiang de bianzhong" 政治庸人是资产阶级思想的变种 [Being politically mediocre is a mutation of bourgeois thoughts], *Beijing pinglun*, February 23, 1967.

rebels echoed with the Central Cultural Revolution Group's decision to let students go back to classrooms in October 1967 under the slogan of "resuming classes while carrying out the revolution" (*fuke nao geming* 复课闹革命). Although a *People's Daily* editorial glorified this decision as a new stage of the Cultural Revolution which could intensify Mao's proposal on the reorganization of the entire education system, there were some practical thoughts underneath the high-sounding words.[73] A document confessed the Party's concern that students who had too much free time under the new temporal discipline could make trouble.[74]

The policy of "resuming classes while carrying out the revolution" gave university rebels a good opportunity to co-opt bystanders now that rebels and bystanders had to live in the same space. In Beijing Institute of Posts and Telecommunications, for example, to rectify the lifestyle of bystanders, rebels started their own version of temporal politics by introducing the activity of "helping each other to make both become red" (*yi bang yi yi dui hong* 一帮一, 一对红) in December 1967. One dormitory asked its residents to report their thoughts facing a Mao portrait every night after 9:30 pm as a measure to "use every minute in the dorm to study Chairman Mao's works." One article depicts this "evening report" (*wan huibao* 晚汇报) ritual: "all students in the dormitory stood in front of a portrait of Chairman Mao in a line… First, let's wish Chairman Mao eternal life without end! Eternal life without end! Then we read quotations of Chairman Mao about some specific issues. Finally, we summarize our day and report to Chairman Mao respectively."[75]

Some less ardent rebels feared that they might not be assigned a good job because they neglected their studies during the Cultural Revolution. Therefore, these people started to follow the bystanders to read professional books. A rebel tabloid reported some rebels' envious attitude toward bystanders in Beijing Institute of Posts and Telecommunications: "These bystanders read a lot of books, and they also have experience assembling radios and electric meters. They know much more than I

---

[73] For the *People's Daily* editorial, see RMRB, October 25, 1967.
[74] MacFarquhar and Schoenhals, *Mao's Last Revolution*, 248.
[75] "Rang Mao Zedong sixiang zhanling sushi zhendi" 让毛泽东思想占领宿舍阵地 [Let Mao Zedong Thought occupy the battle field of dormitory], *Beiyou dongfanghong*, December 16, 1967.

do." These rebels even considered themselves as "goods sold at a reduced price" because they did not learn anything about their majors during the political movement.[76]

As for the helmsman of the Cultural Revolution, Mao did not see bystanders as a potentially subversive force. He also co-opted the bystanders into his own agenda as long as they obeyed his directions when he decided to end the Red Guard movement. One of Mao's secretaries recalls that after the Mao Zedong Thought Propaganda Team entered Tsinghua University to stop violent factional conflicts and establish a university-wide revolutionary committee, there was gossip that most of the members of the new revolutionary committee were bystanders. Mao commented: "There is nothing bad about bystanders. They just disagree with you on factional struggles. You engaged in violent conflicts that couldn't solve the issue, so they had to flee. These bystanders are really good. I agree with them."[77]

Being Loyal to Communist Orthodoxy by Exiting

Some young people who were less enthusiastic about what was going on during the Cultural Revolution exited not because they were politically indifferent or waiting for a comeback, but because they wished to find a meaningful way to pursue their revolutionary ideal, which was highly influenced by orthodox ideology. Between April and May 1967, several music fans in the Beijing University of Technology formed an organization called the "Shajiabang Symphony Orchestra." As Gu Dai, one member of the orchestra, recalls, participants of the orchestra were disappointed with the endless factional struggles between Red Guard factions. "The Cultural Revolution has entered a stabilized stage…but nobody knew how the movement would develop. We were confused about what we should do to 'grasp the orientation of the struggle.'" Although they stopped participating in factional struggles, they did not want to detach themselves from reality. Thus, "a group of literature and art fans in our

---

[76] "Shui shi 'chulipin'" 谁是 "处理品"? [Who are "goods sold at a reduced price?"], *Beiyou dongfanghong*, November 23, 1967.

[77] Xie Jingyi 谢静宜, *Mao Zedong shenbian gongzuo suoyi* 毛泽东身边工作琐忆 [Scattered recollections of the days working by Mao Zedong's side] (Beijing: Zhongyang wenxian chubanshe, 2015), 208.

university planned to do something meaningful."[78] Rumors spread that the participants in the orchestra just wished to live idly.[79] For the music fans, however, joining such an orchestra could let them take leave from the Cultural Revolution without completely divorcing from it. People like Gu Dai might have been tired of factional struggles and their orchestra did not affiliate with any factions, but they did not lose their faith in the revolution. They did not consider their activity as serving factional struggles or simply a way to distract themselves from the boredom. Instead, they followed the fashion of "serving the laborers" by performing for peasants and factory workers.[80]

Some young people chose to live in a way that ideologically aligned with Communist doctrines in general but was not in accordance with the atmosphere of the Cultural Revolution at a certain moment. In December 1969, Pan Jing, a former student from the Beijing Normal University Girls' High School, went back to Beijing from where she was sent down and met three Peking University students who could not be assigned to either the countryside or the factories because of their "mistakes" in organizing a "Society of Communist Youth." These three students, He Weiling, Hu Dingguo, and Wang Yan, led a "communist way of life" in their dormitory at Peking University after they were released from prison and labor camp. They collected all their money, including subsidies from the university and allowance sent by their parents, together and then distributed according to everyone's needs.[81]

PASSING TIME SAFELY BY EXITING

During the Cultural Revolution, people with less political ambitions also found ways to exit the revolution and pass time correctly and safely. This alternative way of life was first available with the rise of faction-affiliated

---

[78] Gu Dai 谷岱, "Huiyi 'Shajiabang bingtuan'" 回忆 "沙家浜兵团" [Remembering the "Shajiabang Corps"], in Li Qinglin, *Nanwang de qingchun*, 374.

[79] Gu, "Huiyi 'Shajiabang bingtuan'," in Li Qinglin, *Nanwang de qingchun*, 384.

[80] Gu, "Huiyi 'Shajiabang bingtuan'," in Li Qinglin, *Nanwang de qingchun*, 380–381.

[81] Pan Jing 潘婧, "Xinlu lichen: wenge zhong de sifeng xin" 心路历程——"文革"中的四封信 [My journey: four letters during the Cultural Revolution], *Zhongguo zuojia* 6 (1994): 177–179.

propaganda teams across Beijing, when many young people formed their own non-factional choruses and propaganda teams to fulfill their natural needs for recreation and social contact. Later practices included self-organized friendship groups.

In April 1967, high school rebels in Beijing divided into two factions over their attitude toward military training in their schools. The "April 3 Faction" was the radical wing of the rebels who demanded a more radical change in the socio-economic structure, while the "April 4 Faction" was more inclined to continue the Cultural Revolution under the leadership of the military training group in their schools to achieve a "great unity" of different rebel groups in their classes.[82] With the split among rebels, people in Beijing witnessed another alternative way of life that was quite different from the mass movement during the first few months of the Cultural Revolution such as printing tabloids, holding rallies, and denouncing people: the rise of self-organized propaganda teams and chorus performances across Beijing.

The performances of some Red Guard propaganda teams were inevitably full of ideological messages. In the summer of 1967, there were two influential chorus performances produced by Red Guards in Beijing. The first one was *Long Live the Victory of Chairman Mao's Revolutionary Line!* (*Mao zhuxi geming luxian shengli wansui* 毛主席革命路线胜利万岁) produced by high school students of "April 3 Faction" from various high schools. The second one was *Suite of Songs on the Red Guard* (*Hongweibing zuge* 红卫兵组歌) produced by children of cadres. On May 29, 1967, the *Suite of Songs* was staged on Tiananmen Square. On June 2, the *Revolutionary Line* debuted. Both were reported to be welcomed by their audience.[83] During this period, self-organized propaganda teams and choruses sprung up in Beijing, leading to a "high tide of Red Guard literature and art."[84]

---

[82] Bu Weihua 卜伟华, *"Zalan jiushijie": wenhua dageming de dongyuan yu haojie 1966–1968* "砸烂旧世界"——文化大革命的动乱与浩劫 (1966–1968) ["Smashing the Old World": Havoc of the Chinese Cultural Revolution (1966–1968)] (Hong Kong: Chinese University Press, 2008), 497–500.

[83] Yang Jian 杨健, *Wenhua dageming zhong de dixia wenxue* 文化大革命中的地下文学 [Underground literature during the Cultural Revolution] (Beijing: Zhaohua chubanshe, 1993), 34–42.

[84] Yang Jian, *Wenhua dageming zhong de dixia wenxue*, 19.

These propaganda teams inherited the tradition of the Party's mass culture policy in the sense that many participants of propaganda teams were activists in state-organized cultural recreational activities before the Cultural Revolution, which made it possible for students to self-produce, self-direct, and self-perform. For example, two students were in charge of choreographing for the *Revolutionary Line*: one student used to participate in the dancing group in a Children's Palace; the other student was the leader of the dance group in Tsinghua University High School. The student responsible for stage scenery had experience participating in a serial musical showing the history of Beijing 101 Middle School.[85]

Propaganda teams with strong factional identity often had clashes with each other, not because they had different views on art, but simply because they were affiliated with different Red Guard factions. The April 3 Faction propaganda team rehearsed at the auditorium of the Institute of Civil Engineering and Architecture (*jiangong xuexiao* 建工学校) and one day, during their rehearsal, members of the April 4 Faction encircled the auditorium and led to a fight.[86] To protect the propaganda team, the two rebel organizations of the Institute of Civil Engineering and Architecture, the "Flying Tigers" (*feihudui* 飞虎队) and the "Boxers" (yihetuan 义和团), guarded the school gate during rehearsals.[87] The "Flying Tigers" also launched an attack on their adversary: the "Old Guard Chorus" (*laobing hechangtuan* 老兵合唱团) organized by children of cadres. One day, when members of the "Old Guard Chorus" were rehearsing at the dining hall of Beijing No. 4 High School, the "Flying Tigers" broke in with catapults and spears. Seeing the well-equipped "Flying Tigers," the "Old Guards" had to flee.[88]

People had diverse motivations when they joined choruses and propaganda teams. For some children of officials, taking part in a chorus was

---

[85] Hu Sheng 胡生, "Chouchu manzhi yu suiyue cuotuo" 踌躇满志与岁月蹉跎 [From "being ambitious" to "a waste of time"], in *Guanghuan yu yinying* 光环与阴影 [Lights and shadows], ed. Mi Hedu 米鹤都 (Hong Kong: CNHK Publications Limited, 2013), 181–182.

[86] Interview with Hu Tong, December 29, 2018.

[87] Hu Sheng, "Chouchu manzhi yu suiyue cuotuo," in Mi Hedu, *Guanghuan yu yinying*, 183.

[88] Tang Xiaofeng 唐晓峰, "Zou zai dachao bianshang" 走在大潮边上 [Walking beside the tide], in Beidao, Cao Yifan, and Weiyi, *Baofengyu de jiyi*, 340.

a way to show their identity after the Old Red Guard as an organization had been marginalized.[89] Yu Xiangzhen was a junior high school student in Beijing No. 49 High School whose parents worked for the Romanian branch of Xinhua News Agency. As a child of officials, in May 1967, Yu participated in the Chongwen District Red Guard Chorus that was organized to celebrate the first anniversary of the establishment of the Red Guard. Her motivation for taking part in the chorus could be best described as both political and apolitical: on the one hand, their repertoire was to commemorate their parents' revolutionary spirit and they constantly emphasized their identity as Old Red Guards during their performance. On the other hand, Yu still thought that activities in the chorus were different from what Red Guards did during the chaotic months during the Cultural Revolution. She later described her experience in the chorus as "a bright colour in my ten-year dark memory" in her blog article.[90]

Yu recalled her motivation for joining the chorus: "I participated in the chorus because several of my best friends participated in it, and we all liked to sing songs."[91] Although the leaders of this chorus did have their own political ambition (they were arrested in October 1967 for "gossiping about Jiang Qing"), most members of the chorus only cared about singing. They perceived the chorus as a way to exit the revolution while still maintaining social ties. Consequently, members of the chorus tried to avoid joining other organizations that had a conspicuous political agenda. "We would chat when we had rests during rehearsals," said Yu. "The topic was: now that there were Red Guard pickets in Xicheng District and Dongcheng District, should we organize our own picket in Chongwen District? Some said that since we already had a chorus, there was no need to organize a picket because otherwise, we would go beyond art and get connected with politics." Although most of the members of

---

[89] One example to show the marginalized position of the "Old Red Guard" was that children of cadres were planning to perform the *Suite of Songs on the Red Guard* in the Capital Stadium which could hold ten thousand audience. Their plan, however, was denied by the Central Cultural Revolution Group. As a result, they had to change their performance into an open-air show at Tiananmen Square. Yang Jian, *Wenhua dageming zhong de dixia wenxue*, 40.

[90] Yu Xiangzhen, "Wo qinli de wenge shinian ba" 我亲历的文革十年 (八) [Ten years of Cultural Revolution that I experienced, part eight], January 26, 2016, http://www.hybsl.cn/beijingcankao/beijingfenxi/2016-01-26/56689.html.

[91] Interview with Yu Xiangzhen, January 25, 2019.

the Chongwen District Red Guard Chorus were children of officials, the chorus did not have a special requirement about people's family background when recruiting new members. One of the reciters of the chorus was from a capitalist family. Even though his father was close to the CCP and was considered a "red capitalist," he still belonged to the "five black categories" from the perspective of the Old Red Guards in the chorus. "We all knew that he belonged to the 'five black categories'," recalled Yu. "We did not know who recruited him, but he was tall and handsome, and he had a sonorous voice. With him, our chorus was upgraded immediately."[92]

For some other high school students, their motivation was simply to entertain themselves. A group of high students in Beijing No. 3 High School organized a joint propaganda team because they felt too bored. As Hu Tong (pseudonym), then an active member of his propaganda team, recalled, "the propaganda team was a major cultural activity for young people during the Cultural Revolution because we all had nothing else to do."[93]

Inspired by city-wide performances organized by other student propaganda teams, Hu, along with his classmates at Beijing No. 3 High School, organized their own propaganda team as a way to kill time. "We had to find something to do," said Hu passionately five decades later. "The school was paralyzed, so we found that we had nothing to do after coming back to Beijing from the 'Great Linkup'." One problem for Hu and his classmates was that No. 3 High School was a boys' school, but to form a propaganda team, they had to find several female performers. They got connected with students at a nearby girls' school (Beijing No. 6 High School) and asked them to send some girls to sing songs together. As a result, they successfully organized a propaganda team with both boys and girls. The joint propaganda team had three major parts: a band of around thirty students who could play the accordion, violin, flute, and erhu; a chorus of around fifty students; and a "stage work team" responsible for stage scenery and lighting. Members of the propaganda team prepared creatively for performances. Hu remembered an episode from

---

[92] Interview with Yu Xiangzhen, January 25, 2019.
[93] Interview with Hu Tong, December 29, 2018.

the stage work team: "During that time, we wanted to cast a shining portrait of Chairman Mao on the curtain. How did we achieve this special effect to let Chairman Mao shine? We put an electric fan in front of a slide projector, and the picture would twinkle when projected on the curtain."[94]

Apart from distracting them from boredom, for teenagers, joining a propaganda team meant that they could have a formal channel to make friends of the opposite sex. Hu Tong considered that "boys and girls were separated for a long time, but young people could not bear that during their adolescence… There were many opportunities for boys and girls to meet with each other in a propaganda team: we needed to rehearse together, collaborate with each other, and there was operatic dialogue between boys and girls in our performance."[95]

The factional affiliations of the Beijing No. 3 High School and Beijing No. 6 High School Joint Propaganda Team were not obvious.[96] Although they were former rebels in their school, when organizing the propaganda team, they paid more attention to the talent of its members. At the same time, while their major purpose of joining the propaganda team was to entertain themselves, they did not refuse calls from state agencies. Hu Tong was proud that his propaganda team was invited by Beijing TV Station to do a live performance in early 1968. The staff at the TV Station, however, asked them to replace their conductor because he came from a capitalist family ("perhaps they feared that our director would turn around and chant a reactionary slogan during the live broadcast," teased Hu). After realizing that they could not find

[94] Interview with Hu Tong, December 29, 2018.

[95] One unexpected outcome of the Cultural Revolution was to blur the boundary between boys and girls in Beijing. As Michael Crook who studied in Peking University High School recalls, before the Cultural Revolution, the school was "lifeless," but with the outbreak of the Cultural Revolution, boys and girls started to connect with each other. See Ke Makai (Michael Crook) 柯马凯, "Laowai Hongweibing" 老外红卫兵 [A foreign Red Guard], in Mi Hedu, *Guanghuan yu yinying*, 365. Several of Chen Donglin's classmates at Beijing No. 3 High School met their future wives when participating in the propaganda team. Interview with Chen Donglin, December 19, 2018.

[96] During my interview with former members of this propaganda team, the interviewees could hardly identify the political stance of the propaganda team. One interviewee (who was the lead singer of the chorus) maintained that "we belonged to neither April 3 Faction nor April 4 Faction." Interview with a former member of the propaganda team, December 29, 2018.

another conductor because nobody else had the skill, Hu wrote a letter of guarantee to confirm that their conductor would not make trouble. For Hu, when deciding who should attend the TV live broadcast, when deciding who should attend the TV live broadcast, the level of people's performance outweighed their family background.[97]

Some choruses served more like a group of people with similar hobbies instead of a real propaganda team. After the Chongwen District Red Guard Chorus dissolved following the arrest of its four key members in October 1967, Yu Xiangzhen had nothing else to do other than reading tabloids and leaflets on the street with her friends. In early 1968, Yu heard that another chorus had been established in Dongcheng District, so she went to ask the leader of the Dongcheng District Red Guard Chorus whether they still needed new members. When doing so, Yu even did not pay attention to the factional affiliation of the chorus; nor did the leader of the chorus care about the factional affiliation of Yu and her friends. The only criterion was whether they could sing. Yu and her friends were asked to sing several songs, and then they were admitted. In Yu's memory, the organizer of the Dongcheng District Chorus was a tall and skinny boy who only cared about how to coordinate different parts in the chorus. Nobody in the chorus talked about one another's political stance.[98]

Performances of the self-organized propaganda teams could often attract a large audience. Some people went to watch performances because they belonged to the same faction, and thus it was an opportunity to make emotional connections by arousing sympathy. On June 2, when *Long Live the Victory of Chairman Mao's Revolutionary Line!* was staged at the Beijing Exhibition Center Theater, it was reported that "there was a lively atmosphere in the theater. People in the audience chanted slogans with performers, and there were people bursting into tears everywhere."[99] Propaganda teams with less factional backgrounds had a more diversified audience. During the debut of the Chongwen District Red Guard Chorus, teachers, students, and residents nearby who heard about the chorus went to watch their performance. After that, they were invited by various work units and even residents' committees in

---

[97] Interview with Hu Tong, December 29, 2018.
[98] Interview with Yu Xiangzhen, January 25, 2019.
[99] Yang Jian, *Wenhua dageming zhong de dixia wenxue*, 37.

Beijing to perform for them.[100] The audience paid more attention to the quality of the performance itself instead of its political implication. In this sense, the audience regarded the chorus as a regular troupe more than a propaganda team. A then audience member who watched the Chongwen District Red Guard Chorus recalled later: when the chorus performed for a residential compound, "all children in the compound went to watch and the auditorium was densely packed… The performance was brilliant!"[101] The Shajiabang Orchestra in Beijing University of Technology, with its feature of playing symphony, could attract a large crowd of audience who enjoyed Western music even during their rehearsals in the university's dining hall.

In addition to joining choruses and propaganda teams, people could also find new ways to entertain and socialize by exiting the revolution and forming self-organized friendship groups. One of these friendship groups was the underground reading club. In spring 1967, the Beijing Library suddenly reopened after having been closed at the beginning of the Cultural Revolution. Hao Yixing, a then student at Beijing No. 41 High School, went to the library with his friends primarily to kill time. They found that most books available were Mao's books and classic writings of Karl Marx, Friedrich Engels, and Vladimir Lenin. Although they were not very interested in theories, they regarded books by Marx and Engels as literary works and enjoyed their poetic styles. Several months later, Hao stopped going to the Beijing Library and started to exchange books with his friends. He read any books that were available to him, regardless of their genres.[102] In March 1969, Yu Xiangzhen was sent to Beijing No. 3 General Machinery Factory as an apprentice. Yu loved reading in her leisure time when she was a student, and thus she volunteered to be the librarian for her factory's reading room so that she could read books there more conveniently after work. Yu quickly finished reading all of the revolutionary novels collected in her factory reading room, so she had to think about other ways to find more books. During this process, Yu, along with several bookworms in her factory, organized

---

[100] Interview with Yu Xiangzhen, January 25, 2019.

[101] Yu Xiangzhen, "Wo qinli de wenge shinian ba."

[102] Hao Yixing 郝一星, "Shamo zaoquan: wenge huimo zhisan," 沙漠凿泉: 文革回眸之三 [Digging for a spring in a dessert: my recollection on the Cultural Revolution, part three], March 9, 2013, https://difangwenge.org/forum.php?mod=viewthread&tid=8184&highlight=%C9%B3%C4%AE%D4%E4%C8%AA.

an informal "underground reading club" to help them find and exchange books.[103] Members of the reading club basically read books for fun. They read classic literature, history books, and also martial arts novels.[104]

Although there were similar "reading clubs" across Beijing, we should not overestimate their subversive power simply because they were "underground." First of all, many members of underground reading clubs never knew the existence of other similar organizations, and thus it was impossible for them to make city-wide connections.[105] Moreover, reading might not lead to a transformation in people's minds. As Bao Kun recalls, although they could read "banned books" in their small circles, because their way of thinking had already been forged by official ideology, most of them could not draw creative conclusions from these books. Sometimes, the new knowledge they got from "banned books" would in turn intensify what they learned from their schools before the Cultural Revolution. Bao provides an example of reading a volume of Khrushchev's speeches: "We had already identified Khrushchev as a traitor of the communist movement, and a revisionist who had betrayed our trust. His speeches only verified the purity of our ideals, and once again proved that he was a 'bad guy'."[106]

While people had chances to get novels depicting the life of young people in other countries during their reading activities, some did not find lifestyles in the United States and the Soviet Union fascinating after they read Chinese translations of J. D. Salinger's *The Catcher in the Rye*, Vasily Aksyonov's *Ticket to the Stars*, and Vsevolod Kochetov's *What Do You Want*.[107] Hao Yixing read both *The Catcher in the Rye* and *Ticket to the Stars* during his underground reading activities. Although he thought that the style of these novels was very new to him, his perception of these two novels was: "I really do not understand why the authors

---

[103] Yu Xiangzhen, "Wo qinli de wenge shinian ba" 我亲历的文革十年 (十七) [Ten years of Cultural Revolution that I experienced, part seventeen], February 16, 2016, http://www.hybsl.cn/beijingcankao/beijingfenxi/2016-02-16/57024.html.

[104] Interview with Yu Xiangzhen, January 25, 2019.

[105] Interview with Yu Xiangzhen, January 25, 2019.

[106] Bao, "Liming qian de yuedong," in Beidao and Li Tuo, *Qishi niandai*, 183.

[107] Yan Li stresses that Chinese readers learned a more colorful way of life in the Soviet Union and the West through reading these novels during the Cultural Revolution, which could let them "make up their own minds about the Chinese government's relentless slander" on these books. See Li, *China's Soviet Dream*, 183–188.

write about such a group of silly young people. For me, they are just making trouble—they are unhappy with their good life, they run away from home, they are spiritually empty, their actions are ill-tempered, and they like to use dirty and obscene words. Hooligans become protagonists."[108] A Peking University student got a copy of *What Do You Want* in 1973 and recorded his feeling in his diary after reading it: "[This book] talks about the education of the young generation and the problem of Stalin's 'cult of personality.' It reveals the evil and decadent side in the society of Soviet revisionism to some extent. It, however, does not touch the reactionary nature of social imperialism."[109]

As an activist of the underground reading club in the Beijing No. 3 General Machinery Factory, Yu Xiangzhen was extremely good at drawing a line between "good" books and "bad" books by herself. When given a handwritten copy of Alexandre Dumas *fils*'s *Camille*, Yu's first reaction was to refuse because she knew that handwritten copies were under investigation, although she still read it once she knew that it was a classic novel. Yu, however, "resolutely refused" to read other popular handwritten copies such as *A Pair of Embroidered Shoes* 一双绣花鞋, *The Second Handshake* 第二次握手, and *Manna's Memoir* 曼娜回忆录 because she knew that the contents of these books were "bad" and reading such kind of hand-copied books would cause serious trouble.[110]

For those who did not read many books, another way to pass time safely was to eat and drink with friends. Hu Tong held this kind of gathering at his home about once a month since the 1970s during which his friends would come to his house with various kinds of deli food. They ate, drank, played poker, and chatted idly. For Hu and his friends, gatherings for meals formed an important part of their leisure time during the Cultural Revolution because they could air their grievances about work.

---

[108] Hao, "Shamo zaoquan."

[109] Sun Yuecai 孙月才, *Beige yiqu: wenge shinian riji* 悲歌一曲: 文革十年日记 [A diary of Sorrow: ten years of the Cultural Revolution] (Hong Kong: Chinese University Press, 2012), 637.

[110] Interview with Yu Xiangzhen, January 25, 2019. Scholars have realized that some handwritten copies became popular during the Culture Revolution not because their contents were rebellious, but simply because they could meet people's needs for entertainment. See Shuyu Kong, "Between Undercurrent and Mainstream: Hand-copied Literature and Unofficial Culture during and after the Cultural Revolution," *Asian Studies Review* 44, no. 2 (2020): 239–257. What is usually ignored is that even for those who were in dire need of leisure reading like Yu Xiangzhen, handwritten copies were not a safe choice.

Nevertheless, the subversive power in Hu's private gathering was highly limited. Although one major purpose of Hu Tong's eating and drinking gatherings was to vent their grievances, Hu and his friends knew exactly where the boundary was: their grievances were only limited to their gatherings because in other places, they might be reported. Going back to their respective work units, everyone behaved obediently.[111]

Privileged Exits

Exiting the revolution was not an easy choice because people had to get access to material resources necessary for living alternatively.[112] In many cases, the very fact that people could exit the revolution revealed their privilege in the People's Republic of China.[113] For them, similar to the Old Red Guards, exiting the revolution resisted the most radical part of the regime that had temporarily deprived them of their privilege, but it did not resist the overall political system under the CCP. When children of officials engaged in alternative ways of life, they were distinguishing themselves from other rebels by showing off their privilege.

One example comes from the reminiscence of a bystander who joined others in eating and drinking as a way to exit the revolution in late 1967, when his acquaintance with a child of officials greatly facilitated his

---

[111] Interview with Hu Tong, December 29, 2018.

[112] While this section mainly focuses on a group of privileged young people, my point can also be verified from a different angle by my interviews with those from working-class families. When asked how they spent their leisure time during the Cultural Revolution, three of my interviewees who were born to working-class families, graduated from less elitist middle schools, and started working in factories in the early 1970s mentioned that at first, they could only go back home after work because there was nothing else to do. Later, they participated in collective leisure activities after the factory started to organize them. One interviewee told me explicitly that he did not observe any "unhealthy" leisure activities during the Cultural Revolution. Workers would usually choose to attend factory-organized ball games. Interviewee 1, October 24, 2018; Interviewees 2 and 3, November 2, 2018.

[113] As Joel Andreas describes, this privilege came from political capital and cultural capital, which means that young people with official or intellectual family background could get access to the resources that they needed for alternative ways of life more easily than others. Even though old political and cultural elites were ousted temporarily during the Cultural Revolution, their political capital and social capital did not vanish, which laid the groundwork for their future coalition. See Joel Andreas, *Rise of the Red Engineers: The Cultural Revolution and the Origins of China's New Class* (Stanford, CA: Stanford University Press, 2009), 9–11.

accessibility to good food. Several decades later he could still remember his experience eating in Xue Manzi's home with several friends. Xue Manzi was the adopted son of the deputy head of the United Front Work Department of the CCP Central Committee. Although Xue's father was ousted during the Cultural Revolution, his house had not been confiscated yet. The feast was magnificent:

> The dining room was in the west wing. There was a large round table filled with dishes. When I sat down, I noticed that all of the tableware was made with Jingdezhen blue-and-white porcelain that was fine and glossy. The tableware was in sets, including all kinds of soup basins, spoons, and plates. A middle-aged maid served the dishes one by one, following the rules of a formal banquet. Such a magnificent and elegant banquet satisfied both my eyes and my stomach. Now I have forgotten what dishes were served that day. But I can still remember the beautiful sets of blue-and-white porcelain tableware.[114]

Literature and art salons in Beijing, as a form of underground youth subculture, consisted of a large group of privileged young people who had exited the revolution. These salons were largely organized and participated in covertly in small circles by those from families of political and cultural elites before the Cultural Revolution. In Beijing, there were several famous and enduring salons organized, respectively, by Li, Xu Haoyuan, Ye Sanwu, and Zhao Yifan.

Li Li was born to an official family whose father participated in the Long March. She became a key figure of the "underground upper-class society" (*dixia shangliu shehui* 地下上流社会) in Beijing after she came back to Beijing from the countryside in 1969 when a group of people started to gather around her and gradually form a literature and art salon. Activities of the salon included "talking about philosophy, Marxism-Leninism, and ideology; playing musical instruments; singing songs; writing literature; sometimes having bicycle outings."[115] One of the participants of Li Li's salon was Bi Ruxie, the author of a "hand-copied" novel, *The Ninth Wave* (*Jiuji lang* 九级浪), which was popular

---

[114] Hao, "Chi he shinian."
[115] Yang Jian, *Wenhua dageming zhong de dixia wenxue*, 75.

among educated youth in the 1970s.[116] Inspired by Li Li, Bi Ruxie wrote this story about how a boy (Lu Zi) and a girl (Sima Li) degenerated from two innocent young students to "problematic" youth who engaged in loose sexual relations. As a member of Li Li's salon, Bi Ruxie showed his acquaintance with Western and Russian literature and art by having Lu Zi and Sima Li discuss Western and Russian artists and writers including Rembrandt van Rijn, Honoré de Balzac, Pyotr Ilyich Tchaikovsky, and William Shakespeare in his novel.[117] Although *The Ninth Wave* is considered by scholars as the first "Chinese novel to expose and criticize social realities in the Cultural Revolution," the author, as a child of officials himself, still revealed his acquaintance with the life of the small circle of officials and his favor of the world view promoted by the CCP before the Cultural Revolution.[118] As Lu Zi says after realizing that he has been living a "decadent life": "I must become the red successor of the proletariat…Have teenagers like us formed our final world view? Obviously, now our world view is not proletarian. What if it is in accordance with the bourgeoisie? That would be too scary!".[119]

From 1967, Xu Haoyuan organized her own salon based in her home at the residential compound of the State Council. Xu was a senior high school student at Renmin University High School when the Cultural Revolution began. As a child of officials, Xu became influential among Old Red Guards during the early stage of the Cultural Revolution, and she was once arrested for mocking Jiang Qing in a poem. Most of the participants in Xu's salon were children of officials, although she also welcomed people from other family backgrounds. The activities in this salon included reading books on political theory, literature, and art; discussing what was going on; studying theories; reviewing literature works; enjoying music and paintings; and exchanging their own works. Formed by children of former elites, members of the salon could easily get access to internal publications that might be difficult for other people

---

[116] Li, *China's Soviet Dream*, 189; Yang Jian, *Wenhua dageming zhong de dixia wenxue*, 78.

[117] Bi Ruxie 毕汝谐, "Jiuji lang" 九级浪 [The Ninth Wave], in *Shiliao yu chanshi* 史料与阐释 [Historical materials and interpretation], vol. 5, ed. Chen Sihe 陈思和 and Wang Dewei 王德威 (Shanghai: Fudan daxue chubanshe, 2017), 36–37.

[118] On the evaluation of The *Ninth Wave*, see Li, *China's Soviet Dream*, 190.

[119] Bi Ruxie, "Jiuji lang," in Chen Sihe and Wang Dewei, *Shiliao yu chanshi*, 62.

to find.[120] Xu and her friends also participated in an art salon organized in Huang Yuan's home in a residential area full of professors and scholars from the Department of Philosophy and Social Sciences of the Chinese Academy of Sciences. Picture albums, books, records, a piano, and even high-quality wine in Huang's home had survived the house raids, which provided salon participants with a highbrow atmosphere.[121]

Xu explained her mentality when organizing the salon: "We had a strong rebellious mind. You do not allow us to do it? You say that I cannot manage to do it? Then I have to do it!"[122] Although Xu considered her motivation rebellious, from the perspective of others she was the embodiment of the revolution: people believed that she was the daughter of an early member of the CCP who used to study in Moscow; during the early days of the Cultural Revolution, she conducted social surveys in northern Shaanxi, the sacred place of the Chinese revolution, disguising herself as a beggar.[123] Others believed that Xu was determined to be a professional revolutionary like Rosa Luxemburg or Vera Zasulich.[124]

Ye Sanwu was the grandson of Ye Shengtao, a famous writer and educator as well as a senior cultural official since the CCP came into power. After graduating from a teaching school, Ye was first assigned to teach in an elementary school and then sent to a forestry center in suburban Beijing, where he had an accident during work and hurt his spine. As a result, Ye had to convalesce at his Beijing home, during which time he read a lot of famous literary works by both Chinese and foreign writers. Ye was good at introducing and telling stories from novels to others, and his personality made his home a salon for other people who were also interested in literature during the Cultural Revolution.[125] Activities in Ye Sanwu's salon were basically apolitical as members were

---

[120] Yin Hongbiao, *Shizongzhe de zuji*, 191–192. Xu Haoyuan maintains that because there was nothing left in her home after the house raid, she usually got together with her friends in parks. See Xu Haoyuan 徐浩渊, "Shiyang nianhua" 诗样年华 [Poetic years], in Beidao and Li Tuo, *Qishi niandai*, 46.

[121] Xu Haoyuan, "Shiyang nianhua," in Beidao and Li Tuo, *Qishi niandai*, 46.

[122] Xu Haoyuan, "Shiyang nianhua," in Beidao and Li Tuo, *Qishi niandai*, 45.

[123] Yang Jian, *Wenhua dageming zhong de dixia wenxue*, 103.

[124] Hao, "Shamo zaoquan."

[125] Pang Yang 庞旸, "Sanwu de shalong, Sanwu de shi" 三午的沙龙, 三午的诗 [Sanwu's salon, Sanwu's poems], in *Sanwu de shi* 三午的诗 [Sanwu's poems], ed. Ye Xiaomo 叶小沫 (Wuhan: Wuhan daxue chubanshe, 2017), 331–332.

interested mainly in listening to music and talking about literature. From the perspective of one participant, the atmosphere in Ye's salon was similar to salons in Paris: "There were always people reading poems loudly in Sanwu's living room. Sometimes poems were read by their authors, sometimes they were read by beautiful girls. These beautiful girls were mostly admirers of the poets. They were versatile. They could sing or play the piano."[126] Ye's attitude toward the regime was not subversive, although people would talk about their grievances during the Cultural Revolution in his salon. For Ye, it was the radicals instead of the entire regime that should be blamed: in April 1976, Ye was excited when people criticized the Gang of Four and commemorated the late Zhou Enlai by posting poems at Tiananmen Square.[127]

In the 1970s, Zhao Yifan, whose parents were both intellectuals who participated in the communist revolution, formed another influential and active literature salon in Beijing. Zhao's salon was famous for his generosity in offering books and grassroots materials he had collected.[128] At first, people exchanged various kinds of novels in Zhao's salon, including internal publications called "grey-cover books" and "yellow-cover books." Zhao's home became a center for many future poets and writers to meet with one another. Among them, there were members of the "Baiyangdian group of poets," consisting of educated youth who were sent to Baiyangdian and who were interested in writing poems.[129] Participants in Zhao's salon were of the elite and privileged: most of them attended Beijing's key high schools before the Cultural Revolution and started to read heavy theoretical books after they were sent down to the countryside.[130] Most members of the "Baiyangdian group" had special advantages compared to educated youth who were sent to other places. As a sent-down youth who worked in Baiyangdian recalls, they could

---

[126] Ye Zhaoyan 叶兆言, "Wenxue shaonian" 文学少年 [A young man loving literature], in Ye Xiaomo, *Sanwu de shi*, 311.

[127] Ye Yonghe 叶永和, "Sanwu yinxiang" 三午印象 [My impression of Sanwu], in Ye Xiaomo, *Sanwu de shi*, 326–327.

[128] Yin Hongbiao, *Shizongzhe de zuji*, 192–193.

[129] Yang Jian, *Wenhua dageming zhong de dixia wenxue*, 86–87.

[130] Xu Xiao 徐晓, "Wuti wangshi" 无题往事 [Untitled past], in *Chenlun de shengdian: Zhongguo 20 shiji 70 niandai dixia shige* 沉沦的圣殿：中国20世纪70年代地下诗歌 [The fallen shrine: underground poems in China during the 1970s], ed. Liao Yiwu 廖亦武 (Urumqi: Xinjiang qingshaonian chubanshe, 1999), 162.

receive the highest salaries and enjoy the best living conditions there. Additionally, most of the educated youth in Baiyangdian were from official or intellectual families, which made it possible for them to exchange internal publications stolen from their parents.[131]

Finally, it is noticeable that the exiting the revolution was highly privileged in the sense that leading an alternative way of life during the Cultural Revolution might not be common among other young people in Beijing because not all of them had enough time or audacity to do that. As Yu Xiangzhen observes, before Lin Biao's downfall in 1971, people hardly had any free time because her factory would occupy all of their leisure time: "There were political study sessions every morning and evening. There were political movements. We also had to work overtime. We did not need to go to work on Sundays, but there were mandatory labor activities. Where could we find the time?"[132] For other young workers in Beijing, even though they had some leisure time, they still did not dare to take part in self-organized leisure activities. As a senior high school student who was sent to a factory in 1968 recalls, "We had nothing to do after work… We had to stay at home. People seemed to be afraid of having fun."[133]

Conclusion: Did Revolution Have Exits?

By viewing alternative ways of life during the Cultural Revolution not as Chinese versions of hippies or samizdat readers, I have argued that in

---

[131] Zhou Duo 周舵, *Zhou Duo zishu: huiyi yu fansi* 周舵自述：回忆与反思 [Zhou Duo's autobiography: recollections and reflections] (Hong Kong: New Century Press, 2019), 32–33. Sun Peidong's study shows that during the Cultural Revolution, reading activities were highly stratified: educated youth from cadre or intellectual families were more inclined to read books compared to young people from peasant or worker families as they usually had channels to get access to books. See Sun Peidong 孙沛东, "Wenge shiqi Jing Hu zhiqing jiecenghua de geren yuedu" 文革时期京沪知青阶层化的个人阅读 [Stratified individual reading activities among educated youth in Beijing and Shanghai during the Cultural Revolution], *Ershiyi shiji* 156 (August 2016): 78–98.

[132] Interview with Yu Xiangzhen, January 25, 2019. Workers in Yu Xiangzhen's factory had to arrive at their posts by 7:00 am, and they could not leave the factory until political sessions ended at 8:00 pm. Sometimes political sessions would last until 9:00 pm. Yu lived in the factory's dormitory, so she had some time to read books before bedtime. According to Yu's observation, it was a norm for many government offices and factories in Beijing to have very tight schedules before 1971.

[133] Interviewee 2, November 2, 2018.

many ways, youth subcultures in China cannot be construed as a means of resistance to the regime. Going back to Ye Weili's "revolution had exits" statement, we might make further enquires: Did revolution really have exits? Where did these exit lead to?

Ye's statement that "revolution had exits" is correct in the sense that as the Cultural Revolution progressed, many young people in Beijing started to find alternative ways of life by deviating from the revolution. When examining the diverse motivations of the youth who did not participate in the Cultural Revolution and lived alternatively, however, Ye's statement is too simple. While some people exited the revolution because they were tired of fierce factional struggles, there were others with different mentalities. The children of officials (the Old Red Guards) were forced to leave the revolution. Nevertheless, refusing to be politically marginalized, they tried every means to resist the rebels and the Central Cultural Revolution Group through their own way of life. While some people who were keen on organizing propaganda teams only did so for fun, there were others who seriously believed that they were doing something meaningful for the Cultural Revolution.

The "exits" were not one dimensional. Many bystanders left the revolution temporarily, but they were still paying close attention to the revolution and eager to stage a comeback. Meanwhile, exiting the revolution did not mean that people started to reshape their relationship with the state by "passively resisting" through everyday life. In general, although these alternative ways of life seemed to contradict the official propaganda, young people did not develop a subversive subculture during the Cultural Revolution. Many of these alternative ways of life had very close connections with the state, and the dominant ideology and narratives still had a huge influence on young people.

Although many young people might have exited the revolution, these exits did not lead to an alternative political system. People were discontented with the abnormal situation during the Cultural Revolution, but for most of them, what they considered "normal" was actually life under the communist regime without Cultural Revolution-style mass movements. In this sense, exiting the revolution and the alternative ways of life that resulted did not contradict their status as benefiting or wishing to benefit from the regime. Although we can find many alternative ways of life during the Cultural Revolution, most young people never fully rid themselves of the establishment because their thought, their taste, and their ideal way of life had already been shaped by the regime.

CHAPTER 7

Epilogue

DAZHAI VERSUS XIAOJINZHUANG: DEBATING POST-MAO LEISURE REGULATION

One day in the mid-1980s, Old Zhang found that he was leading some young workers to remodel a deserted bomb shelter excavated in his factory during the Cultural Revolution into a ballroom. As the head of his factory's Youth League Committee, Old Zhang was keen on organizing leisure activities for workers. "It seems that invigorating workers' life [through organized activities] is a common practice under communist systems," said Old Zhang in high spirits over three decades later, "Otherwise, what else could workers do in their off-duty hours? We organized some cultural recreational activities to let them have a good time." "But couldn't workers find ways to entertain themselves without activities organized by you? It was the 1980s after all!" I asked. Old Zhang looked at me and answered without any hesitation: "They were certainly able to entertain themselves in some ways, but we could elevate their levels (*cengci* 层次) by organizing some competitions. Some talented young people could naturally come through… We the Youth League organized contests of group dancing. And then our factory got first prize in a contest between over one hundred work units belonged to the Machinery Bureau." My interview with Old Zhang culminated in his nostalgia for the comradeship during organized leisure activities: "In 1985 or 1986, we used lunchtime to organize performances. People watched shows with lunch boxes in their hands. If you were late, you could not even jostle your way to the venue. The performances were extremely great. People applauded... Now we cannot hear such applause anymore."[1]

Old Zhang's story reminds us that the death of Mao Zedong in 1976 was not followed by an end of the CCP's leisure regulation.[2] In early 1978, culture cadres across the country gathered in Dazhai Brigade in Shanxi Province to discuss how to refine the interventionist regime by better organizing leisure activities now that radical leaders of the Cultural Revolution had been purged. According to Zhou Weizhi, then the deputy minister of the Ministry of Culture, this meeting was the first "nationwide meeting on cultural work since the smashing of the 'Gang of Four'."[3] Although Dazhai had been famous for Mao's commendation of its experience in agricultural production, culture cadres now found it necessary to learn from Dazhai about its experience in leisure regulation as well.

Cadres who attended the meeting fiercely denounced the "Xiaojinzhuang experience" of leisure regulation as an antithesis of the "Dazhai

---

[1] Interviewee 1, October 24, 2018.

[2] The post-Mao continuities with the Mao years have been acknowledged by scholars and China observers, although many of them are more willing to emphasize the demise of communism. Timothy Cheek notes that while China is one of the most vibrant capitalist economies in the world, "the CCP continues to rule both in name and in fact." The post-Mao reform was not a complete breakaway from Mao's experiments because some reform policies could be traced back to the CCP's "Four Modernizations" proposed in 1964. Deng Xiaoping reinforced, not weakened, the CCP's dictatorship by strengthening Party organizations instead of ruling as a charismatic leader. See Timothy Cheek, *Living with Reform: China Since 1989* (London: Zed Books, 2006), 32, 55.

[3] "Dali tuidong nongcun qunzhong wenhua gongzuo 'xue Dazhai, gan Xiyang,' wei nongye xue Dazhai, puji Dazhai xian fuwu—Wenhua bu Zhou Weizhi fubuzhang zai quanguo qunzhong wenhua gongzuo 'xue Dazhai, gan Xiyang' jingyan jiaoliu xianchanghui bimuhui shang de jianghua (zhaiyao)" 大力推动农村群众文化工作 "学大寨、赶昔阳"，为农业学大寨、普及大寨县服务——文化部周巍峙副部长在全国群众文化工作 "学大寨、赶昔阳" 经验交流现场会闭幕会上的讲话 [Propelling rural mass cultural work to "learn from Dazhai and catch up with Xiyang" to serve learning from Dazhai in agriculture and publicizing the experience of Dazhai: deputy minister of the Ministry of Culture Zhou Weizhi's remarks during the concluding meeting of the national mass cultural work "Learning from Dazhai and catching up with Xiyang" on-spot experience exchange meeting], in, *Xue Dazhai gan Xiyang: quanguo qunzhong wenhua gongzuo "xue Dazhai, gan Xiyang" jingyan jiaoliu xianchanghui wenjian ziliao xuanbian* 学大寨 赶昔阳: 全国群众文化工作 "学大寨 赶昔阳" 经验交流现场会文件资料选编 [Learning from Dazhai and catching up with Xiyang: Selection of documents from the national mass cultural work "Learning from Dazhai and catching up with Xiyang" on-spot experience exchange meeting], ed. Hunansheng wenhuaguan 湖南省文化馆 (n.p., 1978), 1.

experience." As a village in suburban Tianjin, Xiaojinzhuang attracted national attention after Mao's wife Jiang Qing's visit in June 1974. A *People's Daily* article published in August 1974 hailed Xiaojinzhuang for its ten "new things" that emerged during the Cultural Revolution, which included establishing a political night school, organizing a team of poor and lower-middle peasants to write theoretical articles criticizing Lin Biao and Confucius, letting poor and lower-middle peasants teach others about the history of the struggle between Confucianism and Legalism, singing revolutionary model operas, setting up an amateur propaganda team, writing poems, opening a reading room, telling revolutionary stories, organizing sports teams, and promoting gender equality.[4] But for outsiders, perhaps the most prominent feature of Xiaojinzhuang was its practice of asking everyone to sing songs and write poems.[5] This was of course a continuity of the attempts to expropriate all of the people's leisure time through collective activities during the Great Leap Forward. Nevertheless, in the eyes of the culture cadres who strived to justify their new policies after the Cultural Revolution, what was wrong about the "Xiaojinzhuang experience" was not a tight control and radical politicization of people's private time. Rather, they thought that Xiaojinzhuang failed to offer enough proper cultural recreational activities for its villagers, which made the Party's leisure regulation "cold and bleak" (*lengluo xiaotiao* 冷落萧条) on the ground.[6] As Zhou Weizhi revealed, the "Xiaojinzhuang experience" blurred the boundary between work and leisure in the sense that villagers were forced to "leave their work to engage in culture." He cited a villager's complaints: "Commune members sing [model] operas at home; PLA soldiers do farm work on the hillside."[7] In other words, the "Xiaojinzhuang experience" failed to let villagers do the right things at the right time.

Leisure activities organized in Dazhai were in fact astonishingly similar to those in Xiaojinzhuang. During the 1978 meeting, reports delivered to culture cadres across the country by leaders in Xiyang County (where

---

[4] RMRB, August 4, 1974.

[5] Jeremy Brown, *City Versus Countryside in Mao's China: Negotiating the Divide* (Cambridge: Cambridge University Press, 2012), 220.

[6] "Dali tuidong nongcun qunzhong wenhua gongzuo 'xue Dazhai, gan Xiyang'," in Hunansheng wenhuaguan, *Xue Dazhai gan Xiyang*, 6.

[7] "Dali tuidong nongcun qunzhong wenhua gongzuo 'xue Dazhai, gan Xiyang'," in Hunansheng wenhuaguan, *Xue Dazhai gan Xiyang*, 11.

Dazhai located) highlighted singing, painting, poetry, and commentary writing as new models that other places should follow. Then what was the difference between the "Xiaojinzhuang experience" and the "Dazhai experience" in terms of leisure regulation? From the perspective of Guo Fenglian, the Party head of Dazhai, leisure activities in Xiaojinzhuang were merely organized "as a formality" because "even old people in their eighties were asked to sing model operas."[8] This assertion was confusing because when introducing their good experience of collective singing, the leader from the nearby Li'anyanggou Brigade claimed that they let "people from seniors in their eighties to preschool children all got involved in singing activities."[9] Xiaojinzhuang was also criticized for prioritizing "superstructure" over production.[10] This post-mortem was also in an awkward situation when the Party head of the Wujiaping Brigade claimed that their experience of organizing peasants to write short commentaries could facilitate production despite natural disasters in the 1970s: "beautiful flowers of ideology can eventually yield abundant economic fruits…Cadres and commune members have benefited from revolutionary culture."[11]

These similarities in villagers' everyday life in Dazhai and Xiaojinzhuang indicate that they were not the antithesis to each other. Their tensions were largely man-made as a result of the ebbs and flows of their

---

[8] "Fazhan shehuizhuyi wenhua cujin shehui zhuyi geming he jianshe" 发展社会主义文化 促进社会主义革命和建设 [Developing socialist culture, promoting socialist revolution and construction], in *Quanguo qunzhong wenhua gongzuo "xue Dazhai, gan Xiyang" jingyan jiaoliu xianchanghui cailiao* 全国群众文化工作"学大寨、赶昔阳"经验交流现场会材料 [Materials from the national mass cultural work "Learning from Dazhai and catching up with Xiyang" on-spot experience exchange meeting], ed. Henansheng gewei wenhuaju 河南省革委文化局 (n.p., 1978), 17.

[9] Xiyang Jiedu gongshe Li'anyanggou dangzhibu 昔阳界都公社里安阳沟党支部, "Tantan women dadui de geyong huodong" 谈谈我们大队的歌咏活动 [Talking about singing activities in our brigade], Henansheng gewei wenhuaju, *Quanguo qunzhong wenhua gongzuo "xue Dazhai, gan Xiyang" jingyan jiaoliu xianchanghui cailiao*, 3.

[10] Brown, *City versus Countryside*, 218–219.

[11] Xiyang Wujiaping dahui dangzhibu 昔阳武家坪大队党支部, ed., "Women de xiaopinglun shi ruhe wei nongye xue Dazhai fuwu de" 我们的小评论是如何为农业学大寨服务的 [How did our short commentaries serve the learning from Dazhai movement], Henansheng gewei wenhuaju, *Quanguo qunzhong wenhua gongzuo "xue Dazhai, gan Xiyang" jingyan jiaoliu xianchanghui cailiao*, 6.

respective political patrons.[12] The 1978 debate between "Dazhai experience" and "Xiaojinzhuang experience" of leisure regulation was not to reconsider the Party's tight regulation of people's private time but to reaffirm who had the right do this under new circumstances. As Zhou Weizhi emphasized, "We must pay attention to the role of mass culture work... We must grasp it well persistently and thoroughly."[13]

NEW TRENDS AND OLD TRADITIONS IN THE 1980S

Zhou Weizhi's remarks immediately met challenges because, in the early 1980s, some grassroots cadres started to doubt whether it was still necessary to regulate young people's leisure time. A Youth League cadre from a factory in Hubei Province wrote to the journal *China Youth*, asking about whether it was still appropriate to regulate young people's off-duty hours now that people focused more on the economy. According to him, a retired worker wrote to their Youth League branch, suggesting that the League should take some measures to solve problems of young workers making trouble after work. Although the Youth League branch decided to organize more leisure activities, the administrative leader in the workshop had a different opinion: "You have accomplished your mission when regulating the eight on-duty hours... Why bother regulating the time beyond the eight hours? Can't they have fun by themselves?" Editors from *China Youth*, of course, criticized the tendency of having a free hand in young people's leisure time in a militarized tone that was common in the CCP's rhetoric: "It is a noteworthy problem regarding who should occupy the position of young people's leisure time. The Youth League is responsible to study this issue and occupy this position...The Youth League must regulate both the eight on-duty hours and time beyond the eight hours."[14]

Throughout the 1980s, official policies maintained that it was right and proper for the political power to continuously interfere in young people's

---

[12] Brown, City versus Countryside, 225–226.

[13] "Dali tuidong nongcun qunzhong wenhua gongzuo 'xue Dazhai, gan Xiyang'," in Hunansheng wenhuaguan, *Xue Dazhai gan Xiyang*, 14.

[14] "Baxiaoshi yiwai gaibugai guan" 八小时以外该不该管 [Should we regulate people's time beyond the eight hours], in *Zenyang huoyue zhibu shenghuo* 怎样活跃支部生活 [How to invigorate life in Youth League branches], ed. Gongqingtuan zhongyang zuzhibu 共青团中央组织部 (Beijing: Zhongguo qingnian chubanshe, 1981), 50–54.

leisure time. In 1980, the CCP issued a "No. 51 Document," suggesting that "organizing beneficial and variegated leisure cultural and sporting activities is important for the youth to resist ideological influence from the bourgeoisie and all exploiting classes."[15] Compared with the highly politicized and collectivized leisure in the Mao era, however, post-Mao leisure regulation sought to indirectly institutionalize young people's time usage. During the 1980s, the primary goal of leisure regulation shifted from the forging of "new people" to more practical purposes. This trend resulted in ordinary people and not just Party and government officials offering their views on rationalizing the leisure time of youth.

The first purpose of leisure regulation in the 1980s was to let young people acquire professional skills so that they could be better qualified to participate in the economic reform. In 1980, a journal titled *Beyond the Eight Hours* (*Baxiaoshi Yiwai* 八小时以外) was launched with the goal of directing young people's leisure time. Regarding the journal's purpose, the editors called upon its young readers to "cherish the time beyond the eight [on-duty] hours, learn skills, broaden your knowledge, get self-cultivated… to contribute more to the construction of the 'Four Modernizations'."[16] In the first issue of this journal, a then-famous advocate for the "theory of people with talent" (*rencai xue* 人才学) sold his theory that leisure time was vital for those who want to become "talented people." According to the author, "basic civilization" (*jichu wenming* 基础文明), which was an encompassing concept including people's level of knowledge and self-cultivation, was essential in international competition in the sense that the level of basic civilization could reflect the degree of "development" of different countries. Individuals with a higher level of basic civilization could more easily make contributions and become "people with talents." The author, therefore, appealed to his readers that to better serve the national agenda, young people must "make their leisure time tasteful and colourful" so that the level of basic civilization of the whole country would be greatly boosted.[17] Hu Yaobang, head of the

---

[15] Zhongyang tuanxiao qingnian gongzuo jiaoyanshi 中央团校青年工作教研室 ed., *Gongqingtuan gongzuo lilun xuexi gangyao* 共青团工作理论学习纲要 [Outlines for theoretical studies on the work of the Communist Youth League] (n.p., 1982), 168.

[16] "Zhi duzhe" 致读者 [To our readers], *Baxiaoshi yiwai* 1 (1980): 39.

[17] Lei Zhenxiao 雷桢孝, "Rencai, jichu wenming yu yeyu shijian" 人才、基础文明与业余时间 [People with talent, basic civilization, and leisure time], *Baxiaoshi yiwai* (1) 1980: 22–23.

CCP Central Committee who was widely regarded as an open-minded reformist, inherited the tradition of leisure regulation and expressed his concern that young people might use too much time to entertain themselves instead of enriching their knowledge. In October 1981, during a meeting with key members of the Youth League Central Committee, Hu said: "Why do people spend so much time playing poker when they are still young?... Spending too much time on movies, poker, and chess games is a waste of life."[18]

In the 1980s, the leisure time of many young people in Beijing was institutionalized by the state when they fervently studied skills to facilitate their jobs. Old Zhang went to a workers' university to learn enterprise management, and he was not alone in pursuing professional knowledge voraciously in his leisure time. According to a report published in *Beijing Evening News* on February 20, 1984, "studying" had become the most fundamental element in young people's leisure time in Beijing.[19] A survey on leisure allocation of Beijing youth conducted by the Youth League Committee of *Beijing Daily* in 1986 revealed more details about what and why young people participated in studying activities in their leisure time. According to this survey, among the 877 young people who took the survey, 73% of them enrolled in various kinds of training sessions. A young worker who registered in a remedial school for self-taught college entrance examination told the journalist that his dream major was computer science because he wanted to manage a restaurant by using a computer in the future. A female young worker learned English in an extracurricular session, but she was not for a diploma. Instead, she wished to understand what foreign experts in her factory were talking about. A salesperson chose to study sociology in a correspondence college in his leisure time to help him "better understand people and customers."[20] Only 15% of the young people surveyed did not participate in any kind of training session in their leisure time.[21] An American tourist in Beijing recorded people's enthusiasm learning English and other skills in night

---

[18] Gao Yong 高勇, *Wo gei Hu Yaobang dang mishu* 我给胡耀邦当秘书 [I served Hu Yaobang as his secretary] (Beijing: Renmin chubanshe, 2016), 280.

[19] *Beijing wanbao*, February 20, 1984.

[20] *Beijing wanbao*, December 4, 1986.

[21] *Beijing wanbao*, December 7, 1986.

schools.²² The willingness to institutionalize people's time into the state agenda was also reflected by a poem entitled "Farewell, Afternoon Siesta" published in *Beijing Evening News* in January 1985 in which the author expressed his hope that people should reduce their siesta hours to "use this time to its full extent so that rejuvenated China can take off more rapidly."²³

The second purpose of leisure regulation in the 1980s was to distract young people from other activities that might disrupt social order. Using the official language in the Party's "No. 51 Document" of 1980, the purpose of organizing leisure activities was to "maintain stability and unity" (*weihu anding tuanjie* 维护安定团结).²⁴ Social order was connected to the emerging new "atmosphere" (*fengqi* 风气) in people's leisure time that the Party found disturbing. Spontaneous ballroom dance, once again, came under the spotlight. On the one hand, the reshuffled Party leadership regarded dancing as a way to show the changing tide in people's life compared to the stifling life during the Cultural Revolution. In October 1978, during the closing ceremony of the Tenth National Congress of the Communist Youth League, Han Ying, the newly elected Youth League head, danced with young representatives attending the conference. His behavior purportedly aroused heated discussion across the country.²⁵ On the other hand, like the situation in the early 1950s, the Party was attentive to any self-organized dancing activities and whether young people could behave properly when they were dancing. In June 1980, the Ministry of Public Security and the Ministry of Culture jointly issued a notification, ordering the ban of "profit-making dancing parties" (*yingyexing wuhui* 营业性舞会) and "spontaneous dancing parties in public space" (*gonggong changsuo zifa wuhui* 公共场所自发舞会). According to the notification, since 1979, "profit-making dancing parties" emerged in many major cities in China. Although most of these dancing parties were actually organized by official cultural recreational facilities including cultural palaces, clubs, theaters, and parks, the authorities still found it improper for the organizers to "put

---

[22] Paul Theroux, *Riding the Iron Rooster: By Train through China* (New York: G. P. Putnam's Sons, 1988), 102–103.

[23] *Beijing wanbao*, January 26, 1985.

[24] Zhongyang tuanxiao qingnian gongzuo jiaoyanshi, *Gongqingtuan gongzuo lilun xuexi gangyao*, 168.

[25] *Jidang yu huisheng*, 23.

posters publicly to solicit dancers." In parks or even on the streets, young people also gathered spontaneously to dance. Sometimes, their activities could attract "nearly ten thousand onlookers." These dancing parties, as castigated by the authorities, "brought many problems to social order" in the sense that some people "danced in a vulgar style, acted like buffoons, and offended public decency."[26]

The Party paid special attention to the problem of increasing juvenile crimes as well. Unlike the practice that regarded youth delinquency only as ideological problems in the 1950s, in the 1980s, with the criminalization of youth delinquency, the authorities used startling cases of juvenile crimes to warn people about the danger of getting degenerated in their leisure time. In February 1980, the Beijing Municipal Party Committee convened a conference, calling for a "total war" to educate the youth. The Municipal Party Committee asked its grassroots organizations to "enrich young people's spiritual life, and actively occupy the position of young people's leisure cultural activities" so that the problem of juvenile crimes could be better solved.[27] The authorities launched a cooperative propaganda campaign. In April 1980, the *Beijing Evening News* published an article with a sensational title "How Did She Die Exactly," offering details about how a young worker murdered his wife because he engaged in an extramarital affair. The editor of the newspaper wrote in his notes to the readers: "People should not overlook trivia in your life. If you do not resist the corrosive influence of bourgeois thought, trivia in your life can cause crimes."[28] In the meantime, scholars attributed juvenile crimes to the lack of guidance in young people's leisure time and demanded a more interventionist approach from the state.[29]

---

[26] "Gongan bu wenhua bu guanyu qudi yingyexing wuhui he gonggong changsuo zifa whui de tongzhi" 公安部、文化部关于取缔营业性舞会和公共场所自发舞会的通知 [Notification from the Ministry of Public Security and the Ministry of Culture on banning profit-making dancing parties and spontaneous dancing parties in public space] (June 14, 1980), *Gongan jianshe* 12 (1980): 5–6.

[27] *Beijing wanbao*, February 28, 1980.

[28] *Beijing wanbao*, April 7, 1980; *Beijing wanbao*, April 8, 1980.

[29] For a collection of academic studies on juvenile crime in the early 1980s, see Zhongguo shehui kexueyuan qingshaonian yanjiusuo 中国社会科学院青少年研究所, ed., *Qingshaonian fanzui yanjiu ziliao huibian di'erji lunwen xuan* 青少年犯罪研究资料汇编第二辑 论文选 [Collection of materials on juvenile crime studies, vol. 2: research papers] (n.p., 1981).

The third purpose of leisure regulation in the 1980s was to use people's way of life as a tool to showcase China's new look and to justify the reforms. As new economic policies with "capitalist" elements were introduced, Party leaders found it necessary to emphasize the "socialist" affiliations of the regime. In December 1980, Deng Xiaoping highlighted the notion of "spiritual civilization" (*jingshen wenming* 精神文明) to indicate that as a socialist country, China under reform should not only pursue abundant material goods but also meet a high cultural and ideological standard.[30] As Zhao Dingxin, then Beijing's top culture cadre, analyzed in 1982, "to achieve a socialist modernization, we must grasp material civilization on the one hand, and grasp spiritual civilization on the other hand… If we only grasp material civilization and leave spiritual civilization unattended, our regime will be the same as capitalism." Zhao put spiritual civilization over material civilization as he cited a four-point direction on the construction of Beijing from the Central Secretariat of the CCP in April 1980 in which the first three points were all about spiritual civilization (ideology, urban planning, and science and culture). For Zhao, spiritual civilization in Beijing could not be achieved without the regulation of people's leisure activities.[31]

A bolder step came from the Third Plenary Session of the Twelfth Central Committee of the CCP that concluded in October 1984 during which the Party finalized and issued its "Decision on the Reform of Economic Structure." As a part of the umbrella concept of spiritual civilization, the notion of "lifestyle" was mentioned three times at the end of this decision. According to the CCP, economic reform would "lead not only to important changes in people's economic life but also to profound changes in the lifestyle and mentality of the people." This lifestyle should be "civilized, healthy, and scientific" so that it could be "suited to the modernization of productive forces" as well as the "progress of the society."[32] This was considered an innovation by scholars immediately

---

[30] Deng Xiaoping, "Implement the Policy of Readjustment, Ensure Stability and Unity," December 25, 1980, https://dengxiaopingworks.wordpress.com/2013/02/25/implement-the-policy-of-readjustment-ensure-stability-and-unity/.

[31] Zhao Dingxin 赵鼎新, "Zai qunzhong wenhua gongzuo huiyi shang de jianghua" 在群众文化工作会议上的讲话 [Speech during the meeting on mass culture], March 30, 1982, BMA, 164–003-00,304–00080.

[32] "Zhonggong zhongyang guanyu jingji tizhi gaige de jueding" 中共中央关于经济体制改革的决定 [The CCP Central Committee's decision on the reform of economic

because since the CCP came to power in 1949, the Party usually used "lifestyle" or "way of life" in a derogative tone by adding the adjective "bourgeois." Academic studies on the "modern" or "socialist" lifestyle surged shortly afterward.[33]

Numerous newspaper and journal articles sprung up in response to the Party's call for a new lifestyle in accordance with the new era. Tong Dalin, a veteran economic cadre, talked about how to be a "modern" Beijing resident with a journalist from the *Beijing Evening News* in October 1984. Tong proposed that to be a model "modern" citizen, people should live a "modern" way of life, which should be "more and more diversified and colourful."[34] *China Youth Daily*, the mouthpiece of the Communist Youth League, organized a discussion on "youth and modern lifestyle" starting from November 1984 to let people understand that their way of life could reflect the effectiveness of the economic reform.[35] The Youth League also edited and published books teaching young people how to live. For example, in 1987, the Department of Propaganda of the Youth League Central Committee published a *Handbook on Young People's Life* in which various aspects of everyday life, from philosophical investigations on the meaning of life to practical instructions on what men should do to have a healthy and graceful body, were discussed in a Q & A format. The book was organized into five sections (life and concepts about life, social and political life, family life, cultural and sporting life, material life), with a preface written by Liu Binjie, then head of the Department of Propaganda of the Youth League Central Committee. In the preface, Liu asked young people to "live under the logic of history." According to Liu, the ideal way of life under economic reform must "reflect the civilized life of contemporary Chinese people," with both "national characteristics" and "a sense of the new era."[36] Because the Party was anxious to transform

structure], October 20, 1984, http://www.gov.cn/test/2008-06/26/content_1028140_2.htm.

[33] Huidi Ma and Er Liu, *Traditional Chinese Leisure Culture and Economic*, 236–238.

[34] *Beijing wanbao*, October 29, 1984.

[35] Gongqingtuan zhongyang yanjiushi 共青团中央研究室, ed., *Zhongguo qingnian gongzuo nianjian 1985* 中国青年工作年鉴1985 [Yearbook of youth work in China, 1985] (Beijing: Zhongguo qingnian chubanshe, 1986), 227.

[36] Gongqingtuan zhongyang xuanchuanbu 共青团中央宣传部, ed., *Qingnian shenghuo shouce* 青年生活手册 [Handbook on young people's life] (Jinan: Shandong renmin chubanshe, 1987), 1–4.

young people's way of life into a "modern" one, leaders in some work units in Beijing even asked all young people to learn how to dance because dancing was "the symbol of youth" and those who did not dance would become "disabled youth of the 1980s." In another work unit, people who did not dance could not serve as heads of Youth League branches.[37]

Surprisingly, the rising force of Chinese intellectuals in the 1980s did not see the Party's leisure regulation as an outdated practice that should be abandoned during the reform because the Party's effort resonated with their long-lasting desire to be ordinary people's advisors in all aspects. Some intellectuals saw leisure regulation both as a money tree and as a bridge for them to establish direct connections with young people. When China's democracy movement veteran Chen Ziming was raising funds for his nascent independent think tank, he and his colleagues found that books teaching young people how to live could be profitable. One of Chen's colleagues, Li Shengping, jumped on a train from Beijing to Guangzhou just to learn what ordinary people were interested in. Although Li found that people were not interested in lofty topics, he still did not agree with the idea of compiling books with vulgar contents to make quick money.[38] As a result, Li edited and published a heavy book entitled *Handbook on Young People's Social Life in the Modern World* in 1985. The book became a real hit. About 500 million copies were sold, with a profit of over 20 million *yuan*.[39] Compared with other books with the same theme published during the 1980s, this book included a full chapter about how official organizations, including Youth League, Labor Union, and Women's Association, could better organize leisure activities, indicating that even intellectuals who aimed to become an independent force outside the party-state still accepted and even welcomed state intervention in young people's private time.[40]

---

[37] *Beijing qingnianbao*, April 16, 1985.

[38] Xu Xiao 徐晓, ed., *Xundaozhe: mianhuai Chen Ziming* 殉道者: 缅怀陈子明 [A martyr: In memory of Chen Ziming] (New York: Mirror Books, 2015), 225.

[39] Chen Ziming 陈子明, *Jingji lu, duli lu: Chen Ziming zishu* 荆棘路、独立路: 陈子明自述 [A difficult and independent road: Chen Ziming's autobiography] (Taipei: Xiuwei zixun, 2009), 104.

[40] For the contents of the book, see Li Shengping 李盛平, ed., *Xiandai qingnian shejiao shouce* 现代青年社交手册 [Handbook on young people's social life in the modern world] (Beijing: Shuili dianli chubanshe, 1985).

Conclusion

The case of Beijing shows how the Chinese Communist Party achieved much of its interventionist rule not through mass terror, but through the establishment of a way of life that was attractive to many ordinary people through leisure regulation and lifestyle politics. This finding is not to deny the fact that mass terror did exist and was a tool for the CCP to rule its people, as many scholars have previously shown. For those who did not wish to yield to the Party, political terror was genuine when millions were executed or arrested as "counterrevolutionaries." Even for those who did not regard themselves as dissidents, the existence of secret informers around them proved that life was far from easy as the Party was basically suspicious of anyone.[41] Emphasizing these dark sides, however, contributes little to our understanding of the diversity of the CCP's toolbox as they do not explain the widespread nostalgia for life during the Mao era.

Of course, case studies in this book show that throughout the Mao era, persistent elements of subcultures (alternative ways of life) can be observed. One of the major contributions of this book is to position these subcultures between different layers of the Party's leisure regulation to examine what the Party actually achieved, despite so many seemingly defiant phenomena. The Party's policies were never one-dimensional. While the idealist goal that the CCP wished to achieve was to forge ideologically conformist "new people" through a thorough politicization of leisure, this layer of leisure regulation usually backfired because it was almost impossible to transform people's mind, and it was natural for young people to loathe too many political elements in their leisure. The Party's policies of collectivization and institutionalization of young people's leisure, however, met fewer challenges because they were achieved in a silent way. Many people who engaged in subcultures defied the politicization of their leisure, some might have defied the process of collectivization, but few defied the process of institutionalization. The Chinese Communist Revolution might have failed to transform people's minds, but it successfully made people get accustomed to living with the presence of the CCP in their private life.

---

[41] Michael Schoenhals, *Spying for the People: Mao's Secret Agents, 1949–1967* (Cambridge: Cambridge University Press, 2013).

The Party's uninterrupted policy of leisure regulation reveals historical continuity, and this book proposes that the Deng Xiaoping regime did not depart from Maoist interventionism but simply exercised in a more refined manner. Although Party cadres in the 1980s sought to reform many aspects of old structures and institutions from the Mao era, they never considered it appropriate to ease their regulation of young people's leisure and way of life. The effectiveness of the CCP's leisure regulation in the 1980s may be assessed through the response of individuals, such as intellectuals who sought to play an important and independent role in reform. While content with the decreased politicization of leisure, these intellectuals actively called upon the Party to include the rational institutionalization of leisure in its long march toward modernization.

REFERENCES

ARCHIVES

Beijing Municipal Archives

PERIODICALS

Baxiaoshi yiwai 八小时以外 [Beyond the eight hours]
Beijing gongzuo 北京工作 [Work in Beijing]
Beijing pinglun 北京评论 [Beijing review]
Beijing qingnian bao 北京青年报 [Beijing youth daily]
Beijing ribao 北京日报 [Beijing daily]
Beijing wanbao 北京晚报 [Beijing evening news]
Beiyou dongfanghong 北邮东方红 [The east is red in the Beijing Institute of Posts and Telecommunications]
Bingtuan zhanbao 兵团战报 [Battlefield communique of the corps]
Dianying zhanbao/Hongdeng bao 电影战报/红灯报 [Battlefield communique on films/The red lantern]
Dongfanghong 东方红 [The east is red]
Duiwai wenhua zhanbao 对外文化战报 [Battlefield communique on foreign cultural exchange]
Fengleiji 风雷激 [Wind and thunder are surging]
Gongren ribao 工人日报 [Worker's daily]
Hongweibing yundong 红卫兵运动 [The Red Guard movement]
Jiefang ribao 解放日报 [Jiefang daily]
Manhua 漫画 [Cartoon]

Neibu cankao 内部参考 [Internal reference]
Pi Liao zhanbao 批廖战报 [Battlefield communique denouncing Liao Chengzhi]
Renmin ribao 人民日报 [People's daily]
Tianjin wanbao 天津晚报 [Tianjin evening news]
Zhanwang 展望 [Outlook]
Zhongguo qingnian 中国青年 [China youth]
Zhongguo qingnian bao 中国青年报 [China youth daily]

Books and Articles

"1966: Lao Mo de jifeng zhouyu" 1966: 老莫的疾风骤雨 [1966: Storm in Lao Mo], July 13, 2009, http://news.sohu.com/20090713/n265183788.shtml.
A Ying 阿英. *Gongchang wenyu gongzuo de lilun yu shijian* 工厂文娱工作的理论与实践 [Theory and practice of cultural and recreational work in factories]. Beijing: Shenghuo dushu xinzhi sanlian shudian, 1950.
Abrams, Lynn. *Workers' Culture in Imperial Germany: Leisure and Recreation in the Rhineland and Westphalia*. London: Routledge, 1992.
Adorno, Theodor W. *Critical Models: Interventions and Catchwords*, trans. Henry W. Pickford. New York: Columbia University Press, 2005.
"Address of the President to Congress, Recommending Assistance to Greece and Turkey," March 12, 1947, https://www.trumanlibrary.gov/library/research-files/address-president-congress-recommending-assistance-greece-and-turkey?documentid=NA&pagenumber=1.
Andreas, Joel. *Disenfranchised: The Rise and Fall of Industrial Citizenship in China*. New York: Oxford University Press, 2019.
———. *Rise of the Red Engineers: The Cultural Revolution and the Origins of China's New Class*. Stanford, CA: Stanford University Press, 2009.
Arendt, Hannah. *The Origins of Totalitarianism*. New York: Harcourt Brace Jovanovich, 1973.
Aron, Raymond. *Democracy and Totalitarianism*, trans. Valence Ionescu. London: George Weidenfeld and Nicolson, 1968.
Baker, Chris. *The SAGE Dictionary of Cultural Studies*. London: SAGE Publications, 2004.
Bai Zhaojie 白肇杰. "Jiuri Beijing de digunqiu he taiqiu" 旧日北京的地滚球和台球 [Bowling and billiards in old Beijing], *Beijing tiyu wenshi* 4 (1989): 14–15.
Bailey, Peter. *Leisure and Class in Victorian England: Rational Recreation and the Contest for Control, 1830–1885*. London: Routledge & Kegan Paul, 1978.
Beidao 北岛, Cao Yifan 曹一凡, and Weiyi 维一, eds. *Baofengyu de jiyi 1965–1970 nian de Beijing sizhong* 暴风雨的记忆: 1965–1970年的北京四中 [Memories of the thunderstorm: Beijing No. 4 High School from 1965 to 1970]. Hong Kong: Oxford University Press, 2011.

———, and Li Tuo 李陀, eds. *Qishi niandai* 七十年代 [The 1970s]. Hong Kong: Oxford University Press, 2008.

Beijing difangzhi bianzuan weiyuanhui 北京地方志编纂委员会, ed. *Beijing zhi wenhua yishu juan xijui zhi quyi zhi dianying zhi* 北京志 文化艺术卷 戏剧志 曲艺志 电影志 [Annals of Beijing, volume of culture and art, annals of drama, annals of folk vocal art, annals of film]. Beijing: Beijing chubanshe, 2000.

Beijing difangzhi bianzuan weiyuanhui 北京地方志编纂委员会, ed. *Beijing zhi xinwen chuban guangbo dianshi juan guangbo dianshi zhi* 北京志 新闻出版广播电视卷 广播电视志 [Annals of Beijing, volume of news, publication, radio, and television, annals of radio and television]. Beijing: Beijing chubanshe, 2006.

Beijing qingnian she 北京青年社, ed. *Qingnian julebu di yi ji* 青年俱乐部 第一辑 [Youth club, vol. 1]. Beijing: Beijing qingnian she, 1950.

Beijing renmin guangbo diantai 北京人民广播电台, ed. *Beijing renmin guangbo diantai zhi* 1949–1993 北京人民广播电台志 1949–1993 [Annals of the Beijing People's Radio Station]. n.p., 1999.

Beijingshi dang'anguan 北京市档案馆, ed. *Beijing dang'an shiliao: dang'an zhong de Beijing wenhua* 北京档案史料：档案中的北京文化 [Archival historical materials of Beijing: the culture of Beijing in archival documents]. Beijing: Xinhua chubanshe, 2012.

Beijingshi danganguan 北京市档案馆 and Zhonggong Beijng shiwei dangshi yanjiushi 中共北京市委党史研究室, eds. *Beijing shi zhongyao wenxian xuanbian* 1948.12–1949 北京市重要文献选编 1948.12–1949 [Selection of important documents of Beijing, 1948.12–1949]. Beijing: Zhongguo dangan chubanshe, 2001.

Beijingshi danganguan 北京市档案馆 and Zhonggong Beijingshiwei dangshi yanjiushi 中共北京市委党史研究室, eds. *Beijing shi zhongyao wenxian xuanbian 1956 nian* 北京市重要文献选编 1956年 [Selection of important documents of Beijing, 1956]. Beijing: Zhongguo dangan chubanshe, 2003.

Bennett, Andy, and Keith Kahn-Harris, eds., *After Subculture: Critical Studies in Contemporary Youth Culture*. New York: Palgrave Macmillan, 2004.

Berstein, Thomas P., and Hua-yu Li, eds. *China Learns from the Soviet Union, 1949–Present*. Lanham, MD: Lexington Books, 2010.

Bianco, Lucien. *Stalin and Mao: A Comparison of the Russian and Chinese Revolutions*, trans. Krystyna Horko. Hong Kong: Chinese University Press, 2018.

"Biejuyige de yinba gequ," 别具一格的印巴歌曲 [The unique songs from India and Pakistan], January 15, 2013, http://web.archive.org/web/201912042 33831/http:/blog.sina.com.cn/s/blog_5f65e6690101b6zg.html.

Binkley, Sam. "Governmentality and Lifestyle Studies," *Sociology Compass* 1 (2007): 111–126.

Brown, Jeremy. *City versus Countryside in Mao's China: Negotiating the Divide.* Cambridge: Cambridge University Press, 2012.

———, and Matthew D. Johnson, eds. *Maoism at the Grassroots: Everyday Life in China's Era of High Socialism.* Cambridge, MA: Harvard University Press, 2015.

———, and Paul G. Pickowicz, eds. *Dilemmas of Victory: The Early Years of the People's Republic of China.* Cambridge, MA: Harvard University Press, 2010.

Bu Weihua 卜伟华. *"Zalan jiushijie:" wenhua dageming de dongyuan yu haojie 1966-1968* "砸烂旧世界"——文化大革命的动乱与浩劫 (1966–1968) ["Smashing the Old World": Havoc of the Chinese Cultural Revolution (1966–1968)]. Hong Kong: Chinese University Press, 2008.

Cai Xiang 蔡翔. *Geming/xushu: Zhongguo shehui zhuyi wenxue-wenhua xiangxiang 1949–1966* 革命/叙述: 中国社会主义文学—文化想象 (1949–1966) [Revolution and narrative: the imagination of Chinese socialist literature and culture, 1946–1966]. Beijing: Beijing daxue chubanshe, 2010.

Chan, Anita. *Children of Mao: Personality Development and Political Activism in the Red Guard Generation.* London: The MacMillan Press, 1985.

Cheek, Timothy. *Living with Reform: China since 1989.* London: Zed Books, 2006.

Chen Chusan 陈楚三. *Renjian zhongwanqing: yige suowei "hongerdai" de rensheng guiji* 人间重晚晴: 一个所谓"红二代"的人生轨迹 [People treasure after-rain evening sunlight: The trajectory of a so-called "second-generation red"]. New York: Mirrorbooks, 2017.

Chen Huanren 陈焕仁. *Hongweibing riji* 红卫兵日记 [The diary of a Red Guard]. Hong Kong: Chinese University Press, 2006.

Chen Kaige 陈凯歌. *Wode qingchun huiyilu* 我的青春回忆录 [Memoir of my youth]. Beijing: Zhongguo renmin daxue chubanshe, 2009.

Chen Sihe 陈思和, and Wang Dewei 王德威, eds. *Shiliao yu chanshi* 史料与阐释 [Historical materials and interpretation], vol. 5. Shanghai: Fudan daxue chubanshe, 2017.

Chen Xiwen 陈希文. *Fang su zaji* 访苏杂记 [Scattered records of visit in the Soviet Union]. Beijing: Gongren chubanshe, 1951.

Chen Ziming 陈子明. *Jingji lu, duli lu: Chen Ziming zishu* 荆棘路、独立路: 陈子明自述 [A difficult and independent road: Chen Ziming's autobiography]. Taipei: Xiuwei zixun, 2009.

Cheng, Yinghong. *Creating the "New Man:" From Enlightenment Ideals to Socialist Realities.* Honolulu: University of Hawai'i Press, 2009.

Ching, Leo T. S. *Becoming "Japanese:" Colonial Taiwan and the Politics of Identity Formation.* Berkeley: University of California Press, 2001.

Clark, Paul. *Youth Culture in China: From Red Guards to Netizens.* New York: Cambridge University Press, 2012.

Cong Shen 丛深. "Qianwan buyao wangji zhuti de xingcheng"《千万不要忘记》主题的形成 [The formation of the theme of *Never Forget*], *Xiju bao* 4 (1964): 27–28.
Daniel, Ondřej, Tomáš Kavka, and Jakub Machek, eds. *Popular Culture and Subcultures of Czech Post-socialism: Listening to the Wind of Change*. Cambridge: Cambridge Scholar Publishing, 2016.
De Beauvoir, Simone. *The Long March: An Account of Modern China*, trans. Austryn Wainhouse. London: Phoenix Press, 2001.
De Grazia, Victoria. *The Culture of Consent: Mass Organization of Leisure in Fascist Italy*. New York: Cambridge University Press, 1981.
Deng Xiaoping. "Implement the Policy of Readjustment, Ensure Stability and Unity," December 25, 1980, https://dengxiaopingworks.wordpress.com/2013/02/25/implement-the-policy-of-readjustment-ensure-stability-and-unity/.
Deng Yingyi 邓映易. "Women yingdang ba shenmeyang de gequ gei qingnian" 我们应该把什么样的歌曲给青年 [What songs should we give to young people], *Renmin yinyue* 4 (1958): 18.
Dikötter, Frank. *The Cultural Revolution: A People's History, 1962–1976*. New York: Bloomsbury Press, 2016.
Dimou, Eleni, and Jonathan Ilan. "Taking Pleasure Seriously: The Political Significance of Subcultural Practice," *Journal of Youth Studies* 21, no. 1 (2018): 1–18.
Easton, David. *The Political System: An Inquiry into the State of Political Science*. New York: Knopf, 1953.
Ellul, Jacques. *Propaganda: The Formation of Men's Attitudes*, trans. Konrad Kellen and Jean Lerner. New York: Vintage Books, 1973.
Esherick, Joseph W., Paul G. Pickowicz, and Andrew G. Walder, eds. *The Chinese Cultural Revolution as History*. Stanford, CA: Stanford University Press, 2006.
Evans, Christine E. *Between Truth and Time: A History of Soviet Central Television*. New Haven, CT: Yale University Press, 2016.
Featherstone, Mike. "Lifestyle and Consumer Culture," *Theory, Culture and Society* 4 (1987): 55–70.
Fenemore, Mark. *Sex, Thugs and Rock 'n' Roll: Teenage Rebels in Cold-War East Germany*. New York: Berghahn Books, 2007.
Feng Changchun 冯长春. "Jianguo shiqinian guanyu shuqing gequ de piping yu pipan" 建国十七年关于抒情歌曲的批评与批判 [Critiques and criticism on lyric songs during the seventeen years after the founding of the People's Republic of China], *Xinghai yinyue xueyuan xuebao* 1 (2017): 60–74.
Feng Wenbin jinian wenji bianjizu 冯文彬纪念文集编辑组, ed. *Feng Wenbin jinian wenji* 冯文彬纪念文集 [Collected writings commemorating Feng Wenbin]. Beijing: Zhonggong dangshi chubanshe, 2001.

Feng Yuqin 冯玉钦. *Tantan qingnian yeyu shenghuo* 谈谈青年业余生活 [Talking about young people's leisure life]. Wuhan: Hubei renmin chubanshe, 1957.

Finnane, Antonia. *Changing Clothes in China: Fashion, History, Nation.* New York: Columbia University Press, 2008.

Fitzpatrick, Sheila. *Everyday Stalinism: Ordinary Life in Extraordinary Times: Soviet Russia in the 1930s.* New York: Oxford University Press, 1999.

Friedman, Edward, Paul Pickowicz, and Mark Selden. *Chinese Village, Socialist State.* New Haven, CT: Yale University Press, 1991.

Friedrich, Carl J., and Zbigniew K. Brzezinski. *Totalitarian Dictatorship and Autocracy*, 2nd ed. Cambridge, MA: Harvard University Press, 1965.

Fulbrook, Mary. *The People's State: East German Society from Hitler to Honecker.* New Haven, CT: Yale University Press, 2015.

Fürst, Juliane. *Stalin's Last Generation: Soviet Post-war Youth and the Emergence of Mature Socialism.* Oxford: Oxford University Press, 2010.

———, and Josie McLellan, eds. *Dropping out of Socialism: The Creation of Alternative Spheres in the Soviet Bloc.* Lanham, MD: Lexington Books, 2016.

Gao, James Z. *The Communist Takeover of Hangzhou: The Transformation of City and Cadre, 1949-1954.* Honolulu: University of Hawai'i Press, 2004.

Gao Yong 高勇. *Wo gei Hu Yaobang dang mishu* 我给胡耀邦当秘书 [I served Hu Yaobang as his secretary]. Beijing: Renmin chubanshe, 2016.

Gaodeng jiaoyubu bangongting 高等教育部办公厅, ed. *Gaodeng jiaoyu wenxian faling huibian 1949–1952* 高等教育文献法令汇编 1949–1952 [Collection of documents and decrees on higher education]. n.p., 1958.

Gerth, Karl. *Unending Capitalism: How Consumerism Negated China's Communist Revolution.* Cambridge: Cambridge University Press, 2020.

Gold, Thomas B. "Youth and the State," *The China Quarterly* 127 (September 1991): 594–612.

Gongchanzhuyi jiaoyu cidian 共产主义教育词典 [Dictionary for communist education]. Chengdu: Sichuansheng shehui kexueyuan chubanshe, 1986.

"Gongan bu wenhua bu guanyu qudi yingyexing wuhui he gonggong changsuo zifa whui de tongzhi" 公安部、文化部关于取缔营业性舞会和公共场所自发舞会的通知 [Notification from the Ministry of Public Security and the Ministry of Culture on banning profit-making dancing parties and spontaneous dancing parties in public space] (June 14, 1980), *Gongan jianshe* 12 (1980): 5–6.

Gongqingtuan Beijing shiwei wenhua tiyu bu 共青团北京市委文化体育部 and Gongqingtuan Beijing shiwei qingyun shi yanjiu shi 共青团北京市委青运史研究室, eds. *Jidang yu huisheng: Beijing gongqingtuan wenhua tiyu gongzuo sishi nian* 激荡与回声: 北京共青团文化体育工作四十年 [Surges and echoes: Forty years of cultural and sports work of the Beijing Youth League]. Beijing: Beijing gongye daxue chubanshe, 1992.

Gongqingtuan zhongyang xuanchuanbu 共青团中央宣传部, ed. *Qingnian shenghuo shouce* 青年生活手册 [Handbook on young people's life]. Jinan: Shandong renmin chubanshe, 1987.
Gongqingtuan zhongyang yanjiushi 共青团中央研究室, ed. *Zhongguo qingnian gongzuo nianjian 1985* 中国青年工作年鉴1985 [Yearbook of youth work in China, 1985]. Beijing: Zhongguo qingnian chubanshe, 1986.
Gongqingtuan zhongyang zuzhibu 共青团中央组织部, ed. *Zenyang huoyue zhibu shenghuo* 怎样活跃支部生活 [How to invigorate life in Youth League branches]. Beijing: Zhongguo qingnian chubanshe, 1981.
Gorsuch, Anne E. *Youth in Revolutionary Russia: Enthusiasts, Bohemians, Delinquents.* Bloomington: Indiana University Press, 2000.
———, and Diane P. Koenker, eds. *The Socialist Sixties: Crossing Borders in the Second World.* Bloomington: Indiana University Press, 2013.
Gregor, A. James. *Marxism, Fascism, and Totalitarianism: Chapters in the Intellectual History of Radicalism.* Stanford, CA: Stanford University Press, 2009.
Gu Yewen 顾已文. *Guoji jiaoyi wu* 国际交谊舞 [International ballroom dancing]. Shanghai: Wenyu chubanshe, 1953.
———. *Jiaoyi wu qutan* 交谊舞趣谈 [Amusing remarks on ballroom dancing]. Shanghai: Xuelin chubanshe, 2003.
Guizhousheng xiezuo xuehui 贵州省写作学会, ed. *Zhongguo dangdai xiezuo lilunjia* 中国当代写作理论家 [Writing theorists in contemporary China]. Guiyang: Guizhou renmin chubanshe, 1989.
Guo, Sujian. *Post-Mao China: From Totalitarianism to Authoritarianism?* London: Praeger, 2000.
———. "The Totalitarian Model Revisited," *Communist and Post-Communist Studies* 31, no. 3 (1998): 271–285.
Hall, Stuart, and Tony Jefferson, eds. *Resistance through Rituals: Youth Subcultures in Post-War Britain*, 2nd ed. London: Routledge, 2006.
Hamrin, Carol Lee and Timothy Cheek, eds. *China's Establishment Intellectuals.* Armonk, NY: M.E. Sharpe, 1986.
Han Shui 汉水. *Yongwang zhiqian* 勇往直前 [March Forward Without Hesitation]. Tianjin: Baihua wenyi chubanshe, 1961.
Hankiss, Elemér. "The 'Second Society:' Is There an Alternative Social Model Emerging in Contemporary Hungary?" *Social Research* 55, nos. 1/2 (Spring/Summer 1988): 13–42.
Hao Yixing 郝一星. "Chi he shinian: wenge huimou zhi'er" 吃喝十年: 文革回眸之二 [Wining and dining during the ten years: My recollection on the Cultural Revolution, part two], March 21, 2017, https://difangwenge.org/forum.php?mod=viewthread&tid=14104.

———. "Shamo zaoquan: wenge huimo zhisan" 沙漠凿泉: 文革回眸之三 [Digging for a spring in a dessert: My recollection on the Cultural Revolution, part three], March 9, 2013, https://difangwenge.org/forum.php?mod=viewthread&tid=8184&highlight=%C9%B3%C4%AE%D4%E4%C8%AA.

He Dongchang 何东昌, ed. *Zhonghua renmin gongheguo zhongyao jiaoyu wenxian* 中华人民共和国重要教育文献 [Important documents on education in the People's Republic of China]. Haikou: Hainan chubanshe, 1998.

Hebdige, Dick. *Subculture: The Meaning of Style*. London: Routledge, 1979.

He Lu 赫鲁. "Xiao bai lou tiyu huodong yihua" "小白楼"体育活动忆话 [Recollections of sports activities in the "Little White Building"], *Tiyu wenshi*, Z1 (1984): 18–19.

He Lüting 贺绿汀. "Xianchang huiyi gei women de qishi" 现场会议给我们的启示 [Our takeaways from the meeting], *Renmin yinyue* 9 (1958): 2.

He Qiu 何求. "Xiaoyao wenge" 逍遥文革 [Being a bystander during the cultural revolution], December 25, 2012, https://difangwenge.org/forum.php?mod=viewthread&tid=15771.

Hedin, Astrid. "Stalinism as a Civilization: New Perspectives on Communist Regimes," *Political Studies Review* 2 (2004): 166–184.

Henansheng gewei wenhuaju 河南省革委文化局, ed. *Quanguo qunzhong wenhua gongzuo "xue Dazhai, gan Xiyang" jingyan jiaoliu xianchanghui cailiao* 全国群众文化工作"学大寨、赶昔阳"经验交流现场会材料 [Materials from the national mass cultural work "Learning from Dazhai and catching up with Xiyang" on-spot experience exchange meeting]. n.p., 1978.

Hershatter, Gail. *The Gender of Memory: Rural Women and China's Collective Past*. Berkeley: University of California Press, 2011.

Hirschman, Albert O. *Exit, Voice, and Loyalty: Responses to Decline in Firms, Organizations, and States*. Cambridge, MA: Harvard University Press, 1970.

———. "Exit, Voice, and the Fate of the German Democratic Republic: An Essay in Conceptual History," *World Politics* 45, no. 2 (January 1993): 173–202.

Hooper, Beverley. *Foreigners Under Mao: Western Lives in China, 1949–1976*. Hong Kong: Hong Kong University Press, 2016.

Hu Keshi jinian wenji bianweihui 胡克实纪念文集编委会, ed. *Hu Keshi jinian wenji* 胡克实纪念文集 [Collection of essays commemorating Hu Keshi]. n.p., 2006.

Hua Dai 华岱. "Yongwang zhiqian shi zenyang waiqu dangde lingdao de"《勇往直前》是怎样歪曲党的领导的 [How does *March Forward Without Hesitation* distort the leadership of the Party], *Hebei wenxue* 11 (1964): 66–68.

Hunansheng wenhuaguan 湖南省文化馆, ed. *Xue Dazhai gan Xiyang: quanguo qunzhong wenhua gongzuo "xue Dazhai, gan Xiyang" jingyan jiaoliu xianchanghui wenjian ziliao xuanbian* 学大寨 赶昔阳: 全国群众文化工作"学大寨 赶昔阳"经验交流现场会文件资料选编 [Learning from Dazhai and catching up with Xiyang: selection of documents from the national mass cultural work

"Learning from Dazhai and catching up with Xiyang" on-spot experience exchange meeting]. n.p., 1978.

Jianguo yilai Mao Zedong wengao 建国以来毛泽东文稿 [Mao Zedong's manuscripts since the founding of the Republic], vol. 10. Beijing: Zhongyang wenxian chubanshe, 1996.

Jianguo yilai Mao Zedong wengao 建国以来毛泽东文稿 [Mao Zedong's manuscripts since the founding of the Republic], vol. 11. Beijing: Zhongyang wenxian chubanshe, 1996.

Jiefangjun Nanjing budui zhengzhibu renmin qunzhong gongzuobu 解放军南京部队政治部人民群众工作部, ed. *Minbing zhengzhi jiaocai* 民兵政治教材 [Textbook for political training for civilians]. Shanghai: Shanghai renmin chubanshe, 1961.

Jin Yuelin 金岳霖. *Cong duoluo dao fandong de Meiguo wenhua* 从堕落到反动的美国文化 [American Culture from being degenerate to being reactionary]. Shanghai: Pingming chubanshe, 1951.

Johnson, Matthew D. "Political culture in the archive: Grassroots perspectives on party-state power and legitimacy in 1950s Beijing," *The PRC History Review* 3, no. 1 (October 2018): 1–36.

Katz-Gerro, Tally. "Cultural Consumption and Social Stratification: Leisure Activities, Musical Tastes, and Social Location," *Sociological Perspectives* 42, no. 4 (1999): 627–646.

Kenez, Peter. *The Birth of the Propaganda State: Soviet Methods of Mass Mobilization, 1917–1929*. Cambridge: Cambridge University Press, 1985.

Kleiber, Douglas A. *Leisure Experience and Human Development: A Dialectical Interpretation*. New York: Basic Books, 1999.

Kong, Shuyu. "Between Undercurrent and Mainstream: Hand-Copied Literature and Unofficial Culture during and after the Cultural Revolution," *Asian Studies Review* 44, no. 2 (2020): 239–257.

"Lao Fu tiedaobu dayuan huiyilu 78 yang redaiyu" 老付铁道部大院回忆录78: 养热带鱼 [Old Fu's memory of the Ministry of Railway residential compound, part 78: raising tropical fish], October 27, 2017, http://web.archive.org/web/20181207070131/http://blog.sina.com.cn/s/blog_60f72b1c0102y10k.html.

Lao Gui 老鬼. *Xue yu tie* 血与铁 [Blood and iron]. Beijing: Xinxing chubanshe, 2010.

LaPierre, Brian. *Hooligans in Khrushchev's Russia: Defining, Policing, and Producing Deviance during the Thaw*. Madison: The University of Wisconsin Press, 2012.

Lemel, Yannick, and Tally Katz-Gerro. "The Stratification of Leisure: Variation in the Salience of Socioeconomic Dimensions in Shaping Leisure Participation in Two Consumer Societies," *Loisir et Société / Society and Leisure* 38, no. 3 (2015): 399–422.

Lenin, Vladimir. "A Great Beginning: Heroism of the Workers in the Rear 'Communist Subbotniks'," June 28, 1919, https://www.marxists.org/archive/lenin/works/1919/jun/19.htm.

Levi, Erik. *Music in the Third Reich*. New York: Palgrave Macmillan, 1994.

Li Jie 李捷. "Mao Zedong fangzhi heping yanbian sixiang shi dui kexue shehui zhuyi lilun de zhongyao gongxian" 毛泽东防止和平演变思想是对科学社会主义理论的重要贡献 [Mao Zedong's idea on preventing peaceful evolution is an important contribution to the theory of scientific socialism], *Zhenli de zhuiqiu* 9 (1991): 6–13.

Li Ling 李凌. *Rang xinde yinyue shenghuo huoyue qilai pipan huangse gequ jiangzuo tigang* 让新的音乐生活活跃起来——批判黄色歌曲讲座提纲 [Invigorate the new musical life: Outline for lectures criticizing yellow songs]. Beijing: Yinyue chubanshe, 1958.

Li Qinglin 李庆林, ed. *Nanwang de qingchun: beigongda laowujie jishi* 难忘的青春: 北工大"老五届"纪事 [Unforgettable youth: reminiscence from the "old five classes" of Beijing University of Technology]. Beijing: Dangdai zhongguo chubanshe, 2015.

Li Shengping 李盛平, ed. *Xiandai qingnian shejiao shouce* 现代青年社交手册 [Handbook on young people's social life in the modern world]. Beijing: Shuili dianli chubanshe, 1985.

Li Weidong 李伟东. *Qinghua fuzhong gao 631 ban (1963–1968)* 清华附中高631班 (1963–1968) [Senior Class No. 631 in Tsinghua University High School]. New York: Cozy Publishing House, 2012.

Li Weiji 李维基. *Women de lao Beijing: guxi tuzhu de jinghua suoyi* 我们的老北京: 古稀土著的京华琐忆 [Our old Beijing: scattered recollections from a native resident over seventy]. Beijing: Zhongguo qinggongye chubanshe, 2015.

Li, Yan. *China's Soviet Dream: Propaganda, Culture, and Popular Imagination*. London: Routledge, 2018.

Liang Jinghe 梁景和, ed. *Zhongguo xiandangdai shehui wenhua fangtanlu di si ji* 中国现当代社会文化访谈录 第四辑 [Collection of interviews on social culture of modern and contemporary China, vol. 4]. Beijing: Shoudu shifan daxue chubanshe, 2014.

Liao Yiwu 廖亦武, ed. *Chenlun de shengdian: Zhongguo 20 shiji 70 niandai dixia shige* 沉沦的圣殿: 中国20世纪70年代地下诗歌 [The fallen shrine: underground poems in China during the 1970s]. Urumqi: Xinjiang qingshaonian chubanshe, 1999.

Lin Ke 林克, "Huiyi Mao Zedong dui Dulesi heping yanbian yanlun de pinglun" 回忆毛泽东对杜勒斯和平演变言论的评论 [Recollections on Mao Zedong's remarks on Dulles' opinions of peaceful evolution], *Dangde wenxian* 6 (1990): 44–46.

Lin Xili (Cecilia Lindqvist) 林西莉. *Ling yige shijie: Zhongguo jiyi 1961–1962* 另一个世界: 中国记忆1961–1962 [Another World: Memories of China, 1961–1962]. Beijing, Zhonghua shuju, 2016.

Linz, Juan J. *Totalitarian and Authoritarian Regimes*. Boulder, CO: Lynne Rienner Publishers, 2000.

Liu Mingchuan 刘明川, and Bi Dianling 毕殿岭. "Yongwang zhiqian waiqu le daxue shenghuo"《勇往直前》歪曲了大学生活 [*March Forward Without Hesitation* vilified campus life in university], *Zhengzhou daxue xuebao* 4 (1964): 93–102.

Liu Yajuan 刘亚娟. "Shanghai a-fei: gundong de huayu luoji yu jiceng shijian zouxiang (1949–1965)" 上海"阿飞": 滚动的话语逻辑与基层实践走向 (1949-1965) [Shanghai "A-fei:" The rolling logic of discourse and grassroots practical trends], *Zhonggong dangshi yanjiu* 5 (2018): 59–71.

Lu Shuning 卢叔宁. *Jiehui canbian* 劫灰残编 [Fragments from the ashes]. Beijing: Wenlian chubanshe, 2000.

Lu Xueyi 陆学艺, ed. *Qingchun suiyue zai Beida: zhexuexi 1957 ji tongxue huiyilu* 青春岁月在北大: 哲学系1957级同学回忆录 [We were in Peking University when we were young: memoirs of Philosophy students entering school in 1957]. Beijing: shehui kexue wenxian chubanshe, 2012.

Ma, Huidi, and Er Liu. *Traditional Chinese Leisure Culture and Economic Development: A Conflict of Forces*. New York: Palgrave Macmillan, 2017.

Ma Nancun 马南邨. *Yanshan yehua* 燕山夜话 [Evening chats at Yanshan]. Beijing: Beijing chubanshe, 1961.

Ma Zhixiang 马芷庠. *Beiping lüxing zhinan* 北平旅行指南 [Beiping guidebook]. Beiping: Jingji xinwen she, 1937.

Maier, Hans, ed. *Totalitarianism and Political Religions Volume I: Concepts for the Comparison of Dictatorships*, trans. Jodi Bruhn. London and New York: Routledge, 2004.

MacFarquhar, Roderick. *The Origins of the Cultural Revolution, Vol. 3: The Coming of the Cataclysm, 1961–1966*. New York: Columbia University Press, 1997.

———, and Michael Schoenhals, *Mao's Last Revolution*. Cambridge, MA: The Belknap Press of Harvard University Press, 2006.

Mao Zedong sixiang wansui 1961–1968 毛泽东思想万岁 1961–1968 [Long live Mao Zedong Thought, 1961–1968]. Wuhan, 1968.

Marx, Karl. "The Class Struggles in France, 1848 to 1850," 1850, https://www.marxists.org/archive/marx/works/1850/class-struggles-france/ch03.htm.

Mattingly, Daniel C. *The Art of Political Control in China*. Cambridge: Cambridge University Press, 2020.

Meisner, Maurice. *Mao's China and After*, 3rd ed. New York: Free Press, 1999.

McLellan, David, ed. *Karl Marx: Selected Writings*. Oxford: Oxford University Press, 2000.

Mi Hedu 米鹤都, ed. *Guanghuan yu yinying* 光环与阴影 [Lights and shadows]. Hong Kong: CNHK Publications Limited, 2013

———, ed. *Huiyi yu fansi: hongweibing shidai fengyun renwu koushu lishi zhi'er* 回忆与反思：红卫兵时代风云人物——口述历史之一 [Memories and reflections: oral interviews with famous people during the Red Guard Movement, vol. 1]. Hong Kong: Zhongguo shuju youxian gongsi, 2011.

———, ed. *Huiyi yu fansi: hongweibing shidai fengyun renwu koushu lishi zhi'er* 回忆与反思：红卫兵时代风云人物——口述历史之二 [Memories and reflections: oral interviews with famous people during the Red Guard Movement, vol. 2]. Hong Kong: Zhongguo shuju youxian gongsi, 2011.

Ngai, Ngan-Pun, Chau-Kiu Cheung, and Chi-Kei Li. "China's Youth Policy Formulation and Youth Participation," *Children and Youth Services Review* 23, no. 8 (2001): 651-669.

Nowotny, Helga. "Time and Social Theory: Towards a Social Theory of Time," *Time & Society* 1, no. 3 (1992): 421–454.

"On Khrushchev's Phony Communism and Its Historical Lessons for the World," July 14, 1964, https://www.marxists.org/reference/archive/mao/works/1964/phnycom2.htm.

Pan Jing 潘婧, "Xinlu lichen: wenge zhong de sifeng xin" 心路历程——"文革"中的四封信 [My journey: four letters during the Cultural Revolution], *Zhongguo zuojia* 6 (1994): 174–184.

Peng Chao 澎潮. "Yao duoshu shehuizhuyi jitizhuyi zhiqing: tan zhishi qingnian chang shenme ge" 要多抒社会主义集体主义之情——谈知识青年唱什么歌 [We should express more socialist and collectivist emotions: on what songs the educated youth sing], *Renmin yinyue* 5 (1958): 8–9.

Peng Ruifu 彭瑞夫, *Meiguo mianmianguan* 美国面面观 [An overview of the United States]. Shanghai: Liantong shudian, 1951.

Peng Zhen wenxuan 1941–1990 彭真文选（一九四一——一九九〇年）[Selected works of Peng Zhen]. Beijing: Renmin chubanshe, 1991.

Perry, Elizabeth J. "The Promise of PRC History," *Journal of Modern Chinese History* 10, no. 1 (2016): 113–117.

———, and Mark Selden, eds. *Chinese Society: Change, Conflict and Resistance*, 3rd ed. London: Routledge, 2010.

Peters, Olaf, ed. *Degenerate Art: The Attack on Modern Art in Nazi Germany, 1937*. Munich: Prestel, 2014.

Portwood-Stacer, Laura. *Lifestyle Politics and Radical Activism*. New York: Bloomsbury, 2013.

Pospíšil, Filip. "Youth Cultures and the Disciplining of Czechoslovak Youth in the 1960s," *Social History* 37, no. 4 (November 2012): 477–500.

Pu Siwen 濮思温, and Guan Yulin 管玉琳. *Xin jiti wu* 新集体舞 [New group dancing]. Beijing: Shenghuo dushu xinzhi sanlian shudian, 1951.

Putnam, Robert D. *Bowling Alone: The Collapse and Revival of American Community*. New York: Simon & Schuster, 2000.
———, Robert Leonardi, and Raffaella Nanetti. *Making Democracy Work: Civic Traditions in Modern Italy*. Princeton, NJ: Princeton University Press, 1993.
Qian Liqun 钱理群. *Juehuo buxi wenge minjian sixiang yanjiu biji* 爝火不息: 文革民间思想研究笔记 [Tiny flame does not die out: research notes on grassroots thoughts during the Cultural Revolution]. Hong Kong: Oxford University Press, 2017.
Qingnianren zenyang shenghuo caiyou yisi 青年人怎样生活才有意思 [How can young people lead an interesting life]. Beijing: Beijing chubanshe, 1965.
Qingnian tuan Beijing shiweihui wenhua yishubu 青年团北京市委会文化艺术部, ed. *Qingnian julebu* di er ji 青年俱乐部 第二辑 [Youth club, vol.2]. Beijing: Qingnian chubanshe, 1950.
Qingniantuan zhongyang xuexiao gognzuobu 青年团中央学校工作部, ed. *Peiyang wei shehui zhuyi shiye zhongcheng fuwu de laodong zhishi qingnian* 培养为社会主义事业忠诚服务的劳动知识青年 [Nurture laboring educated youth serving the socialist enterprise faithfully]. Beijing: Zhongguo qingnian chubanshe, 1956.
Ramet, Sabrina P., ed. *Rocking the State: Rock Music and Politics in Eastern Europe and Russia*. Boulder, CO: Westview Press, 1994.
"Report to the Second Plenary Session of the Seventh Central Committee of the Communist Party of China," March 5, 1949, *Selected Works of Mao Tse-tung*, vol. 4, https://www.marxists.org/reference/archive/mao/selected-works/volume-4/mswv4_58.htm.
Riordan, Jim, ed. *Soviet Youth Culture*. Basingstoke: Macmillan, 1989.
Risch, William Jay, ed. *Youth and Rock in the Soviet Bloc: Youth Cultures, Music, and the State in Russia and Eastern Europe*. Lanham, MD: Lexington Books, 2015.
Roberts, Margaret E. *Censored: Distraction and Diversion Inside China's Great Firewall*. Princeton, NJ: Princeton University Press, 2018.
Rojek, Chris, Susan M. Shaw, and A. J. Veal, eds. *A Handbook of Leisure Studies* (New York: Palgrave Macmillan, 2006).
Ryback, Timothy W. *Rock around the Bloc: A History of Rock Music in Eastern Europe and the Soviet Union*. New York: Oxford University Press, 1990.
"Sanshou wenge shiqi de shici suoxiang" 三首"文革"时期的诗词所想 [Thoughts on three poems written during the Cultural Revolution], December 19, 2017, http://web.archive.org/web/20181207080526/https://www.douban.com/note/649696309/.
Schoenhals, Michael. *Spying for the People: Mao's Secret Agents, 1949–1967*. Cambridge: Cambridge University Press, 2013.
Schurmann, Franz. *Ideology and Organization in Communist China*, 2nd ed. Berkeley: University of California Press, 1968.

Scott, James C. *Weapons of the Weak: Everyday Forms of Peasant Resistance.* New Haven, CT: Yale University Press, 1985.

Selden, Mark. *China in Revolution: The Yenan Way Revisited.* Armonk, NY: M. E. Sharpe, 1995.

Selznick, Philip. *The Organizational Weapon: A Study of Bolshevik Strategy and Tactics.* New York: McGraw-Hill Book Company, 1952.

Shen Zhihua 沈志华, "Jinshen shiyong huiyilu he koushu shiliao" 谨慎使用回忆录和口述史料 [Use memoirs and oral materials cautiously], March 11, 2013, http://dangshi.people.com.cn/n/2013/0311/c85037-20742242.html.

Shikan bianjibu《诗刊》编辑部 ed. *1958 Shixuan* 1958 诗选 [1958 selection of poems]. Beijing: Zuojia chubanshe, 1959.

Smith, Aminda M. *Thought Reform and China's Dangerous Classes: Reeducation, Resistance, and the People.* Lanham, MD: Rowman & Littlefield, 2013.

Song Bolin 宋柏林. *Hongweibing xingshuai lu: Qinghua fuzhong lao Hongweibing shouji* 红卫兵兴衰录——清华附中老红卫兵手记 [Ups and downs of the Red Guard: diary of an old Red Guard in Tsinghua University High]. Hong Kong: Desai chuban youxian gongsi, 2006.

Song Xinlu 宋心鲁. "Beijing sizhong: wode muxiao, wode muqin" 北京四中——我的母校, 我的母亲 [Beijing No.4 High School: my alma mater, my mother], July 23, 2017, https://difangwenge.org/forum.php?mod=viewthread&tid=14854&highlight=%CB%CE%D0%C4%C2%B3.

Song Yongyi 宋永毅, ed. *Zhongguo wenhua da geming wenku* 中国文化大革命文库 [Chinese Cultural Revolution database], third edition. Hong Kong: Xianggang Zhongwen daxue Zhongguo yanjiu fuwu zhongxin, 2010. CD-ROM.

Swett, Pamela E., Corey Ross, and Fabrice d'Almeida, eds. *Pleasure and Power in Nazi Germany.* Houndmills: Palgrave Macmillan, 2011.

Sun Peidong 孙沛东. "Shiting baoli: jiuping de shengchan chuanbo ji hongweibing yidai de jiyi" 视听暴力:"九评"的生产、传播及"红卫兵一代"的记忆 [Visual-auditory violence: the production and transmission of the "Nine Commentaries" and memories of the Red Guard generation], Harvard-Yenching Institute Working Paper Series, 2018.

———. "Wenge shiqi Jing Hu zhiqing jiecenghua de geren yuedu" 文革时期京沪知青阶层化的个人阅读 [Stratified individual reading activities among educated youth in Beijing and Shanghai during the Cultural Revolution], *Ershiyi shiji* 156 (August 2016): 78–98.

Sun Yuecai 孙月才. *Beige yiqu: wenge shinian riji* 悲歌一曲: 文革十年日记 [A diary of sorrow: Ten years of the cultural revolution]. Hong Kong: Chinese University Press, 2012.

Sung Ping-jen 宋秉仁. "Shengguan tu youxi yange kao" 升官图游戏沿革考 [The evolution of Chinese Promotion Game], *Taiwan shida lishi xuebao* 33 (2005): 27–78.

Tan Youshi 谈有时. *Zenyang tiao jiaoji wu* 怎样跳交际舞 [How to ballroom dance]. Beijing: Minzhi shudian, 1951.

———. *Zenyang xuexi jiaoyi wu* 怎样学习交谊舞 [How to learn ballroom dancing]. Beijing: Unknown publisher, 1953.

Tan Zheng 谭征. *Xunzhao Ma Tieding* 寻找马铁丁 [In search of Ma Tieding]. Beijing: Haiyang chubanshe, 2009.

Tang Xiaobing 唐小兵. *Yingxiong yu fanren de shidai: jiedu 20 shiji* 英雄与凡人的时代: 解读20世纪 [The era of heroes and ordinary people: an interpretation of the twentieth century]. Shanghai: Shanghai wenyi chubanshe, 2001.

Tanner, Harold M. *China: A History*, vol. 2. Indianapolis, IN: Hackett Publishing Company, Inc., 2010.

Theroux, Paul. *Riding the Iron Rooster: By Train through China*. New York: G. P. Putnam's Sons, 1988.

Thompson, E. P. "Time, Work Discipline, and Industrial Capitalism," *Past and Present* 38 (1967): 56–97.

Tian Ying 天鹰. *Yijiu wuba nian zhongguo minge yundong* 一九五八年中国民歌运动 [The Chinese folklore movement in 1958]. Shanghai: Shanghai wenyi chubanshe, 1978.

Timpe, Julia. *Nazi-Organized Recreation and Entertainment in the Third Reich*. London: Palgrave Macmillan, 2017.

Townsend, James R. *The Revolutionization of Chinese Youth: A Study of Chung-kuo Ch'ing-nien*. Berkeley: Center for Chinese Studies, 1967.

Tsipursky, Gleb. *Socialist Fun: Youth, Consumption, and State-Sponsored Popular Culture in the Cold War Soviet Union, 1945–1970*. Pittsburgh, PA: University of Pittsburgh Press, 2016.

Veblen, Thorstein. *The Theory of the Leisure Class*. Mineola, NY: Dover Publications, 1994.

Verdery, Katherine. *What Was Socialism, and What Comes Next?* Princeton, NJ: Princeton University Press, 1996.

Vogel, Ezra F. "From Friendship to Comradeship: The Change in Personal Relations in Communist China," *The China Quarterly* 21 (January–March 1965): 46–60.

Walder, Andrew G. *China Under Mao: A Revolution Derailed*. Cambridge, MA: Harvard University Press, 2015.

———. *Communist Neo-Traditionalism: Work and Authority in Chinese Industry*. Berkeley: University of California Press, 1986.

———. *Fractured Rebellion: The Beijing Red Guard Movement*. Cambridge, MA: Harvard University Press, 2009.

Wang, Ban. *The Sublime Figure of History: Aesthetics and Politics of Twentieth Century China*. Stanford, CA: Stanford University Press, 1997.

Wang Haiguang 王海光. *Zhizao fangeming: Liu Xingfu an yu wenge shiqi de jiceng fazhi shengtai* 制造反革命: 柳幸福案与文革时期的基层法制生态

[Making a counterrevolutionary: The case of Liu Xingfu and China's grassroots legal system, 1949–1979]. Hong Kong: Chinese University of Hong Kong Press, 2021.

Wang Jintang 王晋堂, ed. *Guxiao maixiang 21 shiji Beijing yizhong xiaoshi gao 1644–1990* 古校迈向21世纪：北京一中校史稿 1644–1990 [Old school marching to the 21st century: a draft of the history of Beijing No. 1 High School, 1644–1990]. Beijing: Huayi chubanshe, 1990.

Wang Jiyu 王冀豫. "Beifu sharen de zize" 背负杀人的自责 [I blame myself for homicide], *Yanhuang chunqiu* 5 (2010): 72–75.

Wang, Ning. *Banished to the Great Northern Wilderness: Political Exile and Re-Education in Mao's China*. Vancouver: UBC Press, 2017.

Wang Qianrong 王乾荣, "'Jieji' xin gainian" "阶级"新概念 [New concept of "class"], *Zhongguo qingnian bao*, October 9, 2002.

Wang Renzhong 王任重. "Jiti shenghuo fangshi shi zuixingfu zuimeihao de shenghuo fangshi" 集体生活方式是最幸福最美好的生活方式 [The communal way of life is the happiest and brightest way of life], *Zhongguo gongren* 10 (1960): 8–11.

Wang Shaoguang 王绍光. "Siren shijian yu zhengzhi: Zhongguo chengshi xianxia moshi de bianhua" 私人时间与政治：中国城市闲暇模式的变化 [Private time and politics: changes in the leisure mode in Chinese cities], *Zhongguo shehui kexue jikan* (Summer 1995): 108–125.

Wang, Y. Yvon. "Heroes, Hooligans, and Knights-Errant: Masculinities and Popular Media in the Early People's Republic of China," *Nan Nü* 19 (2017): 316–356.

Wenhuabu chuban shiye guanliju bangongshi 文化部出版事业管理局办公室, ed. *Chuban gongzuo wenxian xuanbian (1949–1957)* 出版工作文献选编 (1949–1957) [Collection of documents on publication work]. n.p., 1982.

Wenhuabu yishu shiye guanliju 文化部艺术事业管理局. *Yinyue wudao gongzuo cankao ziliao 2: huangse gequ wenti zhuanji* 音乐舞蹈工作参考资料 (二)：黄色歌曲问题专辑 [Reference materials for the work of music and dancing, vol. 2: special collection on the problem of yellow songs]. n.p., 1958.

"Wo zai jiefang chu de qiushe jingli" 我在解放初的球社经历 [My experience in a ball game club shortly after the liberation], November 25, 2003, http://web.archive.org/web/20191022235344/http://www.sport.org.cn/sfa/2003/1125/80717.html.

Wu Di 吴迪 ed. *Zhongguo dianying yanjiu ziliao 1949–1979* 中国电影研究资料: 1949–1979 [Materials for studies on Chinese cinema, 1949–1979], vol. 1. Beijing: Wenhua yishu chubanshe, 2006.

Wu, Yiching. *Cultural Revolution at the Margins: Chinese Socialism in Crisis*. Cambridge, MA: Harvard University Press, 2014.

Xi Wuyi 习五一, and Deng Yibing 邓亦兵. *Beijing tongshi di jiu juan* 北京通史 第九卷 [General history of Beijing, vol. 9]. Beijing: Beijing yanshan chubanshe, 2012.

Xian Di 显谛. "Shehuizhuyi qunzhong geyong yundong neng zhi ba bing" 社会主义群众歌咏运动能治八病 [The socialist mass singing movement can cure eight diseases], *Renmin yinyue* 4 (1958): 5–6.

Xie Dingguo 谢定国. "Yige beida xuesheng de wenge riji" 一个北大学生的文革日记 [A Peking University student's diary during the Cultural Revolution], August 17, 2014, https://difangwenge.org/forum.php?mod=viewth read&tid=10029.

Xie Jingyi 谢静宜. *Mao Zedong shenbian gongzuo suoyi* 毛泽东身边工作琐忆 [Scattered recollections of the days working by Mao Zedong's side]. Beijing: Zhongyang wenxian chubanshe, 2015.

Xu Xiao 徐晓, ed. *Xundaozhe: mianhuai Chen Ziming* 殉道者: 缅怀陈子明 [A martyr: in memory of Chen Ziming]. New York: Mirror Books, 2015.

"Xunsu qudi redaiyu he gezi heishe huodong" 迅速取缔热带鱼和鸽子黑市活动 [Immediately ban black markets selling tropical fish and pigeons], *Tianjin zhengbao* 11 (1966): 10.

Yang Jian 杨健. *Wenhua dageming zhong de dixia wenxue* 文化大革命中的地下文学 [Underground literature during the Cultural Revolution]. Beijing: Zhaohua chubanshe, 1993.

Yang, Kuisong, "Reconsidering the Campaign to Suppress Counterrevolutionaries," *The China Quarterly* 193 (March 2008): 102–121.

Yang Xiaogong 杨小工. "Lao 302 de haidi shijie" 老302的海底世界 [Aquarium in old 302], July 5, 2008, http://web.archive.org/web/20181207075420/http://blog.sina.com.cn/s/blog_531b835401009ucw.html.

Ye Weili 叶维丽. *Dongdang de qingchun: hongse dayuan de nü'er men* 动荡的青春: 红色大院的女儿们 [Turbulent youth: daughters of red courtyards]. Beijing: Xinhua chubanshe, 2008.

———, and Xiaodong Ma. *Growing Up in the People's Republic: Conversations between Two Daughters of China's Revolution*. New York: Palgrave Macmillan, 2005.

Ye Xiaomo 叶小沫, ed. *Sanwu de shi* 三午的诗 [Sanwu's poems]. Wuhan: Wuhan daxue chubanshe, 2017.

Yin Hongbiao 印红标. *Shizongzhe de zuji: wenhua da geming qijian de qingnian sichao* 失踪者的足迹: 文化大革命期间的青年思潮 [Footsteps of the missing: youth thoughts during the Cultural Revolution]. Hong Kong: Chinese University Press, 2009.

Youyi de mianli: Zhongguo qingnian bao sixiang erritan xuanji 友谊的勉励: 中国青年报"思想二日谈"选集 [Encouragement of friendship: selected essays from "Talking about thought every two days" column of *China Youth Daily*]. Beijing: Zhongguo qingnian chubanshe, 1955.

Yu Miin-ling 余敏玲. *Xingsu "xinren:" Zhonggong xuanchuan yu Sulian jingyan* 形塑"新人": 中共宣传与苏联经验 [Forging "new man:" the Chinese Communist Party's propaganda and the Soviet experience]. Taipei: Zhongyang yanjiuyuan jindaishi yanjiusuo, 2015.

Yu Na 于娜, and Yu Jia于嘉. *Dangdai Beijing guangbo shihua* 当代北京广播史话 [History of broadcasting in contemporary Beijing]. Beijing: Dangdai zhongguo chubanshe, 2013.

Yu Shichang 喻世长. *Jianguo riji* 建国日记 [Diary during the founding of the republic]. Beijing: Dongfang chubanshe, 2009.

Yu Xiangzhen 于向真. "Wo qinli de wenge shinian ba" 我亲历的文革十年 (八) [Ten years of Cultural Revolution that I experienced, part eight], January 26, 2016, http://www.hybsl.cn/beijingcankao/beijingfenxi/2016-01-26/56689.html.

———. "Wo qinli de wenge shinian shi" 我亲历的文革十年 (十) [Ten years of Cultural Revolution that I experience, part ten], January 28, 2016, http://www.hybsl.cn/beijingcankao/beijingfenxi/2016-01-28/56728.html.

———. "Wo qinli de wenge shinian ba" 我亲历的文革十年 (十七) [Ten years of Cultural Revolution that I experienced, part seventeen], February 16, 2016, http://www.hybsl.cn/beijingcankao/beijingfenxi/2016-02-16/57024.html.

Yurchak, Alexei. *Everything Was Forever, Until It Was No More: The Last Soviet Generation*. Princeton, NJ: Princeton University Press, 2006.

Zerubavel, Eviatar. *Hidden Rhythms: Schedules and Calendars in Social Life*. Berkeley: University of California Press, 1985.

Zhang Baozhang 张宝章. "Sijiu nian shenghuo manyi" 四九年生活漫忆 [Scattered recollections of life in 1949], *Haidian wenshi xuanbian* 11 (1999): 88–100.

Zhang Dazhong 张大中. *Wo jingli de Beiping dixiadang* 我经历的北平地下党 [The Beiping underground Party that I experienced]. Beijing: Zhonggong dangshi chubanshe, 2009.

Zhang Limin 张利民, ed. *Chengshishi yanjiu* 城市史研究 [Studies on urban history], vol. 31. Beijing: Shehui kexue wenxian chubanshe, 2014.

Zhao Di 赵地. "Cong qunzhong geyong huodong kan 'Jiujiu yanyang tian'" 从群众歌咏活动看"九九艳阳天" [Think about "Jiujiu yanyang tian" from the mass singing activities], *Renmin yinyue* (6) 1958: 24–25.

Zhao Heng 赵珩, "Huiyi jiushi de Beijing shangye zhongxin" 回忆旧时的北京商业中心 [A Recollection of the old business center of Beijing], April 5, 2015, http://web.archive.org/web/20191022231036/https://cul.qq.com/a/20150409/027355.htm.

Zheng Guang 郑洸, ed. *Zhongguo qingnian yundong liushi nian 1919–1979* 中国青年运动六十年 1919–1979 [Sixty years of youth movement in China, 1919–1979]. Beijing: Zhongguo qingnian chubanshe, 1990.

Zhonggong Beijingshiwei bangongting 中共北京市委办公厅, ed. *Zhongguo gongchandang Beijingshi weiyuanhui zhongyao wenjian huibian 1958 nian* 中国共产党北京市委员会重要文件汇编1958年 [Collection of important documents of the Beijing Municipal Committee of the Chinese Communist Party, 1958]. n.p., 1960.

―――― ed. *Zhongguo gongchandang Beijingshi weiyuanhui zhongyao wenjian huibian 1960 nian* 中国共产党北京市委员会重要文件汇编1960年 [Collection of important documents of the Beijing Municipal Committee of the Chinese Communist Party, 1960]. n.p., 1963.

―――― ed. *Zhongguo gongchandang Beijingshi weiyuanhui zhongyao wenjian huibian 1961 nian* 中国共产党北京市委员会重要文件汇编1961年 [Collection of important documents of the Beijing Municipal Committee of the Chinese Communist Party, 1961]. n.p., 1965.

Zhonggong Beijing shiwei dangshi yanjiushi 中共北京市委党史研究室, ed. *Peng Zhen zai Beijing* 彭真在北京 [Peng Zhen in Beijing] (Beijing: Zhongyang wenxian chubanshe, 2002.

"Zhonggong zhongyang guanyu jingji tizhi gaige de jueding" 中共中央关于经济体制改革的决定 [The CCP Central Committee's decision on the reform of economic structure], October 20, 1984, http://www.gov.cn/test/2008-06/26/content_1028140_2.htm.

Zhonggong zhongyang wenxian yanjiushi 中共中央文献研究室 and gongqingtuan zhongyang 共青团中央, eds. *Qingnian gongzuo wenxian xuanbian shang* 青年工作文献选编 上 [Selected documents on youth work, vol. 1]. Beijing: Zhongyang wenxian chubanshe and zhongguo qingnian chubanshe, 2012.

"Zhongguo diaoyu xiehui chengli Ye Jianying ren mingyu zhuxi" 中国钓鱼协会成立叶剑英任名誉主席 [The Chinese Fishing Association has been set up with Ye Jianying as its honorary president], *Xinhuashe xinwengao* 4973 (1983).

"Zhongguo gongchanzhuyi qingniantuan" 中国共产主义青年团 [The Chinese Communist Youth League], http://web.archive.org/web/2019102031320/http://www.gov.cn/test/2005-06/28/content_18105.htm.

Zhongguo gongchan zhuyi qingniantuan zhongyang weiyuanhui bangongting 中国共产主义青年团中央委员会办公厅, ed. *Tuan de wenjian huibian 1960* 团的文件汇编 1960 [Collection of documents of the Youth League, 1960]. n.p., 1962.

Zhongguo shehui kexueyuan qingshaonian yanjiusuo 中国社会科学院青少年研究所, ed. *Qingshaonian fanzui yanjiu ziliao huibian di'erji lunwen xuan* 青少年犯罪研究资料汇编第二辑 论文选 [Collection of materials on juvenile crime studies, vol. 2: research papers]. n.p., 1981.

Zhonghua renmin gongheguo jiaoyubu bangongting 中华人民共和国教育部办公厅, ed. *Jiaoyu wenxian faling huibian 1949–1952* 教育文献法令汇编1949–1952 [Collection of documents and decrees on education]. n.p., 1958.

Zhongyang tuanxiao qingnian gongzuo jiaoyanshi 中央团校青年工作教研室, ed. *Gongqingtuan gongzuo lilun xuexi gangyao* 共青团工作理论学习纲要 [Outlines for theoretical studies on the work of the Communist Youth League]. n.p., 1982.

Zhou Duo 周舵. *Zhou Duo zishu: huiyi yu fansi* 周舵自述：回忆与反思 [Zhou Duo's autobiography: recollections and reflections]. Hong Kong: New Century Press, 2019.

Zhou Jing 周静. "Xin Zhongguo 'shiqi nian' Beijing dazhong de yule shenghuo yanjiu" 新中国"十七年"北京大众的娱乐生活研究 [Research on popular entertainment in Beijing during new China's first seventeen years]. master's thesis, Capital Normal University, 2008.

Zhu Mo 朱墨. "Kai le liangnian de 'wan' hui" 开了两年的"晚"会 [A late meeting that was held for two years], *Zhongguo gongren* 5 (1956): 24.

"Zouguo qingchun qi chengchuan huijing guonian de lushang" 走过青春（7）乘船回京过年的路上 [Walking past my youth, part seven: on my way back to Beijing for the Spring Festival by ship], January 24, 2009, http://web.archive.org/web/20181207075640/http://blog.sina.com.cn/s/blog_51d095710100ayqt.html?tj=1.

Index

A
American way of life, 24, 30, 32, 34, 140
Arendt, Hannah, 7, 8
Awaara Hoon, 124, 128, 133

B
backward, 23, 31, 43, 61, 110, 117
balancing work and rest, 109, 142–146, 149, 200, 201
ball game clubs, 24, 38–42, 64, 117, 118
band, 37, 54, 79, 127, 128, 221
Beauvoir, Simone de, 67–69
Beijing 101 Middle School, 207, 219
Beijing Knitting Mill, 88, 89, 100, 102
Beijing No. 3 High School, 201, 221, 222
Beijing No. 4 High School, 95, 183, 184, 188, 190, 198, 201, 219
Beijing Normal University Girls' High School, 88, 89, 182, 188, 217
Birmingham School, 18

board games, 54, 57
bystander, 26, 194, 206–216, 227, 233

C
Central Cultural Revolution Group, 26, 202, 203, 206, 215, 220, 233
Chen, Boda, 206, 210
children of officials, 26, 155, 187–192, 203–206, 219, 221, 227, 229, 233
China Youth, 23, 57, 96, 98, 102, 109, 120, 122, 168, 171, 175, 185, 239
Chinese Communist Party (CCP), 2–6, 8, 13–16, 19, 21, 22, 24–27, 31–33, 36, 37, 53, 59, 64, 69–71, 84, 85, 91, 96, 103–105, 109–111, 117–119, 123, 124, 128, 130, 137, 142, 143, 146, 147, 155, 160, 164–167, 170, 173, 182, 190–192, 196, 200, 221,

227–230, 236, 239–241, 244, 245, 247, 248
chorus, 26, 36, 76, 136, 218–224
class struggle, 75, 151, 152, 154, 155, 169, 171, 172, 174, 187, 191, 205, 210
communal way of life, 141, 142, 150
communist morality, 109, 112, 113, 118–123, 165
cultural leisure, 33, 67, 68, 88
Cultural Revolution, 1, 4, 5, 20, 23, 26, 27, 33, 117, 143, 152, 153, 158, 159, 178, 187, 189, 191, 193, 194, 196–198, 201–222, 224–233, 235–237, 242

D

dancing, 24, 33, 36, 37, 41–46, 48, 50–52, 60, 61, 64, 76, 80, 86, 91, 96, 97, 104, 107, 108, 123, 125, 127, 141, 147, 148, 157, 158, 219, 235, 242, 243, 246
Dazhai, 189, 236–238
difference/three major differences, 25, 26, 153, 158, 159
dormitory, 83, 118, 120, 141, 144, 145, 147, 178, 182, 199, 215, 217, 232
dress reform, 121, 123

E

entertainment, 24, 30, 31, 36, 38, 39, 42, 44, 50, 52–54, 61, 64, 69, 79, 81, 82, 110, 117, 226

G

Great Leap, 130, 131, 133–136, 138–140, 143, 145, 200

H

Haircut, 18, 26, 155, 162, 176, 178, 179, 184, 186, 187, 191, 192
Hirschman, Albert O., 194
Hong Kong films, 155, 160–163
hooligan/hooliganism, 19, 22, 39, 56, 108, 109, 116, 117, 120, 127, 147, 171
Hu, Keshi, 94, 165–167
Hu, Yaobang, 33, 168, 240, 241

J

Jiang, Nanxiang, 72
Jiang, Qing, 203, 206, 229, 237

L

Lai, Ruoyu, 15, 16
Liandong, 202, 203, 206
lifestyle/ways of life/bourgeois lifestyle/communist way of life, 17, 22, 23, 26, 123, 154, 155, 158, 164, 165, 167, 177, 181, 185, 186, 211, 217, 244
Linz, Juan J., 8–10
Liu, Shaoqi, 130, 157, 172

M

Mao, Zedong, v, 2, 4, 5, 8, 12, 13, 43, 55, 82, 145, 152, 154, 156, 165, 166, 169–172, 175, 180, 183, 187, 191, 198, 202, 211, 215, 216
March Forward Without Hesitation, 174, 175
Marx, Karl/Marxist/Marxism, 11, 24, 32, 75, 153, 154, 183, 224
mass culture/mass cultural work, 22, 51, 52, 130, 131, 133–136, 138, 140, 219, 239
Moscow Restaurant, 204, 205

N

Never Forget, 152, 173

O

outlandish clothes, 180, 181
Outlook, 30, 37

P

park festivals, 78–80, 87, 103, 104
participatory totalitarianism/participatory totalitarian model, 6, 7, 11–13, 19
peaceful evolution, 155, 164, 165, 170
Peking University, v, 53, 120, 146, 163, 193, 201, 209, 210, 217, 226
Peng, Zhen, 73, 157–159
propaganda team, 218, 219, 221–224, 233, 237
Putnam, Robert D., 16, 111, 148, 149

R

radio, 24, 52–55, 64, 76, 77, 94, 125, 126, 129, 165, 167, 168, 180, 208, 213, 215
reading club, 19, 88, 224–226
Red Guard, 1, 178, 187, 193, 194, 201, 202, 206–208, 216, 218–220, 222
resistance/resistance model, 3–7, 10–12, 16, 18, 19, 154, 194–197, 233
revisionism/revisionist, 158, 161, 168, 170, 225, 226
revolutionary successors, 170, 172, 178, 185–187, 191
revolutionization, 175, 176

S

salon, 228–231
satellite towns, 159
Scott, James C., 196
social capital, 16, 25, 111, 112, 148, 149, 155, 227
Soviet/Soviet way of life, 7, 24, 33
spiritual civilization, 244
subculture/alternative ways of life, 17, 18, 27, 247
summer vacation, 52, 71–73, 76–78, 200

T

temporal politics, 24, 25, 68–70, 72
tension, 4, 6, 9, 11, 12, 18, 19, 31, 110, 238
terror, 3, 7–9, 11–13, 247
Tianqiao, 67, 68
totalitarian/totalitarianism/totalitarian model, 3–5, 7–13
tropical fish, 210–213
Tsinghua University, 143, 207, 216
Tsinghua University High School, 187–189, 208, 209, 219

V

Verdery, Katherine, 68, 69

W

Wang, Renzhong, 141, 142
Wang, Zhaohua, 82

X

Xiaojinzhuang, 235, 237, 238

Y

yellow books, 113, 120

yellow songs, 108, 124–128, 133, 149

Youth League, 14, 22, 29, 33, 36, 42, 50, 61, 65, 75, 78, 79, 81–83, 87–89, 91–93, 95, 96, 100–103, 110, 118–120, 136, 147, 161, 165, 166, 182, 186, 201, 235, 239, 242, 245, 246
Youth Service Department (YSD), 24, 59–65

Z
Zhou, Enlai, 2, 67, 163, 231

Printed in the United States
by Baker & Taylor Publisher Services